Foreign aid, war, and economic development

T0312011

Foreign aid, war, and economic development

South Vietnam, 1955–1975

Douglas C. Dacy
University of Texas at Austin

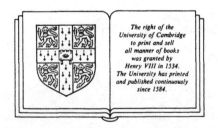

The right of the
University of Cambridge
to print and sell
all manner of books
was granted by
Henry VIII in 1534.
The University has printed
and published continuously
since 1584.

CAMBRIDGE UNIVERSITY PRESS

Cambridge
London   New York   New Rochelle
Melbourne   Sydney

CAMBRIDGE UNIVERSITY PRESS
Cambridge, New York, Melbourne, Madrid, Cape Town, Singapore, São Paulo

Cambridge University Press
The Edinburgh Building, Cambridge CB2 2RU, UK

Published in the United States of America by Cambridge University Press, New York

www.cambridge.org
Information on this title: www.cambridge.org/9780521303279

First published 1986
This digitally printed first paperback version 2005

A catalogue record for this publication is available from the British Library

Library of Congress Cataloguing in Publication data
Dacy, Douglas C.
   Foreign aid, war, and economic development.
   Bibliography: p.
   Includes index.
   1. Vietnam – Economic conditions.   2. Economic
assistance, American – Vietnam.   3. Vietnam – Politics
and government – 1945–1975.   I. Title
HC444.D33   1986   338.9597   86–937

ISBN-13 978-0-521-30327-9 hardback
ISBN-10 0-521-30327-3 hardback

ISBN-13 978-0-521-02131-9 paperback
ISBN-10 0-521-02131-6 paperback

To Mama

Contents

Figures

Tables

xi

Preface

If there is a common impression of the Vietnam war, it is that the United States entered a quagmire from which it was able to extricate itself only with considerable awkwardness. It has been said that the military won all the battles it fought, but lost the war to the political process. If there is a common view on the economy of wartime South Vietnam, it is the one promoted by the popular media that the economy was built around the black market, prostitution, and corruption. If there is a common view on foreign aid to Vietnam, it is that aid was a failure. There may be elements of truth in all of these impressions, but whereas the views and analyses pertaining to military and political affairs have been presented abundantly in books and journals, there is no good source dealing with the economic events that contributed to the final outcome. This book is a modest attempt to inject economic matters into the general analysis of the failed experiment that we refer to as the Vietnam experience.

The experiment to transform a very poor and insecure country into a democratic nation able to stand alone in a relatively short period of time was ambitious. Military, political, and economic activities had to be well orchestrated for the effort to have any chance of succeeding, and rapid economic development was just as important to long-run success as battlefield victories and the general acceptance of democratic political institutions. It seems as if the major contributions of the United States to the experiment were troops, money, and advice, all in abundance, but not out of proportion to the task to be achieved. If we learned anything, it was that troops, money, and advice by themselves cannot secure the loyalty of a people to its government and in excess abundance may even be counterproductive if the enemy is well motivated and patient.

This book is organized around a number of questions dealing with the Vietnam economy during the war. Some are suggestive of the kinds of questions that should be asked in advance of superpower intervention in the affairs of a poor underdeveloped country, but we are more interested in the performance of the Vietnam economy and of U.S. aid in achieving certain goals. To describe and analyze economic events, it was necessary to collect a lot of data and in some instances correct them. A common complaint during the war was that discussions were strongly focused on policy and analysis and were weak on the facts that were needed to support them. I have made every effort to avoid that mistake here.

Chapter 1 is an economic survey of South Vietnam from 1955 to the time of its surrender in 1975. The chapter stands by itself inasmuch as it is more than just a summary of the rest of the book. The problems were distinctly different in the five periods into which the survey is divided. The new nation struggled to get on its feet in the period of resettlement and reconstruction. The period of heightened insurgency that began in 1960 and the assassination of President Diem in 1963 introduced additional problems associated with military insecurity and political instability. The big war began in 1965, and inflation became the major economic problem. After the military defeat of the Communists during Tet, Vietnam achieved remarkable economic growth, and the government began to take serious interest in economic reforms. However, in the end, the economy stagnated as the level of U.S. aid was slashed drastically.

It seems reasonable first to ask the most basic question of fact: What was the overall rate of economic growth of the economy? Real per capita income grew at about 1.4 percent per year. This measure is derived in Chapter 3, which is devoted to national income analysis and the data problems inherent in Vietnam national income accounts. The "top-heavy" structure of the Vietnam economy – more than 60 percent of the gross national product (GNP) in the service sector – is also documented in this chapter.

Was this recorded growth in national income representative of economic development in Vietnam? There is no satisfactory answer to this question. According to some indicators of development, such as improvements in education, administration, and infrastructure, the country moved forward quickly. On the other hand, industrial development was very slow, and there was little deepening in the financial structure of the economy. These and other important indicators of development are discussed in Chapter 4. The history of land reform is laid out in Chapter 5, along with some very tentative conclusions about changes in income distribution. It seems evident that the rural population gained relative to the urban population over the course of the war, but one cannot be sure about the implications of this change for development in the Vietnam situation. Chapter 6 examines the time course of the domestic saving ratio under the assumption that domestic saving rather than total saving is the proper variable to consider for self-sustained growth. Lack of improvement in domestic saving was perhaps the major drawback to economic development in South Vietnam. Finally, if development implies a move in the direction of economic independence, as I think it must, Vietnam made little progress, based on this indicator.

We are concerned with several questions pertaining to foreign aid: How much aid did Vietnam receive? To what extent did aid contribute to the growth of income? What was the role of aid in the war situation? Did aid achieve the goals set for it? Was aid used efficiently? It was hoped that the final report of the Agency for International Development (AID) on Vietnam, *Terminal Report, United States Economic Assistance to South Vietnam, 1954–1975*, would address this set of questions. Because it did not, writers on Vietnam foreign aid are left to answer their own questions. In attempting to assess the effectiveness of U.S. aid, I faced two problems. The first was selecting the major criterion for evaluation. What was aid supposed to have achieved in Vietnam? As for most economists, it was natural for me to assume that the major objective of aid is to promote economic development. However, the use of that criterion to assess the effectiveness of aid in Vietnam would be starting off on the wrong foot and surely would prejudge the result. Vietnam aid had many purposes, but its main purpose was to ensure that the war effort would not collapse because of economic discontentment (Chapter 2). One does not find statements in the official record exactly stating this goal; nevertheless, it is consistent with the manner in which aid was administered. When the Communists attacked the cities during Tet 1968, they fully expected the people to rise up against the Saigon regime, but only a small number responded. Although this single event in no way proves the success of the aid program, it does lend support to a positive assessment of the program on the basis of the major criterion selected.

A related goal of aid was to contain inflation within limits thought to be acceptable by the people. American policymakers were concerned that rampant inflation might contribute to collapse of the war effort. "Stabilization aid," as it was called, no doubt performed the task it was assigned, but it produced some unwanted consequences in regard to economic development. The policy to import rice to keep the price low discouraged production of Vietnam's major crop, and the general policy of importing consumer goods discouraged local industrial development and probably had other adverse consequences that have never been analyzed. For example, the negative impression of Americans that Vietnam was one big corrupt marketplace owes something to the fact that the Vietnam import program featured many items that Americans thought to be unnecessary for a poor dependent country in the midst of a big struggle. Was this at all related to the fact that Americans "soured" on the war? To an economic analyst, much of the imports financed by aid seemed antidevelopmental. Yet, despite unwanted consequences, the central antiinflationary objective was achieved (Chapter 7).

Another problem in assessing aid to Vietnam is that one simply cannot accept the aid figures published in official documents. What appeared to be aid from the point of view of Washington could not always be called aid from the point of view of Saigon, and the economic aid given to Vietnam by the U.S. Military Assistance Command (MACV) directly and through piaster subsidization will not be found in the record books. Even if the dollar value of aid had been recorded unambiguously, there would still be the question of its piaster value. Chapters 8 and 9 deal with the piaster valuation problem and are preparatory to the effort to measure U.S. aid to Vietnam in Chapter 10. Public finance and the role of aid in financing Vietnamese public expenditures are discussed in Chapter 11.

The division of opinion on the Vietnam war frequently distinguished people as either hawks or doves. Similarly, among economists concerned with Vietnam economic policy, there were optimists and pessimists regarding the question whether or not one should expect significant development in that poor country while the war was in progress. The optimists thought that development could proceed with the conduct of the war, whereas the pessimists argued that the war had to come to an end before the country could experience much development. For a person interested in the final outcome, it is useful to ask a different kind of question: What was the probability that the war could be settled in the absence of significant economic development in the South? Day-by-day business was conducted as if it was obvious that a successful conclusion to the war was not related to the question of development.

In my opinion, a certain amount of development was needed to confer legitimacy on the Vietnamese leaders. Development could not wait for the war to end, because it was a precondition. Certainly the government faced a dilemma. In the long run, development was necessary for success. Success also required popular support, which the government believed it would lose if it undertook some of the unpopular reforms necessary for development. The people in power could never make up their minds what they wanted to do on this critical issue. The compromise of some not-so-painful reforms was unsatisfactory, and they came too late at that. The government never really gained legitimacy nor popularity. One aspect of this dilemma is discussed in Chapter 12.

Were the pessimists right? Should we have thought that development had to wait for the war to end? Israel, South Korea, and Taiwan are interesting examples of countries that have developed under conditions of high military threats. Even though none of those countries experienced conditions as severe as those in Vietnam, there are sufficient similarities to suggest comparison. Each of the four countries suffered from high defense burdens, and each received much foreign aid. Why was Vietnam's economic development performance so much worse than that of the other three? In my opinion, the answer to this question must focus attention on the leadership of a country in similar circumstances (Chapter 13). The foreign aid lesson to be learned from the Vietnam experience is that billions of dollars in aid will not buy the economic development that is necessary for a nation's security in the long run unless the leader of the struggling nation is committed to it. The commitment to development and economic independence in wartime South Vietnam, such as it was, came too late to make much of a difference.

Although I have stressed the high military threat in Chapter 13 as a basis for comparing Vietnam's development with that of several U.S. "client" states, there are valid comparisons to be made with other underdeveloped countries. For example, Professor Leroy Jones suggested to me that wartime economic policies in South Vietnam were not essentially different from those in a number of countries that experienced "massive windfall foreign exchange availability." The countries that come to mind immediately are the oil-rich underdeveloped countries that reaped huge windfalls when oil prices escalated in the 1970s. Many of these countries resisted domestic fiscal and monetary reforms and maintained overvalued foreign exchange rates. Like Vietnam, they raised their budgets without regard to long-run consequences, and when the debt crisis replaced the windfall foreign exchange availability, many of these economies began to stagnate. The point is that economic reforms are politically difficult to undertake even in relatively peaceful situations and often require a shock such as a debt crisis. Vietnam's shock was the unexpected severe curtailment in U.S. aid, but unlike the countries today caught up in the debt crisis, it had insufficient time to adjust.

Over the years I have accumulated a number of debts while working on this project. My major debt is to the Institute for Defense Analyses (IDA), which granted me Central Research time to undertake it. IDA provided a stimulating research environment. Because the institute is not faceless, I want to name people. I am grateful to my long-time associate and boss, Dr. Harry Williams. Dr. Alexander Flax, former president of IDA, and Mr. Seymour Deitchman, who was director of research at the time, never turned down a request and were always supportive of my work. I was beneficiary of many discussions with two colleagues, now deceased, Arthur Smithies and William Beazer, and numerous AID officials stationed in Saigon during the war, especially Dr. Willard Sharpe. I am grateful to Betty Johnston Lawson, who encouraged me to go to Vietnam in 1967, my first trip there. Evelyn Cole typed and corrected the manuscript repeatedly, and she finally put an end to it by giving me a deadline.

CHAPTER 1

The rise and fall of the economy

The State of Vietnam became an independent nation when conferees at Geneva in July 1954 partitioned the former French colony of Indochina. It began as a monarchical state, but that condition lasted only fifteen months, until its emperor, Bao Dai, was ousted in a plebiscite by Ngo Dinh Diem in October 1955. From this referendum, which was "a test of authority rather than an exercise in democracy" (Karnow 1984, p. 223), emerged the Republic of Vietnam. The republic survived as a nation for about twenty turbulent years, until April 30, 1975.[1] This chapter traces the rise and fall of an economy shaped by the most expensive foreign aid program in history and buffeted by the tides of a very long and destructive war.

The beginning economic assets of the new nation can be listed quite simply: an adaptive and industrious population of about 11 million, a number of highly productive foreign-owned and -operated rubber plantations, much potential in rice production, and not much else. At the onset of World War II, throughout Vietnam there was a prosperous rice economy able to export 1.2 million metric tons out of its production of 7.7 million tons, or 1,025 pounds of rice per person (Fall 1963, p. 292). By contrast, in 1956 the South portion reported rice production of 2.6 million tons, or 525 pounds per person, and exports of 162,000 tons. Successive disruptive events – the Japanese occupation, the return of the French at the end of World War II, and the First Indochina War – had practically wrecked Vietnamese agriculture as these struggles brought insecurity to the farmers and destruction to the infrastructure. Sixty percent of the road network and one-third of the railroad track had been destroyed, along with much of the river transport system and irrigation canals.

It was an economy "heavy at the top." Aside from agriculture, which engaged about 80 percent of the population, most of the jobs available were due to French operations in the country: 120,000 Vietnamese served in the French army, and 40,000 civilians were employed in military-related activities. In 1954, French expenditures of $500 million created many jobs in commerce and services. By one estimate, the contribution of commerce, services, and government to the GNP (52 percent) was twice as much as that of agriculture (Hoan 1958b, Table VIII). Furthermore, the indigenous Vietnamese did not figure significantly in commerce, because external trade was controlled by the French, and internal commerce and lending by the Chinese

1

minority. Industrial production, which had been located in the North prior to partition, was so limited in the South that Bernard Fall (1963, p. 298) was able to catalogue virtually all industry as consisting of four cigarette factories, two plants producing oxygen and acetylene, two soft drink plants, two small shipyards, a naval arsenal, a distilling plant, a match factory, and two machine shops, altogether employing about 50,000 workers or 1.25 percent of the work force. Evidently, Fall overlooked Vietnam's major industry, rice milling, and the ice plants and sawmills that were prominent at the time. Even so, that was a meager starting point, and Vietnam would need to develop rapidly if it were to have any hope of overcoming even greater obstacles than it had encountered previously.

1.1   Period of resettlement and reconstruction[2]

The new government was confronted immediately with a number of imposing economic problems. The most urgent of these was how to resettle some 900,000 refugees from the North, who were allowed by the Geneva agreements to migrate freely. Next there were the critical financial and technical problems arising from the withdrawal of French forces, technicians, and aid. Agricultural production needed to be expanded quickly if the country was to feed itself, the infrastructure needed to be restored, land tenure arrangements needed attention, and the country had to develop industrial capacity.

A massive resettlement of refugees was accomplished between August 1954 and May 1955 using French and U.S. naval vessels and French aircraft.[3] In that short period of time the population of South Vietnam increased almost 10 percent, with the influx of people characterized by Bernard Fall (1963, p. 336) as "doubly alien" – northern and predominantly Catholic. They were settled in temporary camps in the Saigon area according to previous occupation (e.g., farmers, fishermen, artisans). The plan was to permanently relocate the refugees in groups of 1,000–3,000 on reclaimed agricultural lands primarily in the delta region in the case of farmers and in proximity to fishing areas in the case of fishermen.

The resettlement plan permitted elected officials of the temporary villages to participate in the planning for the permanent settlements along with the General Commissariat for Refugees and the U.S. aid mission called USOM. Once the land had been selected, the refugees were supplied with minimal building materials, some tools, and buffalos. The largest resettlement project was at Caisan, 125 miles southwest of Saigon, where 77,000 hectares of rice land were cleared for up to 100,000 refugees. Most of the financing for resettlement was supplied by U.S. aid, $93 million in the first two years, and much of the organizing and administrative work by Catholic relief organizations (Harnett 1959). By mid–1957, 319 resettlement villages had been built, accounting for about half the refugees who had migrated to the South. The remainder disappeared into the urban population, principally in Saigon. It is an interesting sidelight that the flow of refugees southward did not materialize into the economic debacle foreseen by the Viet Minh's great leader, Ho Chi Minh (Sulzberger 1974). Instead, the situation furnished the new government with a showcase problem that, if properly managed, would go a long way to dispel many of the doubts of its critics. Although some complaints were registered by various relief organizations in regard to reset- tlement financing and other actions, one is impressed with the apparent success and speed with which this difficult first problem was resolved.[4]

Replacing French financial assistance and technicians was perhaps the eas- iest task, with the United States committed as Vietnam's next benefactor. AID's *Terminal Report* states that the first function of the U.S. aid mission in Vietnam (USOM) was to "plug the financial gap" left by the departing French (AID 1976, pt. A, p. 1). There was indeed a large financial gap, mainly because of the need to maintain a large Vietnamese military force to replace the previously provided French security. Maintaining this force, num- bering 250,000 during the first five years, would have been an impossible burden on the budget of the new government, and it became the prime re- sponsibility of the United States. In the period 1955–60, gross U.S. economic aid to Vietnam was $220 million per year on average, or roughly 22 percent of South Vietnam's GNP.[5] Because U.S. military aid supplied arms and equipment, this amount of economic aid was grossly in excess of what was needed to support military operations, and it created a disincentive for the government to engage in any serious effort to raise domestic revenues to finance its own activities. This problem was to persist throughout the war. It was decided very early as a proposition of faith that the standard of living of the Vietnamese must not fall, and therefore much economic aid was used to supply imported consumer goods to support this goal. Probably no economic matter received so much criticism as the "lavishness" of the U.S. economic aid in the early years of the Republic of Vietnam.[6]

A draft of a five-year plan was submitted to the president in June 1957. This plan is interesting because it indicates the priorities of Vietnamese of- ficials at the time. A five-year budget of 17.5 billion piasters ($500 million at the official exchange rate, and half that at a realistic exchange rate) was proposed initially. Of this, 43 percent was earmarked for public works and power, 22 percent for agriculture, 12 percent for health, education, and hous- ing, and 9 percent for industry. Cutting across all sectors, 80 percent of the budget was allocated to the public sector (Rosebery 1959, p. 195). Thus, the government claimed a major role in agricultural development, mainly in land clearing, and was to become a dominant partner in the production of cement, coal, textiles, and sugar. Smaller enterprises planned in paper and glass were left to the private sector. The growth targets of 27 percent in agriculture, 70 percent in fisheries, 20 percent in industry, and 18.5 percent overall were not unrealistic. However, as with most plans, there were controversial projects: The large power plant at Da Nhim in central South Vietnam was overambitious, and rebuilding South Vietnam's part of the old Trans-Indochina Railway seemed cost-ineffective given that its main line was parallel to the coastal shipping lanes. Because most of the financing was to come from U.S. aid, the plan paid little attention to private saving, taxation, and the unhealthy balance-of-payments problem, and this inattention to sources of permanent financing and trade at a time when the country already consumed more than it was able to produce is indicative of a point of view that was not to serve the country well in the coming years. Yet, despite many shortcomings and lack of systematic execution of the plan, many of the goals were met.

President Diem realized almost immediately that something had to be done about two problems that threatened the popularity of his rule. The first was the problem of land ownership. About 3 percent of all landowners and only ⅔ of 1 percent of the million or so cultivators owned 45 percent of all the rice land in South Vietnam, and most of the big landlords were absentee owners, having fled to the cities when the Viet Minh took control of the countryside (Scigliano 1963, p. 121; Fall 1963, p. 308). The second problem was that rents were excessively high, in some places as high as 50 percent, despite a previously enacted cosmetic law that limited them to 15 percent (Wurfel 1957, p. 87). During their struggle with the French, the Viet Minh had initiated a "land to the tillers" reform, giving lands confiscated from large landowners to the tillers. When peace ensued in 1954, the legal basis of these reforms was questioned, and the ex-landlords sent their agents, usually government officials, to collect their rents. Quite understandably, this caused considerable resentment among the peasants.

Reforms in January and February 1955 addressed the issues of maximum rents, interest payments, lengths of contracts on lands under cultivation, and provision for contracts on land that had lain idle. The ordinances that implemented these new arrangements required formal written contracts, but without strict enforcement they proved to be ineffective. Ordinance 57 of October 1956 was addressed to the problem of land redistribution. By this ordinance, a landowner was limited to 100 hectares (plus 15 hectares as ancestral worship land). The government was to purchase all excess land at a price below market value and sell it to the tillers. This reform program required extensive land surveying and legal and other paperwork and proved cumbersome to implement, especially at a later phase when the Viet Cong gained control of the countryside. Thus, a program that grew from good intentions and had a chance of conferring a major political advantage on Ngo Dinh Diem could claim only partial success as a genuine land reform program.

Despite the lack of significant progress in land reform, impressive gains were made in agricultural production with the closing of the First Indochina War and the return of relative security to the countryside. Rice production, reported to be as low as 2.2 million tons in 1954 and 2.8 million tons in 1955, increased to 5.1 million tons in 1960.[7] Although the exactness of these figures is questionable, the remarkable recovery in rice production is not contested. Much of the increase, as would be expected, came from reclaiming land that had been abandoned during the war, about 700,000 hectares, or as much as 45 percent of the land in rice cultivation in 1954 (AID 1976, pt. A, p. 5). Figures on rice production and land in cultivation indicate that the yield per hectare increased from 1.3 tons in 1954 to 2.1 tons in 1960. The latter figure on yield is high in comparison with yields in Indonesia, Thailand, and the Philippines at the time, but low in comparison with figures for the more productive rice countries such as Japan, Korea, and Taiwan (Cole 1959, p. 183), and it is consistent with reported yields for Vietnam in the 1960s. The recovery in rice production permitted Vietnam to export 360,000 tons in 1960, a level probably not achieved during the previous two decades and not to be achieved again. Rubber production increased by about one-third over the period, and production of other crops improved by 40 percent from 1956 through 1960, with the most impressive gains in manioc, sweet potatoes, sugarcane, and copra.[8] The rapid gains in agriculture seem to be unrelated to any major event other than the restoration of peace.

In industry there was no catching up to be achieved, but rather a complete building program to be accomplished. It appears that much of the first five years was spent in discussing and developing an industrial strategy, with the United States supplying technical assistance, feasibility studies, some capital goods, and half a billion dollars in raw materials under the Commercial Import Program (CIP). The section in AID's *Terminal Report* on industry (AID 1976, pt. B), as had many previous AID reports, placed stress on inputs rather than on the more difficult to measure outputs, as if there were a one-to-one correspondence. Most of the imported capital equipment supported infrastructure development rather than manufacturing. In fact, from the beginning there was a conflict between U.S. advisors' emphasis on development through private enterprise and the preference of the government of Vietnam (GVN) for government ownership.[9] Despite the establishment of the Industrial Development Center (IDC) in 1957 to advise on investments and to help finance them[10] and declarations by the president of Vietnam favorable to private domestic and foreign investment,[11] the investment climate was not favorable, and the slowness of industrial development has been attributed to "untimeliness and government inertia and disinterest" (Morrison 1959, p. 225). Relatively little was achieved during this period. A large cement plant was planned at Ha

Tien, the Nong Song coal mine was improved, and new construction in the Saigon area included two textile plants, a tire plant, a glass factory, a paper plant, and a shoe factory employing 8,000 workers (Fall 1963, p. 299). To put these accomplishments in perspective we need only point out that one Vietnamese analyst thought that 400,000–500,000 jobs needed to be created each year just to avoid "urban pauperization" (Fall 1963, p. 301). From 1956 to 1960 the index of industrial production increased 16 percent, but most of that was due to increases in electric power and beverages.

Efforts to build the infrastructure were more successful. First, it was fairly well agreed what had to be done. Second, financing was less of a problem because the local content for some projects was relatively large and the United States was willing to supply the necessary imports in the form of equipment, construction machinery, and technical assistance for projects it approved for the government sector. As early as 1954, USOM developed a highway program whose major objective was to provide assistance for rehabilitation and modernization of the national highway system, consisting of about 6,000 kilometers, and much of that program was completed in the first five years (AID 1976, pt. D, p. 3). By 1959, most of the national railway system was operative, with a continuous line from Saigon to Dong Ha at the seventeenth parallel. The National Institute of Administration was established to train Vietnamese in public administration, and a large effort was expended to improve police operations.[12]

According to Vietnam's rather primitive national income accounts, the GNP increased from 65.4 billion piasters in 1956 (1960 prices) at an annual rate of 4.5 percent to 81.8 billion piasters in 1960.[13] Despite this creditable performance, it appeared to some analysts who were greatly concerned with Vietnam policymaking mistakes, its continuous dependence on U.S. aid, its inability to reduce the percentage of imports covered by exports, and the government's lack of interest in development that Vietnam was on its way to becoming a "permanent mendicant" (Taylor 1961, p. 256). However, a closer look at the components of GNP reveals that the country was making progress in the direction of economic independence. Crude data (in comparison with import and export statistics) show that domestic saving was negative by 8.1 billion piasters in 1955, but by only 0.5 billion in 1960. Essentially, this means that gross investment in the country in 1960 was just about equal to the value of U.S. aid, whereas in 1955 it was considerably below U.S. aid.[14] Alternatively stated, private and public consumption exceeded GNP by 13 percent in the first full year of peace, whereas in 1960 the country consumed its total potential output. Obviously this condition could not persist in the long run, but the record of performance was somewhat better in this period than it has sometimes been made out to be.[15]

1.2 Period of heightened insurgency

Failure of the Diem regime to hold a plebiscite in July 1956 and its further show of contempt for reunification by issuing a republican constitution in the following October led to the Second Indochina War. No notable battle ushered in this war, which Bernard Fall (1963, p. 316) dates to early 1957, and neither the government of South Vietnam nor that of the United States seems to have been much concerned by it up to 1959, despite low-level but continual Communist terrorist activity throughout the country. With its program to move masses of the rural population into "agrovilles" in 1959, the government tacitly recognized that the insurgents had gained the upper hand in the countryside. The year 1960 was marked by a major escalation in terrorist activity and, in December, by formation of the National Front for the Liberation of the South, shortened to National Liberation Front (NLF), and popularly referred to in subsequent years as the Viet Cong. The success of the Viet Cong in wresting control of the rural population away from the government was aided by the frustration, disappointment, and discontentment brought on by failure of the regime to work seriously toward any of its proclaimed social goals.[16] Thus, the time when significant economic gains might have been made relatively easily passed, and the country slipped from bad to worse – from a condition of terror to one of "full-fledged insurrection" (Buttinger 1967, vol. 2, p. 983).[17]

A plan to move peasants away from certain areas of the country and into concentrated population centers called agrovilles was unveiled by President Diem on July 7, 1959. According to the president, these settlements were to be constructed for the purpose of improving the conditions of rural life, and they became the centerpiece for a new drive toward economic and social development (Zasloff 1962–3, p. 327). It is difficult to imagine how anyone could have contended that a plan forcing peasants to move to unfamiliar locations and requiring, in addition, that they pay for them both in money and in conscripted labor time would be bettering their condition. In any event, this program was abandoned in 1961 as unworkable after only about 40,000 peasants had been resettled.

In its place, the regime initiated a much more ambitious plan to move about 10 million peasants into strategic hamlets. The new plan at least had the redeeming feature that the hamlets were to be located in the vicinity of the rice lands already under cultivation. The strategic hamlets were to be fortified by barbed wire, hedges, moats, and fences of pointed bamboo stakes and defended at night by units of the Civil Defense Corps. Like the abandoned agrovilles, the strategic hamlets "were largely just another means of trying to wrest control over the population from the Viet Cong through police coer-

cion, not through reforms that would have taken care of the people's needs''
(Buttinger 1967, vol. 2, p. 988). Although that effort touched the lives of
millions of people and caused much discontentment, it proved ineffective as
a pacification measure, and the strategic hamlet concept was abandoned several years later.

During this difficult period for the country there was a shift in emphasis
in the use of foreign aid in the direction of pacification and away from
development (AID 1976, pt. A, pp. 10–11). Increasingly, AID advisors were
to serve in field operations, and funds were diverted from the CIP to pacification efforts. In addition, there was a substantial reduction in the amount
of economic aid and an increase in military aid. The former dropped to $159
million on average per year in 1961–4 from $231 million for the previous six
years, whereas military aid rose to $191 million in 1964 from $73 million in
1960. A large increase in military advisors accompanied the rise in military
funding. There were 16,000 U.S. military personnel in Vietnam when Diem
was assassinated in November 1963 in a coup d'etat, in comparison with only
700 who had served as advisors in 1960. Vietnamese "regular equivalent"
forces increased by 80 percent from 1960 to 1964,[18] and the GVN budget
deficit rose from 4.7 billion piasters in 1961 to 15.9 billion.

Despite the ominous signs reported earlier, the economy did not collapse,
nor was there runaway inflation. To finance some of the deficit, which an
AID report claims was at least double the value of American aid in 1964
(AID 1976, pt. A, p. 8),[19] the National Bank of Vietnam, founded in 1955
as the country's central bank, printed 10.6 billion piasters in the years 1961–4,
or about one-fifth of the government deficit, causing the money supply to rise
by 70 percent. However, Saigon retail prices rose by only 20 percent over
the same four-year period. It is evident that the Vietnamese people did not
have high inflationary expectations at the time. Physical output increased in
almost every sector, as the following gains indicate: rice 4.6 percent, total
crop production (including rice) 5.5 percent, fish catch 59 percent, industrial
production 54 percent, construction 64 percent. Overall, the economy grew
14.9 percent, or about 1.1 percent per capita per year.

These growth figures do not imply that the economy was developing satisfactorily. The growth in net domestic product was primarily a side effect
of moving the economy to a wartime footing; of the total gain of 11.7 billion
piasters in real product, 7.3 billion piasters were due to increases in public
administration and defense. Thus, the economy was becoming even more
top-heavy than it had been, and that condition could not have been sustained
out of local resources. The domestic saving rate, which had improved up to
1960, sank to a negative 6 percent, and the export/import ratio to 15 percent,
in 1964. The industrial development that occurred during this period was due
mainly to the completion of factories planned or begun in the earlier period.

By the end of 1964, less than two dozen new factories had been built in South
Vietnam since independence (Buttinger 1967, vol. 2, p. 966). Only 12,000
additional jobs were expected to be created in the course of Vietnam's second
five-year plan ending in 1966 (Fall 1963, p. 300).

The only economic reform of any note during this period was the devaluation of the piaster in December 1961 from 35 to 60 piasters per dollar.
Normally, devaluations are expected to stimulate exports. However, this particular devaluation was ineffective in stimulating exports because the new rate
did not apply to rubber, Vietnam's major dollar earner, presumably because
the rubber plantations were under French (foreign) ownership. The land reform
program was not and could not have been pursued vigorously under the
existing condition in which the Viet Cong controlled most of the countryside.

1.3   Beginning of the big war

Americanization of the war in Vietnam brought economic complications to
a country already strained with political problems. We date this period from
the time U.S. Marines set foot on Vietnam soil in March 1965 to the collapse
of the Communist Tet offensive in mid–1968. The difficulty on the economic
front during this period is indicated roughly by the buildup in U.S. troop
strength from 23,000 at the end of 1964 to 543,000 in April 1969, the doubling
of South Vietnamese forces to about 1,000,000, and the growth in other forces
(mainly South Koreans) to 60,000 in the same period.[20] There was, of course,
the matter of how to finance the rapidly growing RVNAF (armed forces,
Republic of Vietnam) without creating inflationary pressure while at the same
time building a government with authority and the administrative capability
to rule. Inflation, then, emerged as the number-one economic problem at the
beginning of this turbulent period. The decline in agriculture, and especially
rice production, was soon to join it at the top of the list of pressing problems.

That the country was already on the verge of political collapse could be
seen through the "revolving door" to the premiership. After the assassination
of Ngo Dinh Diem in November 1963, the government changed hands at
least five times before General Nguyen Cao Ky took the premiership in June
1965. Under these circumstances it is understandable that national economic
policy came to a dead stop. But war conditions had not yet disrupted the
countryside in such a way as to have a major impact on agricultural production.
Rice production and our index of crop output were about the same as they
had been in the late 1950s.[21]

The average rate of inflation up to 1965 was about 4 percent per year.
Within six months after the big war began, prices rose by 20 percent, and it
appeared that there was unlimited scope for further acceleration. To stem this
inflationary potential, the nature of U.S. economic aid to Vietnam changed

drastically. With a change in the character of the war it was recognized that war financing requirements would have to be met almost entirely by U.S. aid. There was no other way. In 1965, Vietnamese domestic tax revenues were less than 7 percent of GNP, and most of those were due to a small tax on production, along with excise taxes on beer, soft drinks, cigarettes, and gasoline, with little potential for significant revenue enhancement. To meet the war deficit, U.S. aid rose from $230 million in 1964 to almost $800 million in 1966.

One must recognize that this massive aid inflow was intended to stabilize the country rather than to promote economic development, although that would have been a welcomed side effect. Importing was the mechanism for turning dollars into the piasters needed to finance the GVN and also to support a considerable American establishment in Vietnam. An economy already dependent on imports became more dependent. Of course, aid and imports did raise the standard of living of the Vietnamese, but they also created a disincentive system that was to work against economic development.

A major problem connected with the aid-finance system was how to fix the foreign exchange rate for a country that hardly exported anything. In 1965, Vietnam was able to export only $36 million, mostly in rubber, while importing about ten times that value. It is obvious that under this condition the international value of the piaster was very low; yet Americans and Vietnamese exchanged their currencies at the official rate established arbitrarily in December 1961 at 72 piasters per dollar (with surcharges). This gross overvaluation of the piaster was a disincentive to local production; it permitted large windfall gains to be made by privileged importers and raised the price of war assistance to the Americans. No single economic problem consumed as much energy among various economics officials and analysts as setting the foreign exchange rate.

In July 1966, the piaster was devalued from 72 per dollar to 118, including a "perequation" tax. The most immediate effect of this move was to slow down the rate of inflation. Prices hardly rose for the next six months. Devaluation was not repeated again during the period of American domination of the war. Prices began rising again in 1967, and in mid–1968 consumer prices were three times higher than they had been at the end of 1964, or an annual average rise of about 40 percent. Aid had done the job assigned it, as even this relatively high rate of inflation did not create a major political problem.

As security in the countryside deteriorated in 1965 and in 1966, rice production began to fall. The response to this problem was to import rice from the United States and to establish a "resources control" program to deny this important foodstuff to the Viet Cong (who lived among the peasants at the time!). Both actions had the unwanted effect of reducing rice production further. U.S. rice was sold at a subsidized price in the cities, and price controls were put on domestic rice, with the result that rice shipments to Saigon declined by two-thirds. It is uncertain whether more rice was consumed by the growers or whether they fed it to pigs, as was reported, and how much was sold to the Viet Cong or taxed away by them. In any event, rice production fell by 20 percent from 1964 to 1968, and this country that had exported 323,000 tons as recently as 1963 imported about 770,000 tons in 1967.

Industrial output followed a somewhat different course. Despite the effort to build industry with aid money in the late 1950s and early 1960s, the country had a very small industrial base when the United States entered the war. Much of this was in beer, soft drinks, and light textiles. These industries continued to grow and perhaps were even stimulated by the war until the Tet offensive in 1968. The index of industrial production increased by 46 percent from 1964 up to the time of the Tet offensive, but this constituted no major change in terms of absolute gains in output.

In 1966, a conference was held in Honolulu for the specific purpose of addressing economic problems.[22] There it was decided that the Vietnam economy and pacification of the countryside would henceforth receive major attention. In May 1967 there occurred a formal change in the organization chart turning pacification over to the U.S. Military Assistance Command Vietnam (MACV). This assured a cutting of red tape and a more vigorous attempt to achieve the hitherto elusive pacification of the peasantry. This change was beneficial in many ways, although it had its brutal side, too, in the elimination of Viet Cong cadres. Many schoolrooms and health facilities were built, and there was a major educational program to introduce farmers to modern agricultural techniques and teach them how to improve their economic return by growing cash crops. During this period of the war, small water pumps and other equipment came into widespread use,[23] there was experimentation with hog cholera vaccine, truck farming was greatly expanded, and new products became available in city marketplaces. U.S. Army captains and majors trained earlier at agricultural colleges in the United States were explaining to Vietnamese farmers how they could make money by growing "sugar babies," the small watermelons found in the southern United States. It is easy to exaggerate these efforts, as some have.[24] At best, they provided a small counterweight to the decline in the production of major crops, but they are indicative of a dynamic period in agriculture, despite many failures.

There was the unseemly side of things, too, as one expects in wartime booms. Active black markets in Saigon and other towns prominently displayed American PX goods and military clothing.[25] Stories about black markets made good newspaper copy, but, in fact, black market activity in consumer products was not really bad for the economy. It gave employment to many refugees from the rural areas and otherwise served as a kind of aid program in which some relatively poor people were allowed to participate. No one in authority really tried to clamp down on the goods black market, because it was recognized that this operation was an important means of keeping prices in check through genuine competition. The same cannot be said for the black market in currency. This obviously had harmful economic effects to the extent that illegal currency exchange was a part of the mechanism for capital flight, as most analysts assumed.

By the time of the Tet offensive, the economy appeared to be turning upward. Political stability had improved with a successful nationwide election in which Nguyen Van Thieu became president. He was to serve in this capacity practically to the end of the war. The GNP, which had been sluggish in 1966, began to grow in 1967. However, a deeper look reveals an economy that was continuing to grow top-heavy in the service sector and was sustainable only with large infusions of foreign aid. Up to this point, development had not been a major goal of aid, but in fact foreign aid had done the job it had been assigned: to bring stability to the Vietnam economy. On the eve of the lunar New Year (Tet), Vietnamese and American officials were very optimistic about the future.

1.4   Period of Vietnamization

In the early mornings of January 30 and 31, 1968, the Communist forces unleashed major attacks against all major cities and towns in South Vietnam. Oberdorfer (1971) has written a fascinating account of this coordinated attack, known as the Tet offensive, which early Communist reports referred to as the General Offensive and General Uprising. The fighting over the next several months resulted in a major psychological victory for the Communist side and changed the course of history in Southeast Asia, even though the expected popular uprising did not occur and the attackers were decisively defeated militarily.

One effect of Tet that had significant implications for future economic activity was that the ranks of the Viet Cong were severely thinned by the fierce fighting that took place. These forces of local origin had conducted an effective antigovernment campaign in many provinces in South Vietnam. After Tet, the character of the resistance movement changed radically, moving more and more to northern (alien) control and reduced effectiveness. As a result, the GVN was able to extend its control over the countryside to a greater extent than previously. The reduction in harassment from the Communist side presented a more favorable environment for economic gains, and the people responded with increased productivity.

Probably the major economic implication in Vietnam following from the Tet offensive was due to the political decision in the United States to pursue peace through negotiations, to disengage from land combat, and to move toward Vietnamization of the war. The withdrawal of half a million troops from Vietnam was to have serious effects not only on the conduct of the battle but also on the performance of the economy. For the first time in the Second Indochina War, Vietnam went to full mobilization and just about doubled the size of its armed forces from 1968 to 1972. In the process of Vietnamization, the GVN became more a legitimate government than it had been previously, partly because it relied less on U.S. support. As Oberdorfer (1971, p. 331) stated in his concluding chapter, "Under the stress of the Tet offensive, the South Vietnamese Government faltered but did not fold, and after the battle it became more of a working institution than it had ever been before."

The validity of that assessment can easily be seen in the economic reforms that took place during the period of Vietnamization. Reforms are never popular, even in developed countries, and it took a certain amount of boldness on the part of the leadership to enact reforms in Vietnam. With respect to economic matters, AID's *Terminal Report* credits much of these reforms to a "change in economic leadership" during the period, the new leaders being American-trained professionals with high regard for the merits of a free enterprise system (AID 1976, pt. A, p. 59). In any event, the same kind of reforms that had been rejected repeatedly by the "old leadership" were discussed seriously and enacted, at least half-heartedly, in most major areas.

Windfall profits accruing to importers were a major problem in Vietnam from the time of introduction of U.S. combat forces in 1965. In an environment of rapidly rising prices with a regime of a fixed exchange rate, privileged importers were allowed to purchase American and Japanese goods at subsidized prices while selling them months later at inflated prices within the country. The devaluation of the piaster in 1966 eliminated the windfalls for a time, but as prices continued to rise in 1967 and rise very rapidly in early 1968, the windfalls increased to new highs. These rents to importers were particularly bad for the economy because (it was thought) they ended up in capital flight rather than being employed in domestic investment.

The obvious solution to the problem was to devalue the piaster at more frequent intervals or to move to a system of flexible exchange rates. Both measures would have transferred the windfalls from importers to the treasury. Although the government resisted both options, it realized that something had to be done in view of the vastly increased expenditures on the war. Instead, the GVN chose to put into effect an "austerity tax" in October 1969. This tax raised the duties on many imported items. The program was poorly designed and did not produce the expected effect. Importers' windfalls did not decline, and government receipts in real terms did not rise, for reasons given in Chapter 8.[26]

The next major economic reform, and perhaps the most important one for stemming inflation and promoting growth, was an interest rate reform in September 1970. Prices rose at annual rates of 24, 32, and 32 percent respectively in 1968, 1969, and the first nine months of 1970. During that period, banks were allowed to pay only 8–12 percent on time deposits, and the lending rate was severely restricted as well. The negative real interest rates discouraged saving and encouraged importers to build inventories of almost all goods for which they could get import licenses. Such a situation promoted "rent seeking" at the expense of productive activity. In the September reform, interest rates were allowed to rise to the range of 14–20 percent. Even though the real interest rate remained negative, the effect of the reform was to encourage saving and time deposits in commercial banks, allowing the government to sell bonds to the private sector, for the first time, to finance its expenditures. The interest rate reform probably was a major factor in slowing the rate of inflation to 13 percent in the year following the reform.

During the period October 1970 to March 1972, a number of decisions were made with respect to the actual foreign exchange rate and the mechanism itself. In a series of moves, the piaster was devalued by at least 50 percent. Initially the government proceeded with characteristic caution, creating a two-tier or "parallel" rate structure. For example, the rate was changed from 118 to 275 piasters per dollar as applied to exports and for the purpose of accommodating U.S. troops serving in Vietnam,[27] while remaining unchanged for other uses.

To increase GVN revenues, the surtax that importers paid on the purchase of foreign exchange (called the perequation tax) was increased. By the end of 1971, the exchange rate system had been so altered that only official foreign government purchases of piasters remained at the 118 rate. Importers of CIP-financed goods paid 275 piasters per dollar, and those who imported from Japan, Taiwan, and other countries under the so-called GVN-financed program paid 400 per dollar. The U.S. personnel "accommodation" rate, as well as the rate on exports, was 410 per dollar. As a result of these upward adjustments in the foreign exchange rate, windfall profits were virtually eliminated, and price discrepancies due to the previous regime were beginning to straighten out. The foreign exchange rate was adjusted frequently from that time on in an effort to retain parity between the piaster and dollar. In retrospect, these adjustments in the foreign exchange rate along with the interest rate reform appear to be routine, but at the time they appeared bold moves because they operated against the vested interests. They provide the best evidence that, at long last, the government was beginning to govern.

Not all of the reforms were of a financial nature. The GVN moved to reduce subsidies to rice consumers and later to consumers of gasoline. They raised duties on sugar and flour, and there were tariff reforms to realign a tariff structure that had long been indefensible.[28]

Probably the major socioeconomic reform of the period of Vietnamization, and even for the entire history of the nation, was the land reform that was put into effect in 1970. This Land-to-the-Tillers program transferred about 1.2 million hectares of land to almost 1 million tenants by the time of South Vietnam's defeat in 1975. Unlike the Diem program, this reform made no demand that peasants pay for the land they received. Rather, the government assumed the burden of reimbursing the landlords, paying them 20 percent in cash and the rest in government bonds that carried a 10 percent return. Given the delayed payment schedules implied in the swap of land for government bonds and the negative real interest rate, it is doubtful that landlords received full market value for their land. Thus, there was some measure of confiscation attendant to the land reform, and this program furnishes another example of the government's ability to act when necessary against entrenched groups.

These favorable remarks should not be taken to imply that all was well on the economic front or that the government made these reforms out of great concern for human welfare. The financial and land reforms had been pressed on the GVN by the American advisors in Saigon, and it was evident that they were necessary if Vietnamization was to have a chance to succeed. On the other hand, they do show that politicians were learning how to deal with the new political process that was emerging and that they were willing to take risks heretofore unknown in South Vietnam. Diem did put down the rebellious sects very early to assure his own survival, but he failed to inaugurate a meaningful land reform program and may even have had contempt for the political aspects of such a program. By contrast, Thieu recognized its political implications and was willing to trade off support from the traditional power structure for votes in the countryside and additional American financial backing.

The period between the Tet offensive and the invasion from the north that was yet to come was the most productive and promising period in South Vietnam's history. Security improved, the government began to take economic actions toward a favorable future, and the economy responded with rapid growth. From 1968 through 1971, net domestic product increased 28 percent, to which the government sector contributed only 6 percentage points. Rice production set the pace during this period, rising to 6.1 million tons in 1971, compared with 4.4 million tons in 1968. Importantly, a meaningful land reform program was initiated, and the government showed its ability to enact financial reforms as well. At no time had the situation ever looked brighter for South Vietnam, but dark clouds were gathering.

1.5   Recession and defeat

Just as the Vietnamese government began to face up to some of its tough economic problems, it was jolted by a major invasion from the north, on March 30, 1972. This Easter offensive by the North Vietnamese, involving some 120,000 main-force troops and thousands of Viet Cong guerrillas (Karnow 1984, pp. 640–3), was repulsed by South Vietnamese ground forces and a massive effort by U.S. airpower. The invasion caused over a million people to flee their homes and created a further economic drain at a time when the economy was already sinking into recession. The successful defense of An Loc and the eventual recapture of Quang Tri, the northernmost provincial capital, were major feats for the South Vietnamese forces. It seemed partly to support the cause of Vietnamization of the war by demonstrating for the time being, at least, that given adequate arms and ammunition the Vietnamese army had become a match for the disciplined army of the North. A big question for the nation was whether or not the economic Vietnamization begun in the previous period would show similar success. The task would be doubly hard in the highly uncertain environment of the next few years.

That environment included a number of adverse elements that contributed to a prolonged recession. The first signs of the recession were not apparent at the time of the North Vietnamese invasion because of a lack of current economic data. One official report argued that early successes by the Northern forces caused a fall in consumer and investor confidence and a cutback in spending. As the process became cumulative, the economic situation worsened (AID-VN 1972b).[29] In retrospect, it is fairly clear that this explanation was naive, because, in fact, the economy had begun to turn down several months before the invasion. Manufacturing and construction activity had been in decline since mid–1971; the number of checks cleared, a proxy for wholesale and retail trade, turned down in December 1971; and a makeshift index of agriculture started to decline in March 1972 (Dacy 1973, p. 19). By the time the bottom was reached in the late summer of 1972, private sector output had fallen from its previous peak by 10–20 percent, and for the year as a whole the private sector components of net domestic product (NDP) were 9 percent below the level attained in 1971, while the total NDP (including public administration and defense) was 5 percent lower.[30] A slight recovery occurred in the late summer, but national income for the years 1973 and 1974 was virtually the same as it had been in the depressed year 1972.[31]

The major factor leading to the recession was the withdrawal of U.S. troops that had begun in 1969. At the beginning of 1972, 157,000 of the 543,000 peak level remained in Vietnam, and by the end of the year another 132,000 had left the country. Associated with the exodus of the American establishment was a direct loss of 150,000 Vietnamese jobs and, adding indirect hires, perhaps 300,000 jobs in all (AID 1976, pt. A, p. 118). To satisfy military requirements, troop spending in the local economy, and pay for Vietnamese employees, the United States purchased $403 million in piasters in 1971. This source of foreign exchange dropped to $213 million in 1972 and less than $100 million in 1973 and 1974 (AID 1976, pt. A, Table 1). The loss in dollar support, of course, had been foreseen by U.S. and Vietnamese officials. However, it was assumed that the difference would be met with increases in conventional aid; but it was not, for as the United States withdrew its troops from Vietnam, it lost interest in unrestrained financial support to the country. The Vietnam economy had been built on the quicksand of imports financed by foreign aid and was bound to falter, if not fail, when that support was removed. Import support, which had averaged $660 million (including piaster purchases) over the 1966–71 period, fell to $616 million on average in the 1972–4 period. The worldwide inflation of the early seventies reduced the real value of this dollar support to $335 million in 1971 dollars (AID 1976, pt. A, Table 2). It is easy to understand why the economy would become unglued with a reduction in the real value of U.S. aid to about half of its previous amount.[32]

The figures given here regarding the depth of the recession do not present an adequate picture of the impact it had on the urban masses. During the late 1960s, most of the accessions to the labor force were preempted by the military, which doubled in size. When the armed forces reached 1.1 million, it stopped growing, thus closing down a major source of employment, and this occurred at the same time the Americans were removing their troops and reducing demand on the labor market. By 1972, a major unemployment problem had developed in Vietnam. Industry had not contributed much to labor market demand in South Vietnam – the whole country employed fewer than 200,000 in industry – and the gains in agricultural production came from using high-yield rice strains and fertilizer; thus, the demand side of the labor market virtually collapsed when government demand eased. Surplus agricultural populations migrated to the cities, where they joined many other unemployed workers. The AID *Terminal Report* estimated that unemployment in 1974 was 1.2 million, or 14 percent of the work force (AID 1976, pt. A, p. 110), and this estimate would be consistent with a figure of about 20 percent urban unemployment. With no growth in sight, the unemployment rate would have been increasing by 3–4 percentage points per year simply because of natural increases in labor force participation. Along with this growing unemployment in the cities there was a drastic decline in real wages paid to employed workers of approximately 30 percent. Combining these figures, the estimate of a decline in per capita income of 36–48 percent (AID 1976, pt. A, p. 118) seems reasonable. Unemployment and poverty in the urban areas were rapidly becoming the major economic problems in Vietnam, and the political implications of this situation were being felt even before the country's defeat in 1975.[33]

Farmers did not fare so badly during this period. The successful land reform program, combined with lessening GVN price intervention as the world price of rice more than doubled, improved the relative welfare of farmers dramatically.[34] Because of unfavorable weather conditions in 1972, the rice crop declined from 6.1 million metric tons in the previous year to 5.9 million tons. The next two years were very good for rice farmers, who increased the area under cultivation by 10 percent and increased production to 6.6 million tons in 1973 and 7.1 million tons in 1974, despite the numerous cease-fire violations that occurred after the Paris agreements. By the time the war came to an end, South Vietnam had become virtually self-sufficient in rice, and that was one of the major economic successes of the twenty-year period.

The export sector also turned in a favorable performance during this period. Stuck at about $12 million per year in merchandise exports during 1968–71, export earnings increased to $85 million in 1974. The factors accounting for this improvement were increases in world prices, a subsidy paid to exporters through the foreign exchange rate mechanism, and new export activities in items such as wood products, frozen shrimp, and other fish products. This is a paltry sum in comparison with the amount that would have been required in the long run, but it was a significant start, and one that had been delayed for many years. Another bright spot was the developing oil situation off the coast of Vietnam in the South China Sea. Exploration began in 1973, and oil was discovered in the summer of 1974. This potential solution to the balance-of-payments problem was making a contribution when the war ended. Drilling rights to foreign oil companies were sold for $17 million in 1973 and $30 million in 1974.

With the severe curtailment in foreign aid and rising budgetary demands due to refugee relief and job works programs, the Vietnamese government made its first move in seventeen years to seriously alter its domestic tax structure by putting into effect a value-added tax in 1973. Domestic revenues, which had covered only 25 percent of government expenditures in 1970–2, financed 41 percent of them in 1975.[35] This is just another example of a theme of the previous section, namely, the increasing audacity of the GVN to govern. The relatively complicated value-added tax was imposed widely, and perhaps unwisely during a recession and in an institutional environment in which it was not well understood. Immediate results included a surge of price increases, confusion and political unrest (AID 1976, pt. A, pp. 128–9), and a drag on demand that contributed to prolonging the recession. Subsequently it was rescinded at the retail level. Despite some undesirable effects, it became Vietnam's major source of revenue at a time when U.S. aid was declining, and it ranks as a major accomplishment of Vietnam politics and economic policy. However, like most of the successful economic reforms, it came too late to be a factor in development.

The removal of U.S. troops and the Paris agreements that the government was forced to accept were demoralizing events in South Vietnam. They created more uncertainty than tranquility. Although the Vietnamese government had never been friendly to the idea of foreign investment, it made an overture in that direction in the early 1970s. In the uncertain environment that prevailed, foreign countries lost interest in some projects that had been under discussion for several years.[36] That these events affected the morale of the armed forces has been documented in a book based on interviews with refugees who fled to the United States (Hosmer, Kellen, and Jenkins 1980). This uncertainty had another curious effect. It contributed to a rise in the velocity of money at a time when the Vietnamese had apparently learned how to keep their money supply under control and how to reduce the inflationary impact of the deficit by selling bonds to the public. Consequently, the inflation rates in the last two years of the war were higher than one would have expected, given the data on money supply. We have already commented on the effect of this inflation on the standard of living of the urban population. It had similar effects on members of the armed forces as the government resisted major pay increases because of tight financial conditions. The severe reduction in real pay to members of the armed forces is thought to have impaired the army's effectiveness (U.S. Senate 1974, p. 8).

In May 1974, the U.S. Senate Foreign Relations Committee sent a team of investigators to report on the situation in Vietnam. Regarding the economy, this team summarized its findings as follows:

Vietnam is rich in agricultural resources but cannot feed herself, has absorbed western technology but cannot afford the imports to operate it, has a well trained labor force but cannot employ it, and provides a wide range of government services but does not have the means to pay for them. [U.S. Senate 1974, p. 30]

This truly dismal appraisal came about a year before the fall of South Vietnam.

At the very end, the economy was to sink to an even lower level than indicated in this gloomy but not totally accurate assessment. According to the AID *Terminal Report*, the GVN appears to have become indecisive, if not paralyzed, in its last year of operation as military and economic assistance continued to decrease. It has been estimated that the budget for 1975 would have been in the neighborhood of 1 trillion piasters, with a deficit of perhaps some 600 billion piasters (AID 1976, pt. A, p. 141), one-fifth of its GNP. Such a deficit would have required at least a 50 percent increase in the money supply, because the increase in government revenues had slowed considerably. Despite declining demand, it is likely that inflation would have accelerated and the standard of living would have continued to fall. When Communist forces marched into Saigon on April 30, 1975, the economy was in a state of collapse.

1.6   The aid economy

Most writers during the war who dealt with Vietnam economic affairs were highly critical of the way the government managed the economy and the manner in which U.S. aid was used. Their criticisms implied that the situation might have been different (better) at the time if certain abuses had been corrected. The abuses usually were thought to be associated with corruption, political indifference to social needs, pampering of the population with un-necessary imports, undue government interference in the economy, hostility toward foreign investment, and a host of policy indiscretions with respect to domestic taxation, interest rates, and the foreign exchange rate. Everyone realized that the war was the major uncertainty affecting economic devel-opment, but one question persisted: Given the war, would it have been possible for the Vietnam economy to have performed significantly better than it did considering the amount of aid the country received?

The word used most frequently to describe the amount of aid was "mas-sive." By one modest measure, U.S. economic assistance to Vietnam was $8.5 billion over the twenty-year period, with an additional $17 billion in military aid. On average, economic aid was about one-fourth of the country's GNP. Calculated in today's prices (1985), the annual figure would be close to $1.3 billion. Because of the tenuous conditions that prevailed, most of the aid was used to stabilize prices, which means it was spent on imports of consumption goods or materials that contributed to domestic production of consumer goods. The standard of living rose by 1.5–2.0 percent per capita per year, and that was sufficient to keep the people from rising up against the government as the Communist side hoped they would.

Only a small share of the aid was directed toward long-run development. The economy grew so long as aid was forthcoming in large amounts, but it never developed a momentum to grow on its own. The agriculture sector was making great strides in increasing output in the last several years of the war, and it was able to release labor for other uses. This desirable and normal outcome became a part of the problem in Vietnam. So long as the military forces were growing, absorption of the surplus labor was easily achieved. Industrial development was too slow to be a major factor in the critical absorption process when the military stopped growing around 1970. One result was increased crowding in cities and a developing unemployment prob-lem that had no easy solution.

Surely, Vietnam needed a balanced economy to solve its long-run needs. For example, just to absorb 100,000 of the 300,000 or so new entrants into the labor force each year in the early 1970s, manufacturing activity would have required an annual investment on the order of $400 million,[37] or a net investment of about 15 percent of Vietnam's national income, *just in manufacturing*. This kind of investment capital was not forthcoming in the environment that existed in the early 1970s, or any other time, in South Vietnam. Not even 100,000 jobs had been created in industry for an entire decade before Vietnam's fall. The economy began in a top-heavy condition when the French left in 1955, and that condition did not improve over the next twenty years. The solution in the beginning was to support this structure with American aid. When that aid started to dry up, the structure began to crumble.

CHAPTER 2

U.S. aid to Vietnam: goals and programming

Two major themes on the purpose of foreign aid are expressed throughout the literature. One is highly pragmatic, realistic, and, in the view of some, even contemptible. The other is idealistic. The first is that foreign aid is (and should be) one instrument of foreign policy used to advance the goals of the donor in the world arena. The second theme is that foreign aid should be given generously to promote economic development in poor countries. Because the first theme can easily encompass the second, they are not necessarily inconsistent. However, it is important to separate these themes, because they suggest the use of different criteria for the purpose of evaluating the effectiveness of a given aid program. The first section of this chapter is given to a discussion of the goals of foreign aid in general, without reference to Vietnam aid.

Next we attempt to define the goals of the massive U.S. economic aid program to South Vietnam. A year after the fall of Saigon, the Agency for International Development (AID) completed a major review of its twenty years of aid to Vietnam (AID 1976). Unfortunately, that report contains no coherent discussion of the criteria by which the effectiveness of the various programs was to be judged. Thus, a necessary first step in our analysis of aid is to identify the principal objectives of U.S. economic aid to South Vietnam, and that is undertaken in Section 2.2. Despite conflicting statements, it seems evident that economic assistance to wartime South Vietnam was one means by which the United States attempted to achieve a military-geopolitical goal, that of keeping the country in the Western sphere of influence. With this purpose in mind, economic development would have to occur as a spillover effect and therefore would proceed at a slower pace than one might expect from the size of the aid program.

Given that the goal of economic aid was to keep the government of South Vietnam (GVN) from collapsing from nonmilitary causes, there was the problem of how much was necessary. Section 2.3 describes a procedure called "gap analysis" that American advisors in Saigon used to produce a rough estimate of the annual aid requirement. The effect of gap analysis was to focus attention on aid as an antiinflation measure, rather than to explicitly promote development, and it created a disincentive system for government economic policy and economic performance. We close out this chapter with a comment on the intriguing question Can aid be harmful?

2.1 Objectives of foreign aid

2.1.1 Promoting general economic development

Many economists would argue that the purpose of foreign aid is to accelerate economic development "up to a point where a satisfactory rate of growth can be achieved on a self-sustaining basis" (Rosenstein-Rodan 1961, p. 107). This view of aid encouraged the construction of a number of Harrod-Domar-type models that were used to estimate the amount of aid necessary and the time required for an underdeveloped country to achieve self-sustaining growth.[1]

To the architects of this theory of foreign aid, the essence of the development problem was insufficient savings and/or exports. To achieve some predetermined or "desirable" rate of growth requires a calculable rate of investment, given information about the incremental capital-output ratio. By this approach, a major reason why an underdeveloped country is not on the desired growth path is that its saving ratio is too small, and therefore the annual amount of savings generated in the economy is insufficient to finance the investment required for the desired rate of growth. Accordingly, the role of foreign aid is to fill the saving–investment gap. By raising the growth rate, foreign aid will contribute to a narrowing of the saving–investment gap, assuming the marginal saving rate is greater than the average, and thereby reduce the need for foreign aid in the long run.[2]

In an open economy it is possible that the constraint to self-sustained growth would be imports (of capital goods). In other words, a country might save enough to meet the required flow of investment but be unable to buy the capital goods abroad because of insufficient exporting and a lack of foreign exchange. In that case there would exist a foreign exchange earnings–expenditure gap, and the purpose of aid would be to fill that gap. If the rate of growth in exports were greater than the rate of growth in required imports, then the foreign exchange gap would be eliminated over time, and aid could be terminated. Or, as income rises, it is possible that the ability to export will increase more rapidly than the need to import, and foreign aid will eventually become unnecessary.[3]

A third constraint could be the inability of underdeveloped countries to "absorb" capital imports. The concept of absorptive capacity is fairly easy to comprehend in an intuitive way, but extremely difficult to formalize.[4] Generally it refers to important constraints such as lack of knowledge, skills, and managerial experience, as well as to other institutional and cultural factors such as bureaucratic inefficiency, poor work discipline, and internal disorder (Adler 1965, pp. 31–3). Given these limitations, it might not be possible for an underdeveloped country to efficiently use all of the foreign aid it might be able to obtain. Thus, elimination of the saving-investment gap and foreign exchange gap might not be sufficient to assure self-sustained growth or, at least, might lengthen the time required. If absorptive capacity were a constraint to development, technical assistance along with capital inflow would be required.

Institutionally oriented analysts of foreign aid are critical of these rather mechanical approaches to foreign aid planning (Mikesell 1968, pp. 91–104; Streeten 1972, ch. 16). They disagree with some of the assumptions that underlie two-gap models and are skeptical about the empirical evidence needed to support some of the functions. Despite certain deficiencies of the models, there have been numerous serious attempts to use them to estimate the aid requirements of specific underdeveloped countries (Chenery and Strout 1966; Fei and Paauw 1965), as well as for the entire underdeveloped world (Rosenstein-Rodan 1961).[5] Gap models that incorporate time as an explicit variable were formulated to estimate the future dependence of the Vietnam economy on U.S. aid (Grimm and Piekarz 1971; Smithies 1972) under the assumption that South Vietnam would survive as an independent nation. In those studies in which emphasis is placed on self-sustaining growth there is an implicit assumption that the purpose of international aid is to promote economic development in general, but without specific reference to the issue of poverty. The question is not "why aid?" but "how much?"

2.1.2   Aid and basic needs

Within the past decade or so, the focus of the development literature has shifted from discussion of investment needs to income distribution and "basic needs." This shift has been so widely accepted that one of the leaders of the basic needs approach has claimed that academicians "are not considered respectable anymore unless the objective of poverty alleviation is woven into their . . . economic writings" (ul Haq 1976, p. 59). Under the "trickle-down" assumption, foreign aid eventually would help to remove poverty; but this assumption has been rejected. In view of the fact that many of the advocates of basic needs also endorse "self-reliance" as a part of the development strategy, it is difficult to see how foreign aid fits into this approach. So long as the focus of development was on investment, the essential role of foreign aid was easy to define. In the new environment, the "theory of foreign aid" has become somewhat amorphous.

The basic needs approach was articulated by high officials during the

MacNamara reign at the World Bank and became the rallying cry for the Third World Forum. Advocates of this view think that world poverty cannot be eliminated under the political conditions that have existed in the developing world up to the present. What is needed is drastic institutional and structural change in the poor countries if they are ever to overcome poverty, and officials who control events in those countries are not likely to change their orientation without intense prodding. Furthermore, in comparison with the requisites for alleviating poverty, the present flow of aid is totally inadequate to do the job, and it is given with so many strings attached as to "sap the initiative and freedom of action of the developing world" (ul Haq 1976, p. 45).

A part of this solution to the problem of poverty is a massive transfer of wealth from the rich to the poor countries, coupled with a genuine interest in both to eliminate poverty. We see here a basic conflict with the theory of aid that was developed in the 1950s and early 1960s. That theory was based on marginalism and trickle-down. In this new approach to foreign assistance, a little aid is worse than none, because it fosters dependency and never touches the poor.

Although there are many new ideas regarding transfer mechanisms for assuring benefits to the poor, a new theory of foreign aid has not emerged. Even though some of the original architects of the theory of foreign aid are quite sympathetic with the move to place poverty and structural change at the forefront of the development literature, there has been little effort to articulate a new theory of foreign aid with new announced goals.[6] Perhaps what is needed is a model based on the Harrod-Domar concept of investment-led growth, but with a threshold requirement for the poor. Growth would not become automatic until the poor reached a certain level of training and wealth. In such a model, the first goal of international transfers would be to fill the poverty gap. Once that was achieved, the conventional approach could be used.

2.1.3   Noneconomic objectives of foreign aid

It is entirely possible that foreign aid will have very little impact on economic development, because the type of aid and the manner in which it is given may be intended to promote noneconomic objectives. To assess the effectiveness of an aid program, therefore, one has to understand the political as well as the economic objectives of aid. Of the many words that have been written and spoken about the objectives of the United States in giving aid,[7] most indicate the paramount importance of noneconomic factors. Furthermore, there can be little doubt that the principal historical rationale for U.S. aid has been international security, not economic development or humanitarian assistance, in spite of expressions by political leaders that the true motive is ethical.[8] Indeed, it has been suspected that aid specifically earmarked as economic, social, and humanitarian has been given as a form of bribery for the purpose of advancing perceived U.S. security needs (Morgenthau 1962, p. 302). That underdeveloped countries must advance economically in order to maintain some kind of free and independent societies is accepted as a tenet of faith in the Western world. Given that approach, the major consequence of insufficient economic progress is assumed to be revolution or internal division leading to "instability and threats to peace." Thus, economic assistance provided by the United States to underdeveloped countries has been considered as a means of forestalling unfavorable political crises. President Eisenhower was explicit on this point. "Our assistance is the *insurance* against rising tensions and increased dangers of war," he said (U.S. Department of State 1957, p. 4).

Charles Wolf (1960, ch. 7) has admirably discussed the objectives of both military and nonmilitary U.S. assistance programs. Even nonmilitary aid, according to Wolf, is intended to serve political as well as economic and humanitarian objectives. Internal political stability, maintaining friendship, and gaining influence are the principal political goals of nonmilitary foreign aid, whereas the economic objectives may be related to the potential gains from trade and the procurement of strategic materials. Humanitarian motives in aid-giving are present to a limited extent and are manifested in programs such as the Peace Corps; however, those motives are hardly an effective rationale for *continuous* aid, because the foreign aid program is formulated and promoted in an administrative and political environment that is highly pragmatic. Members of Congress who favor aid programs have to justify them on an annual basis to the voters, who usually want something in return for their tax payments (Mason 1964, pp. 27–8). On the question of the purely economic objectives of foreign aid, Wolf (1960, p. 681) has concluded that anticipated gains from trade and increases in supplies of strategic materials are unrealistic objectives of economic aid, because the presumed economic gains have never been demonstrated empirically. Thus, there is a strong belief that the objectives of economic aid are predominantly political.

2.2   Foreign aid and U.S. objectives in Vietnam

The contrast between what U.S. officials said about aid in the 1960s and what the State Department actually did is striking. From 1961, when the Foreign Assistance Act replaced the Mutual Security Act, economic development ascended over the ideology of the "cold warriors" as the rationale for foreign aid in the United States. This view was favored not only in academic halls; similar thinking was expressed in the halls of Congress and by officials in the State Department. Samuel Huntington (1972, p. 24) summed up the situation by saying that "aid and development came to be so closely linked as to be about interchangeable."

It is probably true that most thinkers actively concerned with foreign aid rationalized it as contributing to economic development. One is less sure that most members of Congress cared much for economic development, and there is evidence that economic development was not a major reason for giving economic aid to South Vietnam and a number of other countries despite many public statements to the contrary. By 1972, about 35 percent of the funds requested for AID were specifically marked as "supporting assistance" for countries such as Vietnam, Cambodia, Laos, and Jordan,[9] compromising, in reality, the lofty statements of aid spokesmen.

Clearly, aid was used as an adjunct to U.S. political and military strategy in Southeast Asia. In the late 1960s the United States was spending $30 billion per year on the war in Vietnam, and the U.S. government was not disposed to risk this heavy investment by allowing the economy of Vietnam to sink. At the same time, total gross economic assistance was $700–800 million. It is, of course, understandable that the United States should have been willing to pay an amount less than 3 percent of its investment as insurance against collapse of the entire effort.[10] This insurance view of economic assistance to a very large extent shaped the design of the U.S. aid program to Vietnam, including the amount of nonmilitary aid provided, and placed major stress on defense and economic stabilization at the expense of economic development whenever there might be a conflict.[11]

To advance U.S. foreign policy objectives, American aid to South Vietnam was administered in such a way as to (1) supply budgetary support to the Vietnamese government (GVN) while, at the same time, (2) supplying goods to the Vietnamese people in order to improve their standard of living. This double-track approach to U.S. aid policy required specifically tailored programs. Both the Commercial Import Program (CIP) and the PL 480 program, called Food for Peace (FFP), satisfied the requirement. Under the CIP, the aid dollars were sold to Vietnamese importers for piasters, creating counterpart funds owned by the U.S. government. To operate its mission in Vietnam, the United States spent some of the aid-acquired piasters on the local economy and turned the rest over to the Vietnamese government for general budgetary support. Under the FFP program, the counterpart generated by the sale of designated agricultural products was earmarked specifically for the Vietnamese military budget. The imported goods financed by aid dollars were primarily consumer-oriented, because it was assumed that a rise in the standard of living would generate popular support for the government. After 1964, when inflation became the major economic problem in South Vietnam, statements relating aid and inflationary control appear most frequently. However, controlling inflation and providing budgetary support are just different ways of looking at the same problem.

A major worry of U.S. officials was that a severe inflation would cause discontentment among the people, making it virtually impossible for any Vietnamese government to rule. Lack of political stability, undoubtedly, would have jeopardized the GVN's ability to wage war against the enemy, and the key to success for U.S. foreign policy in Southeast Asia was a militarily strong South Vietnam. Thus, the role of foreign aid in Vietnam was fairly straightforward: Keep the people as contented as necessary to support the government. Achievement of that goal required keeping the rate of inflation within tolerable limits and gradually increasing the standard of living of the people under government control.

That the United States should have looked on economic aid as a means of achieving a larger political objective in Vietnam is consistent with stated foreign aid policy at the time. In his written testimony supporting the foreign aid bill, David Bell, the AID administrator, proclaimed Vietnam as one among the "countries in which the short-run objective is to maintain external and internal security with economic development as a long-run goal" (U.S. Senate 1963, p. 69). Aid earmarked for the seven countries listed in this category for fiscal year 1964 was about 10 percent of the total AID request.

The president of the United States expressed keen interest in economic development in Vietnam. In February 1966, when both the military and economic situations in Vietnam appeared threatening, a conference between South Vietnamese officials and Americans took place in Honolulu.[12] Although the conference dealt mainly with pacification, there were some statements about economic priorities. In his final statement, President Johnson warned everyone responsible for carrying out policy that he wanted performance ("coonskins on the wall"), not simply "phrases and high sounding words," toward achieving higher output, more efficient production, and improvements in credit, handicraft, light industry, and rural electrification (U.S. Department of Defense 1971, book C, ch. 8, p. 41). All of these words can be summed up as economic development. Chester Cooper (1970, p. 298) summarized the *intent* of the conference as emphasizing "economic development, social progress, rural construction, and willingness to negotiate a political settlement." Thus, from statements of high-ranking public officials, it appears that economic development was high on the list of priorities. Little attention was given to inflationary control at the time, despite the fact that prices in Vietnam had risen about as fast in the six months preceding the conference as they had risen in the previous four years.

One month after the conference, Mr. Rutherford Poats, assistant administrator for the Far East in the AID, testified before a House of Representatives committee that "AID is engaged in Vietnam in two crucial aspects of the war – the fight against communist subversion and insurgency, primarily in the rural areas; and the fight against inflation and critical commodity shortages in the market place, primarily in the cities and in isolated towns" (U.S. House of Representatives 1966, p. 192). Mr. Poats repeated that theme again in April 1967, but this time he gave the breakdown on fiscal 1967 AID expenditures. Of the $516 million program total, $289 million was intended for "economic stabilization," and only $33 million for "long-range development" (U.S. House of Representatives 1967, pp. 12–13). Finally, in a statement inserted into the record on the Commercial Import Program for the benefit of the Senate Foreign Relations Committee, the Vietnam aid program is described as a "major tool to help cushion the inflationary impact of rapid manpower mobilization and rising Vietnamese military expenditures on the economy of Vietnam" (U.S. Senate 1969, p. 67). Thus, it appears that fighting inflation emerged as the principal goal of the U.S. aid program in word as well as in deed.

2.3   Programming the amount of U.S. aid to Vietnam

The accounting system designed to carry out the political mandate to control inflation was based on the theory of the inflationary or monetary gap.[13] Starting from a position of equilibrium, if monetary demand increases for any reason while real availability does not, inflationary pressure will develop. To eliminate the inflationary pressure, it is necessary to reduce monetary demand or increase availability or achieve some combination of both. Increases in monetary demand are called "injections" (of purchasing power), and increases in availability are called "absorptions" (of purchasing power), in the language of gap accounting as employed at the operating level in wartime Vietnam. The main causes of new injections were the ever-increasing GVN budget and, for a time, the increase in U.S. personnel expenditures on the local economy that accompanied the buildup of U.S. troops and civilians. The principal sources of new absorptions were increases in government revenues and imports. Table 2.1 shows the National Bank of Vietnam calculation of the inflationary gap for 1966–72. The entries in the table are much more aggregated than similar computations made by analysts employed by the AID mission to Vietnam (USAID), from whom the National Bank accountants learned the accounting system.

This technique was introduced by USAID not for the purpose of a posteriori accounting but rather as a tool for predicting the expected rate of inflation and the aid requirement for some future period. By combining a gap calculation with a strict interpretation of the quantity theory of money, theoretically one could estimate the expected rate of inflation for some future period. The

Table 2.1. Inflationary gap, 1966–72 (billion piasters)

	Symbol	1966	1967	1968	1969	1970	1971	1972
Monetary injections								
1. GVN expenditures	E	64.00	109.47	122.63	150.37	206.69	242.18	346.80
2. U.S. expenditures	U	30.00	47.05	45.89	50.36	50.39	100.71	134.18
3. Exports	OI	10.60	3.74	1.33	1.77	1.87	3.67	10.00
4. Financial transfers (purchase of foreign exchange)	OI		6.14	8.79	9.99	9.58	15.75	26.64
5. Increase (+) or decrease (−) in bank credits	OI	20.00	−2.04	0.78	3.85	12.81	21.15	25.92
Total		124.60	164.36	179.42	216.34	281.00	383.46	543.54
Monetary absorptions								
1. GVN revenues	R	42.80	66.93	55.01	100.46	143.11	154.36	224.33
2. Imports	IMP	53.70	66.50	62.30	78.01	80.82	115.99	196.93
3. Financial transfers (sales of foreign exchange)	OA	9.50	12.22	14.08	13.22	8.88	16.58	24.43
4. Increase (+) or decrease (−) in time deposits and capital accounts	OA	0.70	1.92	7.79	11.82	11.91	36.33	75.45
5. Advanced deposits for imports and import credits	OA		0.96	−1.62	−3.84	13.64	9.04	0.85
6. Statistical discrepancy						0.51	5.63	2.15
Total	G	106.70	145.61	137.56	199.67	258.87	337.87	524.14
Inflationary gap		17.90	18.75	41.86	16.67	22.13	45.53	19.40

Source: VN-NBVN (worksheet).

validity of an estimate of inflation based on a calculated monetary gap is predicated on the following four assumptions: (1) There is no change in real domestic output in the forecast period. (2) The only sources of increase in the money stock are those implied in the gap. (3) The velocity of circulation of money remains constant. (4) There is no change in the foreign exchange balance.[14]

To illustrate how gap analysis was used as an input to decision making, some simple algebra is useful. Let

$$E$$ = expected GVN expenditures in piasters
$$U$$ = expected U.S. piaster expenditures in Vietnam
$$R$$ = total expected GVN revenues (taxes)
$$A$$ = value of aid in piasters
IMP = expected value of imports in piasters
OI = other injections expected
OA = other absorptions expected
$$M$$ = stock of money
$$G$$ = inflationary gap
INF* = expected rate of inflation

Gap analysis as applied to wartime Vietnam was based on the following identity:

$$G = E + U + OI - IMP - R - OA$$

For simplicity, assume that IMP $= U + A$ (both U and A generate dollars to finance imports). It follows that

$$G = E + OI - R - A - OA$$

Now, assume that the gap is accommodated by an increase in the stock of money, so that $G = \Delta M$. If the velocity of circulation is held constant, INF* $= \Delta M/M$. Therefore, INF* $= G/M$.

Given this simple model and knowledge of E, OI, R, A, and OA, one could estimate G and INF*. Importantly, inflation could be controlled at some predetermined level by adjusting aid. But A was not the only possible control variable. It is evident that one could try to fix the rate of inflation by adjusting one or a combination of E, OI, R, and OA, as well as A. Suppose we assume that the GVN had little control over OI and OA, but could theoretically control E and R, its expenditures and revenues. Now, it is fairly well established that government expenditures are not cut during a war, and, practically speaking, they are not usually subject to severe constraints. Of course, Vietnamese public officials made speeches about eliminating all nonessential expenditures, as the Americans constantly urged them to do. Despite this, one did not observe much restraint in the actual wartime budgets of South Vietnam. Thus, with the elimination of E as an effective control variable, the only remaining variable under control by the GVN was R.

During the war period, both allies agreed that a desirable military outcome depended on political stability, which in turn depended on economic stability. It seemed rational, therefore, to fix a target for inflation that would fall within a safe limit and then set the control variables in order to achieve the target rate.[15] The weapons available for controlling inflation were to manipulate U.S. aid to Vietnam or to manipulate Vietnamese taxes. In Chapter 12 we point out that the Vietnamese tax base was very limited. Besides, government officials did reasonably argue that high taxes would alienate the urban masses, and a tax revolt in the cities would cause political problems perhaps even greater than inflation. In fact, no serious effort was made to control inflation by raising taxes. In the end, manipulation of U.S. aid appeared to be the only feasible way to fight inflation, and the development goal proclaimed in Honolulu had to be sacrificed.[16]

Once the Vietnamese learned how to play the gap game, they had ready answers to some important questions. They could argue, using an acquired language, that inflation was directly related to the size of the gap, and only a limited number of ways to reduce it were available. The GVN could not reduce expenditures in the war situation, nor could it raise taxes, because that would cause political unrest. The only feasible solution was more aid. The major problem with programming aid by use of gap analysis was that it effectively focused attention on what the Americans had to do rather than what the Vietnamese should have done. To the extent that building a record of solving one's own problems is important for self-sustained growth of a country, the approach used to fix aid levels for Vietnam was antidevelopmental.

2.4   MACV economic aid and the piaster valuation problem[17]

Execution of the plan to use aid primarily to control inflation for short-run political advantage, rather than for long-run development, affected other economic decisions that were only peripherally related to inflation control. An important problem throughout the war period was how to set the foreign exchange rate for the Vietnamese monetary unit of account, the piaster; and the decisions made with respect to the foreign exchange rate were always influenced by the understanding that the U.S. intended to supply enough aid to keep prices from rising much above 30 percent. Vietnamese officials resisted devaluing the piaster when it was clear that its overvaluation was causing misallocation of both domestic and international resources because the foreign exchange rate also influenced the amount of aid they received.

The foreign exchange value of any currency depends on world demand for a country's exports and its demand for imports. From the beginning in 1955, Vietnam had a large export deficit, and the trade gap grew during the war. The export deficit in the 1955–60 period was $176 million per year on average, whereas in the years of relative economic prosperity, 1969–71, it was $625 million on average.[18] Without American aid the piaster would have been worth very little in international trade, because countries other than the United States had little demand for Vietnamese goods and, especially, services. This fundamental proposition was understood by policymakers; nevertheless, there were almost daily discussions on the value of the piaster and what the exchange rate ought to be. The official rates established by the GVN remained unchanged for roughly two periods of five years each between 1962 and 1972, despite the fact that domestic prices rose much faster than world prices over most of that period. The combination of a fixed rate of exchange and significant domestic inflation created conditions under which importers were able to realize large windfall profits[19] and greatly militated against any additional export activity and domestic investment. Almost all of the economic consequences of currency overvaluation were unfavorable for long-run economic development, and these consequences were understood clearly at the time. Why, then, did the government persist in keeping the piaster overvalued?[20]

One reason may be that overvaluation was profitable for some government officials and certain privileged importers. However, there is a second reason of more substance. To understand the second reason, one first has to realize that there were two American aid programs, rather than a single program. The major program was administered by the Agency for International Development. The Commercial Import Program and Food for Peace were the foci of AID (and, technically, the U.S. Agriculture Department) contributions, and these programs required that almost all CIP and FFP dollars be used to purchase U.S. exports. The other aid program drew funds from the U.S. Military Assistance Command Vietnam (MACV), which hired as many as 140,000 Vietnamese civilians (in 1969) to perform numerous construction, maintenance, and service jobs for the command. To pay the Vietnamese workers, MACV purchased piasters from the National Bank of Vietnam at the official exchange rate. These dollars were made available under the "GVN-financed" import program to pay for imports from Japan (primarily), Taiwan, Hong Kong, and a few other countries. The amount of dollar aid made available to the GVN by MACV purchase of piasters depended on the official exchange rate. Given this method of transferring aid, the GVN thought, correctly, it could receive more aid by maintaining a low piaster-for-dollar exchange rate rather than a higher one. Therefore, it resisted frequent devaluation up to 1972, when the currency was allowed to float at short intervals.

How did American officials regard this situation? They frequently encouraged the Vietnamese government to devalue, because they understood how an overvalued piaster could lead to misallocation of resources and, especially, how it reduced exports. Members of the U.S. Congress objected to the overvaluation of the piaster because they knew the policy was costing the United States more than necessary to operate its mission in Vietnam, and they worried, too, because it helped to sustain the currency black market in Vietnam that some congressmen saw as contributing to the "deterioration of the morale and morals of Americans fighting and working in Vietnam" (U.S. House of Representatives 1970, p. 4). (Americans "fighting and working in Vietnam" supplied the dollars to the currency black market!) There was the possibility of forcing devaluation, thereby reducing the size of the MACV aid program and making up the difference with additional CIP or FFP aid. However, U.S. economic advisors recognized that changing the composition away from MACV dollars and toward AID would be detrimental to the cause of inflationary control in the short run, because AID dollars were tied, for all practical purposes, to U.S. exports that were priced about 30 percent higher than comparable Japanese exports.[21] Thus, for a given amount of total aid dollars, the deflationary effect would be greater the higher the percentage of MACV aid to total aid. A MACV dollar was more antiinflationary, and it also raised the standard of living more than an AID dollar. Because both price stability and improvement in the standard of living were integral parts of maintaining political stability, American advisors realized clearly that the effect of devaluation would not be favorable in all respects. That explains, at least partly, why the American advisors did not insist on frequent devaluations. Evidently, devaluation did not serve the immediate U.S. interest in Vietnam,[22] although it probably would have served the long-run interest of economic development.

2.5   Can aid be harmful?

The success of Marshall Plan aid in helping to rebuild Western Europe kindled an enthusiasm among politicians and economists that led to the view that similar achievements might be expected in the Third World. New theories on economic growth stressing saving and the capital–output ratio buttressed this optimistic view. Studies were undertaken to indicate the amount of foreign aid required and the time necessary to raise the growth rates of underdeveloped countries to levels that would be self-sustaining. Agendas for the transfer of aid from developed to underdeveloped areas, suggesting the percentages of GNP developed nations should contribute, were drawn up. Actual events have not justified the early optimism of those analysts.

Of course, not everyone thought that foreign aid was the solution to the problem of economic development. Griffin and Enos have been strong critics of foreign aid, insisting that it generally has neither accelerated growth nor promoted democracy. "If anything, aid may have retarded development by leading to lower domestic savings, by disturbing the composition of investment and thereby raising the capital–output ratio, by frustrating the emergence of an indigenous entrepreneurial class, and by inhibiting institutional reforms" (Griffin and Enos 1970, p. 236). P. T. Bauer has been a long time critic of aid. His main argument is that aid promotes concentration of power in government at the expense of the private sector. This discourages private saving and foreign commercial loans and direct investment, while it encourages capital flight (Bauer 1972, pp. 106–10), and, worst of all, it tends to politicize the developmental process (Bauer 1968, 1972, 1981, 1984). If the government captures a large part of foreign aid and uses it for "government consumption," which then must be maintained even after aid has been discontinued, the growth rate of income can be adversely affected (Dacy 1975). Mikesell has argued persuasively that foreign aid is, at best, only a supplement to domestic resources and of little use in a country that would not have developed without it (Mikesell 1968, pp. 258–61).

From the foregoing it can be seen that the answer to the question that began this section (Can aid be harmful?) is yes. Aid need not have harmful effects, but it can if it is not judiciously used. In the special case of South Vietnam, aid was not given for the purpose of development, and the manner in which it was given promoted economic dependency (Trong 1975). Rather, aid was given for the purpose of supporting the war effort, in large installments and sometimes without regard to its long-run economic consequences. Under such conditions it would be surprising if aid to Vietnam did not have some harmful effects. But this surely is no judgment on its overall effect.

Aside from some of the undesirable features of aid described by the authors mentioned earlier, there was one, perhaps unique to the Vietnam situation, that arose because of the size and character of the aid program. The U.S. aid program was highly visible, and this opened it to inspection and criticism by anyone disposed to criticize it. Also, it was politically sensitive, especially in the United States. Perhaps for these reasons, and because of established laws and other regulations, hundreds of U.S. advisors were sent to Vietnam to supervise, monitor, and report on the program. Alongside most of the Vietnamese officials engaged in economic matters there were AID officials instructing, coercing, and giving friendly advice. The CIP, for example, employed several dozen "commodity experts" (not development experts), whose task was to approve almost every item the Vietnamese wanted to import under the CIP. In effect, the AID officials served as micro control points in the disbursement of aid, but they also influenced how it was allocated, in many instances without regard to market forces or any other economic rationale. From an economic point of view the system was inefficient. It was established to satisfy political concerns, and it operated in the place of well-designed macro rules or policies.

This system of administering the aid program had an adverse effect on economic development for several reasons. In the first place, it was a poor substitute for general policies, such as forcing the Vietnamese to adopt a flexible exchange rate system, that would have permitted the price mechanism to give the proper signals for investment decisions. More important, it had an unfavorable effect on "economic Vietnamization" – placing responsibility for economic performance on the Vietnamese. Frequently, the major concern of Vietnamese officials was to please their American counterparts. Their work was less important than it would have been otherwise, and their incentives to do good work were accordingly reduced. This system of aid administration made the Vietnamese more dependent on the Americans, and that could not possibly serve the cause of long-run development.

2.6   Summary

There is no consensus among political, economic, or social analysts on what foreign aid is supposed to achieve. Narrowing the set considerably, there is not even consensus among economists whether or not aid is a desirable transfer. In the absence of agreement on criteria, it should not be surprising that analysts will disagree on the efficacy of any particular aid program. With reference to Vietnam, one finds conflicting statements on what the United States was trying to achieve with its huge economic aid program. Development, stabilization, refugee relief, "nation building," and other outcomes were all legitimate concerns. Unfortunately, AID's *Terminal Report* (1976) on Vietnam economic aid did not attempt to explain what the agency was trying to achieve, but an outsider writing about aid programs cannot avoid the issue. In the case of Vietnam it seems clear to this writer that economic aid was used as an integral part of the war effort that placed stress on stabilization rather than on development.

In the early literature on the Vietnam economy one sees criticisms of the aid program that are convincing only if one thinks that economic development was the principal goal of aid. It was not. Even so, there is the important question whether or not one might reasonably expect major developmental spillover from this expensive $8 billion program (not including military aid). To the extent that it is possible, we are interested in measuring this spillover effect. Because some economists would not necessarily expect aid to be an important input to development, even if it were intended for that purpose, we are also interested in any observations that will shed light on this topic. The extent to which the country developed economically is the concern of the next four chapters.

CHAPTER 3

The growth of national income

Adjusted national income accounts of the Republic of Vietnam indicate that real income rose at an annual rate of about 4 percent per year from 1956 through 1974. Allowing for population change, this rate of growth would be 1.4 percent per year. To anyone familiar with national income accounting practices in underdeveloped countries, figures such as those quoted should be read with some skepticism. Hence, in the first part of this chapter there is an attempt to remove some of the preconditioned mistrust that a reader might have for our figures by discussing sources of error in the Vietnam national income accounts and making adjustments when they can be justified by other information. The second part of the chapter describes income growth over time and the contribution to growth by sector of origin.

3.1 Economic activity, 1956–72

We are interested in knowing how fast the South Vietnamese economy grew and how major sectors shared in that growth over the two decades ending in 1975. Our search for this knowledge and answers to other questions pertaining to national income was frustrated by known inadequacies in official Vietnamese national income data. At first it seems advisable to present alternative data sets on growth in order to establish a range of estimates that will seem reasonable to many readers. Here are three such sets: (1) The official statistics on gross national product (GNP) as compiled by the National Bank of Vietnam (NBVN). Real GNP, or GNP at constant market prices, was estimated by the NBVN by deflating the expenditure side of the national accounts. (2) A new series on real net domestic product that we have constructed by deflating income originating by sector on the product side of the national accounts. (3) Our own construction of a composite index of economic activity based on physical production in several important sectors of the economy. Ultimately we wish to be more definitive, and this requires joining bits of information to construct a single series that will be free of some of the major objections to the present series.

3.1.1   The national income accounts of South Vietnam

The NBVN began compiling national income statistics in 1955. It discontinued publishing them a year later, presumably because of insufficient data to support the accounts. It resumed compilations again in 1960 and continued, with considerable lags in publication, up to the end of the Republic of Vietnam. The figures for 1973 and 1974 were never more than provisional estimates, and those for 1971 and 1972 were not revised.

The national income accounts were compiled in accordance with procedures established in the United Nations standard system of accounts. Any statement on how accurately the accounts reflect true gross national product or gross domestic product would be a speculation. Okubo (1974) has described and criticized the accounts on a sector-by-sector basis; however, she is silent on their overall accuracy. In an earlier study, Pearsall and Petersen (1971) discussed some conceptual flaws and data problems, but they thought that the accounts were reasonably good for the period of relatively stable prices that existed up to 1965. Both studies are highly critical of the deflators used to derive national income in constant piasters. With regard to the NBVN data on GNP in current prices, one does not gain any impression of consistent and correctable bias from either of the studies.[1] That one should have more confidence in current values than in constant values is hardly surprising, because the latter are derived from the former, and the derivation process adds additional sources of error.

The NBVN's estimates, which we refer to as the official estimates of GNP, are shown in Table 3.1. Estimates translated into dollar values are given in Table A3.5 at the end of this chapter.

3.1.2   Net domestic product

As part of its effort in the area of national income statistics, the NBVN assembled data on gross and net domestic product (NDP) originating by economic sector. These data, which relate to the product side of the accounts, were never, to our knowledge, deflated by the NBVN statisticians. As stated earlier, estimates of real GNP were obtained by deflating the expenditure components of the national accounts. Partly because we are interested in the sectoral distribution of real economic activity, we have attempted to deflate the NBVN's current price data in each originating sector. The major problem in this relatively straightforward procedure is to pick price indexes that can serve as reasonably defensible deflators.

Double deflation is the preferred procedure for generating real series from nominal series in the product accounts.[2] We do not have sufficient data to employ the double deflation technique and have to resort to the less acceptable

Table 3.1. *Official estimates of gross national product in South Vietnam, 1956–74 (billion piasters)*

Year	GNP in current prices	GNP in constant prices (1960 = 100)
1955	63.6[a]	
1956	68.7[a]	65.4[b]
1957	67.0[b]	66.5[b]
1958	71.3[b]	72.2[b]
1959	80.1[b]	79.1[b]
1960	81.8	81.8
1961	84.5	81.8
1962	93.8	88.2
1963	100.3	90.5
1964	114.5	98.8
1965	144.8	108.0
1966	236.2	108.5
1967	356.7	110.7
1968	385.3	105.8
1969	557.6	110.2
1970	804.4	117.5
1971	979.9[c]	120.7[c]
1972	1,102.0[c]	120.4[c]
1973	1,551.0[c]	120.8[c]
1974	2.229.0[c]	121.5[c]

[a]These data were the earliest GNP compilations by the National Bank of Vietnam. The series was not continued in 1957. They are published in the AID *Annual Statistical Bulletin* (AID-VN annual, no. 4, p. 15).

[b]These are not official estimates. They are the author's estimates. See Table A3.3.

[c]Provisional estimates of the National Bank of Vietnam. The estimates for 1973–4 were never officially published.

Source: National Bank of Vietnam data published in the *Vietnam Statistical Yearbook* (various issues) (VN-NIS annual).

procedure of direct deflation. This means that we select a price index appropriate to each sector and directly deflate the value added in each sector by the price index chosen. The principal rationale for the direct deflation method is that it is feasible given our data problems. We cannot comment whether or not and to what extent the resultant series are biased and how the bias (if any) compares with the bias that may exist in the NBVN national income accounts.

The precise deflators used for the sectors are described in a footnote to Table A3.2. The resulting series on real NDP, compiled as the sum of the sector entries, is presented as the third from the bottom row in Table 3.2.

Table 3.2. Net domestic product by sector of origin in constant (1962) prices at factor cost, 1960–72 (billion piasters)[a]

Sector	1960	1961	1962	1963	1964	1965	1966	1967	1968	1969	1970	1971	1972
Agriculture, hunting, forestry, fishing	31.2	26.2	26.2	27.3	29.8	29.8	25.6	28.8	26.7	27.8	32.3	34.3	26.4
Mining and quarrying	0.3	0.4	0.4	0.3	0.2	0.2	0.2	0.4	0.4	0.4	0.3	0.4	0.3
Manufacturing	9.2	9.2	8.6	9.8	9.6	11.4	14.2	14.4	12.3	12.5	15.2	14.9	11.7
Construction	1.3	1.2	1.1	1.3	1.4	1.4	1.6	1.1	1.2	1.9	2.0	1.7	1.5
Electricity, gas, water	0.6	0.7	1.6	0.7	1.2	0.9	0.6	0.6	0.5	0.9	0.8	0.9	1.0
Transportation and communication	3.2	3.4	3.3	3.3	3.4	4.2	3.6	3.8	1.9	3.2	2.9	3.2	3.8
Wholesale and retail trade	9.5	9.4	10.9	11.2	12.7	12.0	16.2	17.1	15.4	22.1	23.8	21.0	24.6
Banking and insurance	0.9	0.8	0.8	1.0	1.0	1.2	1.9	2.1	1.6	1.5	1.4	1.8	1.9
Ownership of dwellings	5.2	4.9	5.2	5.1	5.7	5.5	5.4	4.4	3.2	3.6	3.8	3.4	3.2
Services	4.6	4.8	5.1	5.4	5.9	5.9	6.7	7.3	9.2	7.5	8.0	7.3	7.3
Public administration and defense	12.6	13.1	16.2	16.6	19.9	25.1	32.9	35.2	40.9	44.4	43.6	49.2	50.2
Net domestic product at factor cost[b]	78.6	74.1	78.4	82.0	90.8	97.7	108.9	115.2	113.3	125.8	134.1	138.1	131.9
Public administration and defense adjusted[c]	12.0	13.3	16.2	16.2	19.2	21.4	23.1	24.8	29.7	34.3	38.6	41.4	42.3
Net domestic product at factor cost (adjusted)[b]	78.4	74.3	78.4	81.6	90.1	94.0	99.1	104.8	102.1	115.7	129.1	130.3	124.0

[a]Calculation of net domestic product (NDP) in constant prices: In general, NDP by sector of origin in constant prices was obtained by deflating the sector entries for NDP in current prices (Table A3.1) by appropriate sector price indexes (Table A3.2). The entries for public administration and defense are the exceptions to the deflation procedure. The growth in the public administration sector as given by the deflation procedure is at variance with a series on employment (including military) in the government sector. As explained in Section 3.1.4 in the text, the series on employment appear to be a more reliable indicator of government activity than deflated income originating in that sector. To obtain adjusted row entries for public administration, an index of "permanent civil equivalent" employees (from Table 3.3) was multiplied by NDP in public administration in 1962, the base year for all deflators.

The row entries designated "net domestic product at factor cost" in Table 3.2 were obtained by adding all the deflated incomes originating by sector, including public administration. The row entries designated "net domestic product at factor cost (adjusted)" were obtained by adding the employment-derived series for public administration to the deflated series for all other sectors.

[b]Sum of all the separate sectors. This entry is not strictly comparable with the standard procedure for estimating NDP, which subtracts relevant items from GNP to obtain NDP.

[c]See Section 3.1.5.

Source: Tables A3.1 and A3.2.

The summing-up procedure we used to compile real NDP is not the usual one for deriving it. The accepted procedure is to subtract from GNP the various accounting entries that distinguish GNP from NDP.[3] The residual is then reconciled with the sum of the sectors by a balancing item called a statistical discrepancy. One purpose of our approach was to avoid using GNP statistics in order to obtain an independent series. Thus, we have no statistical discrepancy to compare with that given in the official Vietnamese national income statistics.

3.1.3   Indicators of domestic activity

For underdeveloped countries in which the input–output relations are very simple it is possible to gain a rough check on national income statistics by constructing an index of domestic activity made up of separate sectoral physical indexes. For example, if agriculture and industry contribute little in the way of intermediate inputs to each other, which was the case in wartime Vietnam, a weighted average of physical production indexes for the two sectors will give a good indication of total activity in the two sectors. This method can produce useful information if used cautiously, and we shall construct a weighted index of this type for use in checking yearly estimates of GNP and NDP.

A composite index of physical output is subject to a number of statistical limitations. We wish to emphasize three reasons why our index might be misleading as an indicator of economic growth and welfare over a long period of time:

1. The index uses fixed weights for the components. Over long periods, as tastes and technology change, considerable shifts in the composition of purchases might occur. If the alteration in composition is due to changes in tastes that cause shifts in demand, the physical index will not give a true representation of the economic value of the class of products it is supposed to represent. The same is true for shifts in supply due to technological change. In both cases, relative prices are likely to change. Thus, the quantities purchased and their economic valuations could change, and the latter would not be reflected by changes in the physical indicators.

2. Physical indexes do not allow for the possibility of changes in the mix between value-added and non-value-added components. Of course, the ratio of value added to total value is determined by the state of technology, by the relative prices of all factor inputs, imported raw materials, and semifinished inputs, and by institutional realities such as whether or not free markets are allowed to set prices and the extent

of competition. An index of rice production constructed from data on tons of paddy rice output would overstate its economic value to Vietnam if, during the course of time, most of the increase in output were due to imported (non-value-added) fertilizer.

3. An aggregate index of output necessarily excludes a number of sectors for which no physical measures of output are available. If the index is to serve as an overall indicator of economic activity, it is necessary to assume that year-to-year percentage changes in the excluded sectors are the same as in the included sectors. Because the sectors for inclusion are decided by data availability rather than by truly random selection, there is no a priori reason to believe that the assumption of proportional change in the excluded sectors will hold true.

Despite potential shortcomings, we think it is useful to construct a composite index of physical production. The reader will observe later that there appears to be a significant discrepancy between NBVN's estimates of real GNP, obtained by deflating the expenditure side of the accounts, and our estimates of real NDP, obtained by deflating the product side of the accounts. Evidently the use of inconsistent deflators is responsible for this result, and we know of no objective test to help us decide which series is more trustworthy. As an aid in mediating between the NBVN's official index of national income and our new index of NDP, we construct a third measure – an index of domestic physical activity.

The components for this index were determined by using the following criteria:

1. Data must be available at least for the period 1960–72.
2. Each series must represent an important economic activity.
3. Each candidate must have physical output measures or at least measures not tied to piaster values.
4. Each economic activity selected must be fairly independent of the other activities in an input–output sense.

The first two criteria were selected for very practical reasons. We insisted on physical measures of output in order to eliminate the need to deflate, and we demanded near-zero input–output relationships in order to avoid double counting.

Seven series meet the selection criteria reasonably well and are included as components of an overall index of domestic economic activity. They are crop production, fish production, timber production, industrial production, construction, imports, and government.

3.1.3.1 Description of production indexes: By far the most important economic activity in South Vietnam was agriculture, including animal husbandry, forestry, and fishing. The production index for this sector comprises physical indexes of crop production, tons of fish caught, and cubic meters of timber cut. The index of crop production is a weighted index of production of fifteen different crops. The principal crop was rice, but the index also includes rubber production and relatively minor crops such as sugar, peanuts, and manioc. Whereas estimates of the absolute levels of crop production cannot be considered highly reliable, there is less suspicion regarding year-to-year variations; therefore, the index of crop production is probably more reliable than the raw data from which it is derived. The same comment on reliability of estimates applies to the data on total fish catch and timber.

The index of industrial production is a fixed-weight index made up of seventy-eight separate industrial products divided into classifications representing foodstuffs, beverages, tobacco, textiles, clothing and footwear, wood products, paper products, hides and skins, rubber products, glassware, aluminum products, iron and steel manufactures, machinery, electrical equipment, transport equipment, watches and clocks, plastic articles, miscellaneous products, and production of electricity. This rather inclusive list of manufactured products appears much more impressive than it was economically important in wartime South Vietnam. In fact, the total weight for beverages and tobacco in the index is 59 percent, and textiles, food processing, and electricity add another 32 percent. It is clear from the assigned weights that industrial activity in wartime Vietnam was not well developed.

The index for construction is derived from published data on building permit activity as measured in square meters of floor space. As indicators of construction, these data are deficient in a number of ways: (1) The ratio of construction undertaken without permits to that indicated by permit activity probably fluctuated over time. (2) Not all permits were used. (3) Permit data do not adequately indicate the timing of construction. (4) Permit data ignore the changes in the mix of electrical, plumbing, and other inputs. (5) Our indexes for 1956, 1957, and 1973 are based on building activity in Saigon alone.[4] Thus, in deriving an index of construction from these relatively poor data, we must assume that the ratio of reported to unreported construction was constant and that the percentage of permits fulfilled was constant. Furthermore, these gratuitous assumptions are probably easier to accept than others that deal with the quality of construction and its timing. Despite these severe objections, we believe it is better to include the index, because of its importance to the economy, rather than to exclude it.

Data to compute the previously described indexes were taken directly as published by the National Institute of Statistics.[5] We updated the indexes using the exact techniques employed by the various ministries responsible for them or constructed them as indexes from time series on physical quantities.

Our index of government activity – referred to as public administration and defense in the national income accounts – was never constructed by any agency of the Vietnamese government. Also, there is no physical measure of output in the government sector: All that exist are measures of inputs of labor. However, this poses no more serious conceptual difficulty in computing a measure of physical output than it does in national income accounting, where output of government is measured at factor cost of inputs. Our major problem in constructing an index of government input was that of dealing with the many different types of labor hired by the government and, specifically, how to combine the various classes of civil service employment and military manpower into a single or representative class of employment. Because the government sector was a dominant influence in Vietnamese economic life, we shall dwell at some length on government employment.

In 1960, according to NBVN data, government accounted for 17 percent of net domestic product, second only to agriculture and considerably more than any other sector. Thus, any indicator that purports to measure total domestic economic activity must consider the contribution of government, even if that contribution is measured by input rather than output. Over most of the period of this study, government spent from 80 to 90 percent of its receipts on direct wages and compensation of government employees, including the armed forces; thus, virtually all value added in the government sector was due to the services of people. Given this fact, the growth of employment in the government sector appears to be a reasonable candidate for a physical indicator of activity in the government sector. Accordingly, we used employment data – subject to alterations to be described later – as the indicator of government sector activity. We consider civil employment and military employment separately.

Civilian employment: Vietnamese statistics listed four basic categories of government civilian employees: (1) career government employees, (2) contract government employees, (3) daily wage employees, and (4) temporary employees, sometimes referred to as "floaters."[6] Career civil servants and contract employees were compensated at higher average rates than daily wage and temporary employees. Our problem was to combine the numbers in each category to reflect the fact (or assumption) that wage rates were correlated with output. Our solution to this problem required creating an artificial category called "career equivalent" employees. We assigned a weight to each of the four classes of employees and computed the sum of the weighted employment figures. We counted contract employees on a par with career civil servants, counted each daily wage employee as one-third of a career employee, and counted each temporary worker as one-fifth of a career employee.[7]

Military forces: The Republic of Vietnam classified its armed forces into three groups: (1) The regular forces consisted of the army (called ARVN), navy, marines, and air force; (2) the regional forces (RF) were under the control of the province chiefs and had some maneuver capability; and (3) the popular forces (PF) were strictly local forces who earned some of their income from local economic activities such as farming. Thus, the armed forces were classified basically in accordance with the degree of decentralization of command,[8] and the average pay for the armed forces groups varied considerably. We followed a similar weighting procedure in the military sector as in the civil sector and created an artificial force called "regular forces equivalent." Each RF was treated as 0.6 of a regular force, and each PF was treated at 0.36 of a regular force. The weights were determined by the average compensation scales that existed on January 1, 1965.[9]

The final task was to combine civil government employees and military forces into a single total, which we call "permanent civil equivalent." To calculate this total, we treated each "regular force equivalent" as 0.6 of a "career equivalent." This weight is consistent with the average compensation of career civil employees and regular military forces as of January 1, 1965. These constructed data are presented in Table 3.3, along with the actual numbers in the government civil and military sectors.

The index of imports differs from the others in two significant ways. In the first place, it does not measure directly any national accounts sector. It was included as a proxy measure for commercial activity, especially the national accounts entity of wholesale and retail trade. The high relative importance of the domestic trade sector in the Vietnamese economy calls for its inclusion, in some way, in a composite index of output. To some degree, the inclusion of imports as a proxy for commerce violates the criterion of input-output independence, because imports feed other sectors as well as commerce. This would not be a serious problem if the percentage of strictly consumption-type imports to total imports remained constant. From the available data on composition of imports, and making guesses about whether broad item classes were destined for final, industrial, or agricultural use, we think that the assumption of constant proportion was not grossly violated. The second way in which the import index differs from the others is that it is not based on physical quantities. Rather, it is based on dollar value of imports deflated by a variably weighted index of export prices from the United States, Japan, and Taiwan, the three countries that supplied most of Vietnam's imports during the wartime period. Because of the inclusion of this not wholly appropriate index, the composite

Table 3.3. *Government employment, 1956–72 (thousand)*

Year	Government civil employees		Armed forces strength		Civil and military	
	Total employment[a]	Career equivalent[c]	Total strength[b]	Regular equivalent[c]	Total	Permanent civil equivalent
1956			242	190		
1957			240	188		
1958			244	194		
1959			247	195		
1960	110	62	248	197	358	180
1961	114	54	305	241	419	199
1962	129	61	395	301	524	242
1963	121	61	397	302	518	242
1964	143	66	514	368	657	287
1965	179	72	545	410	724	320
1966	219	89	562	426	781	345
1967	210	92	615	463	825	370
1968	208	108	715	561	923	444
1969	222	113	864	666	1086	513
1970	249	139	986	729	1235	576
1971	308	163	1035	761	1343	619
1972	337	177	1023	757	1360	632
1973		186[d]	1107	833		686
1974			1090	832		

[a]Data from *Vietnam Statistical Yearbook* (VN-NIS 1972, Table 251).
[b]Data sources: 1956–64, Office of the Chief of Military History, U.S. Army; 1965–74, Institute of Strategic Studies, *Military Balance* (annual issues).
[c]See text.
[d]Official data for 1973 unavailable. This figure is based on an assumption that civil employment increased 5% over the previous year.

index of physical economic activity is not derived totally from physical measures. Nevertheless, we shall continue to call it a physical index.

3.1.3.2 Weights for the index of physical output: To combine the six indexes described earlier, it is necessary to assign weights to each sector. Our approach was to make use of both income-originating data, taken from the national income accounts, and employment estimates. We used both sources to avoid extreme bias that might result from using either source separately. The information presented in Table 3.4 illustrates how the weighting schemes will differ depending on whether employment or NDP is used as the basis for weight assignment. Note that agriculture (which includes mining, forestry,

Table 3.4. *Number of workers and net domestic product in five sectors, 1960–3*

	Agriculture	Manufacturing	Construction	Commerce	Government	Total
Number of workers, 1960 (thousand)[a]	5,703	124	50	206	259	6,342
Percentage of 5-sector total	89.9	2.0	0.8	3.2	4.1	
Net domestic product, average for 1960–3[b] in billion piasters	27.9	9.0	1.2	8.5	14.0	23.1
Percentage of 5-sector total	46.0	14.9	2.3	14.0	23.1	
Annual net domestic product per worker in piasters	4,892	72,581	24,000	41,262	54,054	

[a] Data from AID-VN (annual, no. 9, Table A-9).
[b] Data from Table 3.2.

and fishing) employed 90 percent of the labor force engaged in the five sectors listed in the table in 1960, but it accounted for only 46 percent of net domestic product in the years 1960–63. Government employed only 4 percent of the work force in the five sectors, but contributed 23 percent of the NDP. According to the fifth row of Table 3.4, the average net domestic product per worker contribution in agriculture is only one-fifteenth of that in manufacturing and only one-eleventh of the amount in government. To us, these relationships seem implausible and suggest data inadequacies. We do not have an objective way to resolve apparent conflicts in the data and are forced to make a subjective decision on how to take into account both sets of data. For the purpose of assigning weights to the five sectors, we think that the NDP data are better than the data on employment, but we do not wish to ignore the employment data.

Our procedure for determining the weight of the jth ($j = 5$) component in the *composite* index of physical output (w_j^c) is given as

$$w_j^c = 0.2w_j^N + 0.8w_j^{NDP}$$

where w_j^N is the percentage of total five-sector *employment* in the jth sector, and w_j^{NDP} is the percentage of total five-sector *NDP* in the jth sector. Thus, the agricultural weight in the composite index of physical output was computed as 0.2×0.9 plus 0.8×0.46. This procedure generated the following weights: agriculture (0.55), manufacturing (0.12), construction (0.02), imports (0.12), and government (0.19). Of the 0.55 weight for the entire agricultural sector, we assigned 0.5 to crop production, 0.04 to fishing,[10] and 0.01 to timber production.

The composite index of physical production and the contributing sectoral indexes are given in Table 3.5. The base period for the indexes is 1962, whereas the base period for assigning sectoral weights is 1960–3. Had we chosen some later period for the purpose of weight assignment, the weight assigned to government would be much larger than the one actually used, and the weight to agriculture would be smaller. Consequently, the composite index of physical output would indicate a faster growth over the wartime period than that shown in Table 3.5.

3.1.4   Economic indicators compared

The negative appraisals of Vietnamese GNP statistics by previous analysts, as well as our own observations, led us to consider the new NDP series in constant prices and the physical composite index as alternative constructions for measuring real economic growth. They are plotted in Figure 3.1, along with an index of real GNP taken from the official estimates. The indexes representing NDP and GNP began to diverge significantly in the 1965–6

Table 3.5. Indexes of physical production in South Vietnam, 1956–73 (1962 = 100)

Year	Crop production[a]	Fish[b]	Timber[b]	Industrial production[c]	Construction[b]	Imports[b]	Government[d]	Composite[e]
1956	66.5		190.7	73.8	51.8	73.1		
1957	64.5		164.9	71.8	40.8	97.1		
1958	79.3		139.2	69.9	70.5	81.8		
1959	93.0		121.3	73.9	87.8	79.3		
1960	94.6	98.0	110.0	85.7	96.0	84.0	74.4	88.7
1961	90.3	98.0	117.9	88.7	84.0	92.7	82.2	89.3
1962	100.0	100.0	100.0	100.0	100.0	100.0	100.0	100.0
1963	102.9	148.6	125.4	116.5	145.8	109.0	100.0	107.6
1964	99.6	155.7	104.1	132.1	160.6	112.0	118.6	112.1
1965	93.2	147.1	109.3	157.9	177.8	134.2	132.2	117.3
1966	83.3	149.4	90.4	170.8	244.3	210.2	142.6	126.2
1967	87.1	161.2	70.5	189.8	162.0	255.3	152.9	136.4
1968	80.3	161.2	98.3	172.7	89.0	240.4	183.5	133.8
1969	89.2	182.0	158.8	214.4	91.0	272.0	212.0	153.9
1970	98.6	226.3	139.5	244.8	173.3	218.6	238.0	164.0
1971	108.6	230.6	225.7	251.3	180.6	208.4	255.8	173.2
1972	106.7	265.9	260.1	238.4	123.8	197.8	261.2	171.0
1973	117.7	292.2	256.4	211.6	88.7	141.5	283.5	171.1
1974				162.8[f]	80.5[f]			

[a] The index of crop production is a weighted quantity index of the following crops: paddy rice, corn, manioc, mangos, sweet potatoes, sugarcane, copra, soybeans, peanuts, tobacco, rubber, and tea. Paddy rice production dominates this index, accounting for about 80% of the weighting. Data sources: 1957–67, AID-VN (annual, 1967, Table E-1); base year changed to 1962. Figures for 1956 and 1968–73 were computed by the author using production data reported in VN-NIS (monthly and annual, various issues). See also Chapter 4, Section 4.3.1.

[b] Data from Table A3.4.

[c] Data from VN-NIS (monthly and annual, various issues). The Vietnamese National Institute of Statistics began to compute this series in 1962. Figures for the period before 1962 were computed by the author using individual series that are available in various NIS and AID publications.

[d] Data from Table 3.3.

[e] For weights, see text.

[f] These figures are estimates based on the previous year's data and percentage changes taken from data in AID-VN (monthly, Feb. 1975, p. 5).

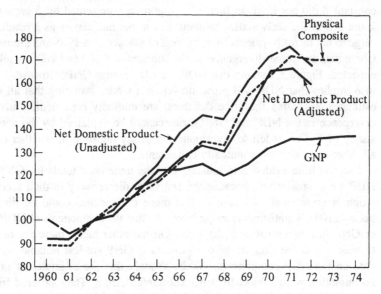

Figure 3.1. Indexes of real economic activity, 1960–74.

period, at the time when inflation became a major problem in Vietnam. This divergence suggests immediately that the deflators for GNP and NDP are inconsistent or that the divergence can be explained by the accounting entries that distinguished the two concepts of national income.

NDP and GNP are closely related concepts, but they are not identical. In the United Nations system of national accounts, the relationship between NDP and GNP is defined in the following accounting identity:

$$\text{GNP} = \text{NDP} + D + T + \text{NFPRW} - \text{SUB} \tag{3.1}$$

where NDP is net domestic product at factor cost, D is depreciation, T is indirect taxes, NFPRW is net factor payments from rest of world, and SUB is subsidies. GNP is equal to *gross domestic product* (NDP + D) at factor cost, plus indirect taxes, plus the (usually) relatively small items NFPRW and SUB. It is calculated at market prices. If we assume that $D + T + $ NFPRW $- $ SUB is some constant proportion δ of NDP, then we can reduce equation (3.1) to

$$\text{GNP} = (1 + \delta)\text{NDP} \tag{3.2}$$

Equation (3.2) is convenient because it allows one to make a direct comparison between *indexes* of GNP and NDP. If $D + T + $ NFPRW $- $ SUB were a constant percentage of NDP, the indexes of GNP and NDP would be identical. Divergence of the indexes must imply that the assumption of a constant δ did not hold. In fact, the proportion represented by δ grew from about 0.2 in the early sixties to about 0.3 in the late sixties as a result of a surge in net factor payments from the rest of the world in 1965 and afterward. Consequently, some divergence in the indexes of GNP and NDP would be expected. Figure 3.1 shows that NDP grew faster than GNP. However, a rise in δ implies that NDP will grow slower than GNP, assuming that all other estimates, including the price deflators, are mutually consistent. Thus, the divergence in the NDP and GNP series cannot be explained by the nonconstancy of δ. One is left to investigate the messy question of whether or not all other estimates were mutually consistent.

There is little evidence to indicate that the undeflated totals for GNP and NDP are contradictory, because the statistical discrepancy in their reconciliation is quite small. Of course, this piece of evidence could be illusory, because NBVN statisticians might have adjusted the components of NDP and/ or GNP in a way to reduce the error. On the other hand, there are reasons to believe that the data on the components of GNP are less reliable than the data on the NDP components. Okubo thought that the estimates of private consumption were subject to rather substantial errors. They suffered from a number of deficiencies in addition to those applicable to estimates of gross value of domestic output (Okubo 1974, p. 95). Regarding net imports, there were always the problems of illegal border trade, improper invoicing, sales of U.S. PX items, and the very serious problem of placing a piaster value on recorded imports (Okubo 1974, pp. 104–5).[11] In addition, the expenditure-side deflators appear to be more difficult to justify than the relatively straightforward deflators we used on the product side of the accounts. Thus, even if the totals for undeflated GNP and NDP are consistent with each other, there is some justification for accepting our own estimates for real NDP as more accurate indicators of economic activity than the NBVN's estimates of real GNP.

This judgment is strengthened as a result of comparing the real NDP index with the composite physical index. Annual variations in the composite are very similar to those in the real NDP index. It is to be expected that the two series would behave similarly over time, inasmuch as they are conceptually related and, significantly, are not totally independent statistically. As an aid in estimating NDP in current prices, the NBVN utilized some of the same physical indexes in the agricultural and industrial sectors of the economy that we used in constructing the physical composite.[12] Yet the conceptual and statistical ties are not so close as to guarantee similar year-to-year movements in the indexes. Thus, it is legitimate to use the composite to further arbitrate between real NDP and real GNP.

For the period 1960–72, the annual increments to the indexes of real NDP and the physical composite, determined as regression coefficients, were 7.4

and 7.6 percentage points, respectively, whereas the average annual increase in real GNP was only 3.9 percentage points. Correlation analysis involving the first differences of the indexes yielded the following coefficients of determination (R^2):

real GNP − real NDP = 0.35
real GNP − composite = 0.23
real NDP − composite = 0.63

These results simply restate what one observes visually in Figure 3.1, namely, that the series on NDP and physical output correspond closely, whereas neither corresponds closely with GNP. Of course, conformity between NDP and physical output is not proof that the NDP series is a better indicator of growth than GNP, but it does provide additional positive evidence. Accordingly, we conclude that the real NDP series is a better indicator of economic activity for wartime Vietnam than the GNP series.

Our opinion favoring the real NDP series over real GNP does not solve the problem of measuring the growth of national income, for there are deficiencies in the NDP series that discourage its unquestioned acceptance. Our task is to point out those deficiencies where they are known to exist and to correct for them to the extent possible.

To determine which components of NDP may be candidates for adjustment, we compare the sectoral indexes of physical activities with the comparable indexes based on NDP data. The following observations are useful:

1. Agriculture (including fishing and forestry): for 1970–2 (average), the physical index was 126 (1962 = 100), and the comparable index based on real NDP was 118. Over the period from 1960, these indexes followed a very similar pattern, deviating by a maximum of 32 percent in 1972.

2. Industrial production: For 1970–2, the physical index was 245, compared with 162 for the real NDP index. Major deviation began to occur in 1968, after which time the physical index grew faster.

3. Commerce (wholesale and retail trade): The import index in 1970–2 was 213, whereas the index based on deflated value added in wholesale and retail trade was 212. However, there was significant divergence between the two indexes for the 1966–9 period.

4. Public administration: For 1970–2, the physical index based on employment was 252, compared with 294 for real NDP. The two indexes diverged by 30 percent in the three-year period 1966–8.

For the agricultural sector, we think the two indexes are consistent enough to rule out adjusting that component of the NDP series.[13] This implies that the combination of the nondeflated series on value added in agriculture and the agricultural deflator yields a believable deflated series. We do not judge similarly for the manufacturing and the public administration sectors. This negative assessment requires that we make another decision about the credibility of the two pairs of indexes.

The divergence in the two manufacturing indexes after 1968 can be explained partly by a shift in the composition of products toward those requiring a high input of imported raw materials. For example, textile, sugar, and paper production increased 87, 113, and 123 percent, respectively, while the overall index increased 46 percent. The combined weight in the index of the three mentioned products plus electricity production, which increased 68 percent, is 28 percent. Each of these products had an input of imported raw materials much higher than average.[14] Consequently, value added should tend to rise slower than the physical index would lead one to believe. Thus, the divergence of the two indexes after 1968 is consistent with the shift in composition known to have taken place. In terms of the assumptions that justify the use of physical indicators, the one that postulates a constant relationship between value added and total output clearly was violated after 1968. Accordingly, we have no compelling reason to reject the NDP estimates on industrial production just because it is inconsistent with the physical index of manufacturing.

From the base period (1962) through 1965 and the first three years in the 1970s, the real NDP component index on wholesale and retail trade corresponds reasonably well with its "physical" counterpart, imports. However, the correspondence was not close in the 1966–9 period. Imports almost doubled between 1965 and 1967 as a result of U.S. policy to finance the accelerated war and to keep the rate of inflation down, whereas the deflated series on wholesale and retail trade rose only 43 percent. In 1967, the index on the deflated value of wholesale and retail trade (1962 = 100) was only 62 percent of the index of imports. Some of this discrepancy can be explained by rapid inventory accumulation. Also, wholesale trade and retail trade are dependent on domestic production as well as imports, and because domestic production rose nowhere near as fast as imports between 1965 and 1969, we think that the import index is not an ideal proxy for the absolute level of commerce for this period. The result is that we do not have a strong reason for rejecting the validity of the NDP component on wholesale and retail trade simply because it fails to correspond closely with the index of imports.

In the case of public administration, there are good reasons to suspect that the NDP figures overstate the contribution of government. The physical index of the growth in government, measured in medium-grade permanent civil servant equivalents, was 30 percent below our deflated estimate of value added in government in 1966–7 and 14 percent below estimated real NDP in 1970–2.

Although there are numerous possibilities that might explain the difference, the following four deserve special attention: (1) NDP at current factor costs was overstated by the NBVN. (2) The implicit government consumption deflator understates the costs of government employment. (3) The productivity of government employment increased over the period. (4) Our index of government employment understated actual employment.

An apparent criticism of our index of government employment concerns the method used for assigning weights to the different categories of civilian and military employment. This is not a severe criticism. A wide variety of weighting schemes would yield approximately the same index series, because the proportions in each employment category did not change radically over the period. In our judgment, changes in the index adequately represent the buildup of the government sector, and therefore we reject possibility 4 listed in the preceding paragraph. We also reject possibility 1. Of all the sectors for which the NBVN estimated income originating, the estimate of public administration should be the best, because that estimate was taken directly from payroll data.

Productivity gains cannot account for the difference either. The reason is that output in government, according to the United Nations (UN) system of national income accounting, is measured by input or in this case by compensation of employees. Indeed, government workers may have become more efficient over time, but that could not be the cause of any measured discrepancy.

The remaining explanation is that the index we chose to use as a deflator of government compensation understated the actual compensation. To check this possibility, we constructed two other deflators based on (1) the computed average (mean) compensation of all government employees and (2) the permanent civil equivalent. We calculated the annual mean compensation for each year between 1960 and 1971 first by using the NBVN estimates on total compensation in government and second by using only 85 percent of total government expenditures.[15] All four resultant series yield compensation indexes whose values exceed the chosen deflator index values. Thus, it is very likely that the implicit government consumption deflator understates the compensation of government employees. If this is true, the growth of government during the war, as measured by official statistics, will be exaggerated.[16]

3.1.5   Adjusted real net domestic product, 1960–72

Among the important sectors of production, as classified in the domestic product accounts of Vietnam, we have sufficient evidence to adjust only the series on public administration and defense. It would be possible to adjust the real NDP series on public administration and defense by picking a different deflator than we previously chose. Another possibility, which we accept, is to build a new constant-price series for public administration and defense utilizing the index of employment in government described in Section 3.1.3.1. To construct such a series, we simply multiply the base-year (1962) value of government output by the index of employment. This procedure generates a real series in constant piaster prices without requiring an explicit price deflator.

The adjusted series on value added in public administration and defense is entered as the next to bottom row in Table 3.2. The bottom row of the table gives the adjusted annual values of real NDP, and these values in indexed form are shown as "Net Domestic Product (Adjusted)" in Figure 3.1 for the period beyond 1963. For all practical purposes, the adjusted and unadjusted series are indistinguishable for the 1960–3 period. Starting in 1964, the adjusted series rises slower than the unadjusted series because the employment-derived estimates of value added in government indicate a slower rise than the deflated NDP series. However, the essential features are preserved, with notable recessions occurring in 1968 and 1972, when by almost universal consensus recessions actually occurred in South Vietnam.

3.2   Overall growth of the economy

From 1956 through 1972, the output of the Vietnamese economy, as measured by adjusted real NDP, almost doubled. The compounded rate of growth was 4.2–4.7 percent per year, depending on the growth measurement technique.[17] If the economy did not grow in 1973 and 1974, as the preliminary estimates of GNP (and our own construction of physical output) indicate, the rate of growth from the beginning to the end of the Republic of Vietnam was 3.7–4.3 percent per year. Growth was not even over the period. Rather, periods of rapid growth were followed by shorter periods, usually of one year, of recession. The temporal pattern of growth of the adjusted NDP series displayed in Figure 3.1 shows that major recessions occurred in 1968 and 1972.

From 1957 through 1960, the average rate of growth was 7.2 percent per year.[18] This period of rapid growth took place in an environment of relative peace and under other conditions highly favorable to growth. The partitioning of Vietnam in 1954 left the South with a number of problems to be solved. Almost all industrial development had been concentrated in the North, where most of the natural resources were located. Saigon had been a major commercial center for all Indochina, but when the Geneva Conference made independent states of Cambodia and Laos as well as North Vietnam, the South lost a good part of its commercial advantage. In support of its administration and military forces in Indochina, France had been Vietnam's major source of foreign exchange; so when the French army pulled out of Vietnam in 1956, that source of foreign exchange was lost. However severe these conditions might have appeared to the newly created nation, there were expectations that the obstacles could be overcome. Scigliano (1963, p. 102) thought that the South Vietnamese "could expect substantial and quick returns from relatively modest efforts. There was idle land to be tilled, a well constructed canal and irrigation network needing only to be restored, a fairly modern road system to be repaired, excellent though aging rubber plantations to be rejuvenated, a nation to be put once more to productive work." Essentially, then, rapid growth in this early three-year period should be associated with reconstruction or a move back to previous levels rather than advancing to new high levels.

The main contributor to growth was agriculture. In 1957, rice production was 3.2 million tons, and it advanced to the level of 5 million tons in 1959 and 1960. That rice production actually increased by more than 50 percent in only a couple of years is difficult to believe,[19] unless 1957 was simply a bad year due to flooding or other climatic events, which, unfortunately, early writers do not comment on. There can be no doubt, though, that the increase in agricultural production was quite large. However, one probably should discount the estimated 9.1 percent average annual gain during this period.

Much of the increase in agricultural production was due to returning to previous levels. According to Bernard Fall's data (1963, pp. 293–4), rice production in 1957 was lower than it had been in 1938, and production of most secondary crops was lower in 1961 than in 1938. There can be no doubt that the fifteen years of warfare between 1940 and 1954 had a devastating effect on agricultural production in South Vietnam, and the returning-to-normal process that followed the restoration of peace was rapid. Whether or not the fast pace of recovery could be maintained once previous levels of output were achieved would depend, at least, on the continuation of peace, assuming all other things remained the same.

The uneasy peace did not continue. In December 1960, the local insurgents organized the National Liberation Front for South Vietnam (NLFSV) and set into motion an intensified campaign to undermine the government's hold over the countryside. Scigliano attributed the recession in 1961 to the increase in the intensity of guerrilla warfare and the loss of security resulting from it (1963, pp. 103, 107). Lack of security was always the major suppressant of growth in South Vietnam, but the decline in agricultural output in 1961 was also due to the excessive flooding of the Mekong Delta in that year.

A new phase of growth began in 1962, despite the year-by-year increases in total NLF (shortened acronym for NLFSV) counterinsurgency operations.[20] The average annual rate of growth for this period through 1967 was 5.9 percent. Growth during the second phase was entirely different from that during the first phase. Guerrilla warfare and open warfare, as it developed after the massive intervention of U.S. troops in 1965, were confined essentially to the countryside, and they adversely affected crop production (and probably all of agriculture).[21] What is noteworthy about economic growth during this period is that very considerable increases took place in industrial production, commerce, and government. Most of these gains were made possible by a very substantial increase in U.S. aid during the period.

The Communist Tet offensive in early 1968 brought an end to the second phase of growth. The Tet attacks brought the war to the cities and thereby removed the exemption that hitherto had applied to industrial production, wholesale and retail trade, banking, and so forth. As a result, all sectors of the economy suffered in 1968, with the exception of government.[22]

The NLF's decisive political victory at Tet cost the Communists a heavy loss in military strength. For the next three years the military balance turned in favor of the South Vietnamese government, permitting it to gain control over much of the countryside, or at least to improve security over a large part of South Vietnam. With the improved security and the continued high level of American aid, the Vietnamese economy performed at its best for the twenty-year period. Recovering from the Tet damage, the economy grew 13.3 percent in 1969 and 11.6 percent in 1970. It could not sustain these high rates, and growth fell to 0.9 percent in 1971.[23] Over the three-year period, the average rate of growth was 8.6 percent, a figure that most observers would accept.

Economic growth in Vietnam during this period was characterized by widespread gains. There were real gains in every sector of the economy listed in Table 3.2. Agriculture, responding, perhaps, to new hybrid rice seed, fertilizer, and land reform, as well as the improved security and government policies that allowed agricultural prices to rise, led the economy into what could have been considered at the time to be a new era for Vietnam. It was an era of Vietnamization of the economy as well as the war, and it began to appear as if Vietnam might be able to succeed as a viable economy and political entity.

The optimism was shattered once and for all by the massive Communist offensive in 1972 along the northern demilitarized zone (DMZ) and in the western part of Vietnam. Our annual data could overstate the decline in agriculture in 1972. According to the data on NDP, agricultural value added dropped by 23 percent, but the index of crop production fell only 5 percent. The Communist offensive in 1972 was directed at areas of only limited agricultural production. Thus, it is not likely that agriculture declined by as much as 23 percent, although few would question that a significant decline occurred.

3.3   Sectoral distribution of net domestic product

Because the discussion of growth in the previous section was unconcerned with the distribution of growth between the various sectors, it could convey an erroneous impression about the health of the economy. As we shall show, the pattern of growth was very uneven and probably would have been detrimental to long-term development had the South Vietnamese government survived. To conduct a sectoral analysis, we divided the economy in two different ways: First, a division of real NDP into private and government sectors is considered. Second, NDP is separated by sectors representing agriculture, industry, and services. Agriculture includes fishing, forestry, and hunting. Industry comprises mining and quarrying, electricity and gas, and transportation and communications, as well as manufacturing. Services include wholesale and retail trade, government, and all other activities. This particular manner of partitioning follows the practice of Simon Kuznets (1971, ch. 3). Data aggregated from Table 3.2 are presented in Table 3.6, which presents annual rates of growth by sector. In order to minimize the effect of grossly inaccurate data for starting and ending points, the rates of growth were determined by linear regressions.

Growth of the Vietnamese economy from 1960 was influenced primarily by growth of the government sector. The growth rate of government (including defense) was over 10 percent per year, and this directly accounted for approximately 55 percent of the total economic growth. If the indirect effects of government growth were added, the percentage would be much higher. For example, much of the growth in wholesale and retail trade undoubtedly was due to the increased payments to military personnel and civil servants. From 1960 through 1972, the government share of NDP grew from 15 to 34 percent. Even the lower figure of 15 percent is abnormally high when compared with other countries. In Kuznets's analysis of sectoral shares for fifty-seven nations, the percentage of gross domestic product (GDP) in public administration for six countries with the highest percentage originating in government was 12.8 percent (Kuznets 1971, p. 108).[24] Further, if one considers only the countries with per capita incomes comparable to that of South Vietnam ($75 to $150), the share of GDP in public administration, according the Kuznets's data, was about 7 percent (1971, p. 104). Even in 1955 (not shown in Table 3.6) the Vietnamese government's share of GDP was about 15 percent in current prices. Thus, at the very beginning, the Republic of Vietnam had an abnormally high percentage of its income originating in government. As the war intensified and became transformed from counter-insurgency operations to full-scale open warfare, the government sector grew to an even more abnormal relative size.

Contrast the growth in the public sector with that in the private sector. As shown in Table 3.7, private sector growth was only 3 percent per year, and there probably was no growth in the private sector from 1972 to 1975. For the fifteen-year period 1960–75, private sector growth was less than 3 percent per year and probably close to the rate of population growth (2.6 per-

Table 3.6. Sectoral distribution of real net domestic product, 1960–72

Year	Real NDP (billion piasters)					Percentage of total NDP				
	Agriculture	Industry	Services	Private sector	Government sector	Agriculture	Industry	Services	Private sector	Government sector
1960	31.2	14.6	32.2	66.0	12.0	40.0	18.7	41.3	85.0	15.0
1961	26.2	14.9	33.2	61.0	13.3	35.3	20.1	44.7	82.1	17.9
1962	26.2	14.0	38.2	62.2	16.2	33.4	17.9	48.7	79.3	20.7
1963	27.3	15.4	38.9	65.4	16.2	33.5	18.9	47.7	80.2	19.9
1964	29.8	15.8	44.5	70.9	19.2	33.1	17.5	49.4	78.7	21.3
1965	29.8	18.1	46.0	72.6	21.4	31.7	19.3	48.9	77.2	22.8
1966	25.6	19.2	53.3	76.0	23.1	25.8	19.4	53.8	76.7	23.3
1967	28.8	20.3	55.7	80.0	24.8	27.5	19.4	53.2	76.3	23.7
1968	26.7	16.3	59.1	72.4	29.7	26.2	16.0	57.9	70.9	29.1
1969	27.8	18.9	69.0	81.4	34.3	24.0	16.3	59.6	70.4	29.7
1970	32.3	21.2	75.6	90.5	38.6	25.0	16.4	58.6	70.1	29.9
1971	34.3	21.1	74.9	88.9	41.4	26.3	16.2	57.5	68.2	31.8
1972	26.4	18.3	79.3	81.7	42.3	21.3	14.8	64.0	65.9	34.1

Source: Table 3.2.

Table 3.7. *Average annual rates of growth by sector*[a]

Sector	Real NDP originating average per year (1960–72) (billion piasters)	Regression coefficient (billion piasters)	Standard error of regression coefficient	Average annual rate of growth (%)
Agriculture	28.7	0.17	0.20	0.6
Industry	17.6	0.53	0.11	3.9
Services	53.8	4.23	0.20	7.4
Wholesale and retail trade	*15.8*	*1.34*	*0.13*	*8.5*
Private	74.5	2.23	0.32	3.0
Government	25.6	2.70	0.15	10.6
NDP	100.1	4.92	0.38	4.9

[a]Computed over the period 1960–72 on NDP in constant (1962) prices.
Source: Tables 3.2 and 3.6.

cent). Thus, goods and services supplied by the private sector per capita were approximately constant throughout the period. In contrast, the rate of growth in per capita public services throughout the period was about 8 percent. In absolute values, real NDP increased by 46 billion piasters from 1960 to 1972. Sixty-five percent of the increase was due to an increase in the public sector. Thus, economic growth in wartime Vietnam can be explained primarily by expansion of government activities to meet the military threat.

Analysis of the sectoral shares to agriculture, industry, and services tells the same story. The growth of agriculture was small but positive, according to our data, and industrial growth was close to 4 percent per year. Over the period, the share to agriculture fell considerably, from roughly 36 percent for the first three years shown in Table 3.6 to 24 percent for the last three years. The share to industry also declined, despite its moderate absolute growth. A fall in the share to agriculture is to be expected in the process of growth, but, in general, the industrial share is expected to grow. At the end of the period, the service sector, including government, accounted for almost two-thirds of the NDP of Vietnam. Almost all of the growth in share to services was due to increases in government and wholesale and retail trade. In the following chapter we attempt to distinguish between growth and development. The abnormal growth in government created a very top-heavy economic structure and most likely would have been a drag on economic development in years to come even if the war had ended on terms favorable to the South.

Table A3.2. Sectoral price indexes used to deflate net domestic product, 1960–72

Sector	1960	1961	1962	1963	1964	1965	1966	1967	1968	1969	1970	1971	1972
Agriculture, forestry, fishing[a]	80.4	94.7	100.0	105.5	109.0	125.4	215.6	353.7	397.4	563.5	785.5	842.5	1,179.2
Mining and quarrying[b]	94.0	95.2	100.0	104.8	108.4	127.7	190.4	281.9	366.3	455.4	579.5	715.7	833.7
Manufacturing[c]	85.7	94.8	100.0	104.3	107.0	111.9	125.2	136.1	174.4	203.6	288.4	389.4	494.3
Construction[d]	91.5	93.6	100.0	100.4	103.7	129.9	214.2	287.5	334.7	490.2	568.3	747.4	792.4
Electricity, gas, water[e]	81.6	91.3	100.0	103.4	104.3	109.9	125.7	143.9	159.3	167.6	229.1	261.1	444.4
Transportation[f]	91.2	97.0	100.0	107.3	110.4	128.4	208.5	299.4	380.0	463.1	633.5	749.0	938.3
Wholesale and retail trade, including restaurants[g]	90.9	95.0	100.0	103.1	107.3	121.4	175.7	255.3	317.9	393.3	510.0	637.2	757.0
Banking, insurance, business services[h]	93.1	95.8	100.0	104.2	108.3	126.4	187.5	280.6	368.1	462.5	593.1	740.3	856.9
Ownership of dwellings[i]	92.0	96.4	100.0	106.0	108.1	124.8	197.1	275.6	349.6	417.7	580.9	689.8	848.7
Services[h]	93.1	95.8	100.0	104.2	108.3	126.4	187.5	280.6	368.1	462.5	593.1	740.3	856.9
Public administration and defense[j]	91.9	96.3	100.0	106.1	107.4	119.9	143.4	180.6	187.0	245.1	299.5	347.1	446.7
NDP implicit deflator[k]	84.6	93.0	100.0	102.0	106.6	120.7	168.7	242.5	274.4	359.3	476.9	568.0	712.1
NDP implicit deflator (adjusted)[l]	85.3	92.7	100.0	102.5	107.3	125.4	185.4	266.6	304.5	390.7	495.4	602.0	757.5

[a]Price index of agricultural products collected by Directorate of Agricultural Economics and published by NIS. This is a composite index of eighteen products, including both plant and animal products.

[b]This is an index of the wage rates of construction workers. See Footnote d.

[c]This is the wholesale price index for manufactured products in Saigon published by the NIS.

[d]Weighted index of labor wages and materials prices in Saigon. The index of labor wages is derived from separate group indexes of average daily wages of male (unskilled) laborers over eighteen yeas of age, female (unskilled) laborers over eighteen, and skilled male workers. The weights for these groups are 0.3, 0.3, and 0.4, respectively. The group indexes were derived from average daily wage data for Saigon (average of wages for December of previous year and December of year under consideration) published in VN-NIS (annual, 1972, Table 239). The materials price index comprises the indexes of wholesale prices in Saigon of bricks, cement, and iron and steel. The prices that form the basis of this index were taken from VN-NIS (annual, 1972, Table 310). The construction deflator is an unweighted average of the indexes of construction wages and materials.

[e]Retail price of electricity in Saigon reported in VN-NIS (annual, 1972, Table 315).

62

[f] Following the practice of Pearsall and Petersen (1971), this is the Saigon working-class index (including rent) published in VN-NIS (annual, 1972, Table 317) reflated to the 1962 base year.

[g] This index was constructed by combining indexes of wages of male laborers over eighteen years of age (0.28), female laborers over eighteen (0.42), and the general wholesale price index in Saigon (0.30). The numbers in parentheses are the assigned weights. See note d for source of wage data. Data on wholesale price from VN-NIS (annual, 1972, Table 313).

[h] Weighted average of indexes of daily wages paid to male laborers over eighteen years of age (0.3), female laborers over eighteen (0.50), male skilled workers (0.15), and female skilled workers (0.05). Weights are given in parentheses. For source of data, see note d.

[i] Following Pearsall and Petersen (1971), this is the consumer price index for middle-class families in Saigon (including rent). The data with base year 1963 are given in VN-NIS (annual, 1972, Table 317).

[j] Implicit government consumption deflator from National Bank of Vietnam. This index was computed by dividing government consumption in current prices by government consumption in constant prices. Both series are given in the national income chapter in VN-NIS (annual).

[k] Last row entries in Table A3.1 divided by row entries called ''net domestic product at factor cost'' in Table 3.2.

[l] Last row entries in Table A3.1 divided by row entries called ''net domestic product at factor cost (adjusted)'' in Table 3.2.

Table A3.1. *Net domestic product at factor cost by sector of origin in current prices, 1960–72 (billion piasters)*[a]

Sector	1960	1961	1962	1963	1964	1965	1966	1967	1968	1969	1970	1971	1972
Agriculture, forestry, fishing	24.0	23.7	26.2	27.1	31.2	36.1	53.0	98.9	101.8	150.1	236.3	289.1	310.9
Mining and quarrying	0.3	0.4	0.4	0.3	0.2	0.3	0.4	1.2	1.6	1.6	1.6	3.1	2.4
Manufacturing	7.5	8.2	8.6	9.6	10.3	12.8	16.5	18.3	20.0	23.8	40.5	58.1	57.9
Construction	1.2	1.1	1.1	1.3	1.4	1.8	3.2	3.1	3.4	7.7	11.6	12.5	11.9
Electricity, gas, water	0.5	0.6	0.6	0.7	1.2	1.0	0.8	0.9	0.8	1.5	1.8	2.3	4.5
Transportation	2.9	3.3	3.3	3.5	3.7	5.4	7.4	11.4	7.3	15.0	18.3	24.3	35.4
Wholesale and retail trade, including restaurants[b]	8.6	8.9	10.9	11.5	13.6	14.6	28.5	43.7	48.8	86.9	121.2	133.5	186.5
Banking, insurance, business services	0.8	0.8	0.8	1.0	1.1	1.5	3.5	5.9	5.8	6.8	8.0	13.6	15.9[c]
Ownership of dwellings	4.8	4.7	5.2	5.4	6.2	6.8	10.7	12.1	11.0	15.0	22.3	23.1	26.9[c]
Services	4.3	4.6	5.1	5.6	6.4	7.5	12.5	20.4	34.0	34.8	47.2	53.9[d]	62.8[c]
Public administration and defense	11.6	12.6	16.2	17.6	21.4	30.1	47.2	63.5	76.4	108.8	130.7	170.9	224.2[f]
Statistical discrepancy[c]	3.0	1.4	0.2	0.4	-1.0	5.3	2.7	-0.1	-10.1	-20.5	-29.3	NA	NA
Net domestic product[c]	69.5	70.3	78.4	84.0	95.7	123.2	186.4	279.3	300.8	431.5	610.2	784.4[g]	939.3[g]

[a]Data sources: 1960–70, VN-NIS (annual, various issues); 1971, derived from data on gross domestic product in United Nations (1973, vol. 2); depreciation subtracted by applying depreciation percentages of GDP by sector; the depreciation factors were determined by comparing NDP and GDP tables in VN-NIS (annual, 1972); 1972, United Nations (1975, April, p. 210); the entries for banking and insurance, ownership of of dwellings, services, and public administration were grouped together, along with net indirect taxes and the statistical discrepancy under "all other"; allocation of the total was made according to footnotes *e* and *f*.

[b]Data for this entry were obtained from United Nations (various issues), except for 1972, as noted earlier. This source includes value added in restaurants and hotels, whereas the data from VN-NIS (annual) exclude value added from these sources. The UN source measures GDP rather than NDP. Adjustments to the GDP data were made by subtracting the value of depreciation (about 3% of GDP) implied in a comparison of NDP and GDP statistics published in VN-NIS (annual).

[c]NDP was obtained from VN-NIS (annual). The statistical discrepancy in this table is a balancing item between NDP and the sum of the entries. Because the wholesale and retail trade entries were taken from the UN source, the statistical discrepancies in this table differ from those given in VN-NIS (annual).

[d]Calculated as follows: [(value of services in UN source in 1971)/(value of services in UN source in 1970)] × [value of services given in VN-NIS (annual,

64

1970)]. This adjustment was necessary because the definition of "services" in the different sources is not the same.

^{f}The change in value added in all other sectors for 1972 was 17% above 1971. These values assume that the same proportional increase applied to the three sectors designated.

^{g}Assumes real value added in public administration increased 2% in 1972. [See 1971 and 1972 entries for "public administration and defense (adjusted)" in Table 3.2.] The derived value for constant-piaster value added (50.2 billion) in public administration was multiplied by the deflator index for 1972 (4.467) to obtain this estimate of value added in current prices.

^{h}Sum of foregoing values assuming no statistical discrepancy.

Table A3.3. *Estimates of gross national product and net domestic product, 1956–60 (billion piasters)*

Year	GNP[a] Current prices	GNP[a] Constant prices (1960 = 100)	NDP[a] Current prices	NDP[a] Constant prices (1960 = 100)	Index of physical output[b] (1960 = 100)	Price deflator[c] (1960 = 100)
1955	63.6[d]					94.5
1956	68.7[d]	65.4	58.7	55.6	80.0	105.6
	69.1					
1957	67.0	66.5	57.1	56.5	81.3	100.8
1958	71.3	72.2	60.7	61.4	88.3	98.8
1959	80.1	79.1	68.1	67.2	96.7	101.3
1960	81.8[d]	81.8[d]	69.5[d]	69.5[d]	100.0	100.0

[a]GNP in constant price is computed as follows: [GNP (1960)] × [index of physical output (*t*)], where *t* is the year of the estimate. GNP in current prices is computed as follows: [GNP in constant price (*t*)] × [price deflator index (*t*)]. Similar calculations apply for NDP.

[b]This index is similar to the one shown in Table 3.5. It differs in that it excludes fish production and that part of government activity related to civilian employment. These exclusions were taken because of data unavailability. The weights for the foregoing index are crop production (0.54), timber (0.01), industrial production (0.12), construction (0.02), imports (0.12), and regular (military) force equivalent (0.19). Data for the series are given in Tables 3.3 and 3.5.

[c]This is the consumer price index for working-class families in Saigon. Data published in VN-NIS (annual, 1972, Table 319).

[d]Official estimates by the National Bank of Vietnam.

Table A3.4. *Production data for physical indexes, 1956–74*

Year	Timber cut (thousand m³)	Fish catch (thousand tons)	Building permits (thousand m²)	Real value of imports[a] ($ million)
1956	555		353[b]	201
1957	480		278[b]	267
1958	405		480	225
1959	353		598	218
1960	320		654	231
1961	343	250	572	255
1962	291	255	681	275
1963	365	379	993	300
1964	303	397	1,015	308
1965	318	375	1,211	369
1966	263	381	1,664	578
1967	205	411	1,103	702
1968	286	410	606	661
1969	462	464	620	748
1970	406	577	1,180	601
1971	657	588	1,230	573
1972	757	678	842[b]	544
1973	746	745[c]	604[b]	389

[a]From data in Table A4.6; the base year for these data is 1962.

[b]These estimates are based on Saigon building permit activity, which in proximate years was 45% of building permit activity for Vietnam.

[c]Extrapolated from 1973 data for seven months.

Source: All data from VN-NIS (annual and monthly, various issues).

Table A3.5. *Dollar value of South Vietnam gross national product,*
1955–74

Year	Piaster value[a] (billion)	Exchange rate[b] (piasters per dollar)	Dollar value[c] (billion)
1955	63.6	70[d]	0.91
1956	68.7	70[d]	0.98
1957	67.0	70[d]	0.96
1958	71.3	70[d]	1.02
1959	80.1	70[d]	1.14
1960	81.8	70[d]	1.17
1961	84.5	70[d]	1.21
1962	93.8	78	1.20
1963	100.3	78	1.29
1964	114.5	81	1.36
1965	144.8	94	1.54
1966	236.2	145	1.63
1967	356.7	189	1.89
1968	383.3	201	1.92
1969	557.6	229	2.44
1970	804.4	325	2.48
1971	979.9	388	2.53
1972	1,102.0	439	2.89
1973	1,551.0	531	2.92
1974	2,229.0	641	3.48

[a]Data from Table 3.1.
[b]Data from Table 9.5, except where noted.
[c]Data from column 1 divided by column 2.
[d]This rate is an assumption by the author. The constant rate is a reflection of stable prices that prevailed during this period. Also, it was the approximate official rate on invisibles.

CHAPTER 4

Indicators of economic development

In this chapter we shall take a more detailed look at some of the economic and social development indicators that lie behind the figures on economic growth presented in the previous chapter. Although it is not really possible to define "economic development" (Little 1982, p. 6), a writer nevertheless has an obligation to make explicit the criteria by which he judges whether or not satisfactory development is taking place. Sustainable growth in per capita income was the focus of attention up to about 1970. Since then, the concern for equity has moved to center stage in the development literature.[1] Both are important criteria for evaluating Vietnam economic development, and two concepts, income distribution and saving, that are important for both concerns are discussed, respectively, in Chapters 5 and 6. A third criterion that we stress is movement toward economic independence. This criterion is not suggestive of the dependency school of development; rather, it is intended to be a reminder that *self-sustained growth* must imply a lessening of dependence on concessional aid, but not mutually beneficial trade and finance. By this third criterion, Vietnam had made little progress at the time of its demise.

4.1 Economic development and economic independence

In the early literature on economic development, writers rarely distinguished between it and economic growth. For example, the overview article on "economic growth" in the *Encyclopedia of the Social Sciences* (Easterlin 1968) uses the terms "growth" and "development" synonymously. Today it is recognized that growth does not assure development, even aside from the consideration of equity. For relatively short periods of time, say one or two decades, it is quite possible for a country to experience rapid growth while hardly developing,[2] and we shall argue that the growth of national income in South Vietnam was an exaggeration of the measure of development.

When considered over very long periods of time, the concepts of growth and development are practically indistinguishable. When the record shows that a country has achieved a satisfactory rate of growth – 2 to 3 percent per capita per year – and has maintained that rate for a number of decades, one can conclude that the country has become developed. This is the approach of Simon Kuznets, and it permits one to distinguish between growth and development by focusing attention on a major implication of development that growth is self-sustaining.

There can be little doubt that Vietnamese economic growth over the war period was not self-sustaining. It was accounted for almost entirely by U.S. aid, and when aid fell off drastically in real terms in the last years of the war, economic growth of the country ceased. The dependence of Vietnamese growth on U.S. aid can be measured crudely in the simplest Harrod-Domar model. Suppose that the only source of saving was U.S. aid, and this was about 20 percent of GNP. With a saving rate of one-fifth, and assuming a capital–output ratio of one-third, the annual growth rate, due *only* to the potential effect of aid, should have been in the range of 6–7 percent. In fact, it was less than 5 percent. Thus, it is evident that almost all economic growth that occurred can be attributed to U.S. aid, rather than to progress in domestic economic conditions (i.e., development).

As was pointed out in the previous chapter, most of the growth in the Vietnamese economy was in the service sector. This sector's growth was due almost entirely to U.S.-supported activities, particularly government functions, including the military. Vietnamese taxes were much too low to support government activities. Without aid, the service sector could not have grown as rapidly as it did, and overall economic growth would have been minimal.

Adelman and Morris (1972, ch. 2) have superbly catalogued the economic, social, and political indicators of development. In addition to these, our criteria demand that the nation should have moved significantly toward economic independence. South Vietnam's growth was dependent on large infusions of foreign aid, the need for which did not decline over time. If anything, aid requirements may have increased over the course of the war. The massive flow of U.S. aid, we suggest, engendered a sense of dependence on the part of Vietnamese officials and, to a lesser extent, the Vietnamese population and potential investors, and that sense of dependence was a major problem in development. After the cease-fire went into effect in January 1973 and the United States began to cut the real value of aid drastically, the Vietnamese economy was in severe trouble.

A useful parallel with Vietnamese military affairs can be drawn. Despite the emphasis placed on Vietnamization of the war after 1968, the military never became self-reliant. It was dependent on U.S. advice, U.S. airpower during the Communist Easter offensive in 1972, and U.S. promises. Even after it became apparent to most analysts that military logistic support would decline following the truce in 1973, high-ranking Vietnamese officers still believed that the United States would intervene to save them from catastrophe. When the high command started to ration ammunition to the field forces, morale worsened, and corrupt practices by military personnel became widespread.[3] The poor performance of the Vietnamese army following the fall of

Ban Me Thout in March 1975 was due to a crisis in confidence that developed with the withdrawal of U.S. forces and subsequent curtailment in logistic support.[4] Among Vietnamese businessmen there was a similar lack of confidence in their economy.

The predominant opinion among U.S. officials up to 1974 was that significant development, usually referred to as "progress," was taking place. In 1972, Henry Kissinger, President Nixon's national security advisor, thought that "the Vietnam economic picture continues to be one of the most encouraging aspects of our efforts in Southeast Asia" (Kissinger 1972). This appraisal came at a time when the Vietnamese economy was in a severe recession. But Kissinger's impression was not contrary to the opinions of his subordinates in the U.S. government. Even as late as mid–1974, the U.S. ambassador to South Vietnam reported to a group of investigators that the country was on the verge of an economic "takeoff" and that the need for massive aid would continue only a few more years,[5] (U.S. House of Representatives 1974a, p. 4). This was almost assuredly a wrong evaluation.[6]

Progress, in the view of public officials, was almost always measured by advances in specific variables. The lack of movement toward economic independence was not mentioned. Rather, they stressed gains made in rice production, infrastructure development, and gains in health and education.[7] Gains in these and other areas undoubtedly occurred, but they seemed to come at the expense of economic independence. They were not generated locally, nor were they sustainable without large amounts of aid.

Most of the remaining sections of this chapter are addressed to special topics in development. In the next section we present the evaluation of Professor Rostow. This view is somewhat more favorable than ours, and it is presented here because it probably is indicative of what high-level officials in Washington were thinking at the time.

4.2   Professor Walt W. Rostow's view[8]

According to Walt W. Rostow,

The development and policies of the 1960's, the response of the South Vietnamese to them, and the evolution of South Vietnam as a society in the widest sense moved the young nation rapidly forward in modernization from where it was in 1954 to the spring of 1972. [1972, p. 470]

In Rostow's terminology, the country emerged from French colonial rule in an early state of "preconditions for takeoff," and by 1972 it was on the verge of takeoff into self-sustained growth. Rostow briefly described the activities supporting his view under the headings of agriculture, urbanization, education, public administration, infrastructure, early industrialization, and foreign exchange.

The progress in agriculture was dominated by the rapid recovery in rice production and the underlying rural attitudes that made it possible. From a deficit of almost 1 million metric tons of rice in 1967 the country moved close to self-sufficiency in 1972. Farming practices had changed. Fertilizer and pesticides were in widespread use in 1972, gasoline-powered irrigation pumps and other farm machinery (small tractors) were commonplace, and new cash crops (particularly vegetables) had gained in importance. Land reform was a reality for the peasants, and self-government had been reinstalled in almost all hamlets and villages in South Vietnam. Also, farmers were enjoying many of the luxuries of city people: radios, television, sewing machines, and motorcycles. "Economically as well as administratively, psychologically as well as politically, the classic barriers between urban and rural life in a country undergoing the preconditions for takeoff were rapidly lowered in the period 1967–1972" (Rostow 1972, p. 472).

Another sign of development was the rapid urbanization in South Vietnam. In 1956, about 15–20 percent of the people lived in "urban" areas. By the end of the war, the urban population was 35–40 percent by unofficial estimates.

Education made rapid gains in wartime South Vietnam. According to Rostow, "starting in 1954 South Vietnam has undergone an educational revolution which has transformed the colonial heritage and the manpower base for modernization" (1972, p. 473). Primary school enrollment increased sevenfold, and secondary school enrollment increased about fourteenfold over the period 1954–72. Over the same period, the number of universities increased to seven from zero, and hundreds of thousands of people acquired new skills as a result of jobs and training connected with American establishment activities in South Vietnam.

Gains in other areas, though less startling than in education, were significant. Rostow argued that proficiency in public administration improved, well beyond that in many underdeveloped countries, because of the conditions imposed on the Vietnam bureaucracy by the war and the many U.S.-sponsored social, political, and economic programs. Many of these programs were American-styled, with a Western-designed approach to public administration and, in some cases, modern technology. Rostow briefly mentioned the buildup of infrastructure in Vietnam during the period, citing the construction of new ports at Cam Ranh Bay and Newport and the modernization of ports at Saigon, Danang, and Qui Nhon, construction of airports and highways, installation of telecommunications, the organization of a national airline, and growth in electric power capacity. He also mentioned some advances in industrialization, but was guarded in his statement about industrialization progress.

Rostow concluded that Vietnam moved "rapidly forward in economic and social as well as political modernization" and stood in early 1972 about where South Korea had been in the early 1960s (1972, p. 475).

Rostow's view was published several years before the fall of South Vietnam. In the author's opinion, the statements made by Professor Rostow on economic development in wartime South Vietnam are valid, and we shall document them in much more detail. However, his facts were too selective and his analysis too uncritical, as the remainder of this chapter and Chapter 6 will make evident.

4.3   Production

In this section we present the facts on the growth of agriculture and industry in wartime Vietnam. Our analysis of the record in these sectors was motivated by a variant of our central question: Did growth in these sectors follow a course indicative that it could have been sustained without large-scale foreign aid?

4.3.1   Agriculture

Rostow and others commented on the rapid growth in rice production between 1968 and 1971. This growth was attributed to the "green revolution" and specifically the introduction of IR–8 rice and the adaptation to modern agricultural techniques, including widespread use of inanimate energy. To support his claim that much progress took place in agriculture, Logan (1971) stated that 400,000 small engines for irrigation were sold between 1967 and 1971. Fertilizer usage increased from 230,000 tons in 1968 to 502,000 tons in 1970. Pesticides were widely accepted. Over a thousand regional and district agricultural technicians were trained in the culture of IR–8 rice. Agricultural credit increased from an annual average of $2.5 million in 1964–6 to $39 million in 1969. This increase followed the reorganization of the Agricultural Credit Office as the Agricultural Development Bank. Logan reported that improved breeds of chickens began to appear in 1968, and livestock death rates were reduced by the use of new vaccines.

Occurring as they did in the midst of a major war, these impressive gains were a source of pride to those who worked hard to promote them. Our concern is whether or not they could have been accelerated or sustained in the face of a declining level of foreign aid that was already becoming apparent in 1972. Most U.S. officials were optimistic with regard to the future of Vietnam agriculture.

In fact, what appeared to be very dynamic conditions in Vietnam agriculture in the early 1970s are not strongly corroborated by the available statistics. The data reported in Chapter 3 show that real value added in agriculture

Table 4.1. *Crop production in South Vietnam, 1956–74 (thousand tons)*

Year	Total			Per capita		
	Rice	Other crops[a]	Total	Rice	Other crops[a]	Total
1956	3,412	1,337	4,749	0.28	0.11	0.39
1957	3,192	1,416	4,608	0.25	0.11	0.36
1958	4,235	1,429	5,664	0.32	0.11	0.43
1959	5,092	1,550	6,642	0.38	0.12	0.50
1960	4,955	1,795	6,750	0.36	0.13	0.49
1961	4,607	1,842	6,449	0.32	0.13	0.45
1962	5,205	1,934	7,139	0.36	0.13	0.49
1963	5,357	1,987	7,344	0.36	0.13	0.49
1964	5,185	1,929	7,114	0.33	0.12	0.45
1965	4,822	1,834	6,656	0.30	0.12	0.42
1966	4,336	1,613	6,949	0.26	0.10	0.36
1967	4,688	1,529	6,217	0.29	0.09	0.38
1968	4,366	1,368	5,734	0.25	0.08	0.33
1969	5,115	1,253	6,368	0.29	0.07	0.36
1970	5,500	1,326	6,826	0.30	0.07	0.37
1971	6,100	1,429	7,529	0.32	0.08	0.40
1972	5,900	1,272	7,172	0.30	0.07	0.37
1973	6,600			0.33		
1974	7,165			0.35		

[a]Computed as "rice equivalent" tonnages.
Source: Tables A4.1 and A4.2.

actually dropped between 1969 and 1972 by almost 18 percent. A decline of that order is of questionable validity, as we previously argued, but any decline in the aggregate is sufficient grounds for discounting the optimistic reports of a decade ago. Aside from the evidence implied by the domestic product statistics, physical production data can be presented to question the hypothesis, based entirely on rice production and anecdotal evidence, that agriculture advanced rapidly during the war. If one considers all the other crops, the development picture looks different. Table 4.1 presents indicators of crop production in South Vietnam for 1956 through 1972.

The "other crops" that have been combined to derive the indicator in column 3 of the table are corn, mungo beans, manioc, sweet potatoes, copra, soybeans, peanuts, tobacco, rubber, and tea. These items, including rice, accounted for almost all of the value of crops in the late 1950s and even in 1971, when rubber and some of the other crops had declined significantly. This group constituted about 80 percent of the value of crop production in South Vietnam.[9] In 1971, the other crops included in Table 4.1 were worth about 15 percent the value of rice.[10] The tonnage figures for the other crops in the table are given in "rice equivalents." A rice equivalent is a unit of equal value in 1957–9 prices. Thus, if the average price of tea per kilogram in the base period were twenty-five times the price of rice, one ton of tea would have a rice equivalent of twenty-five tons. Rice equivalent tonnage for each crop is computed as $P_i/P_r = Q_i$, where P_i is the price per ton of the crop under consideration, P_r the price per ton of rice, and Q_i the rice equivalent per ton of the crop under consideration. The quantities given in column 3 of Table 4.1 are the sums of the rice equivalents of other crops. To the extent that prices measure average utilities, rice equivalent measures are utility equivalent measures. The weight (i.e., P_i/P_r) for each crop and its production is given in Table A4.1.

The data in Table 4.1 indicate no progress by the Vietnamese in their ability to feed themselves over the war period. This is even true of rice production, which at best managed to keep up with population growth. When other crop production is added to rice output (the last column), per capita total output in 1970–1 was lower than it had been a decade earlier.

The statistical performance of the agricultural sector (defined broadly) is improved when yet other products are added to the crops mentioned earlier. From limited data it is apparent that the output of vegetables increased enormously over the period (see Table A4.2). The production of fish and timber also increased in per capita terms. From Table A4.3 we estimate that timber production per capita increased by about two-thirds from the early sixties, and the fish catch per capita doubled over the same period. Another important agricultural product was pigs, the production value of which was about one-third that of rice in 1971.[11] Pig production, according to statistics on controlled slaughterings,[12] did not increase over the 1956–73 period and actually declined from 1960 to the end of the war (see Table A4.3). Adding vegetables, timber, fish, and pigs to the major crops, we can construct a more complete index of agricultural production. According to this index, agricultural production per capita rose by 23 percent from 1956 to the end of the war, or about 1 percent per year. The component breakdown for this calculation is shown in Table 4.2. A word of caution is in order. Although the estimate appears precise, it should be considered only a very crude indicator. The data underlying the estimate probably are poor in quality. The proper interpretation of this increase is that total agricultural output increased slightly faster than the population in a very difficult (war) situation. That alone was an accomplishment that need not be exaggerated.

Two factors can account for most of the observed growth. One was improved agricultural incentives that became embodied in the conscious policy of the government. For most of the war period, the government was concerned with keeping rice prices from rising as fast as they might under strict supply-

Table 4.2. *Percentage changes in per capita production of major agricultural commodities*

Item	Weight[a]	1956–73	1960–73	1964–73
Major crops[b]	55	3	–18	–11
Vegetables	3	240[c]	240[c]	181[d]
Timber[e]	6	–16	62	91
Fish[f]	20	85	107	46
Pigs[g]	16	–20	–57	–36
All agriculture		22	13	9

[a]Based on data in Dacy (1969b).
[b]Calculated from data in Table 4.1. This figure assumes that production of "other crops" did not change between 1972 and 1973.
[c]A guess by the author.
[d]This figure assumes that there was a 10% increase in vegetable production between 1971 and 1973.
[e]Calculated from data in Tables A3.4 and A4.1.
[f]Calculated from data in Tables A3.4 and A4.1; assumes fish catch in 1956 and 1960 of 250,000 tons.
[g]Calculated from data in Table A4.3.

and-demand conditions in order to minimize potential urban discontent. This was achieved by price controls and importing large amounts of rice, particularly from the United States. With the decline in per capita rice production from 1959 to 1966 and the rise in imports, one might expect that the price would have risen relative to other prices, and the farmer response would have been to increase production. Instead, the relationship of paddy and milled rice prices to the GNP implicit deflator remained fairly constant to 1969. After 1969, rice prices began to rise rapidly in relation to other prices,[13] (see Table A.4.4). The rice price/GNP deflator index turned up at approximately the same time that per capita rice production turned up, and this can be attributed partially to the effect on rice production of its price rise.

It is not very likely, however, that a reduction in governmental price-fixing activity fully accounts for the surge in rice production. A major factor, undoubtedly, was the "modernizing" of rice production that encompassed the use of fertilizer, improved methods for pumping water, increased use of farm tractors, and diffusion of knowledge about double cropping. These factors shifted the production function. Yet there is a major question whether or not some of these modernizing influences were proper for Vietnamese agriculture in the long run.

Vietnamese agriculture was increasingly dependent on cheap imports. For most of the war period, fertilizer and pesticides were highly subsidized by the U.S. government through its subsidy of the piaster.[14] The effective price paid by farmers for fertilizer was, at times, only one-third of its value on world markets. If prices paid by farmers for inputs had reflected their true economic costs, it is very unlikely that they would have adopted the methods of production that American agricultural technicians were ever pressing on them. The technology of farming that was spreading in South Vietnam was not reflective of the real costs of inputs and therefore probably was suboptimal from a long-run point of view. It was suitable only to a highly (free) aided economy.

Fertilizer use is a case in point. In 1967, the value of fertilizer imports was approximately equal to the total value of Vietnamese exports, and from 1968 to the end of the war, South Vietnam's total exports of goods[15] were not sufficient to pay for the fertilizer imported (see Table A4.5). It is evident that importation of fertilizer as a basis of increased agricultural productivity was not economically viable, even though it served as an effective expediency. But the real problem became apparent at the time of the quadrupling of oil prices by the Organization of Petroleum Exporting Countries (OPEC). Subsequently the price of fertilizer rose twice as fast as commodity prices in general. This would have exacerbated the basic trade problem of Vietnam. But this unforeseeable event is not a necessary condition for the criticism made.

The fertilizer price/foreign exchange squeeze would have affected the rate of growth of rice production more than the level of production. A number of studies on rice production have indicated that the response of rice yield to fertilizer use varies considerably depending on local conditions and especially on the assumptions about water availability and use.[16] To gain a rough estimate of the rice response to fertilizer withdrawal we have selected a simple production function based on some recent research by the International Rice Research Institute in the Philippines.[17] Using fertilizer import data for Vietnam and allocating one-third of this total to other crops, we have estimated that fertilizer use on rice lands in Vietnam was about sixty-five kilograms per hectare in 1972–4. If that application were cut in half because of a foreign exchange constraint, the expected average yield per hectare would fall 5–6 percent, from 2.36 tons to 2.20 tons per hectare. The total production of approximately 7 million tons in 1974 would be reduced by 350,000–400,000 tons, according to the production function in note 17. New gains would have had to come from reclaiming land or bringing new land under cultivation.

4.3.2 Industrial development

At the time of partition in 1954, industrial production in South Vietnam was confined essentially to beer, soft drinks, and cigarettes. The South, with its rich Mekong Delta, had been an agricultural area in unpartitioned Vietnam, whereas most of the industrial activity of the region had been located around Hanoi in the North. Thus, it was natural that the U.S. foreign aid program in South Vietnam in the early years after partition would place some stress on industrial production. Despite this emphasis, gains in industrial output were disappointing in the first several years. Managerial skills were limited, and there was insufficient expertise in the GVN and the U.S. aid mission to develop and follow through on specific projects. Also, there was disagreement between USOM officials in Saigon and their counterparts at International Cooperation Administration (ICA) in Washington, as well as disagreement between the Vietnamese and Americans over the question of private versus state ownership of enterprises. Ultimately, though, the lack of accomplishment was a result of "untimeliness and government inertia and disinterest" (Lindholm 1959, p. 226).

Data measuring industrial growth are very limited. The index of industrial production from 1956 through 1974 is shown in Table 3.5 in Chapter 3. According to the index, industrial production grew at a rate of 9 percent per year through 1971 and then declined precipitously to the end of the war. This index may understate industrial production, because it does not adequately account for new products such as plastic articles that were being manufactured late in the period. The index declined to 163 (1962 = 100) in 1974 from its peak of 251 in 1971. Even considering the recession of 1972–4, industrial production grew at an annual rate of 4 percent from 1956 to 1975.

Increasing industrialization of an economy in both absolute and relative measures is a familiar fact of economic development. Vietnam contradicted this pattern. There was the expected rapid rise in industrial output up to 1972, but the increase was insufficient to translate into a relative gain in industrial output. Industry's share in net domestic product dropped to 16 percent in 1971 from 19 percent in 1960, according to Table 3.5. Inasmuch as the index of industrial production grew faster than GDP over this period, how could the relative share in industrial production have actually declined? A possible explanation of this apparent inconsistency is that the more rapid increase in industrial production was due to a rise in the proportion of output attributable to imported raw materials. For example, some of the rapid growth items in the index of industrial production, such as paper products, paint, and refined sugar, had a very high import content, whereas some of the slower growth items such as beverages had relatively low import contents (Dacy et al. 1971, p. 17). Thus, the index of industrial production grew faster than real value added in industry. In any case, the quantitative data on industrial output are too limited and ambiguous to be used as the only basis for judging whether or not there was significant industrial development in wartime South Vietnam.

Adelman and Morris stressed *modernization of methods* as an indicator of industrial development. According to their model, "As the country grows economically, domestic consumer goods industries using small power-driven machines tend to be established first. At a somewhat later stage of development, when managerial and labor skills become relatively abundant, the typically developing country finally turns to production of the variety of intermediate goods required for the further expansion of industry" (Adelman and Morris 1972, p. 97). In wartime South Vietnam, handicraft production was giving way rapidly to production using power-driven machinery. However, at no point during the period did the country pass into the stage in which local establishments began to supply a significant variety of intermediate goods to domestic industry.

The reasons for Vietnam's lack of progress in supplying intermediate inputs to its industry are easy to state. Industry came to rely on cheap imported commodities that were encouraged both by AID's Commercial Import Program and by an unrealistic foreign exchange rate policy for most of the war period. There was little incentive for firms supplying intermediate goods to develop in Vietnam. To the contrary, they could not possibly have competed with imports under the conditions that existed before 1971. The political decision to appease the population with cheap imports stultified industrial development. Thus, overall economic policy was essentially antidevelopmental in its effect. Furthermore, managerial and labor skills were never "abundant" to industry, despite big gains in education and training, because the most qualified people in the country were preempted by the armed forces. Said the manager of a plastics manufacturing firm, "We have good machines, but unfortunately we have no capable men to run them" (Dacy 1971, ch. 3). As a consequence, industrial productivity was relatively low in the country. The shortage of managers and skilled workers for industry undoubtedly would have abated had the war been brought to a successful conclusion for the South, but that would not have altered the imbalance in Vietnam's industrial structure and its reliance on imported intermediate products. The major long-run problem with Vietnam industry was that it was built on the assumption of generous and almost unending U.S. foreign aid. Industry was not evolving in such a way as to be competitive and self-supporting.

Adelman and Morris (1972, pp. 96–101) classified seventy-four developing countries into groups depending on level of modernization of industry (in 1961) and change in degree of industrialization (between 1950 and 1961). Their criteria for determining the level of modernization were (1) an estimate of the relative importance of indigenous modern power-driven industrial activities, compared with traditional handicraft production, and (2) the degree of modernity of machinery and organizations in the modern industrial sector. Their highest group (category A) for 1961 consisted of countries such as South Korea and Turkey. South Vietnam, Pakistan, Paraguay, and others were placed in category C, second to lowest. Toward the end of the war, South Vietnam probably had advanced to a position the category B countries had occupied in 1961. At that time, those countries had achieved installed electrical capacity of 25–80 kilowatt-hours (KWH) per capita (Adelman and Morris 1972, p. 98).[18] In 1961, electricity production in Vietnam was 23 KWH per capita per year, but in 1973 it had increased to 82, placing Vietnam in category B on the basis of this single indicator. The rapid rise in electricity production must not be considered a remarkable achievement for Vietnam, because the capacity was a result of foreign aid, but it does indicate the extent to which the country had advanced in the use of electrical power.[19]

Of more relevance for the purpose of analyzing industrial development is the electrical energy used in industrial activity. Vietnamese statistics distinguish between electricity supply for lighting, ventilation, and household use and that used for motor power. Total electricity for motor power use increased from 52 million KWH in 1956 to about 360 million KWH in 1973 (see Table A4.6). This huge percentage gain yields a compound growth rate of 12 percent per year. On a separate calculation, assuming an unchanged consumption rate per government user between 1961 and 1965, we estimate that *private* industrial use grew from 55 million KWH in 1961 to 253 million KWH in 1972, or about 15 percent per year. As the number of users increased from 7,000 to 15,000, the consumption per user in the private sector more than doubled. Although the average consumption per user in the private sector was still relatively small in 1972 at about 17,000 KWH, the upward trend does indicate significant progress in the application of energy in industrial use.[20]

The data on electrical power also indicate that little geographical industrial diffusion took place over the war period. In 1964, 99 percent of the electricity for motor power was used in the southern South Vietnam region (almost entirely in the Saigon area), and in 1972 the figure was 94 percent.[21]

Considering the information on electricity use in motor power, one can conclude that South Vietnam did become more modern over the course of the war. Toward the end of the war, the country would probably have been placed in the Adelman-Morris category B, achieving a state of industrial modernization achieved by Bolivia, Iraq, and Syria in 1961.

The criteria for the Adelman-Morris index of overall change in the degree of industrialization are (1) the average annual rate of increase in real industrialization output, (2) the change in the proportion of domestic gross product originating in industry, and (3) the change in the proportion of total male labor force employed in industry. On these criteria, Vietnam in 1961 was placed in category C, along with Bolivia, Indonesia, and Kenya.

We have already stated that Vietnam had fairly rapid industrial growth (starting from a low base) but that the percentage of domestic product originating in industry actually declined. One should not place much confidence in Vietnam labor force data, but those that are available indicate little movement in industrial employment. According to Vietnam National Institute of Statistics data, 114,000 and 120,000 were employed in manufacturing in 1960 and 1966, respectively. An unsigned study adjusts these estimates to reach a total of 168,000 in 1966, including "nonestablishment" employment. Moody had access to a survey of manufacturing undertaken by the Ministry of Economy in 1970 that indicated employment of only 54,000, with 75 percent of the firms reporting (Moody 1975, pp. 167–9). It is not clear from Moody's work whether this was a nationwide or Saigon-area survey, but, regardless, one gains the very clear impression that industrial employment was a limited source of jobs in wartime South Vietnam. We estimate that all of manufacturing probably did not employ more than 2–3 percent of Vietnam's eligible work force of about 8 million in the early seventies. Over the course of the war, manufacturing employment did not increase much, despite encouragement given industrial development in the form of foreign aid.

By the standards of some successfully developing Asian countries, Vietnam's industry was not competitive.[22] Output per worker was relatively low, but their wages were no lower than those for workers in Taiwan. Consequently, efficiency wages were high, at least in the 1969–71 period. It is understandable how this condition developed. Activities associated with the war drained resources from the economy, resulting in a fall in domestic output. At the same time, the government's requirement for funds grew enormously, increasing the budget deficit, the money supply, and the rate of inflation. To limit the destabilizing political impact of this situation, a decision was made to increase the supply of goods from abroad by raising foreign aid. Consumption per capita rose despite the very destructive conflict. After the surprise Communist Tet offensive in 1968, the government declared a full mobilization of manpower to fight the war, and the mobilization took trained industrial workers as well as others. Firms replaced these trained workers with less skilled workers and with little reduction in real wages. Under normal economic conditions, wages would have fallen in reflection of the decline in productivity. From the industrialist's point of view, an attempt to reduce wages might not have worked in the immediate tight situation and probably would have been opposed by the unions. It was easier for influential businessmen to ask for and to be granted higher protective tariffs on their products.

Finally, there is always a question of how to consider anecdotal evidence in one's analysis. Most of the reports touching on Vietnam's economic development have been written primarily from "firsthand" observations. They have tended to generalize from scattered but observable facts. One such fact is that automobiles were being assembled on a limited scale in Vietnam before the war ended, and automobile production was not a part of the index of industrial production. A major problem is how to temper or adjust an assessment of development that derives from organized data usually published on a monthly or annual basis. Considering only the broad indicators such as national income statistics, the index of industrial output, and the available statistics on manufacturing employment, it seems evident that industrial development in South Vietnam, despite huge infusions of foreign aid, never achieved a momentum characteristic of that observed in successfully developing countries such as Taiwan and South Korea. A judgment must be made on the extent to which inclusion of anecdotal evidence into the measurement will alter this conclusion. In this author's opinion, much of the busyness that impressed wartime visitors to Saigon reflected relatively little improvement in industrial structure, particularly in the last ten year of the war, and therefore cannot be used to significantly alter the conclusion derived from studying the broad statistics. Certainly Vietnam did not develop a very complex input–output relationship and was in no sense self-supporting.

4.4   Imports and exports

No single set of statistics reveals the economic plight of South Vietnam better than that on exports and imports. From the time of partition, South Vietnam was dependent on imported goods far in excess of what it was capable of paying for. In 1956, the country imported $218 million in goods while exporting only $45 million (see Table A4.7), for a merchandise trade deficit that was 18 percent of its national income. The deficit improved slightly to 1961 and then worsened steadily to 1967, at which time it stabilized in the range of $700–800 million, as is shown in Table 4.3.[23]

The foregoing brief statement excludes Vietnam's exported services, which were almost entirely wages paid by U.S. agencies to their Vietnamese employees. These wages were a major source of foreign exchange to Vietnam, and we have estimated their approximate contribution in Table 4.4. These estimates, as most, should be accepted with caution, and one should consult the footnotes to Table A4.8 to understand how they were derived. In the general context of long-run development, these temporary services (wage) exports are irrelevant, because they could not be counted on to generate foreign exchange in the future. In fact, they had already declined greatly by the end of the war because of the withdrawal of U.S. forces.

A closer look at exports reveals that Vietnam was a major exporter of rice up to 1964. In 1963, rice exports were 323,000 metric tons ($36 million), making Vietnam the world's fourth largest exporter, behind only Burma, Thailand, and China. In 1967, Vietnam imported 770,000 metric tons, primarily from the United States. This turnaround of over 1 million tons is a

Table 4.3. *South Vietnam trade deficit, 1956–74ª ($ million)*

Year	Trade deficit[b]	Exports as percentage of imports[b]	Deficit as percentage of national income[c]
1956	172.5	21	18
1957	208.2	28	20
1958	176.9	24	16
1959	149.5	33	13
1960	155.8	35	13
1961	189.8	27	16
1962	219.4	20	18
1963	238.7	24	19
1964	278.2	15	20
1965	352.2	9	23
1966	579.6	5	36
1967	727.6	2	38
1968	695.8	2	36
1969	825.8	1	34
1970	703.6	2	28
1971	692.6	2	27
1972	730.0	2	29
1973	710.5	8	25
1974	802.1	10	23

[a]These figures exclude wages paid by Americans to Vietnamese employees.
[b]From Table A4.7.
[c]National income data from Table A3.5.

good indication of the severity of the rice situation in Vietnam during the period of major escalation of the war.

The principal earner of foreign exchange was rubber. Exports of this commodity declined from 83,000 metric tons in 1959 to 21,000 tons a decade later and remained approximately at the 1969 level to the end of the war. As an earner of foreign exchange, rubber produced about two-thirds of Vietnam's total value of exports over the period 1956–72. Then its primacy gave way to wood products and fish (mainly shrimp). In 1973, these two products accounted for $26 million[24] of the total of $58 million, and fish alone accounted for one-third of the total value of exports in 1974. The pattern of exports was changing when the war ended.

What might have happened to Vietnamese exports in a peaceful environment is a matter of speculation. In a study of development prospects for South Vietnam, the Development and Resources Corporation (1969, vol. 1) thought that the postwar potential for Vietnamese exports was encouraging. The study presented results of a survey of the potential markets for rice, rubber, wood products, fish, feed grain, and several minor commodities. The study foresaw

Table 4.4. *Estimate of wages earned by Vietnamese employees of U.S. agencies, 1967–73*

Year	Average number of employees (thousand)	Total wages paid ($ million)	Merchandise exports ($ million)
1967	135.0	151	16
1968	140.9	154	12
1969	142.4	188	12
1970	135.7	211	12
1971	114.2	152	12
1972	78.2	65	16
1973	26.7	21	58

Source: Tables A4.7 and A4.8.

good markets in most of the major commodities mentioned, but considered the potential markets for rubber, wood products, and fish as excellent. It gave an estimate of market potential for Vietnamese exports in 1980 within the range of $236–427 million. According to the Development and Resources (D&R) study, the export requirement for long-run self-sufficiency was $400–500 million (ten years "after the war"); thus, the general conclusion of the study was that Vietnam had a reasonable chance of achieving economic independence.

The D&R study stressed potential markets. The question, of course, was the ability of the Vietnamese to produce for those markets. We have already pointed out the problem of rice and fertilizer. Some thought that rubber production, which had been devastated by war activities, could not survive as a major export.[25] At the time of the D&R study, Vietnam's cost of producing pulp was three times that in the United States (Development and Resources Corporation 1969, p. 103). Furthermore, the strongest statement to be found in the study about Vietnam's international advantage in producing pulp for export was a tentative one that it "could become one of the low-cost pulp and paper producers in Asia."[26] The evidence supporting strongly positive statements about South Vietnam's export potential on the supply side was very weak. Thus, although foreign markets might have existed for Vietnamese exports, it is questionable that the country would have been able to respond to them on a scale necessary to ensure a rate of growth of exports, say a decade later, compatible with self-sustaining growth.

Vietnam's poor export record during the war jeopardized whatever chances it had for postwar development. We cannot explain the poor performance of exports completely by the physical devastation of war and insecurity. Much of this lack of performance must be attributed to unnecessary and even harmful government policies. For most of the period, the foreign exchange rate policy of the Vietnamese government was calculated to maximize U.S. aid. This policy encouraged imports and discouraged exports, just as it stifled industrial and agricultural development. The significant rise in exports in 1973–4 was due partly to the economic incentives that accompanied the foreign exchange rate reforms in 1971–2. The exchange rate on exports in September 1970 was 118 piasters per dollar, a rate that had been maintained since June 1966.[27] The rate was raised to d 550 per dollar[28] in July 1972. Over a twenty-one-month period, the effective local currency price for a dollar's worth of exports rose 365 percent. In 1973 and 1974 there was a significant rise in the world prices of goods exported by South Vietnam;[29] therefore, real exports were not as high as the figures shown in Table A4.7. Even so, we can conclude that exports responded well to the foreign exchange rate reforms in the 1970–2 period. Whether or not actual exports under the much improved exchange rate had caught up to potential before the end of the conflict we cannot say.

4.5   Demographic changes

A number of changes in demography that are thought to be causally linked with economic development were prominent features of wartime South Vietnam. A major change, the movement of a large part of the population from rural to urban areas was due to the manner in which the war was fought in the countryside and to the lure of many war-induced job opportunities that were created in the cities (Goodman 1975). Another noteworthy process, the growth in educational opportunity, may have been due as much to the desire of Vietnamese officials to please their aid donors and to military requirements as to more conventional causes of educational development. It is evident, therefore, that some demographic changes that occurred in South Vietnam between 1956 and 1975 raced far ahead of economic development and were not as closely linked with development there as in a more conventional setting.

In 1956, the population of South Vietnam was 12,737,000. With population growth slightly over 2.6 percent per year, South Vietnam had about 20,500,000 people when the war ended (see Table A4.1). These figures are not based on census counts, but as reliable approximations they have not been questioned.

Data on the urban-rural mix are more suspect than those on population. Before the war, the urban population was 15–20 percent of the total. The urban ratio grew to 30–35 percent in the early seventies.[30] Because of the large influx of refugees that occurred after the Communist Easter offensive in 1972, the urban population at the end of the war could have been over 40 percent of the total. Again, the large growth in population in the cities cannot be attributed entirely to the normal process of development and would have posed major social, economic, and political problems even if the war had ended on the most favorable terms for the South.

Another change worthy of mention was the improvement in literacy that took place during the war. Lerner stated that literacy is the "basic personal skill that underlies the whole modern sequence" (Lerner 1958, p. 64). There are no authoritative statistics on literacy in South Vietnam; so approximate levels will have to suffice. Scigliano claimed that the French deliberately held down popular literacy and that 80 percent of the people were unable to read or write in 1944.[31] In 1971, Vietnam's National Institute of Statistics conducted a rural household survey for sixteen selected provinces. Among other things, the survey indicated that 76 percent of the population ten years of age and over were literate and that 71 percent of the adult population (age fifteen and above) were literate.[32] These statistics may not be representative of Vietnam as a whole and are improbable for the country if only 20 percent of the adult population were literate in 1958, but it is hardly an exaggeration to state that literacy advanced dramatically.

Indicators of literacy are newspaper circulations and numbers of newspapers published. In 1962 there were thirty daily newspapers "of general information" issued at least four times per week, with a circulation of 540,000. In 1968, fifty-eight newspapers had a circulation of 1,542,000.[33] The increases in newspapers published and their circulations did not follow a smooth curve. Rather, the rise was an up-and-down process probably influenced by the regulations of different governments on the matter of censorship. However, the trend definitely was upward. The newspapers were predominantly in the Vietnamese language, with several in French, English, and Chinese.

Measured by enrollment, classrooms, or teachers, educational growth in wartime South Vietnam was rapid. By the end of the war, virtually every child of school age had been exposed to some formal education. The Vietnamese school system distinguished between primary (first five years of school) and secondary (last seven years) education. Primary education was compulsory, and most students dropped out after completing elementary school. For those who continued, there was a six-year course and an exam, called Baccalaureate 1. For those few students who intended to go to college, there was another year of education, essentially in self-study, to prepare for the Baccalaureate 2 exam.

Total enrollment in primary and secondary education increased from 1,011,000 in 1957–8 to 3,506,000 in 1970–1. More important than the totals are the estimates on percentage of school-age children in school, shown in Table 4.5. Not shown in the table is the steady rise in percentage enrollment that took place over the intervening period. The rise was almost uninterrupted, except in years when the political/military situation was relatively unstable,

Table 4.5. *Children enrolled in school, 1957–70*[a]

| | Number of students (thousands) | | Percentage of school-age children enrolled | |
Year	Elementary	Secondary	Elementary	Secondary
1957–8	887	110	38	4
1970–1	2,718	637	82	17

[a]Excludes students enrolled in kindergarten. School-age children, for the purpose of calculations in this table, were considered to be ages 6–10 for elementary school and 11–17 for secondary school. A survey conducted in fourteen provincial capitals in 1970 revealed that 18% of the population were in the age group 15–19. By linear interpolation we estimated that 18% were in the age group 6–10 and 23% in the age group 11–17. Given the total population for each year, we estimated the school-age population for elementary and secondary schools using 18% and 23%, respectively. This procedure assumes that there was no change in the age composition of the populations in these groups over time and that the survey for the fourteen provincial capitals was representative of Vietnam. We have no information to support or disprove these assumptions. Data on the demographic survey are reported in VN-NIS (annual, 1971, pp. 367–79).

particularly in 1964 and 1968. The figures on enrollment in secondary education are consistent with the increase in number of students examined in the Baccalaureate 1 and 2 exams. In 1957 there were slightly under 10,000 exams given, but in 1970 the number was 145,000.[34] Higher education also advanced during the war. Five times as many students were attending college in Vietnam at the beginning of the decade of the seventies than at the beginning of the sixties. The numbers were approximately 57,000 and 11,000,[35] respectively.

4.6   Development of infrastructure

As a side effect of the war effort, certain components of South Vietnam's infrastructure developed rapidly. Indeed, by 1975, some populous areas in the Mekong Delta were connected by a military superhighway and Vietnam had advanced port facilities that it was only beginning to use. But it is easy to exaggerate the utility to the economy of much of the construction put in place by the U.S. Military Assistance Command. Expensive roads, airports, and telecommunications systems could provide little boost to development if they were inappropriate for the needs of the country, as many of these investments were in wartime South Vietnam.

U.S. military investments in infrastructure were sizable.[36] By early 1971, the military had spent more than $400 million on road construction, over $66 million on harbors, and about $100 million more on waterfront improvements.

Outlays for airfield construction and improvements were $190 million. They cover the five-to-six-year period 1965–70 and therefore indicate an average annual investment of $125–150 million. For the same period, the estimated dollar value of South Vietnam's GNP was about $2 billion per year. Thus, military investments were 6–7.5 percent of GNP, at a minimum, for that period. AID also made sizable investments in infrastructure, contributing $280 million in the form of capital assistance from 1956. Although AID's investments were spread throughout the economy, it made large contributions toward the development and improvement of electrical power capacity, telecommunications, and highways.[37] In contrast to these U.S. contributions, South Vietnam budgetary expenditures on infrastructure were minuscule. For example, for the period 1969–72, total budgeted expenditures for the Ministry of Public Works were less than 0.3 percent of GNP.

Highway development was seen as a critical activity for both military and civil purposes. South Vietnam's original highway system was a part of a general plan for Indochina that, after 1918, distinguished between "local" roads and "colonial" roads. By 1936, Indochina had 27,500 kilometers of roads "usually passable throughout the year," and the system was described as one of the best in the Far East (Robequain 1944, p. 99). In South Vietnam, by a different classification, there were at one time 6,000 kilometers of national and interprovincial roads and 14,000 kilometers of rural and secondary roads, but most of this system had been destroyed or damaged by the time of partition.[38]

Much of the road network had been restored and improved by 1975. Maintenance of the roads and bridges required an extraordinary effort in the insurgency environment of Vietnam, but it was justified on military and pacification grounds. In early 1967 it was decided to restore 4,075 kilometers of highways considered essential for military operations, pacification, and economic development. For all practical purposes, this plan was implemented by the U.S. military command using its own engineering battalions, private contractors, and Vietnamese army engineering battalions. Most of the work was completed by the war's end.[39]

Potable water and electrical power systems were greatly improved during the war. According to AID's *Terminal Report*, the Vietnam Power Company, which produced about 96 percent of the country's power in 1970, had an installed capacity of 813 megawatts (MW) worth $159 million at the end of the war (AID 1976, pt. D, p. 38). Virtually all of this was installed during the war, mostly with U.S. aid, but with substantial contributions from Japan ($56 million) and France ($11 million). Water and sewage facilities increased much faster than population growth. From 1962 to 1971, Vietnamese statistics indicate almost a tripling in the volume of water pumped in Saigon and slightly more than a tripling in all of the rest of Vietnam. After 1971, much additional capacity was added, and systems were upgraded in terms of efficiency of operation and health and sanitation. It is very likely that water supply capacity quadrupled after 1962, and the increase was even larger if nonvolumetric factors are included.

Major improvements were accomplished at the ports of Saigon and Danang, and a deep-water port was built at Cam Ranh. Large and small airfields were constructed throughout the country, establishing an air communications system between all the provinces. A national airline was organized, operating scheduled flights between the principal towns, and it had some international routes to Bangkok, Hong Kong, and Tokyo on which it flew world-standard jet aircraft. The national railroad was rehabilitated, although its service was easily interrupted by insurgent operations. The canal system was not rehabilitated during the war. Finally, there was a modern microwave telecommunications system constructed to serve military needs.

A question concerning the usefulness of much of this infrastructure for economic development remains. It cannot be answered with any confidence. Highways built for military traffic are fine for civilian use if the country is rich enough to maintain them. The deep-water port at Cam Ranh was not even used during the war, and it probably was years ahead of its time in the context of development needs. The relatively expensive air travel system was useful during the war because it was safer than land travel, but it probably would have been cut back in a peacetime setting in which economic considerations would dominate. The growth of the electrical power system was politically rather than economically motivated. Its operating costs were high,[40] and that would not well serve long-run economic development. Yet the infrastructure development during the war was so excessive that loss of even half of it in a peaceful period dominated by economics would still have left much of developmental value. The major temptation has been to overstate its value.

4.7   Money and finance in Vietnam economic development

4.7.1   Monetization of the economy

Monetization of the economy is associated with and may be a necessary precondition for sustained economic growth. Monetization can be defined in a number of ways. One useful definition is the "enlargement of the sphere of monetary economy" (Chandavarkar 1977, p. 665). This definition follows from a two-sector model of the economy in which nonmonetary activities, subsistence and barter, coexist with economic activities requiring money as a medium of exchange. In the process of development, more and more of the nonmonetary activities give way to those that utilize money. A measure of monetization consistent with this definition would be the percentage of national income generated in the monetary sphere.

Chandavarkar (1977) argued persuasively that a commonly used definition of monetization, the ratio of money to income, could be misleading for at least two reasons. In the first place, an increase in the ratio may imply a deepening of the monetary sphere rather than a widening. Second, there does not seem to be any empirically determined systematic relationship between the ratio of money to income and economic development (Chandavarkar 1977, p. 679). Presumably, a measure of real money balance per capita has the same drawback as the ratio of money to income.

Chandavarkar's analysis of national income data for a number of countries indicated that 88 percent of Vietnam's income was generated in the monetary sector in the late sixties. On the basis of these data, this ratio was comparable to those for Thailand and the Philippines and greater than those for India, South Korea, and Malaysia in 1969–70 (Chandavarkar 1977, p. 679). Because earlier monetization ratios for Vietnam are not available, a quantitative statement about the progress of monetization cannot be made. However, one's best guess is that the ratio was much lower at the time of partition. Based partly on speculation, we believe that Vietnam experienced rapid monetization over the course of its existence, using the definition advocated by Chandavarkar.

Although there are objections to using the money–income ratio or the real stock of money per capita as measures of widening of the monetary sector, these indicators are suggestive of monetization when considered along with other variables and a theory that associates development and monetization. Because the use of money reduces the transactions cost of exchange, a money exchange economy is more efficient than a barter exchange economy, and money will emerge in the process of development (Brunner and Meltzer 1971; Niehans 1971). As urbanization accompanies development, assuming that subsistence activities are greatly restricted in urban areas, money becomes a practical necessity of life for people who previously had no need for it. The population movement from rural to urban areas might not at first increase income, but it does increase the demand for money. If money is made available in response to the new situation, the money–income ratio must rise, and that rise is closely associated with a narrowing of the nonmonetized sector. One cannot prove that a rise in the money–income ratio is a true indicator of a receding nonmonetary sector, but if population is shifting from rural to urban areas at the same time, the rise in the money–income ratio will be indicative of a widening of the sphere of monetary economy.[41]

Analysis of a time series on the money–income ratio for 1956–74, using the M_1 definition of money (currency plus demand deposits), in Vietnam is inconclusive as an indicator of monetization (Figure 4.1). In the late 1950s,

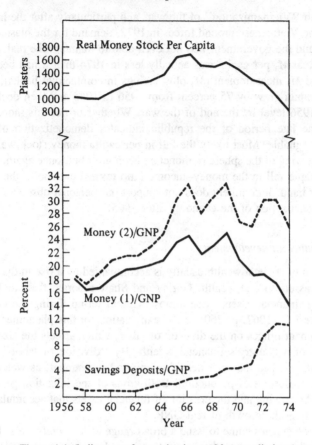

Figure 4.1. Indicators of monetization and intermediation (two-year moving average).

the ratio was about 0.17, and it rose, more or less steadily, to 1965, reaching a high plateau in the range of 0.20–0.30 for the next few years. Then it fell until the end of the war. The fall in the money–income ratio after 1969 might be explained by a rise in inflationary expectations, a loss of confidence by the Vietnamese people in a secure future, or an awakened interest in time deposits once severe interest rate restrictions were removed.[42] In any event, it is not indicative of increasing monetization of the society.

Data on real money stock per capita show the same result. Real M_1 per capita rose about 7 percent per year through 1965. During the "Americanization" phase of the war, 1965-9, per capita real money stock fell only slightly. With "Vietnamization" of the war, and particularly after the heavy fighting of the Vietnamese ground forces in 1972, demand for the piaster fell drastically, and the government was not even able to maintain the real stock of money. Real M_1 per capita was actually less in 1974 than it had been in 1956. On the M_2 measurement (M_1 plus savings in commercial banks), real money per capita grew by 75 percent from 1956 to 1965 and then declined back to its 1956 level by the end of the war. Whether or not this monetary history in the late period of the republic indicates demonetization of the economy is arguable. Most likely the fall in per capita money stock was not due to a narrowing of the sphere of monetary economy, but, once again, only reflects the rapid fall in the money–income ratio toward the end of the war. On the other hand, it definitely does not support our personal observation of increased monetization of the economy after 1965.

4.7.2   Finance in development

Accumulation of societal wealth usually is accompanied by a rise in the ratio of financial assets to real wealth. Gurley and Shaw reported that stocks of nonmonetary financial assets "rise almost without let-up during the development process," (1967, p. 260). Their explanation for this phenomenon is that development hinges on the division of labor, which affects the size and composition of a country's financial wealth. By "division of labor" they mean specialization in the activities of saving and investment, as well as in the physical operations of production. Both kinds of specialization generate lending and borrowing and the creation of financial assets that accumulate at a faster rate than the growth of real GNP.

Over time, countries come to issue a broad range of financial assets. Elaborate financial markets and other institutions are developed to specialize in the transfer of financial assets. The array of financial assets in poor countries is not very large, and it usually is dominated by time and savings deposits. Gurley and Shaw found that the ratio of time and savings deposits to GNP rose from 1–2 percent in very poor countries to about 10 percent in countries with real per capita GNP around $300 and to as high as 50 percent in rich, highly developed countries (1967, p. 260). In Vietnam, the ratio of time and savings deposits to GNP rose from about 1 percent in the late 1950s to slightly over 10 percent toward the end of the war, as shown in Figure 4.1. The rapid rise in this ratio helps to explain the fall in the money–income ratio using the M_1 definition of money. This rise was most likely a response to interest rate reform in September 1970 that allowed interest paid on time and savings accounts in commercial banks to rise from the 8–12 percent level before the reform to a range of 10–21 percent, depending on the term, after it.[43]

The relatively high interest rates still yielded a negative real rate of interest.

It is surprising, therefore, that time and savings deposits grew so rapidly in the early seventies. By the end of the war, per capita real income in Vietnam was approximately $200; yet the ratio of time and savings deposits to GNP had reached the level of those for countries with per capita real GNP of $300. An explanation of this might be that Vietnam had a higher standard of living than other countries with comparable GNPs because it received substantially more aid. In any event, there appears to have been considerable financial development in Vietnam, when that is measured by the crude indicator of ratio of time and savings deposits to GNP.

Also, by the end of the war, banking had expanded, and government bonds were beginning to be accepted by individuals. Treasury bond holdings of individuals increased from 13 billion piasters at the end of 1972 and 24 billion piasters in 1973 to 44 billion piasters at the end of 1974. In real measure, the rise was about 60 percent over the period, and that is significant because it occurred in the face of a deteriorating military situation. Over the same period, credit by the commercial banks actually declined in real terms, while that for the development banks (principally agriculture) rose by 65 percent,[44] although the totals were small, at less than 4 percent of GNP.

The available indicators of financial deepening reveal no significant progress in South Vietnam over the last ten years of its history. The most positive change was the rise in private savings that took place starting in 1970. In general, the financial structure of the economy, that web of financial arrangements that has been described admirably by Shaw (1973), did not develop commensurately with the growth of real income. This simply is another way of expressing the theme that growth was driven by external factors, namely aid, rather than by internal developments. The major conclusion of this section is that finance in South Vietnam was rather "shallow," to use Shaw's expression, at the end of the war.

4.8   Attitudinal factors in Vietnam economic development

4.8.1   Attitude of government toward industrialization

The sequence of economic activities required for rapid industrialization can be promoted or thwarted by the attitudes of the people who run the government. Statements by public officials regarding industrialization or economic development almost always proclaim government support, sometimes enthusiastically. More important than such public statements are the laws and other regulations enacted by government and the day-to-day actions of public officials. In the case of South Vietnam, there was a contradiction between the words and deeds of government officials for all but the last couple of years of the country's existence. That industrialization was not high on the priority list of Vietnamese and American officials is understandable in view of the situation. Ranking Vietnamese officials were preoccupied with the conduct of the war and with efforts to maintain political stability (which meant keeping themselves in positions of influence). Many would have liked rapid economic progress as a by-product of what they considered more important activities, but it was not a focus of their attention. In other instances, specific policies to achieve development went against their own instincts.

This clearly was the case in the early period of the Republic of Vietnam. Bernard Fall (1963, p. 302) explained the relatively poor performance of the industrial sector under Diem in the following way: "In some cases the real reason for the slowness of the industrialization effort was not as much the insurgency or the lack of capital, as the basic philosophy of the South Vietnamese regime, which . . . at first did not attach very great importance to industrial development and is – all protestation to the contrary – basically hostile to foreign investment. [This attitude] has, until very recently, blighted the country's economic development as a whole." The attitude has also been characterized as one of suspicion (Montgomery 1962, p. 93).

Having lived under foreign domination up to the time of partition, it is understandable that the Vietnamese would be suspicious of foreign investment, even if they knew that other developing countries had prospered from it. However, part of the reason for a lack of interest in industrialization, at least in the early years, can be found in Diem's own sense of ethics, on which he attempted to build a new "national culture." Central to the new culture was a philosophy called "personalism."[45]

"Personalism" had a highly moralistic tone. It adopted Confucian values and pressed for a purely Vietnamese culture, although its proponents and teachers were Catholic.[46] With respect to economic organization, "personalism" engendered mistrust in private enterprise, which apparently was viewed as a natural expression of selfish interests. And although economic growth was considered necessary to achieve cultural independence, economic organization justified on the criteria of efficiency and profit was not acceptable (Scigliano 1963, pp. 110–11). Donnell (1959, p. 86) observed no widespread acceptance of this philosophy among the Vietnamese people, but to the public officials picked by the Ngo family it was readily accepted. The result was a deemphasis on industrial output, particularly that requiring large-scale enterprises or foreign investment.

A decade later, the Ngo family was gone, and American influence was overwhelming. Yet the negative attitude toward foreign investment persisted. In 1971, Leroy Jones described a number of institutional impediments to industrial development, just at a time when public officials were making much of economic development by displaying five-year plans, and so forth. In a section on foreign investment (Jones 1971, sect. VI, p. 3) he wrote that "Vietnam today has a reputation as the worst place in Southeast Asia to do business and this judgment is independent of any war-risk factor."

After the North Vietnamese offensive in 1972, war risk may have become the major impediment to foreign investment. Nevertheless, an author of the AID *Terminal Report* commented that "the array of bureaucratic obstacles confronting potential investors" was a major factor inhibiting foreign investment.[47] Thus, virtually to the end of the war the Vietnamese government had not managed to cope effectively with the basic mistrust that its officials harbored for foreign direct investment, despite the presence of thousands of Americans for many years and some $8 billion in aid.

The negative attitude of government officials toward industry did not spill over to agriculture. There never appeared to be a reluctance to promote agricultural development. Perhaps this was due to the fact that agriculture was less subject to foreign penetration, and its smallness of scale was consonant with Vietnamese traditional values.

4.8.2   Modernization of outlook

The attitudes of individuals toward change and, especially, their ability to adapt to it quickly are important requisites for self-sustained growth. We equate these traits with "modernization of outlook." Rostow (1972), Logan (1971), and Silver (1971) stressed some manifestations of modern attitudes in wartime South Vietnam, citing the quickness of farmers to take to gasoline-powered irrigation pumps, IR–8 "miracle" rice, fertilizers, pesticides, and new cash crops, and Popkin (1979) called his book about Vietnam *The Rational Peasant*. The government adopted modern administrative procedures (including the use of computers) and applied modern economic reasoning to complex problems. Adelman and Morris (1972) evaluated dozens of countries in regard to "modernization," depending on whether or not (1) they had advanced considerably beyond Westernized dress and other outward forms of behavior and (2) political, economic, and social programs gained significant support among the urban and rural populations. These are vague criteria, but they convey a sense of direction. As of around 1960, they gave South Vietnam a low score in these aspects of development. The Vietnam land reform obviously had "significant" support among the tenant farmers, but tax-raising programs take many years to become acceptable. At the national level, democracy was taking hold, and village participation was reemerging. By the Adelman-Morris criteria it seems evident that Vietnam had moved a long way toward modernization by the end of the war.

A distinction must be made between the surface forms of modernization so apparent in wartime South Vietnam (dress, television, motorcycles, etc.) and the individual and social attitudes necessary for development. Lerner stressed "psychic mobility" in his search for a model of modernization (1958, ch. 2). Professor Clarence Ayres used to argue that modernization required a positive and, in his language, a "technological" attitude with respect to goal achievement. Here we stress, as key attributes of modernization, independence of mind and a sense of feeling that one exercises considerable control over one's own future or at least can have an influence on events.

Observers in South Vietnam during the last stage of the war were impressed with the level of intelligence and the (apparent) outlook of government officials and people in the street. But their outward optimism covered up a deep sense of fatalism. Businessmen knew that they could not compete with Japan and that the success of their moneymaking schemes was tied to what the Americans would do. Ministers concerned with economic affairs felt that they had to consult with their American counterparts or their American academic friends before taking important actions. The modernization in techniques – the use of fertilizer, IR–8 rice, and hog cholera vaccine – could be attributed primarily to the American presence and American aid. The centerpiece of American aid, the CIP, was conducted in such a way that Americans told the Vietnamese importers which commodities and how much they could import. These regulations did not encourage independence of thought. The American presence fostered a sense of dependence in the Vietnamese, and this feeling was clearly a negative factor in the modernization of outlook.

Nowhere was this sense of dependence more apparent than in the "modern" Vietnamese armed forces, called the RVNAF. Once considered one of the best armies in Asia, the RVNAF had modern weapons and modern staff and command techniques, but the RVNAF never gained a feeling of independence and competence. According to Vietnamese officials, the confidence of the armed forces was severely shattered following the Paris agreements of 1973, which were forced on the government, and once it became obvious that the American shield was being removed. Several years after the war, Vietnam's former ambassador to the United States said that

The presence of American advisors at all levels of the military hierarchy created among the Vietnamese leadership a mentality of reliance on their advice and suggestions. Even though some officers didn't like the intrusive presence of their American counterparts, most of them felt more confident when they had their advisors at their side. [Hosmer et al. 1980, p. 72]

Air Marshal Ky (former premier) thought that the dominant role played by the Americans caused the Vietnamese to lose their "identity" in the end (Hosmer et al. 1980, p. 73).

Military events and economic or social events cannot be regarded as parallel lines, but their underlying psychic drives are too similar to be ignored. The economy depended on millions of individual actors who sought to make a profit whenever they could, and most of them did not rely directly on Americans. Yet to ascribe to the Vietnamese investor or business organizer an attitude that he was in charge of his venture or could make it work independent of American actions would be misleading. The potential Vietnamese investor viewed the future in a very short time frame and was unwilling to take big risks in enterprise. Average Vietnamese citizens had little confidence that their future was secure, with or without American assistance. That pessimistic outlook, the sense that one could only survive, not control events, did not improve over the period of the war nearly so much as the outward signs of modernization might indicate.

4.9   Simulated requirements for self-sustained growth

Previous sections have dealt with developmental factors as isolated problems. One way of bringing these pieces together and of obtaining an overall quantitative impression of economic development in wartime South Vietnam is to present the results of a forecasting exercise that was undertaken in 1971. A dynamic macroeconomic model of the economy incorporating a highly aggregated (5 × 5) input–output structure to constrain production was used to estimate sectoral requirements to sustain consumption under the assumption of a gradual reduction in U.S. aid (Grimm and Piekarz 1971). This model was constructed for the purpose of answering questions of this type: If the United States gradually withdrew its economic aid to South Vietnam, how well would the economy have to perform, year by year, in order to maintain per capita consumption or slightly increase it?

Assuming a reduction in U.S. aid of $50 million per year for ten years and a desired increase in per capita consumption of 1 percent per year, the model indicated the following ten-year annual growth requirements: agriculture 8 percent, industry 9 percent, investment 9 percent, and exports 20 percent. Assuming these simulated requirements were met, GNP growth was projected to be 4.3 percent per year.[48]

The foregoing figures are useful to the extent that they are suggestive of the approximate growth rates necessary for sustaining a consumption path flatter than it had been. In view of the fact that none of the requisite growth rates had been achieved in the previous ten years with foreign aid averaging over $400 million per year, there is little reason to believe that they could have been met with aid declining to less than $100 million at the end of the period. However, this is an arguable conclusion, because, as we have now seen, countries such as South Korea and Taiwan have performed far better than most expected twenty years ago.

The big question, of course, is whether or not the gains made in human capital and administration (which were not allowed to play major productive roles in the war situation) would have been sufficient in a peacetime environment to compensate for the loss of aid and the shaky economic structure built up during the war. The answer to this question is not knowable. In any event, the task of achieving self-sustaining growth would have been an enormous task for South Vietnam.

Table A4.1. *Population of South Vietnam, 1955–74 (thousand)[a]*

Year	Population	Year	Population
1955	12,406	1965	16,124
1956	12,737	1966	16,543
1957	13,077	1967	16,973
1958	13,426	1968	17,414
1959	13,785	1969	17,867
1960	14,153	1970	18,332
1961	14,530	1971	18,809
1962	14,918	1972	19,373
1963	15,317	1973	19,954
1964	15,715	1974	20,553

[a]Data from VN-NIS (annual, 1972, Table 321).
The source table gives population estimates for the
1963–72 period. Estimates in this table were extrapolated backward from 1963 assuming a population rate of growth of 2.6%, the same rate used
in the source for calculating population from 1963
to 1971. Extrapolations for 1973 and 1974 used a
3% growth rate, which is the same as in the source
table for 1972.

Table A4.2. *Major crop production in South Vietnam, 1956–73 (thousand tons)*

Year	Rice	Corn	Mungo	Manioc	Sweet potatoes	Sugarcane	Copra[a]	Soybeans	Peanuts	Tobacco	Rubber	Tea	Vegetables
1956	3,412	31	5	126	104	484	4		13	7	70	4	
1957	3,192	30	5	149	142	870	33	1	16	7	62	4	
1958	4,235	29	6	163	137	761	27	1	22	7	72	3	
1959	5,092	26	6	181	203	824	29	1	19	5	75	4	
1960	4,955	27	7	220	221	1,000	46	3	24	8	78	5	
1961	4,607	32	8	255	236	932	31	4	29	8	78	5	
1962	5,205	38	10	313	273	872	42	4	29	8	78	5	
1963	5,237	37	11	389	300	964	37	5	32	7	76	5	
1964	5,185	46	12	289	301	1,055	35	4	37	7	74	5	108[b]
1965	4,822	44	12	236	278	1,093	37	4	33	8	65	6	133[b]
1966	4,336	35	14	290	246	936	32	8	34	7	49	5	144[b]
1967	4,688	33	20	262	254	770	33	6	34	8	43	4	192[b]
1968	4,366	32	13	260	235	426	28	7	32	8	34	5	
1969	5,115	31	12	233	226	321	25	6	34	8	28	5	
1970	5,715[c]	31	11	216	220	336	30	7	32	8	33	6	218[d]
1971	6,100[c]	34	13	270	230	341	31	8	37	9	20	6	244[d]
1972	5,900[c]	42	14	247	241	331	29	7	39	9	20	5	
1973	7,165[c]												
Weight[e]	1	1.342	2.895	0.737	0.868	0.158	1.237	3.158	2.342	29.474	9.373	24.473	

[a]These figures are derived from data on production of coconuts. The conversion factor is 4,000 coconuts = one ton of copra.
[b]Data from Dacy (1969b, p. 34).
[c]Data from AID (1976, pt. A).
[d]Data from AID-VN (1972a, p. 3).
[e]These weights were computed by the U.S. Department of Agriculture based on prices in 1957–9. These are not normalized weights; rather, they are price relatives, with the price of rice as the numeraire.

Table A4.3. *Controlled livestock slaughterings in Vietnam,
1954–73 (thousand)*

Year	Cattle	Buffalos	Pigs
1954	20.0	11.6	701.8
1955	41.8	13.3	816.0
1956	47.1	15.3	883.6
1957	50.3	12.8	929.5
1958	48.2	15.7	1,025.1
1959	50.4	19.5	1,024.6
1960	56.2	23.0	1,181.1
1961	64.5	28.6	1,139.3
1962	77.7	30.2	955.7
1963	74.0	35.2	909.2
1964	68.6	38.3	1,090.7
1965	76.5	46.7	1,247.5
1966	71.6	48.1	1,093.4
1967	72.3	41.6	1,163.3
1968	67.8	26.1	871.0
1969	80.6	34.0	1,051.0
1970	75.6	39.2	1,171.6
1971	75.8	42.3	1,148.7
1972	56.6	33.5	999.6
1973	53.1	28.6	903.0

Source: VN-NIS (annual, various
issues).

Table A4.4. *Price of rice compared with implicit GNP deflator, 1960–73*

	Rice price index (1962 = 100)		Two-year average			Ratio	
Year	Retail[a]	Paddy	(1) Retail	(2) Paddy	(3) GNP deflator[b]	(1)/(3)	(2)/(3)
1960	76.9	75.2					
1961	104.6	98.9	90.8	87.1	95.7	0.95	0.91
1962	100.0	100.0	102.3	99.5	98.6	1.04	1.01
1963	100.0	95.5	100.0	97.8	102.1	0.98	0.96
1964	118.5	103.0	109.3	99.3	106.6	1.03	0.93
1965	135.4	117.2	127.0	110.1	117.5	1.08	0.94
1966	206.2	195.2	170.8	156.2	165.1	1.03	0.95
1967	418.5	360.6	312.4	277.9	253.5	1.23	1.10
1968	433.8	340.5	426.2	350.6	322.7	1.32	1.09
1969	607.7	559.9	520.8	450.2	455.6	1.14	0.99
1970	818.5	710.9	713.1	635.4	606.4	1.18	1.05
1971	900.0	815.7	859.3	763.3	703.9	1.22	1.08
1972	1,386.2	1,289.1	1,143.1	1,051.9	812.4	1.41	1.29
1973	2,107.7	2,078.8	1,747.0	1,684.0	1,034.5	1.69	1.63
1974	3,473.4		2,790.6		1,471.1	1.90	

[a]Data from VN-NIS (annual, 1972, p. 346). Saigon retail price. The figure for 1973 is from VN-NIS (monthly, Sept. 1974, p. 81). The figure for 1974 was extrapolated from 1974 data for seven months.

[b]Computed from Table 7.1.

Table A4.5. *Fertilizer imports compared with total exports from South Vietnam, 1958–74*[a]

Year	Fertilizer imported[b] (thousand tons)	Value of fertilizer imported[c] ($ million)	Vietnamese exports[d] ($ million)
1958	80	4.9	55.2
1959	159	8.8	75.1
1960	107	6.3	84.5
1961	124	7.1	69.8
1962	116	6.9	56.0
1963	301	21.2	76.7
1964	169	11.3	48.5
1965	179	11.0	35.5
1966	184	12.0	27.6
1967	206	13.4	16.4
1968	373	24.2	11.7
1969	393	25.5	11.9
1970	438	32.9	12.1
1971	384[e]	28.8	12.5
1972	234	27.4	22.7
1973	323	82.8	58.0
1974	NA	122.4	84.9

[a]Different sources give conflicitng data on foreign imports and dollar value in some years. The series in this table were selectively pieced together from diverse sources. The major criteria for selection were that the time series not show drastic (200%) changes from year to year and that the implied price per ton be fairly stable except in years for which large price changes are known to have taken place.

[b]For the period 1958–65, data are from AID-VN (annual, no. 11, p. 101). For the period 1966–72 (excluding 1971), data are from VN-NIS (annual, 1972, p. 317). The figure for 1973 is from VIN-NIS (monthly, July–Sept. 1974, p. 52). The figure for 1973 is an extrapolation from data for eleven months.

[c]Data sources: 1958–65, AID-VN (annual, No. 11, p. 101); 1966–9, estimated by author by assuming a price of $65 per ton; 1970–4, AID-VN (monthly, Feb. 1975, p. 6).

[d]Data from Table A4.7.

[e]This figure was estimated by the author on the assumption that the total dollar value figure as reported was correct and the price per ton was $75.

Table A4.6. *Production and distribution of electricity in South Vietnam, 1954–73 (million KWH)*

Year	Installed capacity[a] (thousand KW)	Production	Distribution to			Number of private subscribers	
			Total	Private lighting	Private and government motor power	Lighting (thousand)	Motor power (thousand)
1954	59.1						
1955	76.0						
1956	75.1	211.9	169.4	80.4	51.8	68.0	2.2
1957	77.0	224.3	177.5	98.8	51.6	78.5	3.0
1958	83.8	244.4	194.7	105.1	57.7	86.9	4.3
1959	95.0	287.4	226.9	119.8	73.5	102.1	5.6
1960	90.1	305.9	242.2	124.1	79.4	97.4	6.0
1961	101.5	329.1	261.3	131.2	88.9	107.1	7.1
1962	107.1	359.4	289.4	138.8	105.6	111.3	8.5
1963	112.4	398.2	325.5	150.6	125.6	113.1	9.2
1964	270.6	469.6	388.6	177.0	154.8	116.2	9.8
1965	294.5	584.9	430.0	192.0	178.5	126.6	10.8
1966	357.3	660.4	532.5	239.1	222.6	133.2	11.2
1967	394.1	779.3	640.0	298.8	258.4	138.3	12.0
1968	453.5	836.4	710.8	309.7	254.0	154.0	12.4
1969	528.7	1,045.9	883.6	352.3	327.9	167.1	14.8[c]
1970	531.1	1,214.5	1,003.0	535.5	302.9	201.6	13.6
1971	573.1	1,340.8	1,096.3	605.4	340.1	242.5	14.5
1972	838.5	1,482.1	1,176.7	632.2	351.6	321.1	14.8[c]
1973		1,627.5	1,190.8[b]				

[a] From 1964–72: This series includes installed capacity of the hydroelectric facility at Da Nhim. It had a capacity of 160,000 KW, but was not used because of wartime disruptions.

[b] Data on supply from VN-NIS (monthly) exclude "free supply," which is included in VN-NIS (annual). This figure is 80 million KWH, approximately the amount of "free supply" in 1972, which is higher than that given in the source in order to make it comparable with reporting in the previous years.

[c] The figure reported in the source cited is 7.4. It is obviously wrong. This estimate was derived by dividing the amount of motor power supplied in 1972 by the average per subscriber in 1971.

Sources: 1954–61, VN-NIS (annual, 1966, p. 238); 1962–72, VN-NIS (annual, 1972, pp. 196–7); 1973, VN-NIS (monthly, July–Sept. 1974, p. 15).

Table A4.7. *Vietnamese imports and exports, 1954–74[a] ($ million)*

Year	Exports[b]	Imports		Import price index[e] (1962 = 100)
		All import arrivals[c]	Commercial import arrivals[d]	
1954	50.6	267.0	235.0[f]	
1955	69.2	263.2	231.6[f]	108
1956	45.1	217.6	191.5[f]	108
1957	80.5	288.7	246.6	108
1958	55.2	232.1	208.8	103
1959	75.1	224.6	198.7	103
1960	84.5	240.3	210.9	104
1961	69.8	259.6	231.9	102
1962	56.0	275.4	230.9	100
1963	76.7	315.4	238.1	105
1964	48.5	326.7	245.8	106
1965	35.5	387.7	297.0	105
1966	27.6	607.2	460.0	105
1967	16.4	744.0	547.4	106
1968	11.7	707.5	473.9	107
1969	11.9	837.7	652.5	112
1970	11.5	715.1	502.3	119
1971	12.4	705.0	598.1	123
1972	15.6	745.6	571.0	137
1973	58.0	716.3[g]	562.4	184
1974	84.9	837.0[g]	659.9	281

[a]The data on exports and imports are derived primarily from customs reports. The annual figures given in the balance-of-payments statements differ slightly from those presented here. See Table 9.2 for balance-of-payments data.

[b]1954–9, AID-VN (annual, no. 9, Table D-3); 1960–72, AID-VN (annual, no. 11, Table 1); 1973–4, AID-VN (monthly, Feb. 1975, p. 6).

[c]Data sources: 1954–9, AID-VN (annual, no. 9, Table D-9); 1960–72, AID-VN (annual, no. 16, Table 1); 1973–4, AID-VN (monthly, Feb. 1975, p. 6).

[d]The figures in this column were derived by the author. They are import arrivals less items that were not contracted through regular commercial operations. The items excluded for the 1957–61 period are identified as public aid, Japanese reparations, French loans, and other non-U.S. and unidentified items, as recorded in AID-VN (annual, no. 9, Table D-12). After 1961, the major items to be subtracted from all imports are listed as Pl 480 rice, Pl 480 (title II) commodities, public aid, aid freight, bartered goods, and unidentified. Data on Pl 480 rice imports are given in VN-NIS (annual, 1972, p. 137) and AID-VN (monthly, Feb. 1975, p. 6). Data on other items are from AID-VN (annual, various issues) and AID-VN (monthly, Feb. 1975).

[e]1955–70: Based on export prices from the United States, Japan, and Taiwan weighted in proportion to Vietnam's imports from these countries. 1971–4: Annual percentage change taken from AID (1976, pt. A, Table 2). These data are based on prices paid for goods actually imported.

It is necessary to make this shift in calculating the index for this period because the worldwide inflation in 1973–4 greatly affected prices paid for goods such as fertilizer and petroleum that were not necessarily imported from the three countries mentioned earlier.

^{f}These data represent import payments rather than arrivals.

^{g}Assumed to be 88% of all imports. (This is the average ratio for the years 1957–71.)

Table A4.8. Calculation of wages paid to Vietnamese employed by U.S. agencies, 1967–73[a]

	(1)	(2)	(3)	(4)	(5)	(6)	(7)	(8)
	Number employ-	Annual wage (thou-			Estimated annual wage (thousand	Total wage bill		Total wage ($
Year	ees (end of year)	sand piasters) Yearly average	Wage index		piasters)	(million piasters)	Exchange rate	million)
1967	141.5	135.0	105[b]	100	105	14,180	94	151
1968	140.0	140.9		123	129	18,180	118	154
1969	144.8	142.4		149	156	22,210	118	188
1970	126.5	135.7		191	201	27,280	129	211
1971	101.8	114.2		233	245	27,980	184	152
1972	54.7	78.2		267	280	21,900	339	65
1973	17.2	26.7[c]		374	393	10,490	503	21

[a]Data sources:

(1) AID (1974b, Apr.–June, p. 7).

(2) Average of end-of-year figures for current and preceding years.

(4) Index applies to skilled workers in Saigon; VN-NIS (annual, 1972, p. 277) and AID-VN (monthly, Feb. 1975, p. 4).

(5) [Column (3) × column (4)]/100.

(6) Column (2) × column (5).

(7) From Table 9.1, column (3).

(8) Column (6) ÷ column (7).

[b]This figure is a yearly average based on total wages paid by U.S. military and civilian agencies in Vietnam and those paid by the major contractors, RMK-BRJ and PA&E for the month of March 1969. Data from Dacy (1967).

[c]Based on quarterly averages.

CHAPTER 5

Land reform and income distribution in Vietnam economic development

In this chapter we trace the history of land reform in South Vietnam during the war and assess how the various programs affected the material well-being of the rural population. A full analysis of income distribution in wartime Vietnam would be a welcome addition to our knowledge of how war policies affected development. In particular, we would like to know if these policies were effective in eliminating relative inequality or absolute poverty as they are usually measured, but an analysis of this sort is not possible because of lack of data. It is possible, however, to infer from nonincome data the progress made in reducing rural poverty and the changes that took place in the relative economic positions of farmers, landlords, and urban wage earners as groups. In addition to its descriptive value in the overall development picture, this kind of information is a useful input to explaining the dynamics of popular support for the government in its political struggle with the Communist forces.

5.1 Income distribution and economic development

At least up to the 1970s, research in economic development stressed growth in per capita income. Development policy, therefore, was concerned primarily with manipulating those variables such as foreign aid that were thought to be effective in speeding up the growth rate in per capita income. In comparison with growth, the concern for equity took a back seat, or it was simply assumed that rapid growth would promote equity, a kind of trickle-down approach. If this were true, obvious value judgments would not play a major role in development theorizing, because there would be no conflict between growth and equity, at least in the long run. The famous inverted-U pattern described by Kuznets (1955) indicated that inequality of income might rise at first, but eventually it would fall. Much of the empirical work of the 1970s tended to cast doubt on this finding or call into question the definition of inequality on which it was based. This work is summarized and the various definitions of income inequality are analyzed admirably by Fields (1980). One important result of the empirical work on income distribution and the rigorous thinking that underlay it was that economists could not avoid making value judgments with regard to integrating income inequality into the definition of economic development.

109

In her reassessment of development goals, Irma Adelman (1975) stated that the objective of economic development is "depauperization."[1] This objective includes the removal of "social, political and spiritual forms of deprivation" as well as the eradication of material poverty (Adelman 1975, p. 306). Actually, this or a similar objective has been stressed for a long time by many institutionally oriented economists, but until recently its acceptance as a development goal was resisted by the mainstream of development economists, who focused on growth as the essence of development.[2] The rush to incorporate equity in the definition of economic development did not begin until the late 1960s.

Its intensity is felt in this often quoted passage from Dudley Seers (1969, p. 3):

The questions to ask about a country's development are: What has been happening to poverty? What has been happening to unemployment? What has been happening to inequality? . . . If one or two of these central problems have been growing worse, especially if all three have, it would be strange to call the result "development," even if per capita income doubled.

The role of land reform in economic development would seem to lose its controversial character once there is agreement that the elimination of various forms of poverty is the central goal to be achieved. By this definition of development, the burden of proof on the advisability of land reform does not rest solely on the argument of economic efficiency. Rationalization for land reform is shifted from technical and empirical arguments based on growth to the broader arena of social equity.[3]

In developing societies that are dominated by agriculture, land reform is a major means for redistributing wealth and for equalizing opportunity. It is advocated as a means for achieving social justice and, therefore, for creating a stable political environment necessary for development. It is argued by some that land reform has a potentially positive impact on creating agricultural employment and slowing the rapid and sometimes destabilizing migration to urban areas (Dorner 1972, ch. 4). Another motivation for land reform might be to increase agricultural productivity, and it is alleged to have done so in some countries (Dorner 1972, ch. 5), although this is a controversial claim.[4] Finally, by increasing the relative wealth position of the rural poor, land reform gives an impetus to local production, assuming the rich have greater taste for imported goods.

5.2   Land reform in South Vietnam[5]

The motive for land reform in South Vietnam from 1945 onward was more political than economic. Both the Viet Minh (early) and the government of the Republic of Vietnam (later) called their land reform programs "land to the tiller" in recognition of the powerful force contained in this revolutionary call to action. However, the means for achieving this goal were radically different. The Viet Minh and Viet Cong resorted to intimidation of landlords and confiscation of lands, as opposed to the GVN's mode of expropriation with compensation, relying on legal arrangements and paperwork.

Land reform was a major goal of the revolutionary and nationalistic Viet Minh from 1945. According to Sansom (1970, p. 55), "they conducted an intensive campaign of terror against landlords and government officials, usually the same persons. The gradual retreat of landlords to the cities that had begun in the 1930s for reasons of role and preferences, in the 1946–1948 period became a panic stricken exodus to escape intimidation, assassination, or trial and probable execution." One might imagine that with the return of the French to Vietnam after World War II and the establishment of puppet regimes, the absentee landlords would have regained their status in Vietnam. In fact, only a few of them returned to their villages, whereas others depended on government officials to collect their rents. The Viet Minh threat was ever present; Sansom (1970, p. 56) stated that "irretrievable power had slipped from the landlord to the tenant."

It appears that history was working in favor of the tenants. In 1945, about 6,500 landowners, including about 500 French citizens, owned almost 1,500,000 hectares of land in the Delta region (Bredo et al. 1968, p. 3). Assume that there were 1,330,000 farmers and 2,000,000 hectares under cultivation in the Delta. Given these assumptions, less than one-half of 1 percent of the farmers owned 75 percent of the land. The available estimates for 1955 are not strictly comparable, but at the time we think that about 15 percent of the owners controlled 75 percent of the cropland (Bredo et al. 1968, p. 12). Despite the lack of strict comparability in the data, it seems evident that some progress was made between 1945 and 1955 in land distribution.

In 1951, Emperor Bao Dai announced a "soft" approach to agrarian reform based on land tenure reform. Basically, this program focused on landlord–tenant relationships in establishing maximum rental rates and squatters' rights in private uncultivated lands. Also, some attempt was made to limit the sizes of holdings, but without any provision for expropriation. This soft approach to agrarian reform avoided major conflict with the landlords, but it was a temporary expedient for a nagging problem.

Land reform started in earnest under the new Republic of Vietnam. Its constitution pledged to make property owners out of the people, to support those with a low standard of living, and to help farmers obtain possession of farmland.[6] The constitution also set out the procedures by which land redistribution would be achieved. The state was to expropriate the land, but was required to make just compensation to the landowners. In 1956, President Ngo Dinh Diem promulgated Ordinance 57, which limited the ownership of rice land to 100 hectares, set out the manner of payment for the expropriated lands, established administrative machinery for transfer of land, and gave first priority of land ownership to those tilling the land. This was the official government program until 1970, when a new land-to-the-tiller program was enacted partly at the urging of the U.S. government and partly because President Nguyen Van Thieu recognized it to be a good political move.

Under Ordinance 57, the government acquired 422,000 hectares between 1958 and 1961 and distributed 244,000 hectares (Bredo et al. 1968, p. 15). In 1968, the accumulated expropriations were only 452,000 hectares, with 267,000 distributed. Thus, the program that showed promise in its early years just about disappeared when the guerrilla war intensified and later escalated into full-scale warfare. Insecurity in the countryside and the requirement for legal transfer of title, necessitating surveys and other actions, were contributing factors to the demise of Ordinance 57.

The Viet Cong land reform program replaced the government's program in areas of the country where the Viet Cong gained control. The Viet Cong land reform program possessed the universality and mass appeal that the Diem land reform lacked, as it was implemented to please the tenant rather than to ease the pain of the landlord. It had three objectives: land redistribution, rent reduction, and higher wages for rural workers (Sansom 1970, pp. 58–9). It is difficult to assess the success of the Viet Cong land reform policies. Sansom thought that their policies were "for the vast majority very effective" (1970, p. 65), whereas AID's *Terminal Report* on land reform (1976, pt. C, pp. 23–6) expressed a less positive view. How much land actually changed hands is not known, but Sansom (1970, p. 65) reported that Viet Cong policies were effective in lowering rents and undoubtedly curtailed the practice of rent collection for absentee landlords by government officials.

Exclusive of Viet Cong distributions in the sixties, further progress in land distribution was made up to 1966–7. Judging from the Lorenz curves presented in Bredo and associates (1968, p. 12), the improvement in land distribution accomplished under the Diem land reform program appears to have been on the order of 20 percent.[7]

The big push for land reform came in 1970, although it had been in planning for several years. As the government began to regain territory in 1967, the status of land reform deteriorated because of the government's policy of returning land to owners of record, in effect evicting tenants who had received land under Viet Cong programs. Indeed, this policy placed the government in an awkward position. To accept the tenant's right to the land effectively would validate the Viet Cong's action, whereas evicting the tenant would incite hostility. Recognition of the adverse political effect of peasant alienation led to the passage of legislation implementing the land-to-the-tiller program.

The law sought to eliminate tenancy completely by expropriating all lands not cultivated by the owner. It limited the right of possession of rice land by any one owner to 15 hectares plus 5 hectares of ancestral worship land and provided for compensation to the previous owner and free distribution to the farmer. The total cost of the program was estimated at 52 billion piasters, with the United States contributing $40 million.[8] The program was to redistribute more than a million hectares over a three-year period.

By the end of 1973, 953,000 titles had been distributed, involving 1,198,000 hectares of land and perhaps 6 million family members. When the war came to an end in 1975, the estimated land cultivated by tenants was only 300,000 hectares.[9] By all accounts, the program was highly successful. One writer (AID 1976, pt. A, p. 113) commented that "the program virtually abolished land tenancy in Vietnam. It raised the living standard of the farmer 30–50 percent and was responsible for a major share of the investment in agriculture that was as noticeable in those years."

Survey research in four villages in different provinces in the Delta conducted between August 1971 and September 1972 provides some evidence on the effect of the land-to-the-tiller program on farmer activities. This study by Callison (1974) indicates that land recipients made more investments in their recently acquired land than tenants and that their output of rice also increased more rapidly. In one of the four villages studied, these results were reversed. However, that reversal was attributed to geography and to the fact that the size of the land parcels distributed there were smaller than average and unsuitable for growing floating rice. On the whole, this study showed very favorable results from the land reform program.

5.3   Land reform and income distribution

It was asserted in a previous passage that land reform raised the income of farmers by 30–50 percent. This statement is not corroborated by any quantitative evidence. Presumably it is based on the assumption that a cessation of rental payments on the order of 30–50 percent, which came about when the tenants acquired land at no cost to themselves, would increase tenants' incomes in that range.

In this section we use indirect evidence to estimate the improvement in farmers' absolute real standard of living and their relative gains in comparison with urban workers. We argue that farmers' incomes increased both absolutely and in relation to those of urban workers. However, it is not clear exactly what a rise in farmer income implies with respect to equality of income distribution. If farmers started out poorer than urban people, a relative rise in their income would imply a reduction in relative inequality at first. But if average farmer income surpassed that of urban people, this could have led again to inequality favoring the rural population. This is a real possibility under the situation that prevailed at the end of the war, when probably 1,500,000 of the working-age urban population were unemployed and the real wages of the million men under arms had been reduced by inflation. Thus, comparing the average income of the farmer with that of the urban population will not necessarily reveal anything concrete about relative inequality. It will only reveal a change in relative status between the rural and urban populations.

The factors to be emphasized in measuring the rise in farmer income per capita in comparison with urban income are as follows:

1. Land reform eventually led to the abolition of rents to landlords.
2. Margins received by middlemen were reduced.
3. Agricultural prices rose faster over the period than the prices of goods purchased by farmers.
4. The rice wage or real wage of urban employed workers declined over the period.
5. The rate of unemployment in urban areas rose dramatically toward the end of the war.

5.3.1   Reduction of rents

Land reform clearly favored the tillers, even if its progress was discontinuous. Reforms under the Viet Minh were reversed once the French returned to Vietnam after World War II. The Diem land reform program bogged down in the insecurity of the 1960–3 period, but it was replaced by the Viet Cong program. When the government began to gain control of much of the countryside in late 1966 and 1967, many of the Viet Cong reforms were reversed, and a period of vacillation ensued up to 1970, when the government's land-to-the-tiller program was inaugurated.

Rents followed the same course. Sansom (1970, ch. 3) traced the progress of rents in the Delta roughly as follows: Before 1956, land rents were in the range of 40–60 percent. They were reduced greatly under Viet Minh rule, but rose again in the early 1950s. In 1954–9, they were 25–40 percent. In government-controlled areas in 1967, they were above 25 percent, but for the Delta as a whole, rents were only 5–10 percent because of the heavy presence of the Viet Cong in this region. However, low rents at this time were offset by Viet Cong taxes, which were as high as 10–20 percent.[10] Before 1965, there were virtually no Viet Cong taxes, and so farmer payments for rent and taxes probably were in the range of 15–25 percent.

In 1966, the Stanford Research Institute Hamlet Survey found that the actual rental payment in the Southern Region was 34 percent (Bredo et al. 1968, p. 60), even though the legal maximum was 25 percent. If 20 percent of the land had fallen into the hands of the tenants by 1967 and therefore was subject to no rent and only negligible taxes in government-controlled areas, the weighted average rent per hectare of land in 1967 was about 27 percent. Thus, the average rent per hectare of land had fallen some since 1956. Because the tenants were not required to pay for land under the land-to-the-tiller program, this land reform program effectively increased farmer income by roughly 27 percent, a significant amount, even if short of the 30–50 percent figure quoted earlier.

5.3.2   Improvement in marketing conditions

Another factor favoring farmers was the erosion of the traditional rice marketing system that had placed middlemen in a strong position. Traditionally the market/finance system of the Delta was controlled by Chinese entrepreneurs who extracted high payments from small farmers for marketing and financial support (Elliott 1971). Sansom (1970, p. 101) reported that by 1967 it was usual to encounter relatively large landowner-farmers doubling as rice merchants in the villages where they lived. Evidently the Cholon Chinese monopoly on rice milling and trade broke down under the insecure conditions that prevailed throughout the Delta of Vietnam. Rice shipments to Saigon were curtailed, and small village mills replaced the larger mills in Cholon and the larger towns. Rice marketing became more a "neighborhood" operation, with the small farmer engaged directly (Sansom 1970, p. 99). The differential between paddy price in the Delta and that in Saigon virtually vanished. In fact, after Vietnam began to import rice on a large scale, Delta prices were 10–15 percent higher than the Saigon wholesale price (Sansom 1970, p. 99).

One activity that somewhat offset these gains by the farmers was "resource control" by the government. The idea of resource control was to limit logistic support to the Viet Cong, and the method of control was to establish checkpoints along the roads of trade to inspect the cargoes being transported. Whether or not these resource control checkpoints denied much to the Viet Cong, they did become focal points for harassment and extortion. Transporters of agricultural commodities were required to pay fees to the government soldiers to continue their commerce. The average amount of these fees (usually in kind) is not known, but they did adversely affect the welfare of both farmers and urban dwellers.

5.3.3   Prices paid and received by farmers

Gains in the economic status of farmers are implied by data on rural–urban terms of trade. Because of data limitations, it is necessary here to stretch the definition of "terms of trade" to mean the ratio of the rice price index to an index of imported goods. In particular, we do not have data on the prices farmers paid for good purchased from urban areas, and we have rejected using general price indexes because they are heavily weighted toward agricultural products. Many of the imports were raw products for industry, but they were purchased by farmers indirectly through trade with urban areas. Deflating the index of rice price by the price index of imported goods yields a measure that we call "units of imports per kilogram of rice," even though, in fact, the ratio is dimensionless. In effect, the farmer sold a kilogram of rice for piasters, which were used to buy varying numbers of "units for imports," where a unit of import is defined arbitrarily as the basket of imports that could be purchased with one kilogram of rice in 1962.

The data in Table 5.1 show that the purchasing power of rice tripled between 1962 and 1973 and then fell off a third in 1974, when world prices for oil and related products rose sharply. The purchasing power of pigs and fish shows a similar pattern. When one recalls that rice production increased by almost 40 percent between 1962 and 1974, it is evident that rice farmers as a group increased their real income during the war. However, a word of caution is necessary for properly interpreting the data. From 1966 to 1970, probably less than 10 percent of the rice grown in Vietnam was shipped to large urban areas. In the two villages studied by Sansom, 43 percent of the rice was consumed by the producing household, and another 13 percent was disposed of as in-kind payment to laborers. Eleven percent went to in-kind payment of rent, and 32 percent was sold for cash, much of which was for payment of rent, and much of this latter part was sold "over the back fence" to neighbors in nearby Delta towns (Sansom 1970, pp. 99–100). Thus, perhaps only 10–20 percent of the rice produced was available to buy imports or domestically produced goods. Of course, after the 1970 land reform, a much larger percentage of rice production was available to purchase the relatively cheap imports.

5.3.4   Urban real wages

From the foregoing discussion it is evident that the rural population made big advances in real income over the war period. By contrast, the real wages of urban workers in Saigon and, presumably, other cities fell: Table 5.2 presents the rice wage or kilograms of rice purchased by a day's labor for skilled and unskilled male laborers in Saigon. The table also shows the real wages of

Table 5.1. *Prices of rice, fish, and pigs relative to imported goods, 1956–74[a]*

Year	Rice	Fish	Pigs
1956	1.19	1.29	1.50
1957	1.08	1.16	1.19
1958	1.17	1.08	1.10
1959	0.95	0.99	1.14
1960	0.94	1.03	0.98
1961	1.12	1.03	0.95
1962	1.00	1.00	1.00
1963	0.97	1.21	1.27
1964	0.96	1.14	1.08
1965	1.09	1.27	1.37
1966	1.47	2.20	1.79
1967	2.43	2.59	2.46
1968	2.29	3.89	3.46
1969	2.93	3.73	3.16
1970	2.83	3.76	3.54
1971	2.52	3.14	2.74
1972	3.16	2.78	2.67
1973	3.20	2.18	2.89
1974[b]	2.29	1.21	1.93

[a](index price of commodity) ÷ (index price of imported goods).
[b]June 1974.
Source: Table A5.1.

workers in terms of all goods and services purchased by the working class. By both measures there was a considerable deterioration in the living standard of workers from the late fifties to the end of the war. Measured by the rice wage, urban workers lost more than half of their daily income.

These data are in marked contrast with those on farm income. People living in rural areas became richer during the war, whereas those living in the cities became poorer.

In the final three years of the Republic of Vietnam, overall urban income worsened even more than the foregoing figures imply. The reason is that unemployment increased dramatically in these last years. Data on unemployment in the major cities could have been as high as 20 percent at the war's end. Three forces converged to generate the very high rate of unemployment. First, the high national rate of labor force growth added over 200,000 each year to the urban work force. Second, refugees from the war zones increased the urban population. Finally, on the demand side, the economy was in a recession, and new jobs were hard to find. There can be little doubt that the

Table 5.2. *Real wages of Saigon workers, 1956–74*

Year	Rice wage[a]		Overall real wage[b]	
	Unskilled	Skilled	Unskilled	Skilled
1956	8.4	14.8	52.4	92.2
1957	11.5	17.9	63.7	99.5
1958	13.4	18.8	80.2	112.5
1959	13.3	19.2	75.0	108.2
1960	14.5	20.5	79.3	112.4
1961	10.8	15.1	76.0	105.9
1962	11.5	16.3	74.7	106.1
1963	11.9	17.0	71.5	102.5
1964	10.4	14.9	72.5	103.6
1965	10.2	14.4	70.2	98.6
1966	9.9	14.2	63.6	91.4
1967	7.7	11.6	69.5	105.0
1968	12.3	13.2	67.1	97.9
1969	9.9	11.4	67.3	97.1
1970	10.4	11.1	65.7	93.5
1971	10.8	13.2	68.9	103.0
1972	9.0	9.7	69.5	92.7
1973	7.5	8.1	67.2	81.4
1974[c]	6.1	7.6	50.1	72.0

[a]Kilograms of rice purchased by a day's labor.
[b]Daily wage in piasters deflated by consumer index for working-class families in Saigon (1962 = 100).
[c]June 1974.

economic condition of the urban population at the end of the war was dismal if not desperate.

Some economists who specialize in the study of land reform think that a successful land reform program is one requirement for significant economic development. It appears that South Vietnam eventually had a successful land reform program, in terms of both land distribution to tillers and the impact this had on their standard of living. At the end of the war, Vietnam's rural population was about 65 percent of the total. For reasons of land reform, removal of government restrictions on rice price, and the breakdown of monopolistic rice marketing practices, a large segment of the population realized significant economic gains during the war. It is most unclear that the growing urban population even maintained its absolute standard of living on average, although "firsthand" observers are likely to contest this statistical evaluation.

Table A5.1. *Selected wholesale prices, 1956–74 (annual average)*

	Rice (d/kg)[a]	Fish (d/kg)	Pigs (d/kg)	Price indexes (1962 = 100)			
Year				Rice	Fish	Pigs	Imported goods
1956	4.6	30.1	28.7	88.5	96.5	112.1	74.6
1957	4.4	28.2	23.8	84.6	90.4	93.0	78.1
1958	4.8	26.5	22.2	92.3	84.9	86.7	78.6
1959	3.9	24.5	23.2	75.0	78.5	90.6	79.2
1960	4.0	26.3	20.5	76.9	84.3	80.1	82.1
1961	5.2	28.7	21.8	100.0	92.0	85.2	89.5
1962	5.2	31.2	25.6	100.0	100.0	100.0	100.0
1963	5.3	39.4	34.1	101.9	126.3	133.2	104.7
1964	5.5	39.0	30.3	105.8	125.0	118.4	109.7
1965	6.5	45.6	40.3	125.0	146.2	157.4	115.1
1966	10.5	94.2	63.1	201.9	301.9	246.5	137.5
1967	20.3	129.8	101.2	390.4	416.0	395.3	160.4
1968	20.7	210.4	153.8	398.1	674.4	600.8	173.6
1969	31.4	240.0	167.0	603.8	769.2	652.3	206.2
1970	40.2	320.4	247.4	773.1	1,026.9	966.4	273.0
1971	48.0	360.0	257.8	923.1	1,153.8	1,007.0	367.0
1972	72.3	382.7	300.6	1,390.4	1,226.6	1,174.2	440.6
1973	111.7	455.2	497.1	2,148.1	1,459.0	1,941.8	670.9
1974[b]	171.3	541.0	710.0	3,294.2	1,734.0	2,773.4	1,436.7

[a] d is the symbol for piaster.
[b] June 1974.
Source: VN-NIS (annual, 1972, Tables 310 and 312) and VN-NIS (monthly, July–Sept. 1974).

Table A5.2. *Vietnam urban workers' average daily wage, 1956–74*[a]
(piasters)

Year	Skilled male worker	Male laborer	Female laborer
1956	88.9	50.5	43.7
1957	91.5	58.6	50.6
1958	101.5	72.3	51.3
1959	100.0	69.3	54.4
1960	102.5	72.3	55.2
1961	102.7	73.7	55.9
1962	106.1	74.7	60.1
1963	110.6	77.2	61.4
1964	114.4	81.0	64.0
1965	126.6	90.1	70.7
1966	190.6	132.6	100.4
1967	314.5	208.2	201.2
1968	371.9	255.0	215.6
1969	449.9	311.6	265.5
1970	592.6	416.4	360.5
1971	772.9	516.5	455.4
1972	870.1	652.1	599.2
1973	1,104.0	843.0	666.0
1974	1,493.0	1,039.0	890.0

[a]Average daily wage as compiled in June of each year.
Source: 1956–72, VN-NIS (annual, 1972, Table 239); 1973–4, AID-VN (monthly, Feb. 1975).

CHAPTER 6

Domestic saving, foreign aid, and economic development

Saving and investment have lost much of their luster in the development literature since the 1950s, when Sir Arthur Lewis declared that saving was "the central problem in the theory of economic development" (1954, p. 155).[1] Their place in the literature needs to be reconsidered, and defining economic development as growth plus improvement in income distribution is a good starting point. It would be unsatisfactory, indeed, to insist that a country was developing if its per capita growth rate were 5 percent per year while the poorest 20 percent of the population were becoming relatively poorer. It would be equally unsatisfactory to insist that a country was developing if its per capita growth rate were negative regardless of what was happening to the relative position of the poor. Saving promotes growth, and that establishes it as a causal factor in development. Thus, saving need not be the "central problem" in development, but as the "engine of growth" it must be a major factor.[2]

6.1 Growth in domestic saving as an indicator of development

One purpose of this chapter is to call attention to the distinction between domestic saving and total saving and to argue that neglect of this distinction is responsible for confusion with respect to the relationship between saving and development. Total saving is the wrong variable of focus. Because total saving includes foreign aid, it is possible for this variable to fuel a kind of mechanical growth for a decade or so that is essentially unrelated to progress in the domestic conditions needed to sustain it. This could produce the classic case of growth without development. However, if growth is generated from local human capital, from organization and administration, as well as from domestic saving, then that growth is also development. In the long run, the only reliable source of saving is the domestic component, so that one looks to improvement in the domestic saving ratio as the major indicator of economic development.

In cases such as that of Vietnam, a major wedge between total saving and domestic saving is foreign aid. In those cases, development need not require a rise in the total saving rate, because, theoretically, one could observe a

121

satisfactory development process in which the domestic saving ratio was rising while the total saving ratio was stationary. In some guise, this possibility furnishes the rationale for giving aid. It has been argued that foreign aid is sometimes necessary to get the growth process started. Subsequently, if growth continues for a number of years, it will become self-sustaining if the marginal saving rate is higher than the average. If foreign aid is performing the task it is supposed to, domestic saving will be rising, and the need for foreign aid will be declining. A successful foreign aid program is one that eliminates the need for foreign assistance, and its measure of success is a rise in the domestic saving ratio.

Growth in the domestic saving ratio would be a necessary and sufficient condition for economic development if it were *causally* related to the socio-political factors in development. That there is an association is commonly agreed, but causality cannot be claimed without a deep study of relationships. Thus, as a single indicator of development, the domestic saving ratio could give a false signal. On the other hand, it seems evident that lack of growth in the domestic saving ratio is an adequate indicator of lack of development.

Some close observers of underdeveloped countries think that foreign aid is ineffective, even "counterproductive" (Griffin and Enos 1970, p. 236), in promoting development. Foremost among these observers is Professor P. T. Bauer, who has written extensively on this subject (1968, 1972, 1981, 1984). Because official aid greatly increases the resources of governments, it has increased their power over the people and strengthened the hands of repressive regimes. This has led to increasing social and political tensions and politi-cization of life in many Third World countries, with the disastrous result of redirecting energies toward "rent seeking" and away from productive activ-ities.[3] Inasmuch as aid favors central planning, according to Bauer, it has subverted entrepreneurship and free enterprise as well as political freedom. By undercutting these sociopolitical determinants of development, aid has played a negative role in some instances. The theory of aid does not deal with Bauer's historical objections, because it usually treats these variables parametrically, if at all. Although most of Bauer's evidence is anecdotal, it serves as a powerful reminder that practice and theory can be poles apart in the economics of development.[4] Our objective in summarizing these kinds of objections to foreign aid is to point out that they apply to the foreign component of saving rather than domestic saving, thereby stressing further the importance of the distinction between total saving and domestic saving.

The well-known criticism that foreign aid may reduce domestic saving (Rahman 1968; Chenery and Eckstein 1970; Weisskopf 1972; Papanek 1973)[5] is further reason for distinguishing between domestic saving and total saving. To understand this point it is useful to break saving into its three major components of private domestic saving, government saving, and foreign saving (or foreign aid in the case of Vietnam). Private saving is determined by individual decisions dealing with allocating income between present consumption and future consumption. Government saving is closely related to the size of government revenues, which derive primarily from taxation. Foreign saving depends on the willingness of foreigners to lend and the willingness of foreign governments to extend aid. The amount of foreign saving desired by an underdeveloped country is determined primarily by its deficit of trade on current account.

Gross investment, the variable most directly related to growth, is the sum of the savings components:

$$\text{gross investment} = \text{private saving} + \text{government saving} + \text{foreign saving} \tag{6.1}$$

All other things being equal, additional taxation will raise government saving, but tend to reduce private saving. However, additional taxes usually do not reduce private saving by the amount they increase government saving. Therefore, improving the tax effort in underdeveloped countries is associated with raising the sum of private and government savings, which we shall designate as domestic saving. Rewriting equation (6.1) as

$$\text{gross investment} = \text{domestic saving} + \text{foreign saving} \tag{6.2}$$

has the advantage of distinguishing clearly between two sources of saving, one strictly under domestic control and the other subject to foreign control. Considered over a long period of time, the former is a more reliable source of investment than the latter in an economy that is growing. Also, a rise in domestic saving is a sign that a country is moving toward economic independence, a factor in development we have stressed previously.

One way to reduce the need for foreign saving is to increase exports relative to imports. Whether this occurs through policies designed to promote exports or import substitution is of no importance in this discussion.[6] Both promotions can occur while gross investment is maintained at some constant level by simply shifting the distribution among the sources of investment toward domestic saving and away from foreign saving. Although foreign trade policy aimed at reducing an import surplus does not raise the rate of total saving or gross investment in the same way that domestic tax policy can, it contributes to the reliability of a given rate of total saving and therefore is an element in the process of economic development.

The impact of foreign aid on domestic saving is ignored in the traditional theory of foreign aid and economic growth. According to that theory, an increase in aid adds to total saving by the full amount of the aid. Thus, in a simple Harrod-Domar type of growth model, an inflow of aid promotes growth on a par with an increase in domestic saving; but strong dissent has been directed against this assumption. As stated earlier, the dissenters have pointed out that there is an observed negative relationship between aid and domestic saving, implying that foreign saving does not add to total saving on a one-to-one basis. Importantly, it might play a role in reducing the reliable domestic saving component.

The channels through which foreign aid might reduce domestic saving are varied. Principally, foreign aid would allow the government to reduce its tax effort. As we argue in Chapter 11, this seems to have happened in South Vietnam. Also, to the extent that domestic saving depends on domestic investment opportunities, an inflow of foreign capital that preempts some of these opportunities will have a discouraging effect on domestic saving (Houthakker 1965).

If an underdeveloped country can reduce its trade deficit, it can eliminate much of the reason for relying on foreign aid. The result is not only a decline in the trade deficit but also a strengthening of the domestic component of saving. Thus, the economic activities related to foreign trade activities are indirectly related to domestic saving. The tax variable is directly related to domestic saving, as stated earlier. Ultimately, both tax and trade policies have effects on domestic saving, and a country will not experience continuing growth unless its domestic saving ratio has reached a level sufficient to sustain it. A country can *grow* rapidly as long as it receives substantial and continuing infusions of foreign aid, but we shall assume that it is *developing* only if a high growth rate is accompanied by a rising domestic saving rate.

6.2   Domestic saving in South Vietnam, 1955–73

Before turning to the facts about domestic saving in South Vietnam, we wish to comment on how the numbers were derived. In the standard national income accounts there is no direct measurement for domestic saving. Values for this variable are obtained by subtracting foreign saving from gross investment, as is suggested by equation (6.2). Although this procedure is straightforward, a user of the derived data should always remain somewhat skeptical of the numbers, particularly for underdeveloped countries that have maintained fixed exchange rates. Because foreign inflows are measured in terms of foreign currencies and gross investment in domestic currencies, it is necessary to find the domestic currency equivalent of foreign saving in order to derive domestic saving as a residual. Using the official exchange rate over a period of time during which a country maintains a fixed exchange rate in the face of a continually depreciating currency would progressively understate the value of foreign inflows and produce an exaggerated measure of domestic saving.

Another problem in the case of Vietnam is how to distinguish between aid to Vietnam and that portion of the dollar inflow that was used to support

American activities in the country. We need to know, first of all, the dollar value of true aid (not necessarily the amount reported in official U.S. Documents) and, second, the "realistic" exchange rate before we can compute domestic saving with any confidence. Chapters 8 and 9 deal with the foreign exchange rate problem, and Chapter 10 deals with the dollar and piaster values of U.S. aid to Vietnam.

Table 6.1 contains the data necessary to calculate domestic saving in South Vietnam for the period 1955–73. This variable is calculated in column 6 as the difference between gross investment and foreign aid, which is called "net resources transferred" in the table. This concept is discussed at length in Chapter 10.

Our calculations reveal Vietnam as a nation that could not support the standard of living that its people enjoyed and one that made virtually no progress in that direction over a period of two decades. For the entire period of our study, the domestic saving ratio was negative. This does not mean that Vietnamese citizens did not save anything. Rather, it means that they consumed beyond their own means to support that consumption out of domestic resources, and if the foreign aid had been eliminated, consumption, gross investment, and national income would have declined. More relevant to our concern for economic development, the domestic saving ratio showed no tendency to improve over time. The implications of this finding for sustainability of economic growth, economic independence, and development are clear. The data presented show that Vietnam made little, if any, progress toward self-sufficiency over the twenty-year period of our study. These data simply corroborate some of the qualitative statements about lack of economic development made in the previous chapters.

The figures in column 7 of Table 6.1 indicate that there was considerable progress from 1955 to 1960. Gross investment was growing, while foreign aid was declining, and the domestic saving ratio increased from minus 13 percent to around zero. With the step-up in insurgency operations in the early 1960s, aid increased and gross investment declined. Later, when the character of the war changed to one of conventional combat with main force units, the domestic saving rate declined further. Finally, we see marked improvement toward the end of the war, when the Vietnamese began to realize that U.S. aid would not be continued forever. The progress of the domestic saving rate in Vietnam is compared with those of its successful neighbors, Taiwan and South Korea, in Chapter 13.

The data in Table 6.1 serve as a prop for reemphasizing the proposition that the domestic saving ratio, rather than the gross investment ratio or the total saving ratio, is the proper indicator of development. Over two decades, aid was about 20 percent of Vietnam's GNP, and the domestic saving ratio was about minus 10 percent. These figures indicate that the total saving ratio

Table 6.1. *Calculation of domestic saving in South Vietnam, 1955–73[a]*

Year	(1) GNP (d billion)[b]	(2) Gross Investment (d billion)	(3) Net resources transferred (U.S. aid) ($ million)	(4) Estimated exchange rate (d/$)	(5) Piaster value of U.S. aid (d billion)	(6) Domestic saving (d billion)	(7) Domestic saving as percentage of GNP
1955	63.6	4.9	192.6	70	13.5	−8.6	−13.5
1956	68.7	4.0	172.5	70	12.1	−8.1	−11.8
1957	67.0		206.8	70			
1958	71.3		176.9	70			
1959	80.1		148.1	70			
1960	81.8	10.4	154.8	70	10.8	−0.5	−0.6
1961	84.5	7.5	198.3	70	13.9	−6.4	−7.6
1962	93.8	9.4	217.4	78	17.0	−7.6	−8.1
1963	100.3	7.6	220.2	78	17.2	−9.6	−9.6
1964	114.5	12.7	239.8	81	19.4	−6.7	−5.9
1965	144.8	13.1	261.3	94	24.6	−11.5	−7.9

1966	236.2	34.5	479.5	146	70.0	−35.5	−15.0
1967	356.7	45.2	550.7	189	104.1	−58.9	−16.5
1968	385.3	31.2	405.5	201	81.5	−50.3	−13.1
1969	557.6	55.5	610.2	229	139.7	−84.2	−15.1
1970	804.4	86.4	614.6	318	194.4	−108.0	−13.4
1971	979.9	95.0	568.9	388	220.7	−125.7	−12.8
1972	1,102.0	115.0	516.8	439	226.9	−111.9	−10.2
1973	1,551.0	172.0	514.9	536	276.0	−103.0	−6.6

*Data sources:

(1) Table 3.1.

(2) 1955–6, see footnote a, Table 3.1; 1960–71, VN-NIS (annual, various issues); 1972–3, International Monetary Fund (monthly, 1975, p. 412); no change in stocks indicated for these years.

(3) Table 10.3.

(4) Table 9.5.

(5) Column (3) × column (4).

(6) Column (2) − column (5).

(7) Column (6) ÷ column (1).

^{*b*}đ is the symbol for piaster.

was about 10 percent over the period. Suppose that the U.S. aid program to South Vietnam had been successful in the sense that it was gradually eliminating the need for aid. In that event it would have been possible for aid to fall from 20 percent of GNP to zero while the domestic saving ratio was rising from minus 10 percent to plus 10 percent, even though the total saving rate was not changing. In such a hypothetical situation there would be little doubt that the country was developing satisfactorily, even though data on total saving would seem to suggest the opposite conclusion.

6.3   Private saving

The domestic saving measure is a reflection of three important economic variables: private saving, annual tax revenues, and annual foreign trade balance. Although it is useful as an overall indicator of development, it is too aggregative to reveal the individual saving behavior of private citizens. A glance at private saving behavior also shows clearly that little progress was made over the period to raise the financing required for economic development.

According to data collected by the National Bank of Vietnam and published by the Vietnam National Institute of Statistics, private saving never exceeded 13 percent and for most of the period was in the neighborhood of 5–6 percent (Table 6.2). In fact, from the beginning, the rate of private saving in Vietnam was one of the lowest in the world. In his well-known article "International Aid for Underdeveloped Countries," Rosenstein-Rodan (1961) listed Vietnam as seventy-third among eighty-nine countries with respect to saving, and almost all the lower-listed countries were very poor African nations. Rosenstein-Rodan's data showed Vietnam's marginal saving ratio to be only 8 percent. This situation did not improve, at least up to 1972.

One explanation of this poor performance in private saving is that the usual rewards for postponing consumption over the period did not exist. In the first place, interest rates that commercial banks were allowed to pay for savings deposits were only 3–4 percent as late as 1967 and had been lower earlier.[7] At the end of 1970, the rates were 8–12 percent. In contrast to these interest rates, the rate of inflation from 1965 to the end of the war averaged about 30 percent. At the time when commercial banks were paying 3–4 percent on savings deposits, *huis*, uncontrolled mutual savings and credit societies that primarily made consumer loans, were paying interest rates consistent with economic conditions, in the range of 48–120 percent (Emery 1970, pp. 679–80). Thus, with negative real interest rates on savings deposits in banking institutions, it should not be surprising that people did not save much.

A second reason for a low saving rate in Vietnam could have been uncertainty regarding the outcome of the war. Saving involves an intertemporal

Table 6.2. *Private saving in South Vietnam, 1960–71 (billion piasters)*

Year	Private saving	Private saving as percentage of GNP
1960	5.9	7.2
1961	0.5	0.6
1962	3.0	3.2
1963	3.2	3.2
1964	9.7	8.5
1965	18.7	12.9
1966	29.7	12.5
1967	16.1	4.5
1968	8.7	2.3
1969	11.7	2.1
1970	43.7	5.4
1971	51.2	5.0

Source: VN-NIS (annual, various issues). Private saving in this table is the sum of household saving and corporation saving as given in tables on domestic capital formation in the national income accounts.

decision. It is a decision to postpone consumption to some future period. All other things being equal, a pessimistic view of the outcome of the war would be cause for limiting saving in the present. It is possible that many Vietnamese thought that a Communist victory would be accompanied by confiscation of wealth, as well as limited opportunities for future consumption. This would serve as a disincentive to save. In Chapter 7 we hypothesize that there was an improvement in confidence in the period following the military defeat of the Communist forces in their Tet offensive and that this was a factor in the decrease in the velocity of money. Such a situation would tend to promote saving, and we do see some sign of this in the figures for 1970–1 as compared with private saving in 1968–9. Of course, this casual observation is no test of the hypothesis.

In September 1970, a government decree on interest fixed the rates on savings deposits in the range of 10–21 percent, and in May 1972 they were raised slightly higher, to 24 percent for deposits over twelve months. These reforms are described in Chapter 7, along with data showing how effective they were in stimulating saving in commercial banks. The reforms were useful in raising the rate of saving in Vietnam, as well as encouraging the transfer of funds from neighborhood-type arrangements (*huis*) to commercial organizations that served as a better conduit between investors and savers. We hold the opinion that the interest rate reforms would have been even more effective in raising the saving ratio toward the end of the war had they not come at a time when confidence was declining. Also, the last reforms were implemented when the economy was in a severe downturn. In effect, the interest rate reforms in South Vietnam were too timid and too late to have a dramatic effect on domestic saving through private saving. And this lack of progress in private saving was a major blemish on the overall development picture in wartime South Vietnam.

CHAPTER 7

Wartime inflation

A major political concern in South Vietnam was that an escalating Vietnamese war budget would cause a rampant inflationary condition promoting serious discontentment among the people. Under the worst scenario, they might rise up against the government, or, at best, they would be ripe for political manipulation by the enemy. Thus, economic policy stressed inflation control rather than long-run development. No one knew exactly what rate of inflation would be politically destabilizing, but it was thought that a rate of around 30 percent would be safe. Hyperinflation was to be avoided.

The history of inflation in South Vietnam is usefully separated into two distinct periods: an early period beginning with the founding of the republic and extending through 1964, and a late period lasting until the end of the war. The dividing line between these two periods is, just coincidentally, about the halfway mark in the political life of the Republic of Vietnam. The real divide, of course, is marked by the significant escalation of the war in South Vietnam in early 1965, when U.S. combat troops were introduced on a large scale. In the early period, the rate of inflation was 4.5 percent on average. It hardly seems to have been a problem. In the late period it varied between 16 and 60 percent and was a major concern of Vietnamese officials and U.S. advisors.

7.1   Programmed inflation

We characterize the post–1964 period as one of programmed inflation, to distinguish between what actually happened in that ten-year period and what some choose to call "rampant" or "runaway" inflation. The words "rampant" and "runaway" usually imply that prices are out of control and that in due course hyperinflation will occur. Except for very short periods of time, such as during the early weeks of the Communist Tet offensive in 1968, or earlier in 1966 when there was much speculation that the piaster would be devalued, prices were never out of control. There was virtually no chance that hyperinflation would develop, because the United States stood ready to supply aid in the amount necessary to prevent it.

The procedure for estimating the amount of aid necessary to keep price rises in check was discussed earlier in Section 2.4. Briefly restated, analysts estimated in advance the gap between monetary injections such as government expenditures (including U.S. piaster expenditures) and absorptions of purchasing power such as taxes and imports. The difference is called the monetary gap. According to conventional monetary analysis, the ratio of the gap to the nominal supply of money is an approximate measure of the expected near-term rate of inflation. By supplying resources from the outside, the gap, and hence the expected rate of inflation, theoretically could be reduced to any amount consistent with the targeted or programmed rate.

The programming of inflation obviously was not an exact science. It could not be exact for the following reasons: (1) No one fully understood the process through which the known causal variables operated on price. (2) It was not possible to anticipate many price-sensitive events such as curtailment of supplies to urban markets due to a sudden flare-up of the war in the countryside. (3) There was no precise understanding or measure of the lags in the effects of monetary and import policies. (4) There was slippage between U.S. and Vietnamese policy intentions and the actual implementation of policy. The slippage can be attributed to inefficient Vietnamese administration, as well as logistical, military, and political problems. A final reason is that the U.S. Congress did not decide aid levels this way and could not be counted on to rubber-stamp figures drawn up by bureaucrats. Despite all the obstacles to attaining a precise programming of inflation, the policy did achieve its goal of containing inflation within politically tolerable limits. For the eight-year period 1967–74, the average annual rate of inflation was 27 percent. Maintaining the programmed rate was difficult in 1973 and 1974, when prices rose 59 and 40 percent, respectively. These larger-than-desired rates were due partly to an unexpected rise in the velocity of money, and worldwide inflation was a contributing factor.

7.2   Vietnamese price indexes

In the foregoing discussion, the "consumer price index for working-class families in Saigon" has been used as the basis for measuring inflation. This index and others suffer from two severe handicaps that must be noted: (1) Virtually all Vietnamese price indexes were based on price quotations taken in Saigon, rather than weighted averages from all regions in the country. (2) The market basket of goods and services on which the indexes were based underwent rather significant changes during the period. Scattered information suggests that prices outside of Saigon moved in line with Saigon prices when measured over a year or so, but considerable differences could have occurred over short periods. The war touched different regions of the country at different times with varying intensities; thus, one would not expect short-term price variations to be the same in all regions.

In addition to the working-class price index, the Vietnam National Institute of Statistics (NIS) compiled the "consumer price index for middle-class families in Saigon" and the "Saigon wholesale price index." The Joint Economic Office of USAID published data on the "Saigon retail price index," and the National Bank of Vietnam (NBVN) compiled the "implicit GNP deflator" as an outcome of national income accounts activities. The behavior of four of these indexes since 1960 is shown in Table 7.1. Data for the three indexes published by the NIS have been available since at least 1951. The indexes shown in the table are averages of twelve monthly figures and therefore cannot be used to measure calendar-year rates of inflation.[1] The series for the GNP deflator begins in 1960, when the NBVN started to estimate national income, and the USAID index (not shown) was initiated in 1965. It is clear from the table that the two consumer price indexes moved closely together each year as well as over the entire period. The implicit deflator advanced imprecisely along with the consumer price indexes. The wholesale price index, which moved much more sluggishly than the others, was based largely on official price quotations (fixed by the government) rather than transactions prices. That explains why it did not move up as rapidly as the others.

The implicit deflator has no monthly or end-of-year values.[2] The two NIS consumer price indexes were compiled monthly, and the USAID index was compiled weekly.

None of the indexes is ideal for measuring inflation. The availability of the working-class index in a long series, plus the advantage of broader inclusion, makes it the best candidate for use in statistical analyses. For convenience, we shall refer to the working-class index simply as the "price index" or "price level" in the remainder of this chapter.

7.3 The determinants of inflation

What were the causes of inflation in wartime South Vietnam? How strongly did each contribute to it? To answer these questions, we need a theory to suggest the variables to be tested and the manner in which they might be entered into the analysis of inflation. There is no lack of theories of inflation, as the survey literature on theories of inflation shows (Bronfenbrenner and Holzman 1973; Laidler and Parkin 1975; Frisch 1977). Of all the theories, the quantity theory of money is the oldest and most frequently tested. It has a major advantage of simplicity. Also, it specifically indicates not only the direction but also the strength of influence of each variable. More so than the alternative theories, it supplies a hypothesis that can be tested directly. Accordingly, the following analysis is conducted along the line of the quantity theory.

Table 7.1. Vietnamese price indexes, 1956–74ᵃ (1962 = 100)

Year	(1) Middle-class index[b]	(2) Working-class index[b]	(3) Wholesale price index[b]	(4) Implicit GNP deflator	(5) Implicit NDP deflator
1956	92.9	96.4	86.5		
1957	92.3	92.0	86.5		
1958	90.2	90.2	87.8		
1959	92.2	92.4	83.0		
1960	92.1	91.2	87.0	94.1	85.3
1961	96.4	97.0	97.4	97.2	92.7
1962	100.0	100.0	100.0	100.0	100.0
1963	106.0	107.9	103.3	104.2	102.5
1964	108.2	110.4	106.8	109.0	107.3
1965	124.8	128.4	115.5	126.0	125.4
1966	197.1	208.6	150.1	204.1	185.4
1967	275.6	299.4	199.9	302.9	266.6
1968	349.6	380.0	216.9	342.4	304.5

1969	417.7	463.1	259.1	568.8	390.7
1970	580.9	633.5	321.1	644.0	495.4
1971	689.8	749.3	382.4	763.7	602.0
1972	848.7	938.3	510.3	861.1	757.5
1973	1,205.1	1,355.5	755.1	1,207.8	
1974	1,786.8ᶜ	2,004.5ᶜ	1,232.6ᶜ	1,734.3	

[^a]Data sources:

(1) VN-NIS (annual, 1972) and VN-NIS (monthly, 1974, July–Sept.). This price index is called the "consumer price index for middle-class families in Saigon."

(2) VN-NIS (annual, 1972), VN-NIS (monthly, 1974, July–Sept.), and AID-VN (monthly, (1975, Feb.). This price index is called the "consumer price index for working-class families in Saigon."

(3) VN-NIS (annual, 1972) and VN-NIS (monthly, 1974, July–Sept.).

(4) Computed from data in Table 3.1.

(5) Table A3.2.

[^b]These indexes have been computed as averages of the monthly values and reflated for 1962 as the base year.

[^c]End of April 1974. Data for September–December not available. The April figure was selected because it is probably more representative of the yearly average than any other monthly figure.

The quantity theory of money

The quantity theory can be expressed as

$$MV = PQ \qquad (7.1)$$

or

$$P = MV/Q \qquad (7.2)$$

to stress the price variable (P). M is the stock of money, V is income velocity, and Q is real national income. These equations are expressions of the quantity theory when additional information about V and Q is supplied. For example, if V is assumed to be fixed by the institutions of society, and Q is the full-employment level of national income, then price varies proportionally with the money stock.

In many countries over long periods of time, velocity has remained fairly constant. However, given the turbulent war environment that existed in South Vietnam, there is no reason to assume that velocity would have remained unchanged. In fact, it did change over time in a U-shaped pattern, declining to the mid-1960s and then rising, as the data in Table A7.3 show and Figure 4.1 implies. Because other variables did not remain constant in South Vietnam, the simple quantity theory cannot be expected to explain year-by-year price changes, although the long-term relationship between the money stock and the general price level is indicated clearly in Figure 7.1.

Ever since Friedman (1956) stressed that velocity is a functional relationship rather than a constant, much empirical research dealing with the demand for money or inflation has employed the flexible velocity model, namely,

$$P = v(\cdot)(M/Q) \qquad (7.3)$$

where $v(\cdot)$ is a functional relationship explaining income velocity. In this formulation of the quantity theory, emphasis is placed on the independent determinants of velocity as well as on money and real output. We have no explicit model of real income determination for South Vietnam. Our basic assumption is that it was driven toward full employment as a result of U.S. aid policy and wartime mobilization.

Use of the simple quantity theory in empirical research requires another critical assumption regarding the causal relationship between the money supply and the income-generating process. Specifically, a quantity theorist assumes that the money supply is an exogenous variable and that its size is determined by the monetary authority, not by some endogenous cause. Recent monetary research has addressed the question of the causal relationship between the money supply and national income or other variables. This is a controversial issue in monetary analysis. In the case of wartime South Viet-

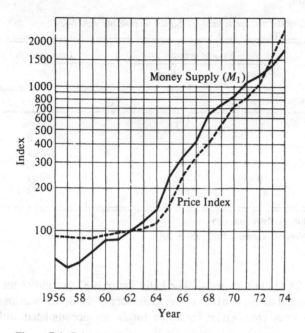

Figure 7.1. Prices and money in South Vietnam, 1956–74. *Sources*: Tables A7.1 and A7.2

nam, one can state fairly confidently that the causation from national income to the money supply was insignificant or that the money supply in any given year was exogenously determined, and, following the quantity theory, we shall consider the money supply and the determinants of velocity as the causes of inflation.

7.3.2   The money stock in Vietnam

Money stock figures defined both as M_1 (currency in circulation plus demand deposits) and as M_2 (currency in circulation plus demand deposits plus savings deposits in commercial banks) are given in Table A7.2. The money stock at the end of each year, defined as M_1, is shown in Figure 7.1. Over the period 1956–74, M_1 increased at an average annual rate of 21 percent, and M_2 at 24 percent. For the two principal subperiods 1956–65 and 1965–74, the average annual growth rates were 9 and 29 percent, respectively, for M_1 and 9 and 35 percent, respectively, for M_2.

The major source of money supply increase was the government deficit. By our estimate, the total government deficit after aid was 598 billion piasters in the 1962–74 period. Advances by the National Bank of Vietnam to the

Table 7.2. *Interest rate structure in South Vietnam, 1967–74*

	Savings deposits		Term deposits	
Period	With lottery (%)	Without lottery (%)	3 months (%)	12 months (%)
November 1967[a]		2–3	3	
August 1969[a]			5	8
March 1970[b]	3	5	8	12
September 1970[b]	8	10	14	20
August 1971[b]	9	12	16	21
May 1972[b]	13	17	19	24

[a]Data source: Emery (1970, pp. 645–7).
[b]Data source: VN–NIS (annual, 1972, Table 201).

treasury were 289 billion piasters.[3] The latter figure is 87 percent of the total M_1 stock at the end of 1974. Much of the remainder of the deficit was financed by borrowing from commercial banks on funds that accumulated with the growth of M_2.

M_1 and M_2 grew at virtually the same rate until the end of 1970. In some sweeping economic reforms in September of that year, interest rates were liberalized. Prior to these reforms, interest rates on savings deposits had been in the range of 3–5 percent. Table 7.2 shows the interest rate structure from 1967 to the end of the war.

The September 1970 and subsequent reform measures had a major impact on the growth of savings and time deposits in commercial banks and, hence, on the growth of M_2. The data assembled in Table 7.3 can be interpreted in a way to support this assertion. Column 1 in Table 7.3 was derived by averaging the figures in Table 7.2. By this measure, the nominal interest rate in 1973–4 was six times as high as it had been in 1968. Furthermore, if we tentatively accept the previous year's rate of inflation as the expected rate of inflation in the current year and define the ex ante real rate of interest as the nominal rate less the expected rate of inflation, then the ex ante real rate of interest was positive for the first (and only) time in 1972.

Savings and time deposits in commercial banks increased by large multiples after 1970. In real terms, savings and time deposits more than tripled. The noticeable response of savings deposits to changes in the nominal rate of interest is impressive, considering that the real rate of interest was negative in 1971, 1973, and 1974. Of course, a positive real rate is not necessary to stimulate savings deposits if the only option is holding currency and demand

Table 7.3 Savings deposits in commercial banks, M_2 and related data, 1967–74[a]

Date	(1) Nominal rate of interest (%)	(2) Expected rate of inflation (%)	(3) Real rate of interest (%)	(4) Change in savings deposits (billion piasters)	(5) Savings deposits (billion piasters)	(6) M_2 (billion piasters)
1967	3	31	−28	0.7	9.0	91.2
1968	3	48	−45	6.4	15.4	139.5
1969	5	28	−23	9.7	25.1	165.8
1970	10	22	−12	8.8	33.9	196.8
1971	14	28	−14	31.1	65.0	273.4
1972	16	14	2	70.1	135.1	362.9
1973	18	24	−6	31.2	166.3	429.0
1974	18	46	−28	96.7	263.0	597.0

[a]Data sources:
(1) Unweighted average of data in Table 7.2.
(2) Actual rate of inflation in previous year.
(3) Column (1) – column (2).
(4) Table A7.2.
(5) Table A7.2.
(6) Table A7.2.

deposits that yield a worse real rate. The fact is that M_2 grew rapidly after 1970, and most of its growth was due to a rise in savings and time deposits.

The cause of the rapid rise in M_2 also contributed to the decline in the rate of increase in M_1. Private savings deposits in commercial banks provided the funds that these banks used to purchase higher-yielding government bonds. In this manner, the government was able to finance a larger share of its deficit through bond sales, rather than borrowing from the Central Bank.

7.3.3   The income velocity of money[4]

Monetary analysis has identified a number of variables that bear on an individual's demand for money. Because these influence the aggregate demand for money, they are also determinants of the average number of times the money stock turns over per year to support a given income. By far the most discussed and tested variable in studies of the demand for money is the cost of holding money. Institutional determinants such as the length of the payment period and demographic variables such as urbanization and population density were stressed by the Fisher school.[5] Per capita income is an important variable in theories on the transactions demand for money (Baumol 1952; Tobin 1956). Fisher also posited that the ratio of currency to the stock of money would be a determinant of velocity, and, more recently, Melitz and Correa (1970) have claimed to have demonstrated its importance, but this claim has been questioned by Hanson and Vogel (1973). A previous study by the author was unable to support hypotheses that population change, per capita real income, and the currency ratio affected velocity in Vietnam (Dacy 1984). Here, only two variables will be considered: the cost of holding money, and U.S. troop strength in South Vietnam during the war.

7.3.3.1 Cost of holding money: The cost of holding money equals the income-generating opportunities forgone. In comparison with the situation in a highly developed nation, those opportunities in developing nations are limited; this was particularly true for Vietnam. As alternatives to holding money, a Vietnamese could invest in real estate, durable goods, gold jewelry, savings accounts, and treasury bonds. For most of the period, holding financial assets was an option inferior to holding real goods, because the rates of return on most financial assets were negative in real terms, because the government fixed their nominal legal rates below the rate of inflation (Table 7.3). The cost of holding money in a period of rising prices and when real interest rates on financial assets are negative is the expected rate of inflation. That is the rate at which the nominal value of goods or physical assets is expected to rise, and therefore it is a measure of the cost of holding money.

7.3.3.2 U.S. troop strength: U.S. troop strength as a determinant of velocity in Vietnam has both a theoretical economic justification and a psychological appeal. Its economic justification is evident when viewed as a demographic variable affecting spending and money-holding activities. These activities produced a "pure economic" effect on velocity. The psychological aspect depends on the influence U.S. troops had on the expectations of Vietnamese citizens regarding the political outcome of the war. This we refer to as the "confidence" factor.

7.3.3.2.1 Troop strength as a "pure economic" factor: Perhaps the most prominent event of a demographic character to take place in wartime South Vietnam was the rapid buildup of American military forces and their equally rapid exodus. Between 1965 and early 1969, American and other non-Vietnamese personnel associated with the war grew in strength to 8–9 percent of the adult population of South Vietnam.

When U.S. forces were entering Vietnam in large numbers, economic analysts were concerned that their spending on the local economy would pose an inflationary threat. Translated into an explanation that fits our current frame of reference, velocity was expected to increase to accommodate the troops' demand for local currency. So convinced were the American advisors of this ultimate inflationary impact, the military command spent millions of dollars on out-of-country R&R trips for service personnel, partly to improve their morale, but also because AID officials were anxious for the troops to spend their incomes in places like Hong Kong, Singapore, and Bangkok, rather than in Vietnam.

An analysis of the impact of American troops on inflation is a complicated matter. One cannot be sure that their introduction was highly inflationary, as was asserted at the time. In terms of standard macroeconomic theory,[6] an inflow of foreign troops should produce the following partial effects: (1) Their spending, treated in macroeconomic models as an increase in exports, should cause an increase in aggregate demand. (2) Troop spending should generate additional foreign exchange reserves and stimulate imports, thus having the effect of reducing aggregate demand for domestic goods. (3) The willingness of troops to hold piasters can be treated as an increase in liquidity preference, causing a reduction in aggregate demand. If the effects of (1) and (2) simply cancel, the overall impact of troop spending and money-holding activities should be deflationary, on balance. In other words, troops would supply foreign exchange to stimulate imports just enough to cancel out the inflationary impact of their spending on the local economy, but the additional fact that they were willing to hold piasters would tend to slow velocity and retard inflation. On the other hand, the effect of (1) could have been greater than the combined effects of (2) and (3). This outcome would be most likely if the government used the dollars exchanged by U.S. troops to build up foreign exchange reserves, rather than for additional importing. Because the GVN did increase its foreign exchange holdings in the 1965–7 period, we conclude that the buildup of U.S. troop strength during that period was probably slightly inflationary, but not to the degree feared by economy managers at the time.[7]

7.3.3.2.2 Troop strength as a confidence factor: Economic analysis frequently proceeds from an assumption of some utility function that properly includes variables such as uncertainty. War conditions, particularly those that prevailed in South Vietnam, induce greater population movement than would be normal in peacetime. This increases feelings of insecurity and uncertainty among the population, while reducing the range of assets feasible for them to hold and increasing their precautionary demand for cash, thereby reducing velocity.[8]

In the special case of Vietnam, it seems likely that velocity would have been affected by the confidence the people had in the ability of their country to survive as a free enterprise state. A major factor in the decision of a citizen to hold wealth in the form of money, rather than in other assets such as securities, real capital, and consumer goods, would be the individual's expectation about the outcome of the war. In the event of victory by the enemy, all of these assets would be subject to varying degrees of confiscation. Thus, a rational citizen would have to consider the subjective probability of defeat in making portfolio decisions. With regard to fiat money, it is probably true that confidence in the government to maintain itself in war promotes the demand for it, whereas a sense of defeat spurs the holding of consumer goods. Thus, velocity would be expected to rise when the government appears weak and to fall when it appears strong.[9]

Although fluctuations in confidence can be noted, they cannot be measured directly. Our approach to measuring Vietnamese confidence is to assume that it was influenced primarily by current military events. Battlefield defeats would engender pessimistic expectations, whereas victories would generate optimism. As was stated in Chapter 4, the Vietnamese were highly literate and seemed well informed on military events by reading newspapers and listening to radio. Even though their sources frequently were propagandizing, truth and falsity could be separated on the basis of objective events (as when a town does not fall even though its capture was reported to be imminent; or when government troops, Viet Cong cadre, or North Vietnamese troops are seen in the vicinity or go into hiding). The major influence on military events was the engagement of American troops and the number and intensity of American troop strength. But even without major engagements (1970, for example), most Vietnamese felt more secure about the future when the troops were there. The troops were highly visible throughout the country, and one can assume that their presence greatly influenced the subjective judgments of the Vietnamese regarding the outcome of the war. Specifically, it was difficult for average Vietnamese to think seriously that they would lose the war to the Communists so long as America was resolved to prevent it. A critical assumption of our analysis is that the Vietnamese measured U.S. intentions (rightly or wrongly) by the presence of American troops, and their expectations about the future were directly related to U.S. troop strength in South Vietnam.[10] Given this assumption, one would expect to observe a fall in velocity with the buildup of U.S. troops, and a rise in velocity as the troops departed the country, assuming other things to be equal.

7.3.4   Estimating velocity (V_1)

On the basis of the foregoing discussion we write the function for velocity in wartime South Vietnam as

$$V_1 = f[r, (\Delta P/P)^e, \text{DEM}, \text{EXP}] \tag{7.4}$$

where V_1 is velocity ($= \text{GNP}/M_1$), M_1 is the money stock defined as demand deposits plus currency in circulation, $(\Delta P/P)^e$ is the expected rate of inflation, DEM is U.S. troop strength as a demographic variable affecting velocity and EXP is expectation about the outcome of the war. For much of the period, r was fixed at a very low rate. As pointed out earlier, it was negative in real terms in all but one year from 1960 on. Under the circumstances, r will be dominated by $(\Delta P/P)^e$ as a measure of the cost of holding money. Accordingly, r will be dropped as an argument of velocity in our analysis of V_1. As classified earlier, U.S. troop strength (TROOP) was the major demographic variable. It was argued earlier that the number of U.S. troops in Vietnam should be weakly but positively related to velocity. TROOP is also taken as a measure of Vietnamese expectations (EXP) about the outcome of the war. By our reasoning, V_1 and EXP should be inversely related. Because TROOP represents both DEM and EXP, it will not be possible to separate the "pure economic" effect (the aggregate demand effect) from the confidence effect, and the present analysis cannot measure the importance of these variables separately. However, because we think that the pure economic effect of troop presence was weak in comparison with their effect on confidence, we have a hypothesis that velocity was inversely related to U.S. troop strength in Vietnam. This hypothesis is contrary to that widely held at the time. Dropping r and combining DEM and EXP into TROOP, we have

$$V_1 = g[(\Delta P/P)^e, \text{TROOP}] \tag{7.5}$$
$$+ \qquad -$$

The expected partial effects of the independent variables are indicated by the signs below the variable designations.

If there is no observable trend in the rate of inflation, the expected rate of inflation can be measured as a distributed lag of past rates of inflation.[11] In those studies in which data were limited to relatively short series, the rates of inflation in the previous two periods have been used to measure the expected rate of inflation in the current period.[12] Our data are limited to fifteen annual observations, 1960–74,[13] and that practically precludes using a longer lag structure. Consequently, the lag structure for estimating the velocity function was limited to the previous year's rate of inflation and the previous two years' rates of inflation.

Problems of measurement abound. Which price index should be used? Should price be measured as of the end of the year on average for the year? As previously noted, the working-class family price index is used. It is the most extensive of the options, and possibly the most reliable one. It clearly suffers from all the problems of Laspeyres indexes, and its use introduces a minor inconsistency in the analysis. Recall that V_1 is calculated as GNP/M_1 or PQ/M_1, where Q is real national income and P is the price level. P in this expression should be the implicit GNP deflator, not the working-class price index. Thus, the choice is between using an index that better measures the phenomenon it proposes to measure and another that is more consistent with the measure of velocity required to do any empirical work. Another consideration favoring the more reliable working-class index deals with timing. There is no end-of-year measure for the GNP deflator. Therefore, strictly speaking, if one wishes to measure a calendar-year change, one cannot use the implicit deflator, which is an average measure over the year and represents more the actual price at midyear than at the end. Because we have no overwhelming reason for selecting one index over another, or a midyear measure as compared with an end-of-year measure, tests were performed with different price indexes. The best results were derived using the working-class index when measured at the end of the year, and these results are reported here.[14]

Theory is not instructive with regard to specifying the functional forms of the estimating equations. It is conventional to measure the variables in logarithms, but there is no particular reason to do so except for the convenience of interpreting the regression coefficients as elasticities. Our preference is to measure the troop variable in natural units. If TROOP is to reflect an expectation about the outcome of the war, it might better serve this purpose if significant changes are not damped, as would be the case for logarithmic measures. But our preference is not strong. Therefore, TROOP is entered in the regressions both ways.

The results pertaining to V_1 are shown in Table 7.4. A suggested independent variable, the rate of inflation two periods past, $d \ln P(t - 2)$, is not

Table 7.4 *Results of V_1 regressions for South Vietnam*[a]

Dependent variable	Independent variables								
	$d \ln P$ $(t-1)$	$[d \ln P)$ $(t-1)] -$ $[d \ln P$ $(t-2)]$	$\ln$ TROOP	TROOP	$d \ln$ TROOP	d TROOP	c	R^2 (adj.)	D.W.
$\ln V$	0.49 (2.73)[b]		−0.051 (5.52)				1.63 (32.66)	0.70	1.56
$\ln V$	0.97 (5.52)			−0.0009 (6.37)			1.53 (38.74)	0.75	1.49
$d \ln V$		0.80 (2.92)			−0.039 (2.05)		−0.09 (0.24)	0.45	2.34
$d \ln V$		1.06 (3.83)				−0.0008 (2.55)	−0.01 (0.36)	0.52	2.50

[a]Troop strength is measured in thousands, and the working-class price index has a base of 1.00 in 1962.
[b]Figures in parentheses are t values.

included in the table because the estimated coefficient on that variable is not statistically significant. This implies that a lag structure extending over two years is too long, an implication that appears to be reasonable given the rapidly changing economic and social conditions of wartime South Vietnam.

Based on the t values, the hypothesis that the immediate past rate of inflation and American troop strength in Vietnam were major determinants of velocity should not be rejected. For one-tailed tests, both variables are statistically significant at better than the 5 percent level almost regardless of how the variables are measured and whether they are entered as originally specified or as first differences.[15] With respect to the form of the equations, one should notice, particularly, the regression results when TROOP is measured in natural units rather than in logarithms. Switching from logarithms to natural units marginally improves the adjusted R^2 values. One possible interpretation of this result is that a logarithmic transformation tends to reduce the effects of big changes that may have had major effects on confidence because of their "shock" value.

Two variables – the previous year's rate of inflation and U.S. troop strength – account well for the movement in V_1 over the period 1960–74. The previous year's rate of inflation is taken to be a measure of the current year's expected rate of inflation and represents the expected cost to the Vietnamese of holding money. U.S. troop strength in Vietnam had potentially offsetting influences on the velocity of money. By far the more significant influence was due to the rise in confidence the Vietnamese felt in the ability of the GVN to survive so long as U.S. troop strength was increasing. This was manifest in their willingness to hold larger amounts of piasters rather than spending them more rapidly. The result was a slowdown in the velocity of circulation. However, when the U.S. troops began to leave Vietnam, confidence was affected adversely, and velocity rose. At the time, the downward movement in velocity up to 1968 in the face of inflation and the upward movement after 1969 were puzzling to the economy watchers. Our hypothesis explains this phenomenon well.

7.3.5   Money and inflation

During 1960–74, the major contributor to inflation was the growth in the money supply. The long-term relationship between money and prices is clear in Figure 7.1. Over the period, both prices and money stock increased at an average compounded rate of 24 percent per year. According to the quantity theory, the rate of inflation is expected to be approximately equal to the rate of change in the money stock plus the rate of change in velocity minus the rate of change in real income, or $d \ln P = d \ln M + d \ln V - d \ln Q$. The average rate of increase in real income was 3 percent. Thus, 88 percent of the annual rise in prices was accounted for by changes in the money stock and velocity. Although the long-term relationship between prices and money is not in doubt, there is a question of how well changes in the money supply explain changes in price in the short term. In particular, what was the year-to-year relationship between money growth and inflation?

We attempt to answer this short-run question by testing equations of the following types:

$$P = f[M, Q, (\Delta P/P)^e, \text{TROOP}] \tag{7.6}$$
$$P = h(M, Q, \hat{V}) \tag{7.7}$$

where the variables are price (P), money (M), output (Q), expected rate of price changes $(\Delta P/P)^e$, troop strength (TROOP), and estimated velocity $(\hat{V})$. Equation (7.6) is typical of models employed in monetary analyses. It is simple to estimate by ordinary least squares and can be useful as a predictive model of price, but it is a misspecification of the quantity theory, because in the quantity theory coefficients on M and Q are restricted. Equation (7.7) can be estimated by two-stage least squares, and it is a direct test of the quantity theory. The variables in parentheses are those specified in the quantity theory, and we expect the coefficients on M, Q, and V to be 1, -1, and 1, respectively.[16]

The results of both approaches are presented in Table 7.5. The money stock is defined as M_1. As expected, regressions pertaining to the levels of the variables show good results. Regression no. 1 shows a strong relationship between money and price, but the exact relationship is not that predicted by the quantity theory, nor should one expect to obtain the predicted value from this form of regression equation. In the two-stage least-squares regression, no. 2, all of the estimated coefficients are sufficiently close to their expected values, including the constant term expected to be zero. Thus, there is no reason to reject the quantity model. In the case of regressions with first differences, the misspecified model, regression no. 3, yields poor results, but the properly specified model yields good results. In regression no. 4, the estimated coefficients all lie within two standard errors of their expected values. Overall, these results indicate a strong relationship between price and the explanatory variables, both over the total period (regression no. 2) and in the shorter period (regression no. 4).

7.4   Summary

The major long-term goal of economic policy in wartime South Vietnam was to keep the people sufficiently satisfied that they would not rise up against the government. The proximate goal was inflation control. Although significant price rises occurred during the war, they were always kept within tol-

Table 7.5. *Regressions pertaining to price level and rate of inflation*[a]

Regression number	Dependent variable	Independent variables							
		ln M	ln Q	d ln P(t-1)	TROOP	ln V	c	R^2	D.W.
1	ln P	1.21	-2.08	0.99	-0.001			0.995	2.49
		(15.80)[b]	(3.70)	(3.50)	(6.83)		(5.65)		
							(2.44)		
2	ln P	1.07	-1.14			1.19	0.04	0.996	2.19
		(15.92)	(2.32)			(8.22)	(0.02)		
		d ln M	d ln Q	[d ln P (t-1)] −[d ln P(t−2)]	d TROOP	d ln V	c	R^2	D.W.
3	d ln P	0.52	-1.42	0.65	-0.0002		0.14	0.454	1.73
		(1.52)	(1.50)	(1.98)	(0.56)		(1.61)		
4	d ln P	0.80	-1.92			0.70	0.10	0.747	2.14
		(3.67)	(2.95)			(3.11)	(1.84)		

[a]Troop strength is measured in thousands, and the working-class price index has base of 1.00 in 1962.
[b]Figures in parentheses are *t*-values.

erable limits, and economic policy on inflation control must be judged to have been successful. It will not surprise anyone with a basic knowledge of the theory of inflation that price rises can be controlled even with large government deficits if enough goods are supplied from the outside. If inflation is due to "too much money chasing too few goods," it can be controlled by supplying goods through foreign aid to neutralize money creation due to government deficits. The antiinflation policy worked reasonably well in South Vietnam.

There are two other ways in which American activities helped to keep prices under control. First, the large economic aid program was a major cause of the real growth of the Vietnamese economy that took place during the war. The real growth rate of about 3 percent per year would permit an expansion of the money stock at that rate without causing inflation. Second, the buildup of U.S. troop strength in Vietnam allowed the government to print up additional piasters insofar as the troops were willing to hold them, but, more significantly, the buildup dampened monetary velocity by raising the expectations of the public regarding the survivability of the political regime. The withdrawal of U.S. troops reinforced the inflationary pressures that were building up toward the end of the war.

Table A7.1. *Consumer price index for working-class families in Saigon, 1956–74 (first quarter 1962 = 100)*

Date	End of quarter			
	1	2	3	4
1956	96.6	102.6	105.8	92.6
1957	93.3	97.5	96.7	93.4
1958	90.7	92.1	96.0	93.9
1959	96.6	95.3	97.3	93.6
1960	91.9	93.0	96.7	97.4
1961	96.4	98.6	103.0	101.8
1962	100.0	100.8	106.3	104.9
1963	106.1	111.3	116.4	111.6
1964	111.0	112.8	116.9	117.7
1965	116.8	125.6	142.4	159.1
1966	174.8	207.2	243.0	256.7
1967	293.8	304.2	336.1	338.8
1968	372.8	383.8	410.9	421.3
1969	430.8	466.5	510.9	554.9
1970	589.0	642.9	688.2	736.4
1971	749.5	757.3	777.9	850.0
1972	909.6	940.8	1,016.4	1,079.7
1973	1,215.2	1,288.5	1,571.4	1,718.8
1974	2,042.0	2,143.0	2,323.5	2,413.7

Sources: VN-NIS (annual, 1966, 1972), VN-NIS (monthly, July–Sept. 1974), and AID-VN (monthly, Feb. 1975).

Table A7.2. *Money stock in South Vietnam, 1956–74 (billion piasters)[a]*

	End of year					Average over year				
Year	Currency	Demand deposits	M_1[b]	Quasi money	M_2[c]	Currency	Demand deposits	M_1[b]	Quasi money	M_2[c]
1956	8.3	3.9	12.2	1.0	13.2			12.3[d]	1.0	13.3[d]
1957	7.6	3.4	11.0	0.7	13.2			11.6[d]	1.1	12.7[d]
1958	7.9	3.9	11.7	0.9	12.6	7.9	3.5	11.4[d]	0.8	12.2[d]
1959	8.9	5.2	14.1	0.9	15.0	8.6	4.7	12.9[d]	0.9	13.8[d]
1960	11.2	5.5	16.8	0.9	17.7	10.4	5.6	15.5[d]	0.9	16.4[d]
1961	12.2	5.0	17.2	0.9	18.1	12.3	5.3	17.0[d]	0.9	17.9[d]
1962	13.2	6.3	19.5	0.9	20.4	12.9	5.8	18.7	0.6	19.6
1963	15.5	6.8	22.3	2.0	24.3	15.3	7.0	22.3	1.5	23.8
1964	19.0	8.4	27.4	2.2	29.6	17.8	8.2	26.0	2.1	28.1
1965	32.8	14.8	47.6	2.9	50.5	26.8	12.0	38.9	2.6	41.5
1966	46.0	17.4	63.5	8.3	71.8	42.1	18.6	60.7	5.4	66.1
1967	61.3	20.9	82.2	9.0	91.2	55.0	18.9	73.9	8.3	82.2
1968	91.8	32.3	124.1	15.4	139.5	87.2	27.1	114.3	11.0	125.3
1969	108.1	32.6	140.7	25.1	165.8	101.8	31.8	133.6	19.4	153.0
1970	125.9	37.0	162.9	33.9	196.8	119.5	34.1	153.6	28.1	181.7
1971	162.1	46.3	208.4	65.0	273.4	149.1	41.5	190.6	51.4	242.0
1972	183.7	44.1	227.8	135.1	362.9	182.2	41.6	223.8	103.3	327.1
1973	200.0	62.6	262.7	166.3	429.0	193.7	54.9	248.6	150.1	398.7
1974	245.7	88.3	334.0	263.0	597.0[e]	231.3	81.2	312.5	238.0	550.5[e]

[a] Data sources: Data from VN-NIS (annual, various issues), except for 1956 and 1974; data from 1956 from International Monetary Fund (monthly), and data for 1974 from AID-VN (monthly, Feb. 1975). Data are averages of figures for March, June, September, and December unless otherwise noted.
[b] M_1 = currency in circulation plus private demand deposits.
[c] M_2 = M_1 + savings and time accounts in commercial banks (quasi money).
[d] Average of December figure for previous year and December figure for current year.
[e] Estimated from data on quasi money in International Monetary Fund (monthly).

Table A7.3. *Income ve-locity in South Vietnam, 1960–74*

Year	V_1	V_2
1960	5.1	5.0
1961	4.8	4.7
1962	5.0	4.9
1963	4.5	4.2
1964	4.4	4.1
1965	3.7	3.5
1966	3.9	3.6
1967	4.8	4.3
1968	3.4	3.1
1969	4.2	3.6
1970	5.2	4.4
1971	5.1	4.1
1972	4.9	3.4
1973	6.2	3.9
1974	7.1	4.0

Source: Derived from Tables 3.1 and A7.2.

CHAPTER 8

Windfall gains from importing

The principal "rent-seeking" activity in wartime South Vietnam, and particularly in the period 1965–70, was importing.[1] Continually rising domestic prices in a regime of a fixed foreign exchange rate and controlled interest rates allowed a Vietnamese entrepreneur to reap huge windfall gains in the relatively riskless enterprise of importing. The system permitted these privileged traders to buy goods at subsidized prices and sell them later at inflated prices. Foreign aid played a major role in this operation.

Most of the economic aid received by Vietnam was channeled through relatively few private importers who were licensed by the government. They purchased the foreign exchange from the government, placed orders for imports, and sold the imports many months later at inflated prices. Under competition and free market interest rates, this possibility would not have existed. However, given the institutional arrangements that did exist, the financial incentives in importing completely dominated those in production, attracting the cream of Vietnam's entrepreneurial pool, as well as their capital, to the importing business rather than to other enterprises that might have contributed more to long-run economic development of the country.

It was thought that 85 to 90 percent of all lending by Saigon banks until August 1970 was for the purpose of importing (AID 1976, pt. A, p. 59). Understandably, importers preferred low interest rates, and it is assumed that they used their considerable influence with their friends in government to delay needed interest rate reforms. From time to time they received unwitting assistance from AID officials who were concerned primarily with inflation control. For example, in late 1969, some of these officials argued for the suspension of the Vietnamese "commercial consumables" program, according to which local industry was encouraged to manufacture light supplies such as boots, barbed wire, canteens, and so forth, for the armed forces. The Joint Economic Office of USAID in Vietnam argued that "with overfull employment and a high level of inflation these goods were best supplied from outside" (AID, 1976, pt. A, pp. 46–7).[2] This is an instance in which preoccupation with inflation control favored importers at the expense of long-run development. The relatively small group of licensed importers had an influence beyond their economic contribution and, as will be shown later, derived much personal gain from the inflationary process. In the remainder of this chapter we develop a theory and an accounting procedure for estimating importers' "rents of privilege."

8.1   The motives for importing

The usual motive for importing is profit. In a wartime inflationary economy the profit motive may be dominant, but others undoubtedly exist. With regard to the situation that existed in Vietnam for the period 1965–70, wealth protection was another motive. Its consideration is useful, if not essential, for understanding the behavior of importers during that period.

With prices rising 30 to 40 percent per year, it is understandable that people will look for a means to protect their wealth. They will want to hold as little as possible in the form of cash and as much as possible in some asset that appreciates in terms of money. Holding financial assets, such as a savings account or bonds, in wartime Vietnam was no way to hedge against inflation, because those assets earned (by law) considerably less than the rate of inflation. Practically the only hedge against inflation during the war was the holding of goods or nondepreciating currencies, and the importing business furnished good opportunities for the trader to hold both.

8.1.1   Holding goods

Commercial Import Program (CIP) analysts thought that the Vietnamese importer lacked sophistication as an importer. He frequently knew or cared little about the particular market for which he imported. If he could not obtain a license to import steel, then he would try for one to import chemicals, and so forth. Of course, as a businessman (not a trade specialist), the importer knew exactly what he was doing. He quite simply wanted to hold goods rather than cash, and, profit potential aside, he was willing to take whatever goods he could get. No other line of activity in wartime Vietnam afforded such a good opportunity to flee from a depreciating currency to stocks of goods.

8.1.2   Obtaining nondepreciating currencies

In wartime Vietnam it was illegal to hold foreign currencies. Thus, most people who wished to hold them resorted to the flourishing currency black market. Importing opened up a distinct and less risky way to obtain foreign currency through deliberate overinvoicing of imported goods. Suppose an importer took out a license to import a high-unit-price item such as a fishing boat. If the exporter agreed to overprice the boat for official purposes, the importer could obtain excess foreign exchange from the National Bank on a legitimate import license.[3] The amount in excess or some part of it could then be deposited in a foreign bank. This would have been advantageous for any importer who desired to transfer depreciating currency into hard currency so long as the effective piaster cost of importing (official rate of exchange plus tariffs) was less than the black market rate for the hard currency.

8.2 The economic theory of windfall gains and taxation in Vietnam inflation

8.2.1 Windfall gains, rents, and excess profits

A windfall gain is distinguished from profit in that it accrues to an individual without his performing any economically productive service. In the pure theory of competition, windfalls are not possible as a general condition, for if they did accrue temporarily, output would increase in response to the entry of new firms, price would decline, and the windfall would disappear. We refer to windfalls alternatively as excess profits and rents.

Windfalls usually persist as a result of special privileges or when institutional factors (including imperfect knowledge of the market) prevent the forces of competitive supply and demand from operating fully. Under certain conditions it is possible for the government to tax away windfalls. However, for the actual political-economic environment that prevailed in Vietnam between 1966 and 1970, it is difficult to imagine any practical governmental measure that could have completely eliminated windfalls due to importing. On the supply side, the level of imports was constrained by the amount of foreign exchange made available by U.S. aid, so that market prices were not set by competitive supply. On the demand side, inflation and price expectations continually caused monetary demand to exceed whatever level of imports might have been established by the government.

The amount of windfalls at any given time was set by a combination of institutional factors. For the period of the late sixties, the volume of imports was fixed by the government, and it allocated imports to a relatively few through licensing. With the knowledge that world export prices were rising slower than domestic prices, and with the foreign exchange rate fixed for long periods of time, it was fairly riskless for an importer to purchase almost any commodity on the "approved list" in anticipation of capturing a widening difference between the inflated domestic price and the relatively fixed import price.

The hypothetical level of excess profit and the way it would be affected by inflation are shown in Figure 8.1. Let SX represent the supply of imports at some fixed exchange rate (plus tariff), and let D be the demand curve at the same time. Under competitive conditions, the import quantity would be OF and the market price FF'. Suppose that the quantity OF required an

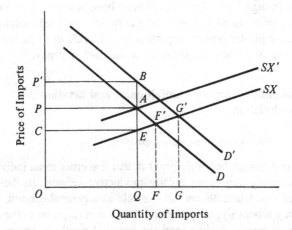

Figure 8.1. Supply and demand for imports under competition.

amount of foreign exchange in excess of what the government had to sell. To conserve foreign exchange, suppose the government restricted imports to OQ and allocated that quantity to the licensed importers. The importer's cost per unit (including provision for normal profit) would be EQ, but the unit selling price would be AQ. Excess profit per unit would be AE, and total windfalls from importing would be $CEAP$.

Subsequent domestic inflation would tend to increase the *monetary* demand for imports, and maybe real demand as well, if import prices were rising slower than domestic prices. This situation can be illustrated by an outward shift in the demand curve to D'. Importers would raise their price to BQ, thereby capturing additional rents of $P'BAP$. This amount will clearly be a rent of privilege, because it accrues to the importer without his performing any additional productive service whatsoever. If there were no constraints on the volume of imports, and if licenses were issued freely to anyone who wanted them, the quantity imported would expand to OG, the price would be $G'G$, and there would be no rents.

8.2.2   Taxing of rents: simple analysis

Would it not be possible for the government to tax away the rents? Under the foregoing conditions, this possibility would depend on the organizational structure of the import business. If only a few large importers controlled most of the business, then the government might not be able to tax away all the rents. On the other hand, if entry were unrestricted, then it would be possible to transfer the rents from the individuals to the government. For the theoretical analysis, we shall distinguish between two extreme cases.

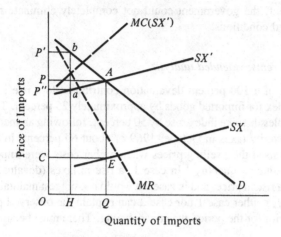

Quantity of Imports

Figure 8.2. Importing under oligopoly.

Case 1: Government issues licenses to anyone. Once again, suppose that the quantity were set at *OQ* in Figure 8.1. By raising the foreign exchange rate or tariff, the government could shift the supply curve to the importer upward by any amount it wished. Thus, it would be possible for the government to shift the supply curve to *SX'*. For the amount of foreign exchange sales corresponding to the given volume of imports, *OQ*, the government could raise its local currency collections from *OQEC* to *OQAP*. In other words, it could just exactly tax away the undesirable excess profits of the importing community, *CEAP*.

Case 2: The government issues licenses to a relatively few importers who collude tacitly, and the government sets the volume of imports lower than the importers would have done on their own. The second condition is simply a modification that will allow the government constraint to be binding. Figure 8.2 is Figure 8.1 reproduced with the marginal curves that are pertinent to *D* and *SX'*. As before, the rents that the government wishes to tax are indicated by the area *CEAP*.

In this case, if the government were to raise the cost of importing to *SX'*, importers would respond by reducing their purchases by *HQ* and charging the demand price for the new quantity, *OP'*. The new desired level of imports would be *OH*, because *H* is the quantity at which marginal cost equals marginal revenue. Importers would not take all the foreign exchange offered them. Their new level of rents, *P"abP'*, would be smaller than the former amount, and it is also possible that total government collections would be smaller than before. In any event, the government could not completely eliminate rents under the postulated conditions.

8.2.3   Taxing of rents: extended analysis

In 1966, the event of a 100 percent devaluation contributed to a rise in the wholesale price index for imported goods by approximately 25 percent. Three years later, the wholesale price index rose by 50 percent, following an increase in customs and austerity taxes in October 1969 of about 60 percent. In both events, importers raised their selling prices when higher costs were imposed on them without reducing quantity.[4] In case 1, a rise in taxes (devaluation) would not suggest a rise in price, and in case 2 it would not suggest maintaining quantity. Evidently, neither case 1 nor case 2 can explain the observed price and quantity behavior for the period we are analyzing. There must be another explanation.

It was suggested earlier that an important motive for importing in an inflationary situation is the desire to protect wealth. The desire to maximize rents could account for a price rise accompanying a rise in the cost of importation. But, all other things being equal, this behavior for maximizing rents would lead to a reduction in the volume of goods desired by importers. After the new demand was satisfied, an importer might have additional reserves that he would desire to protect. Those additional reserves could be converted into additional goods that would not clear the market at the higher price. However, the importer would have the option to store them in anticipation of future price increases.

Interest rate policy favored the importer during the late sixties. Generally, the importer had to deposit only about 20 percent of the value of goods on his licenses and could borrow the rest from his bank. The bank was restricted by law from charging more than 12 percent interest. Under those conditions, and with an expected rate of inflation of 30 to 40 percent, turning cash into goods could be very profitable, even if the trader had to wait several months in order to sell his goods at some desired preestablished price.

In this context, suppose that the government were to attempt to capture the rents by, say, a one-stroke devaluation. Such a measure might be successful in raising additional revenues for the government, but it would not necessarily be successful in abolishing all rents. By devaluing, the government would raise the supply price of the imported goods, and that would tend to reduce rents. However, the importer could counter by raising his selling price, selling immediately a smaller quantity than he imported, and store the remainder for sale at some future date.[5] Figure 8.3 illustrates the economic reasoning behind this analysis.

D is the demand curve at a given time, and SX is the supply curve as in

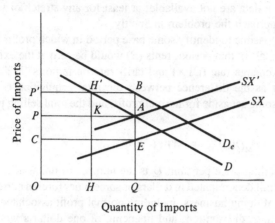

Figure 8.3. Importing in extended analysis.

the previous discussion. OQ is the volume of imports established by the government. The price for OQ quantity is AQ (or OP), and rents to importers are given by the area $CEAP$. With devaluation, the supply curve shifts to SX', and importers respond by raising the selling price to OP', a price that will allow them to sell OH given the demand curve D. If importers expect monetary demand to increase in the future to D^e, then they might order the additional quantity HQ rather than hold any financial assets that have a rate of return less than the rate of inflation. The rate of inflation determines how rapidly the demand curve shifts to D_e. Importers must estimate the future rate of inflation, because it is an important consideration in calculating the storage and financing costs for holding inventories valued at $HQAK$.

As importers sell off OH goods and acquire a cash position, they will want to turn the cash into more goods and will do so if they can obtain licenses. The repeated process will lead to inventory accumulation beyond the amount HQ indicated in the static diagram. Under the assumptions we have made, there is no limit to their accumulation. However, a practical limit is set by the availability of warehouses. Also, practically, the importers' business horizons are not infinite, and they may be guided by some upper limit based on past experience.

8.3 Accounting procedure for estimating windfall gains

In this section we outline an accounting procedure based on the economic theory outlined in Section 8.2. Our goal is to derive estimates of the rents from importing from 1962 through 1970. If data were available on unit costs and selling prices for a variety of goods, then direct calculations could be made. Because those data are not available, at least for any stretch of years, it is necessary to approach the problem indirectly.

Suppose it were possible to identify some base period in which profits from importing were normal. In that period, rents (R) would be zero at the existing (official) foreign exchange rate (OFX) and tariff rate on imports (MT). Let us define total rent as the difference between the total acquisition cost of imports, including some set aside for normal profit, and the total selling price. Hence,

$$R = PQ - P_M Q(\text{OFX} + \text{MT} + B) \tag{8.1}$$

P is the domestic selling price per unit, Q is the number of units, and P_M is the import cost per unit denominated in dollars or some other foreign currency. B is all other costs of doing business, including normal profit associated with handling, warehousing, distribution, and financing of one dollar's worth of imports. Because OFX and MT are measured also as piasters per dollar, $P_M Q(\text{OFX} + \text{MT} + B)$ is the total cost of importing measured in local currency (piasters).

Define the effective *legal* exchange rate as the sum of OFX and MT. Assuming that importers paid the posted tariff rates, the effective *legal* exchange rate would be equal to the *effective exchange rate* (EFX), which is defined implicitly. The *effective exchange rate* is discussed in Appendix 8.1 at the end of this chapter. For the purpose of calculating rents, it is clearly the relevant concept. Therefore, the theoretical equation (8.1) must be replaced with the effective equation (8.2):

$$R = PQ - P_M Q(\text{EFX} + B) \tag{8.2}$$

In the base period, when rents are zero,

$$R_0 = P_0 Q_0 - P_{M(0)} Q_0(\text{EFX}_0 + B_0) = 0$$

and

$$Q_0 = (P_{M(0)}/P_0)Q_0(\text{EFX}_0 + B_0) \tag{8.3}$$

[or $1 = (P_{M(0)}/P_0)\,(\text{EFX}_0 + B_0)$]. Likewise, in period j,

$$R_j = P_j Q_j - P_{M(j)} Q_j(\text{EFX}_j + B_j). \tag{8.4}$$

Divide by $P_{M(j)} Q_j$:

$$R_j/P_{M(j)} Q_j = (P_j Q_j/P_{M(j)} Q_j) - (\text{EFX}_j + B_j) \tag{8.5}$$

Let $Q_j = sQ_0$ ($s \neq 0$), so that (8.5) becomes

$$R_j/P_{M(j)} Q_j = (P_j sQ_0/P_{M(j)} sQ_0) - (\text{EFX}_j + B_j) \tag{8.6}$$

Substitute (8.3) into (8.6):

$$R_j/P_{M(j)}Q_j = \frac{P_j s Q_0 \, (P_{M(0)}/P_0) \, (EFX_0 + B_0)}{P_{M(j)} s Q_0} - (EFX_j + B_j)$$

which reduces to

$$R_j/P_{M(j)}Q_j = (P_j/P_0) \, (P_{M(0)}/P_{M(j)}) \, (EFX_0 + B_0) - (EFX_j + B_j)$$

$$(8.7)$$

Let $R_j/P_{M(j)}Q_j = R_j^* =$ windfall gains per dollar of imports. $P_j/P_0 = n_j$, an index of domestic selling price of imports, and $P_{M(0)}/P_{M(j)} = 1/e_j$, where e_j is an index of the foreign price paid for imports. Thus,

$$R_j^* = (n_j/e_j) \, (EFX_0 + B_0) - (EFX_j + B_j)$$

$$(8.8)$$

Equation (8.8) is an approximation to the amount of rents collected per dollar of imports by the importing community in some period assuming that no rents existed in the base period. All other things being equal, rents derive from a situation in which n rises faster than e. If there is no change in dollar import costs, the foreign exchange rate, taxes, or handling charges, then rents become inevitable if there is any rise in the domestic price paid for imports.

The expression n/e is the ratio of the domestic inflation rate of imported goods to the inflation rate of exported goods from the rest of the world. It is the key to the measurement of rents. However, the reader should note that the ratio of n to e will understate the potential for rents if the value of e is established when the order is placed. The reason is that there must be a delay between the time orders are placed and their arrival, and n can grow during this period. In Vietnam, the delay time was three to nine months. If we knew the exact lag structure, we would not want to choose synchronous n and e values. However, because we do not know the lag structure, we choose for practical reasons to measure n and e at the same time, and thus the ratio tends to understate the true value of rents.

8.4 Windfall gains from importing, 1962–70

8.4.1 Picking a base period

The first requirement for estimating windfall gains is to pick a base period during which it can be assumed, reasonably, that excess profits were non-existent or at least small relative to later periods. A reasonable argument can be made for selecting 1962–3 as the base period. In December 1961, the government devalued the piaster by 70 percent. If excess profits existed previously, this act probably eliminated most of them. Following the devaluation, the price index of imported products increased only 12 percent on

Table 8.1. *Estimated windfall gains from importing for selected periods, 1962–70 (piasters per dollar)*

Period	Windfall Profit (d/$)
1962–3	0
1964	−0.6
1965 (1st half)	6.5
1965 (2nd half)	23.3
1966 (1st half)	34.6
1966 (2nd half)	−17.2
1967	20.5
1968	27.3
1969 (1st half)	14.9
1969 (3rd quarter)	44.2
1969 (4th quarter)	127.9
Oct. 1969 to June 1970	104.7

Source: Data for calculations from Table A8.1.

average from 1961 to 1962. The relative stability of the period can be judged by the fact that the black market rate for the dollar hardly changed. From January 1962 to January 1964, domestic prices, as measured by any of the price indexes, changed by less than 8 percent. Price rises in 1964 for the consumer indexes were almost double their annual rates in 1962–3, and at the same time the black market rate for the dollar increased over 30 percent. Although not excessive by later year standards, the price increases in 1964 were large in comparison with those in 1962–3. Given these facts, we assume that importers' profits were normal in 1962–3.

8.4.2   Estimate of windfall gains

The periodic estimated values of windfall gains are given in Table 8.1. The particular period divisions were chosen with some consideration to the economic history of the eight-year time span for which windfall profits were an important economic factor. In 1964, the consumer price index for working-class families rose only 6 percent. In the first part of 1965, the United States began its combat troop buildup, but for the first half-year, prices rose only 13 percent. Inflation became a major problem in the second half of the year as prices rose 27 percent. The first six months in 1966 are distinguished from the previous period by the addition of a surcharge on foreign exchange or "perequation tax" for some imports early in March 1966, and the latter half of the year is distinguished from the first half by the devaluation of the piaster that took place on June 18. After an initial increase, associated with the

Table 8.2. *Windfall gains as percentage of effective exchange rate by period, 1964–70*

Period	Effective exchange cost (d/$)	Windfalls as percentage of effective exchange cost
1964	81.4	−0.7
1965 (1st half)	78.5	8.2
1965 (2nd half)	77.4	30.1
1966 (1st half)	84.4	41.0
1966 (2nd half)	186.2	−9.2
1967	168.8	12.1
1968	173.8	15.7
1969 (lst half)	189.3	7.9
1969 (3rd quarter)	191.4	23.1
1969 (4th quarter)	223.8	57.2
1970	267.5	54.9

Source: Table A8.1.

devaluation, prices leveled off for the rest of the year. They began to rise significantly again in early 1967. The year 1969 is divided into three parts because of various economic measures taken in that year. The perequation tax was extended in June 1969, and the austerity tax reform came in October of the same year.

8.5 Analysis of results

8.5.1 Historical overview

Table 8.2 presents the estimated windfall gains for each period as a percentage of the implicitly derived effective exchange rate. Clearly, there was a rise in windfall gains to the second half of 1966. An abrupt decline followed the midyear devaluation in 1966. Evidently, importers were not earning even "normal" profits immediately following the devaluation. Excess profits were fairly small – in the range of 8–16 percent of the effective exchange rate – for the three years after the devaluation. They increased perceptibly in the third quarter of 1969, but the very high estimate shown for the fourth quarter of 1969 should be considered in only the grossest sense, because the errors in calculation associated with the data could be very large for such a short period. Nevertheless, windfalls undoubtedly were considerably higher in that quarter than in the preceding one. Then they dropped sharply in the first half of 1970, but remained high for the year on average. The inability to control windfall gains, which were assumed to be significant at the time, was a contributing factor in the decision to devalue the piaster in October 1970 and to effectively free it in June 1971 (although the "official rate" was not changed until early 1972).

The following subsections examine in more detail the change in windfalls for the period in which they were a troublesome economic and political problem.

8.5.2   Effect of the 1966 devaluation on windfall gains

In a country that relies heavily on imports, devaluation is one prescription for inflationary control. It is a means of taxing domestic consumers of imported goods, but more pertinent to our analysis is the fact that if the devaluation is effective, it will result in transferring excess profits away from the privileged importers to the government. Usually a program that operates directly on the foreign exchange cost will be more effective than one that raises taxes, because the government is more sure of collecting the former. This is particularly true of underdeveloped countries.

The devaluation in June 1966 unquestionably was successful in transferring excess profits away from the importing community to the government. By our estimate, excess profits rose significantly from practically nothing in 1964 to 30 percent of the exchange value of imports during the last half of 1965 and first half of 1966. For the second half of 1966, they fell to a negative amount of d17 per dollar. Requests for licenses of U.S.-financed imports decreased from $318 million in the first six months of 1966 to $191 million in the last six months (AID-VN annual, no. 10, Table D–8).[6] Another indication of the effectiveness of the devaluation is that it helped to wipe out the government deficit almost completely,[7] with the end result that prices rose only slightly the rest of the year.

Between June 1 and the end of 1966, the import price index rose by 25 percent. Most of this rise came in anticipation of the devaluation that raised the cost to importers by about 60 percent. It would appear, therefore, that importers were able to shift a significant part of the cost increase to the consumers. Their desire and ability to do so would be consistent with the theory developed in Section 8.2.3. Interest rates were very low, the number of importers increased only slightly – despite publicity to the contrary at the time – and some other conditions were favorable. However, two conditions, the limitation on storage space and the long delay of up to eighteen months between ordering and arrival, were unfavorable to importers and advantageous to the GVN tax system. The government placed a retroactive levy called the equalization tax[8] on all orders in the pipeline at the time of devaluation. This tax netted the government more revenue in 1966 than the perequation tax and almost as much as that received in customs duties (Dacy 1969a, sec. 1.1.2). The tax resulted in a direct transfer from importers to the government of approximately $50 million, most of which was collected in the last half of the year. Evidently, the equalization tax *in addition* to the devaluation contributed to the final effect of driving windfalls from a significant level to a negative amount.

8.5.3 Windfalls in 1967 and 1968

Windfall gains in 1967 and 1968 were not large enough to generate serious concern. For those years, excess profits were about d12 to d16 per dollar of imports, or less than 10 percent of the import cost. Our method for estimating windfalls depends on the relationship between domestic price changes and the cost of importing given a fixed exchange rate. With a fixed exchange rate, the cost of importing will rise when import taxes are raised. The theoretical tariff was increased early in 1968 by about 50 percent on the average. For the two years, the implicit tariff on dutiable imports was approximately d30 per dollar, whereas the theoretical tariff was only slightly higher. It appears that the collection of customs revenues was quite efficient during the period, and the author believes that one reason for the inconspicuous level of windfall gains during the economically stable period up to the summer of 1969 was that importers were paying most of the taxes they were legally bound to pay.[9]

8.5.4 Windfalls following the austerity tax reform in 1969

Inflation became a serious problem once again in 1969. To cope with the problem, the government decided to raise import taxes. In June, the perequation tax was raised by d20–d30 per dollar on most items subject to the tax, and, additionally, the tax was placed on some CIP and PL 480 (Title I) commodities for the first time. In October, an austerity tax reform was put into effect. The new schedule raised the theoretical import costs (exchange rate and all taxes) by 60–70 percent. The anticipatory response to this measure was a 25–30 percent jump in the imported commodity price level. The reader should note the similarity in the cost–price behavior at the time of devaluation in 1966 and the austerity reform in 1969. We can only speculate that the government thought the results would be similar. They were not. After the austerity reform, windfalls rose to their highest level for the period.

We offer three reasons for the dissimilarity in results: (1) In 1969, storage space was not the same problem it had been in 1966. (2) There was no retroactive tax to capture the windfalls. (3) The administrative organization for handling and enforcing a fourfold tariff increase simply did not exist. And perhaps the opportunities for bribery within the customs office were so pronounced that the collection system broke down. This statement is not based on the author's intimate knowledge of the customs process following the austerity reform, but rather is an inference from data. For the nine months October 1969 to June 1970, the implicit tariff rate (customs plus austerity) on dutiable imports was in the range of 50–60 percent of the theoretical (or schedule) rate. This performance of customs is by far the worst in the decade of the sixties. Thus, prices were raised in anticipation of a larger cost increase that never came. The result, of course, was that windfall gains soared to their highest level.

Windfall gains to importers were not a factor in the Vietnam economy after 1970. In a series of exchange rate moves, the government raised the rate, and by the end of 1971 the country had adopted a virtually flexible system. In the framework of our analysis, the cost of imports to the importers rose about as fast as the spread between their selling price and the imported price, eliminating the major source of windfalls.

Appendix 8.1:   The effective exchange rate

The *effective exchange rate* is the piaster cost to the importer at the port of discharge after payment of all import taxes. It includes the official exchange costs and all taxes *actually paid* by the importer, less any other payments made as bribes to speed up action, to avoid legal costs, or simply to keep someone of influence happy, or, as one Vietnamese businessman said, "the costs of public relations." Of course, the extent to which these illicit payments were made or their amounts were never recorded. Some of them undoubtedly have been included in what we have called windfall gains (excess profits) from importing, but they are not included in the *effective exchange rate*. Total piaster costs of importing were equal to the government's piaster income from selling dollars to importers and collecting the taxes on the imports. The *effective exchange rate* can be determined implicitly only by dividing the total government collections by the dollar value of imports.

The *effective exchange rate* differs from the effective *legal* exchange rate in that the former is defined by actual collections and the latter by theoretical or scheduled collections. Actual tariff collections were always less than an amount implied by data on the composition of imports and the tariff schedule. For the 1962–5 period, actual customs collections were perhaps only 75 percent of the amount estimated had everyone paid the legal rate (Dacy 1969a, pp. 16–17). The percentage probably improved after 1966 and then severely deteriorated following the disastrous austerity tax reform measures of October 1969. For the next nine months, it is doubtful that the actual tariff collections were more than 60 percent of the theoretically possible collections. There were many ways importers could evade paying the intended rates. It was easy to misclassify goods, because the Vietnamese had their own classification system, called Nhap Cong (NC), but they also used the Brussels Tariff Nomenclature (BTN code). Goods declared on one system could not be adequately checked on the other. Some fraudulent invoicing was practiced, and there was also the prospect of simply paying off a customs official to avoid the tariff. Because the Vietnamese government was not able to collect the amount implied in the tariff schedules, it would be wrong to use the effective *legal* exchange rate as a measure of importers' piaster costs per dollar of imports.

There are several problems in computing the *effective exchange rate*, even though the concept is straightforward and simple. The *effective exchange rate* is the ratio of the total piaster cost of imports and their dollar cost. One problem is that published statistics pertaining to piaster costs and dollar costs are not matching. Balance-of-payments data show the value in dollars for *all* imports, including those that did not enter commercial channels, such as project aid and PL 480 (Title II) commodities. Statistics gathered by the Vietnamese customs office refer only to items passing through customs. Although those goods were primarily commercial, they did not entirely exclude direct government imports such as rice, which was a very large item, and some goods destined for the military commissaries. A proper calculation of the *effective exchange rate* must use data only on goods imported for profit.

Another problem is the timing of customs payments. In the statistics, the dollar cost of imports was generated from import arrivals, not when customs duties were actually paid. The payment of duties was made several weeks or months after the goods arrived, and whereas duties paid early in a given year should be applied to import arrivals late in the previous year, in our calculations they are treated as sychronous. It is thought that the lag between arrivals and payment of import duties was not long; so although the nonsynchronous nature of the data probably causes some distortion, it is not likely to be gross. The magnitude of distortion depends on the length of the period covered and the stability of the variable to be measured. If the level of imports and the payment of all taxes are steady over a long period, then the fact of a lagged relation will cause little error in measurement. If the level of imports and tax payments are irregular, the distortion could still be small if the period for which measurement is desired is relatively long – say a couple of years. However, the distortion could be large if the period of measurement is only a quarter of a year.

There are three relatively accessible series on the dollar value of imports into Vietnam. The one that we used as the closest representation of commercial-type imports was reported by the Vietnam customs office (Directorate General of Customs).[10] These data account for imports delivered to a licensed importer for his own disposition, which was, presumably, to sell for profit. Almost all in this class of imports carried some kind of duty in the war period. We call this class commercial imports, and their dollar value serves as the

Table A8.1. *Data for computation of windfall gains*

Period	(1) Effective exchange rate (EFX) (d/$)	(2) Import price index (1962–3 = 1.00) (n)	(3) "World" export price index (1962–3 = 1.00) (e)	(4) Cost of doing business (B) (d/$)	(5) $n/e(EFX_0 + B_0)$ (d/$)	(6) Windfall gains (R^{**}) (d/$)
1962–3	78.3	1.000	1.000	15.7	94.1	
1964	81.4	1.075	1.040	16.4	97.2	−0.6
1965	77.9	1.220	1.025	18.4	110.7	15.5
1st half	78.5	1.119	1.030	17.1	102.1	6.5
2nd half	77.4	1.307	1.020	19.7	120.4	23.3
1966	139.2	1.873	1.024	36.0	170.9	5.7
1st half	84.4	1.546	1.020	23.5	142.5	34.6
2nd half	186.2	2.200	1.030	31.8	200.8	−17.2
1967	168.8	2.517	1.040	38.2	227.5	20.5
1968	173.8	2.770	1.045	48.9	248.2	27.3
1st quarter	166.5	2.690	1.040	46.6	243.2	30.1
3rd quarter	175.4	2.797	1.050	48.4	250.4	26.6
1969	196.8	3.550	1.110	58.0	300.6	45.0
1st half	189.3	2.991	1.090	53.7	257.9	14.9
3rd quarter	191.4	3.445	1.100	58.8	294.4	44.2
4th quarter	223.8	5.018	1.130	65.8	417.5	127.9
1970	267.5	6.178	1.170	81.9	496.3	146.9
1st half	280.5	5.545	1.160	74.9	449.3	93.9
2nd half	253.0	6.858	1.180	87.8	546.3	205.5

Explanations and data sources:
(1) Table A8.2.
(2), (3), (4), see Appendix 8.2.
(5) [Column (2) ÷ column (3)] × 94; $(X_0 + T_0 + B_0)$ = 94.
(6) Column (5) − column (1) − column (4).

denominator in the implicit calculation of the *effective exchange rate* [i.e., (piasters collected by the government)/(dollar value of imports)].

Appendix 8.2:   Data computation and sources

A major prerequisite for calculating windfall profits is to estimate the values of variables required by equation (8.8). The following is a discussion of the sources of raw data and the manner in which they were converted into the specific forms required for the calculations. All values are shown in Table A8.1.

(1) EFX_0: This constant is a measure of the average cost of foreign exchange for commercial-type imports in the base period, 1962–3. The cost for the base period is implicit: It was obtained by dividing the number of piasters collected by the National Bank of Vietnam for sale of dollars plus the number of piasters collected by the customs office as import taxes by the dollar value of commercial imports arriving in the base period. Because tariff rates varied between commodities, this implicit cost is an average cost. For the base period, the average implicit foreign exchange cost was 78.3 piasters per dollar.

(2) $EFXj$: This is the average implicit exchange cost for the jth period. It is computed as shown in Table 8.2.

(3) B_0: This is the piaster business cost per dollar of importing in the base period. There are no direct observations on B_0. CIP analysts in Vietnam were of the opinion that this cost was approximately 20 percent of all exchange costs in a normal period, and GVN officials in the Ministry of Economy thought that 20 percent was a good guess. The cost of doing business includes financing, warehousing, and labor costs, as well as "normal" profits. Given our calculation of EFX_0 = 78.3, we fix B_0 at 15.7 piasters per dollar. To determine the periodic values of B, it is divided into two components:

The first, b_1, is an index of the noninterest costs of doing business. By assumption, this was 90 percent of total costs. Item b_1 applies to profits, wages, local transportation, and warehousing (rent) expenses. Of these expenses, it has been assumed that 75 percent were nonrental expenses, and 25 percent were rental expenses. Further, it has been assumed that profits, wages, and other nonrental costs rose in line with the middle-class price index and that rental expenses rose along with the rent components. The estimated piaster cost of these components in period j would be $0.9 \times b_{1j} \times B_0$.

The second, b_2, applies to financing or interest costs. These costs depended on the interest rate, the amount of deposit (down payment) required for purchasing foreign exchange, and the length of the period (in advance) of deposit, which generally was the time elapsed from down payment to time of arrival of imports. Because measures on none of these variables are avail-

Table A8.2. *Calculation of effective exchange rate, 1962–70*

Period	(1) Dollar value of commercial imports ($ million)	(2) Piaster value at official rate (d billion)	(3) Import taxes (d billion)	(4) Total piaster collections (d billion)	(5) Implicit or effective rate (d/$)
1962	230.9	13.854	4.318	18.172	78.7
1963	238.1	14.285	4.275	18.560	78.0
1964	245.8	15.287	4.719	20.006	81.4
1965	297.0	17.819	5.322	23.141	77.9
1st half	137.8	8.268	2.555	10.823	78.5
2nd half	159.2	9.551	2.767	12.318	77.4
1966	460.0	41.956	22.067	64.023	139.2
1st half	212.5	12.751	5.186	17.937	84.4
2nd half	247.5	29.205	16.881	46.086	186.2
1967	547.4	64.593	27.789	92.382	168.8
1968	473.9	55.920	26.435	82.355,	173.8
1st quarter	85.3	10.065	4.141	14.206	166.5
3rd quarter	388.6	45.855	22.294	68.149	175.4
1969	652.5	76.995	51.415	128.410	196.8
1st half	358.9	42.350	25.590	67.940	189.3
3rd quarter	161.8	19.092	11.879	30.971	191.4
4th quarter	131.8	15.552	13.947	29.498	223.8
1970	502.3	59.271	75.080	134.351	267.5
1st half	263.7	31.117	42.863	73.980	280.5
2nd half	238.6	28.155	32.217	60.372	253.0

Explanations and data sources:

(1) Same as for Table A4.7. Values for subperiods were obtained by prorating the annual figures. The percentage for any subperiod was determined as the ratio of all import arrivals in Vietnam over the subperiod to the total of all import arrivals for the year. Import arrivals by month were published in VN-NSI (monthly, various issues). Note that "all import arrivals" exceeded "commercial imports" by 30–40% over the period covered in this table. See Table A4.7.

(2) The official rate was d60/$ to July 1966 and d118/$ for the rest of the period of this table. The figures in this column were obtained by multiplying these rates by the figures in column (1).

(3) Import taxes are the sum of regular customs duties, the austerity tax, the perequation tax, and other "extra budgetary" receipts related to importing: (a) The customs and austerity duties are net of export duties. Data compiled from various issues of VN-NIS (monthly, various issues), on a current or "cash" basis. The data used for customs receipts do not correspond exactly with data found in AID (1974b) or VN-NIS (annual). The latter publication records fiscal-year (rather than calendar-year) information for 1966–9, and AID (1974b) apparently records fiscal year information for 1966–7 without comment, and it is not evident what data it records for 1968 and 1969. Export data for tax exclusion taken from VN-NIS (annual, 1971, Table 168, p. 163). (b) Data on perequation tax collections were compiled from worksheets supplied by Mr. Nguyen Uyen (in 1971), a statistician at the Joint Economic Office, Agency for International Development, Saigon, Vietnam. These compilations differ from the numbers published in AID (1974b), particularly for 1967–9. Examination of the work-sheets led the author to suspect that there might be some transcription errors in the series in AID (1974b). (c) Other non-budgetary receipts related to importing were taken from AID (1974b, p. 10). These data measure essentially the "equalization tax" collections and are not broken down by subperiod. Subperiod values were derived by multiplying the annual totals by the percentage of import arrivals for the subperiod. The figure for the first half of 1966 was taken from Dacy (1969a; p. 21).

(4) Column (2) + column (3).

(5) Column (4) ÷ column (1).

able in a consistent time series, it was necessary to improvise series based on general knowledge and inference. Between December 1961 and June 18, 1966, the official exchange rate – including the five-sevenths surtax – was unchanged at 60 piasters per dollar, and the official nominal rate of interest was unchanged also. Assuming no change in the deposit ratio and no change in the length of the deposit period, the nominal interest cost probably did not vary significantly during the 4.5-year period. Given our previous assumption that nonfinancing costs were 90 percent of B_0, we calculated that financing costs were 10 percent of B_0, or 1.6 piasters per dollar up to mid-1966. When the piaster was devalued by 100 percent in 1966, financing costs would double, all other things being equal, because the absolute size of the down payment would double even if the ratio were unchanged. The official nominal interest rate was raised from 3 to 8 percent in subsequent years (through September 1970). Without specific information on the changing deposit ratios and down payment periods, and not trusting the official interest rate as a true representation of what importers actually had to pay for money,[11] we must rely on assumptions. The critical assumption here is that after devaluation of the piaster in 1966, the interest costs of importers rose proportionately with the rate of inflation, as measured by the middle-class index. Although our procedures for estimating the b_2 costs are not totally satisfactory, the index applies to a very small component in the total cost and has only minor influence on the calculation of windfall gains.[12]

(4) n: This denotes the index of prices of imported goods. For 1962 through June 1965, we use the National Institute of Statistics price index of imported products. This is one of the component indexes in the general index of wholesale prices in Saigon. In July 1965, USAID began to compile a different index of imported products. Whereas the NIS index was computed from *quoted* import prices plus constant markup, the USAID index was computed from selling prices. When domestic prices were rising, the NIS index might have been an inadequate measure of prices paid by Vietnamese wholesalers, and therefore it is a poor index to use for the purpose of estimating windfall gains, particularly for the high inflationary period after mid-1965. The USAID index has two disadvantages: It applies only to CIP imports, and the list of items is small relative to the NIS index. Beginning in 1968, USAID broadened the list of imports and also included some non-CIP imports. With the larger and improved list, USAID started a new index. However, it is a hybrid between a wholesale price index and a retail price index, but it probably is the best of the three. Our index fuses together these three indexes into one continuous series.

(5) e: This is an index of export prices. During the period 1962–70, over 70 percent of the imports into Vietnam came from the United States, Japan, and Taiwan. Index e is a variably weighted index of export prices from these

three countries, as reported in *International Financial Statistics* (International Monetary Fund monthly), with weight determined as the ratio of each country's imports into Vietnam to the total imports from the three countries. We call it the "world" export index for convenience.

CHAPTER 9

The international value of the piaster

In this chapter we attempt to measure the value of the Vietnamese piaster, or dong (d),[1] for the period up to 1972, when, for all practical purposes, it was allowed to float to seek its market value. Specifically, "international value" means the price of the piaster in terms of dollars or its exchange ratio. A method for deriving an approximation for the market value is laid out, rationalized, and employed later to compute a series called the "approximate market clearing rate of exchange" for the period 1964–70. Our calculated exchange rate series is then compared with a reported black market rate series. For those periods in which a marked difference is observed, an explanation is sought. Both series are then subjected to a test of consistency that utilizes national income data. Finally, a judgment is made on how the two rates, along with another derived from national income accounts, might be fused together to establish one series, the dollar "value of the piaster." This series has already been used to translate piaster national income into its dollar equivalent, and it will be used subsequently in estimating the value of foreign aid to the Vietnamese economy.

9.1 The official exchange rate and misinformation

It is difficult to think of any major economic problem in wartime Vietnam that was not related in some way to the foreign exchange rate. Solutions and approaches to these problems were frequently limited because the Vietnamese government maintained a fixed exchange rate that grossly overvalued the piaster most of the time. Some consequences of this economic policy were a severe curtailment of exports, a higher rate of inflation than was necessary given the amount of U.S. aid, weakened incentives on the part of the GVN to limit expenditures and to raise revenues through taxation, probable misallocation of imported and domestic resources, misallocation between consumption and investment, and promotion of speculative or rent-seeking activity in the import sector at the expense of productive activity in the domestic production sector. The overvaluation of the piaster probably had no socially beneficial consequence.

If the consequences of the overvalued piaster were as alleged here, why, then, did the government stick to a fixed rate policy until 1972? We do not accept as an explanation that GVN officials were not aware of the adverse consequences mentioned earlier, for those officials had access to many foreigners well trained in economic analysis. One suspects that Vietnamese officials were more interested in maximizing the dollar value of foreign aid out of belief that the country needed this strategy to prosper in the short run. In any event, arguments that this policy adversely affected development do not seem to have been persuasive.

As pointed out in Chapter 7, a major short-run objective of U.S. aid was inflation control. The amount of aid required for this purpose was determined by a monetary gap calculation.[2] The gap that had to be filled by foreign aid to control inflation was a piaster gap, and the size of this gap measured in dollars depended on the foreign exchange rate selected. Because the amount of dollar aid in this system would be inversely related to the exchange rate, anyone who wanted to keep the dollar value of aid high would attempt to fix a low (piaster-for-dollar) exchange rate. Thus, it is easy to understand why the Vietnamese would argue for a low official foreign exchange rate. Why the Americans accepted such a formula for calculating required economic aid must be considered in the much broader context of the overall war effort.[3]

Setting an unrealistic exchange rate also conveyed misinformation that could have deceived U.S. lawmakers. As a condition for aid, U.S. senators wanted to know to what extent the Vietnamese were bearing the financial burden of their budget deficit, as compared with Americans. At a hearing before the Senate Foreign Relations Committee, Chairman William Fulbright probed Mr. David Bell, the AID administrator, on this question. By Mr. Bell's calculation, 24 billion piasters out of a budget of 55 billion was being financed out of aid. Senator Fulbright wanted to know if the 24 billion piasters included import taxes, which he thought ought to be considered a part of aid. Bell replied that Vietnamese import taxes should not be considered a part of aid because they were "a tax on the people of Vietnam and in no sense a tax on the people of the United States."[4]

In this interchange, the AID official unwittingly misrepresented the extent to which the Vietnamese people were bearing the financial burden of their budget. The exchange rate that underlay his calculation of 24/55 was arbitrary and bore little relation to real supply and demand factors that would legitimize its use as an economically meaningful conversion ratio. At the time of the hearings, the official exchange rate was 60 piasters per dollar, and so the $400 million in aid that the United States was giving Vietnam translated into 24 billion piasters. At that time, the average tariff rate was 25 piasters per dollar of imports. It is obvious that the Vietnamese people would have been equally well off if the official rate had been 85 piasters per dollar with no import taxes. But in that case the AID administrator would have reported that the United States was supplying 34/55 of the budget. Given the fact that the black market rate for dollars in Vietnam was 170 piasters per dollar, it is safe to assert that even an exchange rate of 85 to 1 would overvalue the piaster, implying that the calculated ratio of 34/55 also would have been too low. In any event, a proper calculation of burden sharing requires a realistic conversion rate. In its economic use, "burden" implies losing something, which the Vietnamese were not, by exporting to pay for imports.[5] This probably was Senator Fulbright's point.

9.2   Measures of the value of the piaster

There are several competing approaches for measuring the "true" value of the piaster during the war period. Two possibilities are considered here: (1) The black market rate for dollars is one candidate, and this measure has been used by some economists interested in the economy of South Vietnam (Smithies 1970; Pearsall and Petersen 1971), essentially in the absence of anything else to use. (2) A hypothetical "auction rate" is the second candidate. To calculate the auction rate, one would need to know the number of piasters that might have been collected if the U.S. dollars had been auctioned to all bidders rather than exchanged at the official rate to a limited number of licensed importers. The purchasing power parity approach is an obvious third possibility. Although this approach would be accepted by many economists as a valid measure of the value of the piaster, the data for computing it for Vietnam are unavailable, and therefore it will not be considered here.

9.2.1   Black market rate as a proxy

The reasoning for using the black market rate as the proper measure of the value of the piaster, evidently, is that it reflects preferences of both buyers and sellers for the two currencies involved. The trouble with this explanation is that it assumes that a black market is a free market, when in fact it might be affected by many factors that may limit its size and produce asymmetrical risks to buyers and sellers.

The black market for currency in Vietnam developed because the GVN prescribed how dollars were to be used and who could obtain them legally. With minor exceptions, only licensed importers had access to dollars. American servicemen and civilians supplied dollars to the black market in order to purchase goods and services on the local economy.[6] They used the black market because the rate of exchange there usually was much more advantageous than they could obtain legally at the exchange windows of U.S. installations. The buyers of dollars and suppliers of piasters on the black market were Vietnamese who, we assume, wanted to take their money out of the country for safekeeping and investment or to avoid depreciation caused by a very rapid domestic rate of inflation.

Theoretically, whether or not the black market rate is a good indication of the true value of local currency depends on both institutional and economic factors. The most important institutional factors are the intensity with which the government acts to curb black market activities and the penalty it imposes on apprehended violators. The probability of catching a violator is causally related to the first factor. The product of the probability of apprehension and the penalty is the expected cost of a violation. Importantly, the expected cost of violation may not be the same for buyers and sellers because the apprehension probabilities and/or the penalties may not be the same. Ordinarily, strict policing would tend to reduce both the supply of foreign currency and the demand for it. Although that would definitely affect the quantity of currencies exchanged in the black market, there might not be a price effect. The situation would be different if policing were asymmetrical, as it was in wartime Vietnam. The political situation there made it unlikely that the government would attempt to find or punish an American violator with the same intensity that it would seek out and punish a local citizen. Consider the probable punishment as an example. Suppose that the expected punishment for an American civilian caught supplying dollars was deportation to the United States, but that the Vietnamese violator expected to be sentenced to a jail term or worse if caught. In this case, the expected penalty would appear to be much greater on the demand side (buyers of dollars) than on the supply side, and the black market price for dollars would be relatively low. Of course, under opposite conditions, the black market price for the dollar would be relatively high.

To decide analytically if the black market rate was an adequate measure of the true exchange rate, one needs to know also who used the market and for what purpose. If the black market were used by Vietnamese *solely* to acquire dollars for capital flight, so that there were zero substitutability for capital flight and importing dollars, then the black market rate would be irrelevant for the purpose of estimating the value of imported goods. In that case the goods and financial markets would be completely separate, and supply and demand factors in each would determine the foreign exchange rate for legal trade activity on the one hand and the financial black market rate on the other.

The result would be different if licensed importers of goods used the black market as an adjunct to legal purchases of foreign exchange in order to import amounts beyond the licensed authorization, or if they used importing as a cover for capital flight. Underinvoicing in order to import more than the licensed amount would be profitable, theoretically, whenever the official exchange rate plus the tariff rate exceeded the black market rate.[7] The mechanics are the following: An importer takes out a license to import one dollar's worth of some commodity. He enters into an agreement with an exporter to bill him at the rate of eighty cents per dollar's worth (or some other amount below one dollar). The exporter sends 1.2 units at a stated total cost of one dollar. The importer pays the official exchange rate plus tariff for one dollar's worth and procures the other twenty cents he owes the exporter on the black market at a price cheaper than the *effective exchange rate*, defined as the official exchange rate plus all import taxes. Of course, the importer would like to buy all of his foreign exchange on the black market, but would not do so because he needs the official foreign exchange purchase receipt to validate the importing activity. Without this receipt, the goods might be confiscated on arrival, and the importer might be punished. It is evident that the temptation to underinvoice varies directly with the difference between the *effective exchange rate* and the black market rate. The act of underinvoicing will tend to reduce the difference between the *effective exchange rate* and the black market rate.

Overinvoicing is motivated by a desire for capital flight. In this case the importer arranges to have the exporter certify a higher price than the actual one. To pay this fictitiously high price, an importer will take out a license allowing him to purchase more foreign exchange than necessary to import some good. When the exporter is paid the fictitious price in foreign exchange, he reimburses the importer's agent for the difference, which is deposited in a foreign bank. Theoretically, overinvoicing will occur whenever the black market rate is higher than the *effective exchange rate*, and it will tend to pull the black market rate down because it reduces demand for foreign exchange on the black market.

Overinvoicing and underinvoicing can occur simultaneously whenever there is a relatively large spread in tariff rates. This situation allows some importers to underinvoice on goods that carry high tariff rates, whereas others who prefer capital flight might overinvoice on goods that carry low tariff rates. The conditions in wartime Vietnam were ripe for both of these operations. To illustrate this point it is useful to allude to the tariff schedule in effect from October 1969 to June 1970. The legal tariff rate on fertilizer was zero, and only 8 piasters per dollar on textile raw materials (as a group average), but it averaged 306 piasters per dollar on motor vehicles. There were additional levies or perequation taxes of 20 piasters per dollar on textile raw materials and 60 piasters per dollar on vehicles. Thus, at that time, when the official rate was 118 piasters per dollar, the *effective (legal) exchange rate* for textile raw materials was 146 piasters per dollar, and that for vehicles was 484 piasters per dollar. (Of course, the range for specific items was much broader.) During the same period, the currency black market averaged 355 piasters per dollar. Although conditions seem to have been ideal for overinvoicing and underinvoicing, one should not jump to the conclusion that these activities were, in fact, occurring on any grand scale. The point is that conditions in wartime Vietnam were conducive to overinvoicing and underinvoicing, and therefore the financial black market and the legal import market probably were connected to some extent. Thus, the assumption that the black market rate is a reasonable first approximation to the true exchange rate, given the actual situation of wartime Vietnam, has some merit.

9.2.2   A measure based on a hypothetical exchange auction

We now propose a mental experiment in order to justify the auction method of calculating the value of the piaster. This experiment is suggestive of a method for calculating an exchange rate to be called the *approximate market clearing rate* (AMCR).

Suppose that there were no official fixed exchange rate in Vietnam during the war, but rather the dollars accruing to the government through U.S. aid had been auctioned off to the highest bidder. What piaster price would Vietnamese importers have been willing to pay for those dollars? Or suppose that the government maintained a complete monopoly on importing goods and sold the goods in blocks to the highest bidder. How much would wholesalers have been willing to pay for the goods? Either price could be used properly to value imports, because, in a gross kind of way, the price would be set by conditions of supply and demand. In this sense, the foreign exchange auction is analytically equivalent to the mechanism of flexible exchange rates.

Suppose the Vietnamese had abolished customs duties on imports and instituted a system of multiple exchange rates, different rates on different items. In that hypothetical state, what rates would importers have been willing to pay for the purpose of obtaining import licenses in various commodity lines? If the government had known the relevant demand elasticities, it could have established multiple rates at which importers would have purchased all the available foreign exchange. Those rates would have just cleared the market for the various commodities.

After June 1966, many, if not most, goods were priced to the importer in a multiple-tier system. To obtain a dollar, the importer paid the official exchange rate, the economic consolidation surtax, a perequation tax, customs (and austerity) duties, and sometimes a "special" perequation tax. For the moment, assume that importers had no way of avoiding payment of these taxes. (This implies that no difference existed between the *effective exchange rate* and the *effective legal exchange rate*.) Had the government consolidated all components into one composite payment, call it the effective legal exchange rate, would importers' demand for commodities have fallen? The obvious answer is no, because under the assumed conditions, importers would have been paying the composite rate all along, in piecemeal fashion. If foreign exchange were not rationed, importers might have desired to purchase additional dollars at the effective legal exchange rate, but it is not likely that they would ever purchase less under the hypothesized condition.

The composite rate method allows one to calculate a lower bound on the value of imports. The basic rationale for this method is that a free exchange rate system unencumbered by tariffs and other add-ons would produce, on balance,[8] a volume of imports at least equal to that under the existing system.

Another relevant question arises: Would the government have been able to raise the composite rate without causing the volume of imports to decrease? The answer to this question depends on whether or not importers were earning any excess profits. If there were excess profits from importing, theoretically the government would have been able to tax the excesses without reducing the volume of imports.[9] In any event, the value of imports to the importers would be their value at the composite rate plus excess profits. At this price the government would have been able to auction off all the foreign exchange it actually sold; that is, this price would have just cleared the market, and it is called the *market clearing rate* of exchange. Where conditions are not so clear, it can be called the *approximate market clearing rate*, the designation chosen here.

In the mental experiment, it has been assumed that importers actually paid the official rate plus all legal taxes. It was commonly believed, in contrast, that there was considerable avoidance of customs duties over most of the period. For most of the period, actual customs collections were considerably less than those implied by the legal tariff schedule. To properly consider this source of error, it is necessary to assume that the composite rate would include the actual customs collection rate. Thus, the *effective legal exchange rate* must be replaced by the *effective exchange rate*. The calculations that follow use an implicit effective exchange rate derived by dividing total *actual* piasters collected from selling foreign exchange by the dollar value of commercial imports.[10]

9.3   The approximate market clearing rate, 1963–70

The foregoing discussion suggests that a series of the approximate market clearing rate can be constructed from the following elements: the official foreign exchange rate (OFX) measured in piasters per dollar, all import taxes (MT) measured in piasters per dollar, and windfall gains from importing (R) measured the same way. Recall that the effective exchange rate (EFX) is given as

$$EFX = OFX + MT$$

Table 9.1. *Approximate market clearing rate, 1962–70*

Period	Effective exchange rate	Windfall gains per dollar	Approximate market clearing rate
1962–3	78.3	—[a]	78.3
1964	81.4	−0.6	80.3
1965	77.9	15.6	93.5
1966	139.2	5.7	144.9
1967	168.8	20.5	189.3
1968	173.8	27.3	201.1
1969	196.8	45.0	241.8
1970	267.5	146.9	414.4

[a]By assumption, there were no windfall gains during this period.

The approximate market clearing rate is

$$AMCR = OFX + MT + R$$

or

$$AMCR = EFX + R$$

Insofar as Vietnamese importers actually paid the effective exchange rate to conduct their enterprises, AMCR could not be below EFX unless R were negative. This could not happen out of free choice by the importers, but it was possible as a result of the government imposing retroactive rules such as was done when the piaster was devalued in 1966. The calculation of windfall gains was discussed in the previous chapter. All that remains to be done to derive the approximate market clearing rate is to add those to the effective exchange rate, as shown in Table 8.2 and reproduced in Table 9.1.

To gain some overall idea of the extent to which some official Vietnamese statistics are distorted by using the official exchange rate of the piaster, the reader need only compare the figures derived in Table 9.1 with the official rate of d35 per dollar from 1961 through July 1966[11] and d80 per dollar from August 1966 to October 1967. The surtax of d38 per dollar was absorbed into the official rate in October 1967; so the rate became d118 per dollar, and it remained there until March 1972, when all pretense to a fixed rate was removed.[12]

9.4 The black market rate and the market clearing rate[13]

During the period to which the estimates in Table 9.1 apply, the official policy of the Vietnamese government was to limit the sale of foreign exchange to direct importing activities. Official sale of dollars for nonimporting activities was limited to a few minor purposes, such as financing the education of students in foreign countries and traveling expenses of businessmen (Beazer 1970, p. 2). The only way a nonlicensed importer or someone interested in investing abroad could obtain dollars was in the black market.

Given efficient markets, two prices for the same good cannot exist side by side. With respect to the value of the piaster in two markets – legal and illegal – any difference would not be permanent so long as arbitrage were possible. Thus, in a situation permitting arbitrage, any divergence between the calculated market clearing rate and the black market rate could be explained only by measurement errors. Certain implications follow from a comparison of the two rates:

1. If the two rates are close and move together, this supports the efficient market hypothesis in the case of wartime Vietnam.
2. If one believes that some scope for arbitrage existed and accepts the efficient market theory, then an observed close association between the two rates is supportive of the method used in computing the market clearing rate.

Figure 9.1 shows the relationship between the calculated market clearing rate and the black market rate. The numbers of observations are confined to annual averages, because using shorter periods increases the probable distortion in the computed values due to timing considerations. The general pattern that emerges is quite clear: Before 1967, the black market rate was considerably above the market clearing rate. Starting in 1967, the two rates are close together, remarkably so, given the crudeness of the raw data and the procedure used to estimate the market clearing rate.

A relatively simple explanation of why the black market rate was higher than the market clearing rate before 1967 and why the ratios changed as they did can be advanced by introducing political uncertainty and opportunity for arbitrage as explanatory variables. It was asserted previously that arbitrage would wipe out price differences. Whenever the black market rate was above the market clearing rate, it would have been advantageous for Vietnamese importers to buy dollars at the official rate of exchange and sell them on the black market, driving the black market rate in the direction of the official rate. In fact, there was only limited scope for this kind of direct arbitrage through 1965. Most of the goods that entered Vietnam were financed through the Commercial Import Program, with fairly tight auditing, and a relatively small percentage was financed through a Vietnamese government program (GVN financing), with fairly loose auditing. CIP financing required that the importer satisfy the Agency for International Development in Saigon (USAID) concerning the ''need'' for the import and then find an American exporter, who had to be certified by the agency's Washington office (AID Washington).

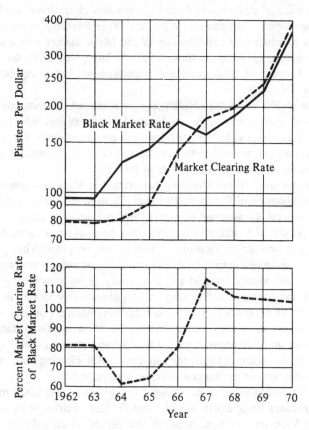

Figure 9.1. Black market rate compared with market clearing rate.

On certification that the goods were shipped, AID Washington would pay the exporter in dollars, and on receipt of the goods, the importer would pay the GVN the piaster price at the official rate plus various taxes (the effective rate of exchange). Given this procedure of double checks, arbitrage would require that a Vietnamese and an American exporter act jointly. Although arbitrage could be achieved in this way, the institutional constraints were severe, and to overcome them would require a learning process of some duration. Under GVN financing, the importer could make an agreement with an exporter in, say, Japan, Taiwan, or Hong Kong, who could hardly be checked in detail by the Vietnamese government. Thus, under the GVN financing procedure, which imposed much less severe constraints than the CIP procedure, the opportunity to profit from arbitrage through overinvoicing and underinvoicing would be more apparent. The learning process would be shorter and the risk of engaging in illegal deals reduced, and the practice of arbitrage would be more fully developed. Accordingly, under the GVN financing system, one would expect to observe a convergence of the black market rate and the market clearing rate to some common level. At any given time, the rates might differ, because of disruptions and imperfections, but in equilibrium they would be the same.

Uncertainty would affect the convergence as it altered the motivation of those buyers of dollars who were not licensed importers and who had no access to legal exchanges. In the period we are concerned with, two major causes of uncertainty can be identified as changes or expected changes in the political situation and changes in the rate of inflation.

In the unstable political environment that existed in Vietnam starting just before the assassination of President Ngo Dinh Diem in November 1963 and lasting until General Ky assumed power in 1965, we assume that there were a number of people of wealth with much to lose by a takeover either by the Viet Cong or by a new South Vietnamese government. People who had gained through favoritism in one regime could fall into disfavor under a new regime. These people, we assume, would think seriously about transferring their wealth out of the country, and lacking any legitimate way to buy dollars, they would turn to the black market. Under this assumption, political uncertainty would cause an increase in the demand for black market dollars and drive their price up. One consequence of this uncertainty would be a divergence between the black market rate and the market clearing rate, which depends critically on the unchanged effective exchange rate.

Inflation also would increase the demand for dollars on the black market and, all other things being equal, would cause the black market price to rise. In the actual Vietnam situation, inflation also served as an inducement to increase the supply of dollars on the black market as well as to increase the demand. The reason is that the principal suppliers of dollars, Americans, were required to buy piasters at a fixed "accommodation" rate. Understandably, as the spread between the black market rate and the accommodation rate widened, more and more Americans would resort to the black market as a source of piasters. There is no a priori way of knowing how the black market rate would respond on balance to both increased supply and demand without being able to quantify the increases. Regarding the effect of inflation on convergence, there is an additional complication. Domestic inflation would cause the price of imports to rise if their supplies were restricted (the Vietnam case), and this would increase windfalls from importing. The market clearing rate, as a consequence, would rise. That would tend to promote convergence whenever the market clearing rate was below the black market rate and promote divergence whenever the market clearing rate was above the black market rate, all other things being equal.

Table 9.2. *Market clearing rate/black market rate ratio and explanatory information*

Year	(1) Market clearing rate/ black market rate	(2) Black market rate minus market clear- ing rate	(3) Percentage GVN financing	(4) Political situation[a]
1962	0.81	20.6	0.29	S
1963	0.81	20.6	0.27	U
1964	0.62	49.9	0.32	U
1965	0.64	52.7	0.24	U
1966	0.80	35.2	0.35	S
1967	1.16	−25.4	0.54	S
1968	1.06	−12.1	0.61	S
1969	1.06	−13.3	0.56	S
1970	1.05	−21.4	0.52	S

[a]S denotes a relatively stable political situation; U denotes an unstable political situation.

Information on two of the factors discussed earlier is given in Table 9.2. This information can be used in a qualitative way to explain the behavior of the ratio curve plotted in the lower half of Figure 9.1. Column 3 shows the percentage of total imports financed through the GVN system. The percentage is intended to serve as a proxy measure for the institutional constraint against freedom to arbitrage. Low values indicate severe restrictions, and higher values indicate more freedom to arbitrage, because, as stated earlier, the GVN system was more amenable to overinvoicing and underinvoicing than the AID-financed CIP. Without some freedom to arbitrage, one should not necessarily expect the black market rate and the market clearing rate to be the same. Based on the foregoing discussion, one would expect a positive correlation between the ratios in column 1 and those in column 3. The symbols in column 4 are intended to convey some idea about political stability. U denotes an unstable political situation; in comparison with that, S denotes stability. If one or more forcible changes of government took place during a year, the U symbol is entered. For those years in which there were no changes, or if a change was not due to a coup d'etat, such as, for example, the nominal change of government in 1967 when Nguyen Van Thieu replaced Nguyen Cao Ky as president, a symbol of S is entered.

In 1962, the low GVN financing percentage implies a limited scope for arbitrage. The 25 percent premium in the black market rate was not easily reducible. In the following year there was a change for the worse in the political situation. The black market rate started to move upward in the last half of the year, though this is not shown in the table. The widening between the two rates in 1962–5, on our theory, was due to the very frequent changes of government that stimulated interest in capital flight. In 1966, the percent of total imports accounted for by GVN financing began to rise, opening up opportunities for arbitrage, and the political situation became more stable, easing demand pressure on the black market. Also, in mid–1965, prices began to rise rapidly, exerting some upward pressure on the market clearing rate. After 1967, all of the factors favored an equalization of the two rates.[14]

This briefly sketched history lends support to the following propositions:

1. Before 1967, conditions were such in Vietnam to caution against using the black market as a general measure of the value of the piaster.
2. After 1967, the closeness of the market clearing rate and the black market rate serves to build confidence in either one as an indicator of the value of the piaster under the assumption of efficient markets.
3. If one accepts, a priori, the method and data used to compute the market clearing rate, the closeness of this rate and the black market rate is supportive of the efficient markets hypothesis.
4. Because none of the evidence gives cause for rejecting the validity of the market clearing rate, taken over the entire 1962–70 period, it can be more readily justified as an indicator of the overall value of the piaster than the black market rate.

The discussion in this section does not *prove* that either rate is a *true* indicator of the value of the piaster, nor was it intended to do that. The intent is much more modest – simply to build confidence for the acceptance of the market clearing rate as a reasonable proxy for the unknown *true* value of the piaster over the period. This does not mean that each value in the series is equally acceptable as any other. Yet another test is suggested in the next section of this chapter to build more confidence.

9.5   A test of consistency using national income data

In the foregoing discussion, an explanation was advanced regarding why the black market rate and the market clearing rate moved closely together after 1967. Both rates appear to be reasonable candidates as measures of the true value of the piaster. But the fact that two logically appealing measures tend to support each other is no foolproof evidence that either is correct. To obtain an estimate of the market clearing rate, many assumptions were made, and data of unknown reliability had to be used. This is particularly true of the data used to estimate the market clearing rate for 1970, as will be seen later.

In this section we shall use the national income data in such a way as to question the validity of the market clearing rate series. Annual changes in

Table 9.3. *Indexes of net domestic product in constant U.S. dollars and constant piasters, 1962–72 (1967 = 100)*

Year	Indexes of NDP in constant dollars based on		Index of NDP in constant piasters
	Black market rate series	Market clearing rate series	
1962–3	53.6	76.7	76.3
1964	46.2	86.1	86.0
1965	52.2	94.3	89.7
1966	62.5	89.1	94.6
1967	100.0	100.0	100.0
1968	90.3	98.0	97.4
1969	102.4	111.7	110.4
1970	80.4	88.1	123.2
1971	100.3		124.4
1972	103.1		118.3

real net national product were discussed in much detail in Chapter 3. Any series that purports to show the value of the piaster in terms of dollars must pass, at least, in a rough sort of way, the following test: Movements in the real value of net domestic product measured in dollars must show a reasonable correspondence with movements measured in piasters. This test is based on the assumption that the series on real NDP measured in piasters is more reliable than any series of the value of the piaster in terms of dollars.

Formally, the proposed test proceeds in three stages: (1) Translate nominal piaster income into dollar equivalent income using some conversion ratio such as the market clearing rate and the black market rate. (2) Deflate the dollar equivalent series by a U.S. deflator to obtain a series of real income measured in dollars. (3) Compare the real dollar equivalent income series in an indexed form with an index of the real piaster series taken from Vietnamese national income accounts. Correspondence between the derived series lends support to the selected piaster value series chosen to translate piaster national income into dollar value of national income. Noncorrespondence signals that there is an inconsistency between the national income data and the piaster value data. Three series are compared in Table 9.3.

Recall that 1968, the year of the Communist Tet offensive, and 1972, the year of their Easter offensive, were periods of recession in Vietnam. In between those years, real national income grew. This history is shown in the index of NDP in constant piasters. Note that the index of real dollar values of NDP derived from the market clearing rate shows a close correspondence with the constant piaster series up until 1970. In 1970, both dollar value series indicate a major recession in South Vietnam, despite the fact that strong growth, rather than recession, occurred that year. Consistency demands the verdict that neither the calculated market clearing rate nor the black market rate is a satisfactory measure of the international value of the piaster in 1970.

Analysis of the figures in Table 9.3 indicates that the black market rate appears to be an unreliable measure of the foreign exchange rate up to 1967. This conclusion was reached from a different argument in Section 9.4. Note from the table that the real NDP implied in the black market rate is lower in 1964 and 1965 than in 1962–3. To the contrary, the Vietnamese national income accounts show that it was significantly higher in 1964 and 1965 than in the earlier period. Further, according to the black market series, NDP took a huge jump in 1967, and a jump of the indicated size is not consistent with the other data, even approximately.

From 1971 on, it is not feasible to calculate a market clearing rate. Given similar movements between the black market rate and the market clearing rate from 1967 to 1970, it is assumed that the former will serve as a reasonable measure of the value of the piaster from that time. Note that the index of NDP based on the black market rate increased in 1972, whereas income actually declined that year. However, a similar dollar-denominated index computed from GNP data, rather than NDP, shows a drop in 1972. Thus, in our judgment, whereas national income data do not positively support use of the black market rate series, neither do they call for decisively rejecting it after 1967, with the exception of 1970.

Just as it is possible to uncover inconsistencies in the estimate of the value of the piaster by analyzing national income data, working in a reverse manner it is possible to construct a series on the foreign exchange rate using national income data as a source. Let $y'(t)$ be real income in piasters for the period t (prime indicates piaster magnitudes), and let $y^*(t)$ be real income in dollars for the period t (asterisk indicates dollar magnitudes). Consistency requires that an index of piaster real income be the same as an index of real dollar income, or that

$$y'(t)/y'(0) = y^*(t)/y^*(0) \tag{9.1}$$

Define the international value of the piaster (VOP), or free foreign exchange rate, as the relationship between nominal piaster income and nominal dollar income,

$$VOP(t) = Y'(t)/Y^*(t) \tag{9.2}$$

where Y' is nominal piaster income and Y^* is nominal dollar income. From (9.1) and (9.2) it is possible to compute an index of the value of the piaster with the equation[15]

$$VOP(t) = [P'(t)/P^*(t)]VOP(0) \tag{9.3}$$

Table 9.4. *Three estimates of the international value of the piaster (piasters per dollar)*

Year	Black market rate	Market clearing rate	Series based on NDP accounts
1962-3	96.9	78.3	78.3[a]
1964	130.3	80.8	80.7
1965	146.2	93.5	89.5
1966	180.1	145.9	121.1
1967	163.9	189.3	169.1
1968	189.0	201.1	183.2
1969	228.5	241.8	228.3
1970	393.0	414.1	287.7
1971	387.9		326.0
1972	439.2		392.3

[a]This figure is assumed to be the same as the market clearing rate.

where P' is the Vietnamese price index and P^* is the American price index.

A third series using equation (9.3) is shown along with the black market rate and the market clearing rate in Table 9.4. The key to the new series is the implicit definition of the value of the piaster as VOP $= Y'/Y^*$. This definition focuses attention on the ratio of prices in the two countries, when, actually, the demand and supply of foreign currencies depend on the prices of traded goods and services rather than all goods and services. Thus, there is no persuasive reason for accepting the new series over the black market rate or market clearing series. The fact that the series in column 3 advances faster than the other two could mean that the ratio of Vietnamese general prices to U.S. general prices rose faster than a like ratio pertaining only to tradeables (by some nonconventional definition). It could mean simply that the Vietnamese NDP accounts have been improperly deflated. Or it could mean a number of other things. Despite serious misgivings about this series derived from national income data, it is supportive of an argument to accept the market clearing rate up to 1970 and to reject both the market clearing rate and the black market rate for 1970.

9.6 International value of the piaster, 1962–74

The task at hand is to piece together two series on the dollar value of the piaster in a manner that is consistent with the arguments advanced earlier. Those arguments are summarized in the following statements:

1. The black market rate as an indicator of the international value of

Table 9.5. *International value of the piaster and other series, 1955–74[a]*
(piasters per dollar)

Year	(1) Official exchange rate	(2) Black market rate	(3) Market clearing rate	(4) NDP data rate	(5) International value of piaster
1955	35				
1956	35				
1957	35	88			
1958	35	81			
1959	35	82			
1960	35	91			
1961	35	99			
1962	60	97	78	78	78
1963	60	97	78	78	78
1964	60	131	81	81	81
1965	60	146	94	90	94
1966	104[b]	180	145	121	145
1967	118	164	189	169	189
1968	118	189	201	183	201
1969	118	229	242	228	229
1970	118	393	414	288	325
1971	118	388		326	388
1972	356[c] 435[d]	439		392	439
1973	494	531			531
1974	633	641[e]			641

[a]All figures are annual averages. Data sources:
(1) 1955–65, International Monetary Fund (monthly, various issues); 1966–73, AID (1974b; p. 26); 1974, AID-VN (monthly, Feb. 1975, p. 3).
(2) 1957–65, AID-VN (annual, no. 9, p. 43); 1966–72, VN-NIS (annual, 1972, Table 199); 1973, AID (1974b, p. 9, "U.S. 10 Green"); 1974, AID-VN (monthly, Feb. 1975, p. 3, "U.S. 10 Green").
(3) and (4)   Table 9.4.
(5)   See text.
[b]Three months at d60/$, and nine months at d118/$.
[c]Full-year average. First three months at d118/$.
[d]Average for last nine months.
[e]This rate is d5/$ less than the black market rate based on $100 transactions. Other data in this table pertain to black market rates based on $10 transactions, which, on average, brought d5/$ less than the larger transactions.

the piaster is indefensible up to 1968. A good case can be made for accepting the black market rate as an indicator for the international value of the piaster from 1968 to 1974, with the single exception of 1970, for which period it is clearly inconsistent with an implied rate based on national income data.

2. A good case can be made for using the calculated market clearing rate as an indicator of the international value of the piaster for the period 1962–9. It is consistent with the implied series based on national income data for that period and with the black market rate for the period 1967–70.

Our preferred solution to the problem is to use the market clearing rate for 1962–8 and switch to the black market rate for 1969–74, with the exception of 1970. For 1970, an interpolated value is selected. The interpolation procedure uses the implicit rate based on national income data. The value of the piaster for 1970 is assumed to lie equiproportionately between the black market values for 1969 and 1971, as the 1970 figure for the series based on national accounts lies between its adjacent years. The value so computed, d325 per dollar, implies a very slight rise in the dollar value of real NDP in 1970 over 1969, and that is consistent, at least in direction of change, with actual events in South Vietnam.

Table 9.5 displays the fused series called the "international value of the piaster" measured in piasters per dollar. This table includes the contents of Table 9.4. The first column shows the average annual official exchange rate. On April 1, 1972, the government went off a fixed rate system, allowing the piaster to seek its free market level in orderly steps. The average "official" exchange rate for the last nine months in 1972 was d435 per dollar. Note how close the official and black market rates were from 1972 to the end of the war. It was not until December 1974, when there were threatening signs in South Vietnam, that the closeness between the black market rate and the official (controlled floating) rate vanished. In that month, the black market rate was about 20 percent above the official rate. There are no data available on the path of the black market rate over the final months of the war. This precludes pursuing the intriguing relationship between the black market rate and political uncertainty.

CHAPTER 10

Vietnam foreign assistance

The wartime economy of South Vietnam was foremost an *aid economy*. This relatively underdeveloped country could not possibly have met the demands of a long and destabilizing war out of its own resources, and the glue used to hold the country together was foreign aid. Foreign aid is a concept, like charity, with which almost everyone is familiar, but its meaning in the Vietnam situation is not clear. The reason is that the United States reserved some of what it reportedly gave to the Vietnamese for its own purposes, and whether or not this kind of "gift" should be called aid is a controversial issue. In this chapter we propose a concept of aid that is at variance with officially recorded statistics and attempt to measure it by that definition. In the next chapter we shall discuss the efficiency of aid in Vietnam public finance.

10.1   Defining aid

In discussing Vietnam aid, two kinds of problems arise: (1) the conceptual problem of specifying what aid is, and (2) the problem of accounting for aid, or measuring it. The following discussion will show that neither of these problems has a neat and definitive solution.

Among other things, aid can be considered as international charity. In giving charity, the donor presumably expects no reward other than the satisfaction gained from helping someone else. If this were the definition of aid, one would have to analyze the motives behind every international transfer to determine if the resource involved should be classified as charity (aid), and that would be an impossible task. Yet, Little and Clifford found it difficult to define aid in a reasonable way without considering the motives of the donor nation (1965, ch. 3). When financial assistance is given for the *pure* purpose of economic development, they define the transfer as aid. On the other hand, when the donor's main interest is in buying something, such as political support, they think the transfer ought to be treated as any purchase rather than aid; but such a definition invites trouble. For example, they concede that a transfer could count as aid even if the donor's main interest in financing *economic development* is a hope that the recipient nation will develop institutions and positions in world politics favorable to the donor. Thus, transfers that are *intended* to promote economic development should be classified as

192

aid regardless of any other motive of the giver. Unfortunately, the stress on intention renders it almost impossible to determine from data sources alone whether or not any particular international transfer should be classified as aid.

The motives behind U.S. economic assistance to Vietnam were discussed in Chapter 2. Some transfers were made for the purpose of helping the Vietnamese improve their material well-being, but it is evident that the dominating motive was to "buy something" in the sense of Little and Clifford. Inasmuch as the data do not permit one to disentangle these motives, it is not possible to ascertain what share of the total transfers ought to be considered as aid. A definition of aid that requires knowledge of underlying motives cannot be applied in the case of wartime Vietnam.

Charles Wolf, Jr., divided aid into three classes: economic, technical, and military support (1960, p. 190). His classification of aid depends on the sector in which counterpart funds are spent. Consider, for example, the case of PL 480 (Food for Peace) commodities given to the Vietnamese. By agreement between the American and Vietnamese governments, PL 480 counterpart funds were destined to support the military budget. Although Food for Peace commodities (rice, corn, cooking oil) were sold in the economic marketplace and generated local economic activity, the receipts from their sale directly supported the defense budget. By Wolf's definition, PL 480 aid would be considered as military support rather than economic aid. On the other hand, imports under the Commercial Import Program, which were hardly distinguishable from PL 480 commodities in terms of economic activity generated, would be considered as economic aid, because the counterpart funds derived from them were destined for general government support. For the purpose of analyzing the effect of aid on economic development and how the donor might control the distribution of aid to a country, a procedure for separating military and economic aid is of limited value. The reason is that the aid donor usually cannot determine how aid funds will be used so long as the recipient country has a domestic source of revenue. Because revenues are fungible, an underdeveloped country could easily augment its military budget with nondefense support funds by shifting local tax revenues from the civil budget to the defense budget. However, the earmarking of funds for military support does demonstrate the intention of the donor, and that revelation would disqualify these funds from counting as aid in the sense of Little and Clifford.

There is an additional problem in using the donor's intentions in the definition of aid. As was pointed out in Chapters 2 and 7, the major objective of nonmilitary aid to Vietnam was to guard against any political unrest due to destabilizing rates of inflation. U.S. intentions in giving aid had very little to do with economic development. Nevertheless, aid certainly was expected to promote favorable economic results, namely, price stabilization. Clearly, if price stabilization were the primary objective of U.S. economic support, one would find it very difficult to distinguish between the effects of CIP and PL 480 aid. The distinction between military and civil budgetary support is not valid in a context in which inflation control is a major objective of economic aid.

We do not find any of the distinctions made earlier to be very useful in classifying U.S. grants to Vietnam. Under the most restrictive definition of aid, the one requiring that the donor is not attempting to buy anything for himself, very few of the billions of dollars the United States gave Vietnam would be considered as aid. Under the broadest definition, namely, anything that has an impact on a major economic variable such as price, almost all transfers would be considered as aid. A satisfying definition of aid, after many years of study, remains elusive.

10.2   Four U.S. aid programs to Vietnam

Jacob Viner is reported to have quipped that "Economics is what economists do." No doubt, in the record books, aid is whatever bureaucrats choose to call it. With regard to wartime Vietnam, the bureaucrats were preponderantly American, and most of what they called aid was supplied under three institutionally defined programs. They were (1) the Commercial Import Program (often referred to as Commodity Import Program) or CIP, (2) Food for Peace (FFP), alternatively called PL 480 aid after the public law enacting it, and (3) Project Aid (PA). In Vietnam, there was a substantial fourth "program" that will not be found in the record books anywhere, but its omission would call into question the adequacy of any discussion on aid to Vietnam. We shall call the fourth source of economic aid the "piaster subsidy aid" program (PSA). Each source of aid will be discussed later. Figure 10.1 may be useful as an orientation. It indicates the manner in which dollars were turned into piasters and how and whether or not the funds were channeled through the Vietnamese budget to support military and civil end uses. Recalling Wolf's classification of aid, the figure implies that much of the American aid to Vietnam would be called military support rather than economic assistance. However, as an antiinflation measure, this distinction is not valid.

10.2.1   CIP aid

A major U.S. aid program to underdeveloped countries is known as the Commercial Import Program. The essential feature of this program is that the United States furnishes dollars to a recipient to finance the importation of U.S.-manufactured commodities. In the case of South Vietnam, the United States allowed 10 percent of the CIP funds to be spent for third-country purchases. In the process of deciding how much aid the United States would

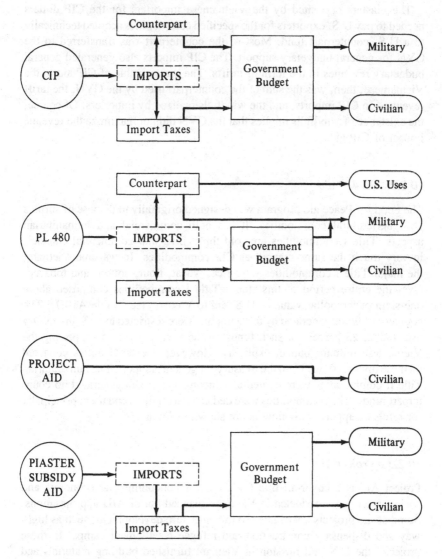

Figure 10.1. Sources and uses of aid.

grant to Vietnam, a definite CIP amount was fixed, usually in the range of one-third to two-thirds of the total aid package (see Table A10.1). CIP aid was broken down into separate commodity subclasses (such as iron and steel products, industrial machinery, chemicals) based on the ''needs'' of the economy as determined by U.S. commodity analysts.

The piasters deposited by the Vietnamese importers for the CIP dollars needed to pay U.S. exporters for the specified commodities accrued technically to a U.S. counterpart fund. Most of the counterpart was transferred to the GVN for general budgetary support. The CIP imports also generated general budgetary revenues in the form of tariffs. The piaster value of CIP aid to the Vietnamese, then, was the sum of the counterpart used by the GVN, the tariff revenues on CIP imports, and the windfalls realized by importers. Of course, the existence of windfalls implies that the GVN did not maximize the revenue impact of CIP aid.

10.2.2   PL 480 aid

The Food for Peace aid program was designed originally to dispose of surplus U.S. agricultural commodities. It has both commercial and humanitarian aspects. Title I commodities are sold through regular commercial channels in very much the same manner as CIP commodities. In wartime Vietnam, the major Title I commodities were rice, wheat, flour, cotton, and tobacco. Over the entire period of this study, Title I commodities composed about one-sixth of the dollar value of U.S. aid to Vietnam (see Table A10.1). The counterpart funds generated by these imports were restricted to U.S. in-country uses (about 23 percent of such funds on the average) and to supporting the Vietnamese military budget explicitly. However, the tariff duties collected on these imports flowed into the treasury for general support. The humanitarian Title II commodities were treated as noncommercial and generated no counterpart funds. The commodities were dedicated to civilian end uses, principally for refugee support. This flow is not shown in Figure 10.1.

10.2.3   Project Aid

Project Aid is a cover-all title for a host of noncommercial economic and social enterprises conducted in Vietnam financed out of AID appropriations. Some of the projects contributed to infrastructure development, such as highway and dispensary construction and refugee resettlement camps. In these projects, the U.S. aid mission in Vietnam furnished building materials and technical and supervisory services. Many of the rural development projects thought to be essential to general social development or "nation building," as it was called, were financed out of Project Aid. A very large part of the Project Aid total was used for "technical assistance" or, more exactly, to support the very large AID establishment in Vietnam. As shown in Table A10.4, there were over 2,000 people associated with the AID mission in the 1967–70 period. Technicians representing almost every imaginable activity were present or on call to Vietnam. Agricultural specialists, railway engineers, labor organizers, financial experts, programmers, health and educational personnel, political analysts, census statisticians, public administrators, and others were present in Vietnam to some degree. There was hardly a desk in the Vietnamese government that did not have an advisory desk on the American side. Project Aid generated no counterpart funds and therefore no revenues for the Vietnamese treasury in support of its budget.

10.2.4   Piaster subsidy aid

The U.S. Military Assistance Command (MACV), other U.S. agencies, and most of the U.S. military and civilian personnel serving in Vietnam gave economic aid to Vietnam as a result of U.S. acquiescence to subsidize the piaster. To support its widespread operations in Vietnam, MACV purchased billions in piasters to pay the thousands of Vietnamese it and its contractors employed. In 1971 alone, the MACV disbursing officer, acting for the entire U.S. presence, bought 74 billion piasters at a cost of over $403 million. Had those piasters been purchased at an approximate market clearing (or some realistic negotiated) rate, their cost in dollars would have been millions of dollars less than actually paid. This policy affected the purchasing power of American service personnel and civilians who bought piasters for their own use at official windows, in contrast to the rising numbers who patronized the currency black market. The "accommodation rate" paid for personal use was more favorable than the official rate, but still imposed a penalty. The sum of the penalties paid by official agencies and individuals we call "piaster subsidy aid" (PSA). By this procedure, it was not necessary for the U.S. Congress to appropriate as much "official aid" as the total thought to be necessary.

The dollars collected from GVN piaster sales (primarily) to Americans were used to finance imports not subject to USAID approval or regulations. Most of the goods imported under this "GVN-financed import program" originated in Japan and Taiwan, and they carried relatively high tariffs. PSA supported the Vietnamese budget via tariff revenues and National Bank of Vietnam noninflationary lending to the Vietnamese government.

10.3   Measures of foreign aid to Vietnam

10.3.1   Gross dollars transferred

The simplest measure of U.S. aid to Vietnam is the sum of the four programs briefly described. We call this measure *gross dollars transferred* by the United States. It is the dollar value of aid as recorded in U.S. sources plus the value of PSA.

PSA can be calculated as the "unearned" dollars received by the Vietnamese because of overvaluation of the piaster. Let r^* be the implicit piaster-per-dollar exchange rate used in piaster purchases by the United States; r is the appropriate market clearing rate, called AMCR in Chapter 9; r^*/r is the percentage of the market clearing rate at which transactions were made. This can be called the "earned" percentage of the total dollar purchases by the Vietnamese government. A value of $r^*/r = 1$ would mean that all piaster purchases took place at an exchange rate of 100 percent of the market clearing rate, and consequently the subsidy of the piaster would be zero. PSA can be calculated as $(1 - r^*/r)$DPP, where DPP is dollar value of piaster purchases. This simple procedure for calculating PSA is carried out in Table 10.1 for the period 1964–74. Before 1964, the values were negligible.

The measure of gross dollars transferred by year from the United States to Vietnam is shown in Table 10.2. The column headed by AID combines CIP and Project Aid. PL 480 includes both Title I and Title II. The amount of military assistance is also included in the table. The figures on military assistance include only military hardware, ammunition, and relatively minor items such as gear and clothing. Importantly, it excludes the billions of dollars spent on U.S. military operations in Vietnam, the millions spent on U.S. servicemen working on economic and pacification projects, and millions spent out of the Military Assistance Service Funded (MASF) account.

10.3.2   Net resources transferred

Another concept of foreign assistance is *net resources transferred*. In the simplest balance-of-payments statement, *net resources transferred* is equal to the deficit or surplus in goods and services in the current account. In the case of South Vietnam, where international capital flows, exclusive of foreign aid, and gold movements were negligible, the deficit on goods and services was compensated by foreign aid. Thus, the deficit on goods and services in the Vietnam case, which measures net resources transferred, is also a measure of foreign aid received on a current basis.

Unfortunately, one cannot adequately determine the amount of foreign aid received by Vietnam from a straight reading of the country's balance-of-payments accounts. The reason is that currency translations at the official exchange rate yield a biased estimate of net resources transferred. However, the balance-of-payments framework is useful for calculating net resources transferred. To make such a calculation, we assume that the dollar values of merchandise imports and exports as recorded in the balance-of-payments accounts are fairly accurate. We also assume that the imports of commercial services were negligible. To estimate net resources transferred, then, an estimate of the value of services exported is required.

Table 10.1. *Estimates of U.S. economic aid due to piaster subsidy, 1964–74[a]*

Year	(1) Piasters purchased (d billion)	(2) Piasters purchased ($ million)	(3) Implicit exchange rate (r^*) (d/$)	(4) Estimated market clearing rate (r) (d/$)	(5) r^*/r	(6) Earned exchange from piaster purchases ($ million)	(7) Subsidy on piaster purchases ($ million)
1964	2.5	42.2	59.2	81	0.73	30.7	11.5
1965		74.0	69.6[b]	94	0.74	54.8	19.2
1966		233.1	85.8[b]	145	0.59	137.5	95.6
1967	19.1	202.8	94.2	189	0.50	101.4	101.4
1968	36.7	310.8	118.1	201	0.59	183.4	127.4
1969	40.9	346.7	118.0	229	0.52	180.3	166.4
1970	41.2	318.3	129.4	325	0.40	127.3	191.0
1971	74.0	403.1	183.6	388	0.47	189.5	213.6
1972	77.6	228.9	339.0	439	0.77	176.3	52.6
1973	64.3	127.9	502.7	531	0.95	121.5	6.4
1974	n.a.	97.0[c]	n.a.		0.95[d]	92.2	4.9

[a] Data sources:

(1) and (2) AID (1974b, Oct.–Dec. 1973, p. 21).

(3) Column (1) ÷ column (2).

(4) From Table 9.5.

(5) Column (3) ÷ column (4).

(6) Column (2) × column (5).

(7) $(1 - r^*/r)$ × column (2), or column (2) − column (6).

[b] Assumes one-third of transactions made at average personnel accommodation rate (118d/$) and two-thirds at average official rate.

[c] This figure was taken from AID (1976, pt. A).

[d] Assumes the same as previous year.

Table 10.2. *U.S. economic and military assistance to South Vietnam by fiscal year, 1955–75 (million dollars)*

Fiscal year	AID[a]	PL 480	Piaster subsidy	Total economic aid	Military assistance	Total assistance
1955	320.2	2.2		322.4		322.4
1956	195.7	14.3		210.0	176.5	386.5
1957	259.4	22.8		282.2	119.8	402.0
1958	179.4	9.6		189.0	79.3	268.3
1959	200.9	6.5		207.4	52.4	259.8
1960	170.6	11.3		181.8	72.7	254.5
1961	140.5	11.5		152.0	71.0	223.0
1962	124.1	31.9		156.0	237.2	393.2
1963	143.3	52.6		195.9	275.9	471.8
1964	165.7	59.1	5.8	230.6	190.9	421.5
1965	225.0	49.9	15.4	290.3	318.6	608.9
1966	593.5	143.0	57.4	793.9	686.2	1,480.1
1967	494.4	73.7	98.5	666.6	662.5	1,329.1
1968	398.2	138.5	114.4	651.1	1,243.4	1,894.5
1969	314.2	99.4	146.9	560.5	1,534.0	2,094.5
1970	365.9	110.8	178.7	655.4	1,577.3	2,232.7
1971	387.7	188.0	202.3	778.0	1,945.6	2,723.6
1972	386.8	67.8	133.1	587.7	2,602.6	3,190.3
1973	313.3	188.3	29.5	531.2	3,349.4	3,880.6
1974	384.3	269.9	3.2	657.4	941.9	1,599.3
1975	191.3	49.6		240.9	625.1	866.0
Total	5,954.4	1,600.7	985.2	8,540.3	16,762.3	25,302.6

[a]Prior to 1962, U.S. economic aid was administered by the International Cooperation Administration (ICA). Data for AID (and ICA prior to 1962), PL 480, and military assistance are the revised figures as of May 1976. They were supplied to the author by the Statistical Reports Division, Office of Financial Management, U.S. Agency for International Development. Data for piaster subsidy are linear interpolations of figures in column (7) of Table 10.1, converting calendar-year data into appropriate fiscal years.

The value of services exported by Vietnam is the sum of two broad components. The first component is made up of the piasters purchased by MACV for its own operations and on behalf of all the American personnel who wished to spend on the local economy. Recall that the United States hired over 140,000 Vietnamese at one time, and there were over half a million Americans stationed in Vietnam in 1968–9 who spent, on average, ten to fifteen dollars per month on local goods and services. The second component involves American piaster expenditures from counterpart and trust funds set aside for American use. Thus, the value of services exported is the sum of the "earned" portion of piasters purchased by Americans (and other foreigners) plus U.S. agency spending out of set-aside funds.

As before, let DPP be dollars used to purchase piasters, r be the approximate market clearing rate of exchange, and r^* be the implicit exchange rate for piaster purchases. NRT(d) is net resources transferred measured in piasters, and E(d) is U.S. piasters spent out of counterpart and trust funds. Then,

$$\text{NRT(d)} = rM - r[X + (r^*/r)\text{DPP} + \text{E(d)}/r] \qquad (10.1)$$

M and X are merchandise imports and exports, respectively, as measured in dollars, and (r^*/r)DPP is the "earned" foreign exchange gained from selling piasters (i.e., the market value of the labor and other services purchased by Americans). E(d)/r is the dollar value of the services purchased by American agencies out of piaster set-aside funds. The expression in brackets is the dollar resource cost of goods and services exported by Vietnam. This value is translated into piasters when multiplied by r. The dollar-denominated equivalent of equation (10.1) is

$$\text{NRT(\$)} = M - X - (r^*/r)\text{DPP} - \text{E(d)}/r \qquad (10.2)$$

In equation (10.2), E(d)/r = E($). The piaster value of E is used in our calculations of NRT($) because that is the way the data were recorded. Our annual estimates of net resources transferred are given in Table 10.3. They are derived in a straightforward way from equation (10.2).

10.3.3 Total aid

Neither *gross dollars transferred* nor *net resources transferred*, as measured earlier, exhausts the total received by Vietnam. Aside from inaccuracies in the basic data, *gross dollars transferred* excludes, among other things, foreign aid from third countries, and *net resources transferred* excludes much infrastructure development by MACV that was not included in import statistics. *Gross dollars transferred* exceeded *net resources transferred* by 20 percent over the 1955–74 period. Subperiod comparisons are shown in Table 10.4. The differences in the overall subperiod averages were due to the following facts:

1. Some of the obligated funds (AID and PL 480) were not recorded in import statistics and therefore are excluded in our calculations of net resources transferred. For example, about one-third of AID funding to Vietnam supported Project Aid. Project Aid in the form of "technical assistance" or direct materials support and PL 480 Title II commodities for humanitarian (refugee) assistance were not counted in Vietnam import statistics.
2. Some of the obligated funds were set aside for U.S. uses in Vietnam. About 23 percent of PL 480 (Title I) aid was set aside, and about

Table 10.3. Calculation of net resources transferred to South Vietnam, 1955–74[a]

Year	(1) Merchandise imports [M] ($ million)	(2) Merchandise exports [X] ($ million)	(3) Export of services [(r*/r)DPP] ($ million)	(4) U.S. uses of PL 480 (d billion)	(5) U.S. uses trust fund (d billion)	(6) Value of piaster (d/$)	(7) Total U.S. uses [E(d)/r] ($ million)	(8) Net resources transferred ($ million)
1955	263.2	69.2			0.1	n.e.	1.4[b]	192.6
1956	217.6	45.1				n.e.		172.5
1957	288.7	80.5			0.1	n.e.	1.4[b]	206.8
1958	232.1	55.2				n.e.		176.9
1959	224.6	75.1		0.1		n.e.	1.4[b]	148.1
1960	240.3	85.5				n.e.		154.8
1961	272.6	71.7		0.2	0.1	n.e.	2.6	198.3
1962	268.7	48.7		0.1	0.1	78	2.6	217.4
1963	307.3	83.3		0.2	0.1	78	3.8	220.2
1964	325.5	48.8	30.7	0.4	0.1	81	6.2	239.8
1965	370.5	40.5	54.8	0.4	0.9	94	13.9	261.3
1966	656.6	25.2	137.5	0.5	1.6	146	14.4	479.5
1967	753.7	37.7	101.4	8.1	4.0	189	63.9	550.7
1968	668.7	41.5	183.4	3.7	4.0	201	38.3	405.5
1969	853.2	33.0	180.3	2.0	4.8	229	29.7	610.2
1970	778.8	12.7	127.3	3.0	4.7	318	24.2	614.6
1971	802.7	14.7	189.5	6.6	4.9	388	29.6	568.8
1972	742.9	23.8	176.3	8.9	2.5	439	26.0	516.8
1973	717.0	60.6	121.5	n.a.	n.a.		20.0[c]	514.9
1974	887.0	75.0	92.2	n.a.	n.a.		20.0[c]	699.8

[a] Data sources:

(1) and (2) 1955–60, VN-NIS (annual, 1964–5, Table 253). Data from this source were converted to dollar values using the exchange rate 35/1. The derived figures are consistent with trade data for 1957–60 published in AID-VN (annual, no. 9, Tables D3 and D12); for the 1961–72 period, AID-VN (annual, no. 12, Table II); for 1973–4, AID-VN (monthly, Feb. 1975, pp. 6–7). Imports are "earnings" rather than "payments."

(3) Column 6, Table 10.1.

(4) 1962–72, AID-VN (annual, no. 16, Table IV); 1955–61, AID-VN (annual, no. 9, Table H-5).

(5) 1962–72, AID-VN (annual, no. 16; Table IV); 1955–61, AID-VN (annual, no. 9, Table H-8).

(6) Table 9.5.

(7) [column (4) + column (5)]/column (6).

(8) Column (1) − column (2) − column (3) − column (7).

The data on merchandise imports and exports are not from consistent series. For the period 1961–72, the data are from balance-of-payments tabulations. In the earlier period, 1955–60, the data are customs reporting of import arrivals and exports. For most of the years prior to 1965 for which balance-of-payments data are available, there are only minor differences in the annual figures. After 1964, the differences are substantial in some years. Because balance-of-payments data presumably account for some noncommercial imports, the data are a better accounting of total imports. However, before 1961, noncommercial imports were relatively insignificant.

[b] Converted from piasters to dollars at the rate of 70 to 1.

[c] These are the author's guesses.

Table 10.4. *Annual average amount of aid from the United States by selected periods*

Aid defined as	Annual average for period ($ million)			
	1955–60	1961–4	1965–71	1972–4
Net resources transferred	175.1	218.9	498.2	577.4
Gross dollars transferred*a*	217.9	200.9	649.2	574.4
Military assistance*a*	89.4	224.5	1,301.4	1,968.4
	As percentage of gross national product*b*			
Net resources transferred	17	17	24	20
Gross dollars transferred	21	16	32	19
Military assistance	9	18	63	67

*a*These calculations were made by using one-half the fiscal-year entries in Table 10.2 for the beginning and terminal years of the periods indicated.

*b*Average annual GNP in dollars calculated from data in Table A3.5. Average dollar values in GNP in billions were 1.05, 1.27, 2.06, and 2.95 for the periods 1955–60, 1961–4, 1965–71, and 1972–4, respectively.

11 percent of CIP counterpart went into the trust fund to support USAID and U.S. embassy local currency needs. These funds were a part of *gross dollars transferred*, but are not included in *net resources transferred*.

3. Foreign aid from other countries was included in imports in some instances and therefore in *net resources transferred*, but obviously not in *gross dollars transferred*.

The two major omissions from gross dollars transferred are non-U.S. aid and U.S. military expenditures in support of Vietnam infrastructure. In the 1960–72 period, non-U.S. aid was $231 million. Contributions from various countries were as follows: Japan, $72 million; France, $57 million; Germany, $53 million; other countries, $49 million. In addition, South Vietnam received $23 million from the Asian Development Bank and various United Nations activities (AID 1974, p. 49).

The other major omission from gross dollars transferred is the aid South Vietnam received from the United States but not provided for under the Foreign Assistance Act. With funds appropriated for the U.S. military budget, much infrastructure development in South Vietnam was completed during the war. A previous study undertaken at the Institute for Defense Analyses estimated from available sources that expenditures on road construction were more than $400 million as of January 1971. Harbor and coastal improvements performed out of U.S. military funds cost about $166 million, and airfield construction cost $190 million (Beazer et al. 1972, p. 24). There was no estimate available on the cost of military communications systems. Investment in infrastructure not included in gross dollars transferred probably exceeded $1 billion. Most of this aid, and certainly the investments in roads, port facilities, and some airport construction, could easily be considered as economic development assistance. In addition to this visible infrastructure investment, MACV personnel performed many services in the form of technical support. The U.S. military provided advisors in many areas of development, particularly at the district and provincial levels.

Including all aid sources – aid provided under the U.S. Foreign Assistance Act and Mutual Security Act, aid provided directly and indirectly with U.S. military funds, and that from other countries – South Vietnam received close to $10 billion of economic aid over the twenty-year period. By this "gross resource" measure, the amount of aid supplied would be above thirty-one dollars per person per year, on average, or 25–30 percent of South Vietnam's measured GNP. By contrast, Jordan, another war-torn country in the 1960s, received aid in the amount of 19 percent of its GDP. Israel received 10 percent of its GDP for the same decade, and the U.S. "client nations" South Korea and Taiwan received 8 and 5 percent, respectively (Papanek, Jakubiak, and Levine 1969).[1]

10.4 The real value of aid

Whatever hopes the people of Vietnam had regarding the survival of their nation, they sank markedly in the last several years of the war. The sagging morale of Vietnam's armed forces and its people has been reported admirably in Snepp's book *A Decent Interval* (1977).[2] Officials in the Nixon administration were constantly frustrated by U.S. congressional actions to cut back on military aid to the country. Less well known is the fact that economic aid in real terms was drastically cut back in the last few years of the war. Attempted Vietnamization of the economy coupled with fading support by the American public made the Vietnam outcome inevitable.

The real value of aid measured as real net resources transferred is displayed in Table 10.5. After 1969, there was a steady decline in aid to about 50 percent of its highest level. This decline was due to rapid rises in the prices of Vietnamese imports (shown in Table A4.7) rather than a decline in the nominal dollar value of aid received. Prices of Vietnamese imports more than doubled from 1969 to 1974, while the dollar measure of aid rose slightly. However, the real GNP of Vietnam was higher in 1974 than in 1969. Thus, the real value of aid as a percentage of GNP fell faster than the real value of aid. As a percentage of GNP, the real value of aid fell from 36 percent in

Table 10.5. *Real net resources transferred, 1956–74ᵃ (million dollars)*

Year	(1) Real net resources	(2) Real import support	(3) Real net resources as percentage of GNP
1956	150.6		16.9
1957	191.5		21.2
1958	171.7		17.5
1959	143.8		13.4
1960	148.8		13.4
1961	194.4		17.5
1962	217.4		18.1
1963	209.7		17.0
1964	226.2	176.4	16.8
1965	248.9	301.9	16.9
1966	456.7	792.5	30.9
1967	519.5	498.0	34.5
1968	380.0	529.2	26.4
1969	544.8	491.5	36.3
1970	516.5	541.5	32.3
1971	462.5	685.8	28.2
1972	377.2	423.6	23.0
1973	279.8	284.0	17.0
1974	249.0	238.7	15.1

ᵃData sources:
(1) Column (8), Table 10.3, divided by column (3), table A4.7.
(2) Basic data for this column taken from AID (1976, pt. A, Table 2). Data in source table were divided by 1.06 to move the base year from 1964 to 1962. "Import support" is defined as the sum of CIP, Pl 480, direct dollar support, and U.S. piaster purchases. CIP, PL 480, and direct dollar support data in the source table conform to fiscal years, and this series is closer in concept to our "gross dollars transferred" than to "net resources transferred."
(3) Let the 1962 value in column (1) of this table divided by the 1962 value in column (3) of Table A3.5 equal x. Let $I(RNR)_t$ be the index of real net resources with base year 1962, and let $I(GNP)_t$ be the index of real GNP with base year 1962, as computed in Table 3.1. The figures in column (3) of this table are computed as $[I(RNR)_t/I(GNP)_t]x$.

1969 to 15 percent in 1974. The rapid decline in aid undoubtedly was the major reason for the sluggish performance of the Vietnamese economy in the late years of the war.

10.5   The uses of Project Aid

The various goals of U.S. aid as stated in AID documents and congressional hearings were (1) economic stabilization, (2) relief, (3) political development, (4) economic development and reconstruction, (5) social development, (6) technical support, and (7) other. In previous chapters we have emphasized stabilization because most attention was focused on that goal. Generally speaking, all of the funds that generated counterpart piasters for GVN budgetary support can be classified as stabilization aid. Those funds accounted for about one-half of total U.S. aid, including infrastructure aid supplied out of the U.S. military budget. All of the value of PL 480 (Title II) commodities, $88 million of Project Aid, and an estimated $129 million of "other" aid can be classified as refugee and war victims relief, rehabilitation, and resettlement aid. Most of these funds were used in the very early years of the Republic of Vietnam (1955–6) to aid in the resettlement of refugees from the North and in the late years of the republic (1972–5) to support war victims and resettlement that became necessary because of large population movements associated with the 1972 Communist Easter offensive. The rest of Project Aid funds served to advance the goals listed as items (3)–(7) earlier. These goals were frequently referred to as "nation building" by high-ranking U.S. politicians and other people working in the pacification programs. Piaster subsidy support, to the extent that it advanced any of the goals listed earlier, must be classified as stabilization aid. However, some of it undoubtedly went into capital flight.

Project Aid financed several hundred different kinds of projects in Vietnam. The broad project classes, along with the dollars spent in each class, are shown in Table 10.6. Project Aid funds were used primarily to supply "technical assistance" in the form of U.S. advisors in Vietnam. At the peak of U.S. involvement in Vietnam, there were close to 3,000 American technicians (excluding military personnel and contractor civilians paid with military funds) and 700 participants associated with the AID mission functions in Vietnam (see Table A10.4). There were advisors or monitors in virtually all conceivable activities. Indeed, one could easily conclude from the American (civilian) presence in South Vietnam that Americans were there not only to teach the Vietnamese how to do things but also to instruct on which things were worthwhile to undertake, and this circumstance contributes to explaining why it was difficult for Vietnamese civil operations to become "Vietnamized." The amount spent on capital assistance was only about one-sixth of the total Project Aid expenditures.

The entries in Table 10.6 on "technical support" and "discrepancy" require some explanation. Some of the cost of American technicians, supplies, and services was not allocable to specific projects and was charged to an overhead account called Technical Support. This entry also includes the costs associated with managing the CIP, for which there was no specific Project Aid account. "Discrepancy" is the difference between the total Project Aid figure reported in Table 10.5 and that compiled by the AID comptroller's office.[3] Under consistent definitions and accounting practices, the totals in

Table 10.6. *Noncommercial aid to South Vietnam by class of project, cumulative to end of period (million dollars)*

Class	Project Aid	Project-type aid	PL 480 (Title II)	Total
Relief & rehabilitation	87.7	128.7	330.6	547.0
Political development	284.5			284.5
Public Safety & public adm.	159.0			
Pacification	125.5			
Economic development	516.0	58.9		574.9
Agriculture & natural resources	85.5	58.9		
Industrial & mineral development	103.9			
Labor	6.0			
Transportation	320.6			
Social development	267.4			267.4
Health & sanitation	209.9			
Education	57.5			
Technical support	231.5			231.5
Other	192.8	197.1		389.9
Discrepancy[a]	−25.3			−25.3
Total	1,554.6	384.7	330.6	2,269.9

[a]This discrepancy is the difference between Project Aid reported in Table A10.1 and that in Table A9.3 in Dacy (1985).

Sources: Project Aid and project-type aid compiled from a detailed table (Dacy 1985). PL 480 figures from Table A10.1.

these tables should be the same. In presenting their proposed programs to Congress, officials of AID's Vietnam Bureau frequently rearranged items in a way they thought would give Congress a clearer picture of the areas of expenditures than they might gain from conventional accounting of how obligations were to be spent, and this resulted in keeping two sets of records that differ slightly. A more detailed explanation is attempted in a footnote to Table A10.1.

The major programs in the economic development category were associated with highways and roads, electric power generation, crop production, and land reform.[4] However, all of Project Aid was freed from heavier (capital) expenditures on infrastructure, because, as pointed out earlier, MACV made many of those investments out of the U.S. military budget in support of military operations in Vietnam.

Table A10.1. *U.S. Economic aid to South Vietnam by program, 1955-75, by fiscal year*[a]

Year	AID				PL 480		
	Total	CIP	Project Aid	Other[b]	Total	Title I	Other
1955	320.2	253.7	7.0	59.5	2.2		2.2
1956	195.7	174.7	23.9	-2.9	14.3		14.3
1957	259.4	210.9	48.9	-0.4	22.8		22.8
1958	179.4	151.9	29.8	-2.3	9.6	4.4	5.2
1959	200.9	146.4	42.9	11.6	6.5		6.5
1960	170.5	135.6	29.8	5.1	11.3	5.0	6.3
1961	140.5	111.2	11.8	17.5	11.5	7.0	4.5
1962	124.1	94.1	16.8	13.2	31.9	26.8	5.1
1963	143.3	95.0	14.3	34.0	52.6	23.7	28.9
1964	165.7	113.0	14.6	38.1	59.1	34.3	24.8
1965	225.0	150.0	23.7	51.3	49.9	41.4	8.5
1966	593.5	399.3	82.4	111.8	143.0	98.2	44.8
1967	494.4	160.0	321.2	13.2	73.7	73.3	0.4
1968	398.2	160.1	232.1	6.0	138.5	96.6	41.9
1969	314.2	130.0	169.1	15.1	99.4	60.8	38.6
1970	365.9	238.5	122.7	4.7	110.8	75.6	35.2
1971	387.7	281.0	103.1	3.6	188.0	164.9	23.1
1972	386.8	313.0	73.8		67.8	62.5	5.3
1973	313.4	226.2	87.2		188.3	179.0	9.3
1974	384.3	332.9	51.4		269.9	268.9	1.0
1975	191.3	143.2	48.1		49.6	45.7	3.9
Total	5,954.4	4,020.7	1,554.6	379.1	1,600.7	1,267.1	330.6

[a]Data sources: With the exception of "Project Aid" and "Other," these data were supplied by the Agency for International Development, Vietnam Residual Group (deactivated). Data on Project Aid are from the Agency for International Development (Statistics and Reports Division), "AID Projects, By Country and Field of Activity" (various fiscal-year reports).

[b]Data in "Other" column are computed by subtracting CIP and Project Aid figures from "Total." "Other" is attributed primarily to funds obligated as "contingency funds" or CIP funds that were used to finance AID programs requiring local currency, such as refugee resettlement ($55.8 million in FY 1955), land reform, and war victims relief. These expenditures were treated as Project Aid expenditures in AID's congressional presentations but were not accounted for as Project Aid expenditures in AID's comptroller reports.

Table A10.2. Number of technicians supported by AID project funds, 1966–73

	1966	1967	1968	1969	1970	1971	1972	1973
Number of U.S. technicians	1,014	2,074	2,780	2,864	2,177	1,649	1,109	882
AID-employed	781	1,591	1,908	1,771	1,480	1,248	912	579
Participating agency	97	219	371	306	255	108	67	81
Contractor technicians	136	264	501	787	442	293	130	222
Number of participants	344	1,160	643	691	974	1,039	1,223	1,030

Source: Agency for International Development, submissions to Congress for various fiscal years.

CHAPTER 11

Financing public expenditures

An interesting and unresolved question of the Vietnam war pertained to economic "burden sharing." At appropriations hearings on foreign aid, U.S. congressmen wanted to know if the Vietnamese people were bearing "their share" of the economic burden of the war. This was not an ethical question, but was intended to elicit only the simple response that x percent of the war budget was being financed by Vietnamese taxation and $1 - x$ percent by U.S. aid.

As seen earlier, witnesses were not able to answer this "simple" accounting question because of the lack of consensus on the foreign exchange value of the piaster. Better answers to this and other questions of Vietnam public finance depend on the kind of information provided in Chapters 9 and 10.

With the situation that prevailed in wartime South Vietnam, it would not have been possible for the Vietnamese to raise sufficient revenues to finance government operations at the expenditure levels recorded. Basically, there were three sources of financing: domestic revenues, deficit (or inflationary) financing, and foreign aid. We have seen that foreign aid was programmed in a way to keep the deficit under control. Foreign aid generated counterpart funds for budgetary use and promoted growth of income that potentially increased the domestic tax base. But foreign aid cannot be counted on to fill the budgetary gap or to fuel growth over an indefinite period. Eventually the people of a country must pay for the activities of government that contribute to economic development, and taxation must replace foreign aid. In this chapter we describe the Vietnamese tax structure, estimate the extent to which local financing contributed to central government operations, assess the efficiency of foreign aid in Vietnam public finance, and, importantly, analyze Vietnam's tax effort to replace foreign aid.

11.1 Expenditures and revenues

Although insurgents operated in South Vietnam from the time of partition, the country was relatively peaceful in the early sixties. Even so, defense was a heavy burden, and total central government expenditures were about 20 percent of the gross national product. In most other respects Vietnam resembled many other underdeveloped countries. Per capita income was about

211

eighty-five dollars, the dualism between the big city and countryside existed, exports were confined to agricultural products (rice and rubber), and the base for taxation was thin. The total domestic tax rate of under 10 percent of GNP obviously was insufficient to finance government operations. Vietnam was spared runaway inflation only because U.S. aid filled the budgetary gap. When the big war started early in 1965, the fiscal situation worsened as the budgetary gap increased more than the inflow of aid. The situation hardly improved in the prosperous years 1969–71, and after 1972, when the Vietnamese government finally moved to improve its tax collections, the situation became even more difficult because of severely declining U.S. aid.

11.1.1 Central government expenditures

By the end of the war, the government had over 1.5 million persons on its payroll, and that represented over a fourfold gain from the early sixties. The requirement to support this very large government sector had a dual effect on the economy: It removed resources from productive employment, thus reducing the tax base, while at the same time increasing government obligations. One cannot overstress the enormity of this fiscal problem. In the productive age span of fifteen to forty years, we calculate roughly that the government absorbed one-half of the country's effective male manpower resources after the Tet offensive in 1968. Furthermore, if some factor were used to adjust for health, the figure would be higher.

Table 11.1 represents data on government expenditures over a nineteen-year period. The extraordinary rise in central government spending was divided fairly evenly between military and civil, although civil expenditures, which started at a lower base, rose faster than military expenditures. Overall, about 80–90 percent of these expenditures were due to payroll costs. Because the United States supplied most of the war-related materials, there was relatively little need for the government to buy war equipment. Civil expenditures, particularly toward the end of the war period, were tied primarily to the activities of four ministries: Interior, War Veterans, Education, and Agriculture and Land Development. For the three-year period 1970–72, expenditures on these activities accounted for 60 percent of all civil expenditures. The percentages attributable to each were Interior 21 percent, War Veterans 14 percent, Education 13 percent, and Agriculture and Land Development 12 percent.[1] For the last two critical years of the Republic of Vietnam, no systematic breakdown of civilian expenditure data is available. However, much of the civil expenditure was for the purpose of relief, rehabilitation, reconstruction, civilian public works programs (in Saigon and Da Nang), and rice subsidy. According to AID's Terminal Report on Vietnam, these pro-

Table 11.1. *Government expenditures, 1956–74ᵃ (billion piasters)*

Year	National budget expendituresᵇ Defense	Civil	Total	Otherᶜ	Total Expenditures
1956	8.5	5.1	13.6		13.6
1957	8.0	6.2	14.2		14.2
1958	7.3	6.5	13.8		13.8
1959	7.4	7.9	15.3		15.3
1960	7.0	8.2	15.2		15.2
1961	8.3	8.0	16.3		16.3
1962	12.0	10.0	22.0		22.0
1963	13.6	12.3	25.9		25.9
1964	14.2	14.4	28.6		28.6
1965	21.9	22.2	44.1	−1.3	42.8
1966	29.5	29.5	59.0	2.4	61.4
1967	55.3	46.2	97.5	−1.4	96.1
1968	74.6	46.6	121.2	8.4	129.6
1969	91.7	41.7	133.4	14.3	147.7
1970	122.0	65.0	187.0	19.0	208.0
1971	151.0	105.0	256.0	16.3	272.3
1972	205.0	161.0	366.0	−19.2	346.8
1973	283.0	232.0	515.0	n.a.	515.0
1974	346.0	374.0	720.0	n.a.	720.0

ᵃData sources: National budget expenditure data: 1956–60, VN-NIS (annual, 1964–5, Table 241); 1961–4, AID-VN (annual, no.`11, Table C–11); 1965–74, AID (1976, pt. A). Other data from VN-NBVN (annual, various issues).

ᵇThe data for the period 1956–60 are on a fiscal-year basis. The Vietnamese fiscal year was the calendar year, excluding some expenditures the first five months but including some expenditures for the first five months of the following calendar year. For the years in question, the difference in accounting periods is probably insignificant.

ᶜData in this column are net expenditures due to the budget of Saigon Port, the budget of Saigon and other municipalities, provincial budgets, and rural reconstruction budgets.

grams took about one-third of all civilian public spending in 1972–4 [AID 1976, pt. A, sect. 12(Q)].

In Chapter 3 we pointed out that real government expenditures rose over 200 percent from 1960 to 1973, while net domestic product was rising only 60 percent. Financing a rise of this magnitude out of domestic resources in a relatively poor country with a shrinking private sector base (over part of the period) could have been achieved, if it was possible at all, only by reducing per capita consumption to some very low level, perhaps to one-half of its previous level. The drastic action required for that approach was not considered to be a political possibility by officials of the U.S. government, and, accordingly, the United States continued to supply the amount of aid needed to avert political collapse.

11.1.2 Central government revenues

The revenue system of wartime Vietnam consisted of a large assortment of special taxes levied on domestic activities, administrative revenues, import duties, American aid, and deficit finance. With regard to taxes, one is hard pressed to imagine a type of tax not on the books in some form.[2] However, there was never any systematic attempt to eliminate nuisance taxes or to strengthen those that proved effective. The income tax was revised in 1966, and a value-added tax was imposed in 1973. These modern-style taxes, little understood by the Vietnamese, coexisted with anachronistic levies that irritated the taxpayer out of all proportion to the revenues they raised.

In a sweeping indictment of the tax system, Stockfisch (1971, pp. 1–2) wrote the following:

It may be said that relative to the near and long term problems that face it, the Republic of Vietnam does not have an effective tax system . . . in some respects the national government comes pretty close to not having a tax system at all. Grave deficiencies in tax administration and enforcement, the reliance on deficit spending sustained mainly by central bank money creation, a foreign-aid supported import base which generates "pseudo" tax revenues in the form of import related duties, and a set of tax laws that might have been designed to discourage the rational conduct of business and to maximize administrative difficulties . . . .

It is probable that responsible ministries of the Vietnamese government were informed and understood the shortcomings of their tax system, even if not totally agreeing with the strong language of Stockfisch. Then, if they knew, why did the government not make some effort to remedy the situation? The answer to this question, in part, is an explanation of the fiscal dilemma discussed in the next chapter. Before proceeding to an explanation, we first present some data that will verify in a general way the passage quoted earlier.

11.1.2.1 Domestic revenues: Domestic revenue collections are shown in Table 11.2. The only entry in the table that may not be evident is the one called "administrative revenues." Administrative revenues were raised from proceeds of government agencies, earnings from the national lottery, and, in 1972, a war relief tax. Only four taxes listed in the table were significant revenue earners. The income tax was a minor source of revenue before 1967. Note the progression in earnings from this tax. In 1967, the collections more than doubled because of a newly enacted withholding provision. Subsequently, income taxes rose steadily to the end of the republic. The percentage increases appear significant. However, when deflated or compared with total

Table 11.2. *Domestic revenue collections in South Vietnam, 1956–74[a] (billion piasters)*

Source	1956	1957	1958	1959	1960	1961	1962	1963	1964	1965	1966	1967	1968	1969	1970	1971	1972	1973	1974
Direct taxes	0.7	0.7	0.8	0.8	0.8	0.9	1.3	1.6	1.0	1.0	1.4	3.1	4.1	5.4	8.0	10.0	16.3	28.5	39.8
Income tax							0.9	0.9	0.7	0.8	1.1	2.5	2.9	3.6	6.7	8.7	14.0	25.4	38.3
Patente							0.2	0.5	0.2	0.2	0.3	0.4	0.5	0.6	1.0	1.3	1.9		
Other							0.2	0.2	0.1			0.2	0.7	1.2	0.3		0.4		
Indirect & excise	3.7	4.6	4.3	4.3	4.6	5.4	3.4	4.0	4.2	5.5	9.1	12.8	13.6	19.7	28.2	37.8	49.1	133.4[b]	203.6[b]
Production tax							0.6	0.9	1.0	1.3	1.9	2.5	3.0	5.8	9.3	12.7	16.3		
Beer & beverages							0.2	0.3	0.5	0.9	2.2	3.4	3.4	4.9	6.6	8.4	9.4		
Tobacco							0.9	1.0	1.1	1.6	2.7	4.1	4.4	5.2	7.4	11.6	17.7		
Gasoline							1.1	1.2	1.1	1.1	1.4	1.7	1.8	2.9	3.3	3.6	3.8		
Motor vehicles							0.1	0.1	0.1	0.1	0.2	0.2	0.2	0.2	0.3	0.3	0.3		
Entertainment							0.1	0.1	0.4	0.5	0.7	0.3	0.2	0.4	0.5	0.8	0.9		
Other							0.4	0.4				0.6	0.6	0.3	0.8	0.4	0.7		
Registration taxes	0.6	0.5	0.6	0.6	0.7	0.6	0.7	0.9	0.8	1.1	2.3	3.0	3.0	4.9	5.8	6.8	8.2	7.4	7.5
Registration & inheritance							0.4	0.5	0.4	0.5	1.1	1.3	1.1	2.9	3.2	3.6	3.8		
Dividends							0.2	0.3	0.2	0.2	0.4	0.6	0.7	0.9	1.2	1.6	2.4		
Super rent										0.1	0.4	0.6	0.7	0.9	1.1	1.0	0.9		
Other							0.1	0.1	0.2	0.3	0.4	0.5	0.5	0.2	0.3	0.6	1.1		
Total taxes	5.0	5.8	5.7	5.7	6.1	6.9	5.4	6.5	6.0	7.6	12.8	18.9	20.7	30.0	42.0	54.6	73.6	169.3	250.9
Administrative revenues[c]	0.9	1.1	1.0	1.2	1.1	1.6	1.6	1.7	2.1	3.2	4.0	5.9	6.6	5.9	9.0	13.9	25.7	29.3	46.1
Total revenues	5.9	6.9	6.7	6.9	7.2	8.5	7.0	8.2	8.1	10.8	16.8	24.8	27.3	35.9	51.0	68.5	99.3	198.6	297.0

[a] Data sources: data for 1956–61 from AID-VN (annual, no. 9, p. 49). These data are for overlapping seventeen-month periods corresponding to the Vietnamese fiscal years. During periods when the annual receipts did not change significantly, the seventeen-month period corresponded reasonably well with the calendar year. Data for 1962 and 1963 from Dacy (1969a, Tables 1 and 2). Data for 1964–72 from AID (1974b, Apr.–June, p. 14). Data for 1973 and 1974 from AID (1974b, Oct.–Dec.).

[b] These figures include the value-added tax put into effect in 1973.

[c] Figures in this row comprise receipts form government agencies, miscellaneous receipts, reimbursements, refunds, and special receipts as listed in AID-VN (annual, no. 9, p. 49).

personal income in Vietnam, income tax revenue is seen to be small and the
rise less spectacular. From 1967 through 1972, the ratio of income tax collection to national income (roughly equal to personal income in Vietnam)
rose from 0.8 percent to 1.5 percent. The production tax, a flat percentage
tax (levied against some manufacturing firms on the value of output), the
cigarette tax (an ad valorem tax, paid at the site of manufacture), and the
excise tax (per liter) on beer and beverages were the other three major con-
tributors to government revenue before 1973. Taxation on beer and tobacco
had the advantage of ease of collection, and, importantly, these items were
considered luxuries (despite the fact that they were consumed by the poor).
It was easy to raise collection rates because of the luxury connotation in the
minds of moralistic officials. Domestic taxes as a whole (exclusive of administrative revenues and import duties) were 7.3 percent of GNP in 1956
and 5.6 percent in 1971. After the much heralded reforms in the fall of 1971,
the percentage rose to 6.7 in 1972. In the summer of 1973, the government
finally made a move in the direction of tax reform by putting into effect a
value-added tax. Primarily as a result of this tax, all revenues climbed to 10.9
percent of GNP in 1973 and 11.3 percent in 1974.

11.1.2.2 Revenues from customs duties: Up to 1972, Vietnamese official
statistics show that customs and austerity taxes on imported goods exceeded
domestic revenues. In the critical 1966–71 period, import taxes even exceeded
counterpart aid according to conventional accounting practices. However,
these statistics are based on an accounting illusion. It is this illusion that
Stockfisch had in mind when he used the phrase "pseudo revenues" as a
description of revenues raised through customs and austerity taxes.

Import duty collections appear high in the official Vietnamese statistics
because the government chose to collect piasters through import taxes rather
than through official sale of dollars to importers. They chose a mixture of
high formal tariffs and low official exchange rate because that combination
had the effect of maximizing foreign aid.[3] In principle, the government could
have converted the dollar value of aid into spendable piasters by charging
importers a high exchange cost and low (or zero) tariffs or low exchange cost
and high tariffs. By arbitrarily choosing the latter, they simply engaged in an
accounting fiction that made it appear that the piaster value of aid was low
in relation to import taxes. For a country that does not receive aid and responds
to an exchange rate that properly values its currency, exports rather than aid
will pay for imports. In this situation, the duties collected on imports are
properly to be considered a true tax on the consumers and producers in the
country,[4] but that was not the situation in wartime Vietnam.

During the war period, the Vietnamese exported some commodities and a
rather substantial amount of services. Thus, the country did gain exchange

earnings above the amount of aid it received. It follows, then, that not all of the import-derived revenues ought to be counted as "pseudo revenues." The immediate task is to determine the amount of "earned" import revenues, in contrast to the amount we have called pseudo revenues. Let X equal the dollar value of exports, M the dollar value of imports, and T the nominal piasters collected as import taxes. Define

$$R = (X/M)T$$

X/M is the percentage of imports paid for by exports. R can be interpreted as "earned import taxes," that is, earned in the sense that they derive from utilization of local resources rather than aid.

In estimating the value of U.S. aid to Vietnam in the previous chapter, it was assumed that U.S. purchases of Vietnamese (personnel) services were a legitimate export of Vietnam. The problem there was to determine what percentage of U.S. piaster purchases constituted a subsidy (aid) to the Vietnamese government. Here we follow the same procedure in order to determine the value of all Vietnamese exports.

The estimate of earned import tax revenues is given in Table 11.3. Note that the percentage of imports financed by exports was close to a third in most years. All recorded import revenues not attributed to exports should be classified as aid. If one wished to argue that all of the U.S. piaster purchases were a subsidy to the Vietnamese government, rather than a legitimate cost of its operations in Vietnam, virtually all import taxes would be called pseudo revenues. We do not take this extreme position.

11.1.2.3 Aid: The third source of government revenues was U.S. aid. The value of aid measured as net economic resources transferred and gross dollar resources transferred was estimated in Chapter 10. Unfortunately, neither of these concepts serves the present purpose of determining how much aid was available to support the Vietnamese budget. Budgetary aid was only that part of net resources transferred that could be converted into piasters for use by the GVN.

Thus, from the point of view of the Vietnamese treasury, the actual spendable amount of aid was much less than its value to the economy. Budget support aid was governed by the amount of funds deposited in the GVN counterpart account by the U.S. disbursing officer, and there is some ambiguity in the data on this important series, as is seen in the three different series presented in Table A11.1. We have constructed a "compromise" series in column 4 of Table 11.4.

Total foreign aid for budgetary use is taken as the sum of official (counterpart) aid and import duties that cannot be attributed to Vietnamese exports, or "unearned import taxes," as they are called in Table 11.4. Once again,

Table 11.3. *Tariff revenues attributable to Vietnamese exports, 1956–74*[a]

Year	(1) Foreign exchange earned from sale of piasters to U.S. ($ million)	(2) Regular exports ($ million)	(3) Total exports [(1) + (2)] ($ million)	(4) Dutiable imports ($ million)	(5) Percentage imports financed by exports [(3) ÷ (4)]	(6) Import tax receipts (d billion)	(7) Revenues attributable to exports [(5) × (6)] (d billion)
1956		45.1	45.1	191.5	23.6	2.1	0.5
1957		80.5	80.5	246.6	32.6	2.8	0.9
1958		55.2	55.2	208.8	26.4	2.1	0.6
1959		75.1	75.1	198.7	37.8	1.8	0.7
1960		84.5	84.5	210.9	40.1	2.0	0.8
1961		69.8	69.8	231.9	30.1	2.9	0.9
1962		56.0	56.0	230.9	24.3	4.9	1.2
1963		76.7	76.7	238.1	32.2	4.7	1.5
1964	30.7	48.5	79.2	245.8	32.2	6.1	1.6
1965	54.8	36.5	90.3	297.0	30.4	5.6	1.7
1966	137.5	27.6	165.1	460.0	35.9	25.9	9.3
1967	101.4	16.4	117.8	547.4	21.5	28.4	6.1
1968	183.4	11.7	195.1	473.9	41.2	26.7	11.0
1969	180.3	11.9	192.2	652.5	29.5	52.9	15.6
1970	130.5	11.5	142.0	502.3	28.3	71.7	20.3
1971	189.5	12.4	201.9	598.1	33.8	110.4[b]	37.3
1972	176.3	15.6	191.9	571.0	33.6	47.2[b]	15.9
1973	121.5	58.0	179.5	562.4	31.9	53.5	17.0
1974	92.2	84.9	177.1	659.9	26.8	42.6	11.4

[a] Data sources:
(1) From column (6), Table 10.1.
(2) From Table A4.7.
(4) From Table A4.7. "Commercial import arrivals."
(6) 1956, VN-NIS (annual, 1964–5, Table 241, "Custom duties"); 1957–63, AID-VN (annual, no. 9, Table C-8); 1966–9, AID (1974b, Jan.-March, p. 14); 1970–4, AID-VN (monthly, Feb. 1975, p. 2).

[b] The drop from 1971 to 1972 is due to a reform in 1971 raising the foreign exchange rate and lowering customs duties.

Table 11.4. *Total GVN revenues by source, 1956–74[a] (billion piasters)*

	(1)	(2)	(3)	(4)	(5)	(6)	(7)	(8)	(9) Aid contributions
Year	Domestic revenues	Import taxes earned	Import taxes unearned	Counterpart aid	Foreign aid	Deficit finance	Total	(5)/(7) (ratio)	(5)/[(7) − (6)] (ratio)
1956	5.9	0.5	1.6	8.1	9.7	−2.5	13.6	0.71	0.60
1957	6.9	0.9	1.9	8.4	10.3	−3.9	14.2	0.73	0.57
1958	6.7	0.6	1.5	6.7	8.2	−1.7	13.8	0.59	0.53
1959	6.9	0.7	1.1	5.5	6.6	1.1	15.3	0.43	0.46
1960	7.2	0.8	1.2	5.8	7.0	0.2	15.2	0.46	0.47
1961	8.5	0.9	2.0	4.2	6.2	0.7	16.3	0.38	0.40
1962	7.0	1.2	3.7	7.6	11.3	2.5	22.0	0.51	0.58
1963	8.2	1.5	3.2	8.8	12.0	4.2	25.9	0.46	0.55
1964	8.1	1.6	3.5	8.2	11.5	7.4	28.6	0.40	0.54
1965	10.8	1.7	3.9	11.4	15.3	15.0	42.8	0.36	0.55
1966	16.8	9.3	16.6	21.1	37.7	−2.4	61.4	0.61	0.59
1967	24.8	6.1	22.3	24.9	47.2	18.0	96.1	0.49	0.60
1968	27.3	11.0	15.7	22.3	48.0	43.3	129.6	0.37	0.56
1969	35.9	15.6	37.3	25.8	63.1	33.1	147.7	0.43	0.55
1970	51.0	20.3	51.4	28.2	79.6	57.1	208.0	0.38	0.53
1971	68.5	37.3	73.1	33.5	106.6	59.9	272.3	0.39	0.50
1972	99.3	15.9	31.3	102.8	134.1	97.5	346.8	0.39	0.54
1973	198.6	17.0	36.5	128.0	164.5	134.9	515.0	0.32	0.43
1974	297.0	11.4	31.2	253.0	284.2	127.4	720.0	0.39	0.48

[a]Data sources:
(1) Table 11.2.
(2) Table 11.3, column (7).
(3) Table 11.3, column (6) − (7).
(4) Table A11.1.
(5) Column (3) + column (4).
(6) Column (7) − column (5) − column (2) − column (1).
(7) Table 11.1, "Total expenditures."

these duties are counted as aid rather than import duties because they were due to U.S. aid as defined in the previous chapter. Foreign aid available for budget support is shown in column 5 in Table 11.4.

11.1.2.4 Deficit financing: Deficit financing is the difference between total government spending and total budgetary receipts including foreign aid. Our definition of deficit financing simply as a balancing item is incompatible with Vietnam treasury statistics as reported in the National Bank of Vietnam's annual reports. In those reports, the deficit was obtained by adding various items, some of which were derived from dubious accounting practices, without any regard to whether or not the total was consistent with other accounts in the fiscal system of accounts.

In any given year, the government could borrow from the National Bank or the public. About 60 percent of the cumulative deficit after foreign aid was financed by borrowing from the Central Bank, and 30 percent was raised by selling bonds, principally to commercial banks. The remaining 10 percent is an unexplained accounting residual. Data from which these calculations were made are presented in Table A11.2.

Official government figures on borrowing from the Central Bank are lower than those stated earlier. The difference is due to accounting procedures related to the major devaluations that took place in 1966 and 1972. In 1966, international assets were increased by 6.8 billion in terms of piaster valuation, and the gain in 1972 was 62 billion piasters (VN-NBVN annual 1966, 1972). Technically, the government owned the foreign exchange. In both years, it "repaid" the National Bank the amount of the accounting gains, thereby masking significant borrowings in those years.

Sale of government bonds played only a slight role in public finance until 1971. In the six-year period before 1971, government bond sales financed only 2.5 percent of national budgetary expenditures. In 1971 and 1972, bond sales financed 6.7 and 10.5 percent of government expenditures, respectively. Commercial banks were virtually the complete "public" market for bonds, buying 85 percent of the total. Bank participation, for all practical purposes, was forced by a requirement installed in 1966 that commercial banks subscribe to treasury bonds in amounts fixed by the government. Through 1968, they held the minimal amounts required by law. Given that interest rates were between 1.5 and 2.5 percent, bank behavior in the 1966–8 period is understandable. Interest rates rose slightly in 1969, and banks were allowed to use bonds in excess of the minimal requirement as collateral against loans from the National Bank. In 1971 and 1972, banks purchased about three times the minimum requirement. In 1972, interest rates on treasury bonds were raised to the range of 13–18 percent. The low statutory interest rate that existed up to 1971 was undoubtedly the main reason for failure of the government to finance much of the debt with bonds.

11.2 Tax effort

"Tax effort" refers to the amount of taxes collected in relation to the population's ability to pay and the administrative ease in collecting them. Conceptually, it can be measured as a ratio, with taxes collected in the numerator and the value of some function in the denominator. The simplest such measure is the ratio of taxes collected (T) to GNP. Because this measure is easy to obtain, it has been used in intercountry comparisons of tax efforts, but it has serious limitations. One problem is that the simple ratio T/GNP does not consider the state of economic development. A given ratio will indicate a higher tax effort for a poor country than for a rich one. In poor countries, taxes are difficult to extract from the people because the surplus available for taxation beyond minimum living conditions is small.[5] Another variable that bears on tax effort is the relative importance of foreign trade in the economy. Lotz and Morss (1967) have argued that the more a country is open to trade, the easier it is to collect taxes, because governments find it more convenient to collect taxes on trade flows than on domestic income. Record keeping is better on trade flows, the number of inspection points is limited, and the tax is paid only indirectly by the final purchasers. Furthermore, the "degree of openness" – measured as value of trade flows to GNP – is an indication of the internal structure of an economy that probably correlates with the government's ability to collect taxes internally as well as externally (Lotz and Morss 1967, p. 482).

The value in the denominator of the tax effort equation can be interpreted as an "adjusted" GNP. Large trade flows and high per capita GNPs would yield adjusted GNPs above the actual one, whereas small trade flows and low per capita GNPs would have the opposite effect. Thus, for those countries in which taxes are relatively easy to collect, a given T/GNP ratio would indicate a lower tax effort than for one where local conditions make it difficult to collect taxes. Lotz and Morss solved this additional variable problem by regression analysis, as will be explained in the following subsection.

Suppose a country makes little "effort" to collect taxes through explicit tax programs, but takes the politically expedient approach of financing its public expenditures through money creation and inflation. Inflationary finance clearly is a tax on the population, but in the customary accounting framework it raises no taxes. This method would not register as a contributing factor to tax effort. At the same time, it would increase the tax burden on the population.

It is important to recognize that tax burden and tax effort are not simply two sides of a coin.

11.2.1   Vietnam's tax effort

To measure tax effort in Vietnam and to gain some perspective on its progress over time, we divide the nineteen-year history into five periods. This break-down assures some smoothing in the data, but more important, it yields some information on the relation of tax effort to changes in political/military conditions. The five periods are delineated as follows:

1956–60: A period of relative peace in South Vietnam. The country was beset by many problems, but, in general, they were political and economic rather than military.

1961–4: A period of increasing insurgency operations by the Viet Cong, growing uncertainty, and political disintegration of the South Vietnamese government.

1965–9: A period of large-scale warfare, with a buildup of U.S. forces in Vietnam and U.S. influence. After initial gains in 1965–6, the Communist forces suffered military setbacks in 1968, and the economy grew rapidly in 1969.

1970–2: A period of many announced economic reforms. "Major reforms" were said to have occurred in the fall of 1969, throughout 1970, and in the fall of 1971. It was also characterized by "Vietnamization" of the war as U.S. forces were withdrawn. A major Communist offensive took place in 1972, and the economy suffered a major economic recession.

1973–4: Marked by the cease-fire agreement. It was a period of declining levels of real U.S. aid and of realization on the part of the Vietnamese that they would have to bear a larger share of the financial burden of the war than previously.

Period average data are presented in Table 11.5. Note the column headed by *T/GNP*, the simplest indicator of tax effort. According to this measure, Vietnam's tax effort in the first four periods was very poor. In comparison with about fifty low-income countries listed by Lotz and Morss (1967, Table 1), Vietnam's *T/GNP* ratio exceeded only those of Haiti, Guatemala, Ethiopia, Afghanistan, and Korea (for data in 1962–5). More important for our analysis is the fact that this simplest measure of tax effort did not improve until the final period. It is interesting to note that the much heralded economic reforms

Table 11.5. *Vietnam tax effort in relation to other less developed countries*[a]

Period	T/GNP (%)	Per capita GNP ($ U.S.)	Index of openness (%)	Expected T/GNP (%)	Deviation from expected (%)	Rank
1956–60	10.0	78	26.0	12.7	−21.3	37
1961–4	9.6	84	23.7	12.6	−23.8	39
1965–9	9.5	111	26.9	13.1	−27.5	41
1970–2	9.8	133	22.8	13.0	−24.6	40
1973–4	13.9	157	21.4	13.1	+6.1	23

[a]Expected T/GNP = 10.21 + 0.0085(per capita GNP) + 0.0712(index of openness). See Lotz and Morss (1967, Table 6). The index of openness is the ratio of imports plus exports to GNP.

of the 1969–72 period were not effective in raising the tax ratio. To a large extent, these were enacted to satisfy U.S. advisors and perhaps as preconditions for maintaining the large aid program. But the aid program was contradictory to the notion of economic reforms. The guaranteed inflow of aid reduced the incentive of the GVN to actually put into effect any burdensome economic reforms, including those related to tax effort.

In 1973–4, the simple tax effort ratio was increased by about 40 percent over previous periods. The *complete* withdrawal of U.S. combat troops from Vietnam and the growing unpopularity of any kind of aid to that country in the U.S. Congress were properly interpreted by the Vietnamese government as signals that real economic reforms must be made. With the implementation of the value-added tax in 1973, the first genuine tax reforms of the war period were executed. Indirect and excise taxes increased from 4.5 percent of GNP in 1972 to 8.5 percent in 1973 (see Table 11.2). The T/GNP ratio achieved in the 1973–4 period by Vietnam is comparable to levels achieved by Ghana, Uganda, Costa Rica, and Tanzania a decade earlier, and those countries are in the bottom half of the listing of effort by *poor* countries.

As stated earlier, the simple T/GNP measure of tax effort could be misleading for the purpose of international comparisons. To adjust for relative poverty and ease of raising tax revenues, Lotz and Morss (1967) regressed T/GNP on per capita GNP and the index of openness, using fifty-two underdeveloped countries in their sample. "Degree of openness" was defined as the ratio of trade (imports plus exports) to GNP. Per capita GNP was a proxy for relative poverty or stage of development. Using the parametric values estimated in their regression, they calculated the value for tax ratio each country would be expected to have assuming constancy in degree of openness and per capita income. The percentage deviation from the expected tax ratio was computed for each nation. Countries with expected T/GNP ratios lower than those observed were thought to be countries with relatively high tax efforts, and the converse was assumed when the expected T/GNP ratio was higher than observed. On the basis of these deviations, they ranked the countries according to tax effort. We used the Lotz and Morss regression coefficients to calculate Vietnam's expected T/GNP ratio and its deviation from the observed ratio. Comparing Vietnam's deviation with those of the fifty-two low-income countries, we were able to establish Vietnam's rank with respect to tax effort.

Ranked with the other poor countries (fifty-three counting Vietnam), Vietnam's position on the list, measured by deviation from the expected ratio, is low. The last column in Table 11.5 shows its rank to be between 37 and 41 for all except the last period. Excluding the last period, its rank would be still lower had we computed per capita income (in dollars) by using the official exchange rate as the Lotz and Morss study did for the other countries. Instead, we used the market clearing rate estimated in Chapter 9 to convert piaster GNP to dollar GNP. Had we used the official rate, we would have observed higher per capita incomes in Vietnam (and higher expected T/GNP ratios) than those shown in the table. Consequently, the percentage deviations would have been more negative than shown in the table, and the rank listings lower. In other words, we presented the best case for Vietnam.

If tax effort can be measured in the manner indicated earlier, tax effort in Vietnam prior to 1973 was comparable to that in Nicaragua, Costa Rica, Haiti, and Malasia and probably better than that in Guatemala and Afghanistan. However, in 1973–4, Vietnam's rank was about midway in the Lotz and Morss list and comparable to the effort in Peru, India, and South Africa.[6] No doubt, Vietnam's tax effort improved during the last two years of its existence. It is likely that this increase would have been permanent had the South Vietnamese nation survived, because improving their tax effort became a necessity with declining aid levels.

11.2.2 Domestic taxes compared with U.S. aid

We now address the question that opened this chapter: What percentage of the Vietnamese budget was borne by the people of Vietnam? Estimates presented to inquiring congressmen at the time were confused. We previously cited the lowest estimate of 44 percent. Another witness testified five years later that 71 percent of the GVN budget was supported "directly and indirectly" by the United States,[7] excluding that part of the budget financed by deficit. A U.S. congressional study stated that "at least 80 percent" was provided directly and indirectly by U.S. aid (U.S. House of Representatives

1971, p. 6). If the assumptions and calculations consistent with the data presented in Table 11.4 are reasonable, it is clear that U.S. officials had little appreciation of the relative contributions of aid and domestic revenues to total budgetary expenditures.

Our calculations on "burden sharing" are given in columns 8 and 9 of Table 11.4. On the definition of foreign aid implied by the figures in the table, the U.S. contribution to GVN expenditures was smaller than the foregoing citations, and in relative terms it declined over time. By averaging the figures in column 8, the U.S. contribution in the period of reconstruction and rehabilitation (1955–60) was 58 percent, whereas in the period of recession and defeat (1972–5) the U.S. contributed 37 percent toward the budget. Column 9 shows the U.S. contribution before considering deficit financing. Under the assumption that a deficit is not a burden,[8] U.S. participation declined from 53 percent in the 1955–60 period to 48 percent in the last years of the war, not a significant change given the crudeness of our data. Nevertheless, our figures are considerably less than those claimed by U.S. officials during the war. One reason for the difference is that our calculations assume that some of the piasters purchased and U.S. uses of counterpart funds were war-related U.S. expenditures rather than aid.

11.3 Efficiency of aid in public finance

By any measure, aid played a most important role in financing Vietnam's public expenditures. This section is concerned with the question whether or not Vietnam used the enormous amount of aid it received in a way that would maximize its budgetary impact. We measure "efficiency of aid" in public finance as the ratio of funds actually converted to budgetary use to the potential maximum. Specifically, how well did the GVN turn dollar aid into piasters for budgetary use?

The administration of aid did not permit some of it to support the budget. The commodity portion of U.S. Project Aid, PL 480 Title II commodities, and some third-country capital project aid were not transferable into counterpart funds. Although these kinds of aid contributed to economic welfare as a part of net resources transferred, there was no way the government could sell these items to accumulate funds to pay its bills.

"Maximum potential aid for budgetary use" is defined as the piaster value of net resources transferred less the value of nonbudget support items (those mentioned earlier). Call this "net budget resources transferred." Piaster value is obtained by multiplying dollar value of net budget resources transferred by the market clearing rate of exchange. A major difference between "maximum potential" and actual budget support aid is due to the exchange rate the GVN

Table 11.6. *Indicators of efficiency of aid in public finance*[a]

Period	(1) Potential aid for budgetary use (d/billion)	(2) Potential aid lost (d billion)	(3) Aid lost/ potential aid	(4) Aid lost/deficit	(5) Potential aid/military budget
1962–4	43.7	8.9	0.20	0.63	1.10
1965–8	237.0	88.8	0.38	1.19	1.31
1969–72	670.6	287.2	0.43	1.14	1.18

Data sources:
(1)   Table A11.3.
(2)   Table A11.3.
(3)   Column (2) ÷ column (1).
(4)   Column (2) ÷ column (1) in Table A11.2.
(5)   Column (1) ÷ column (1) in Table 11.1.

actually used to convert dollars to piasters and the rate that could have been used.

Some data on "aid efficiency" are presented in Table 11.6. Data in the table are focused on aid lost rather than aid utilized, to highlight the negative side of Vietnamese policies. Note that much of the aid potentially available to support the budget was not used. Between 20 and 43 percent was lost for various reasons. Some imply mismanagement or neglect, but some loss in aid efficiency was accepted as the cost of reducing political risks.

In the critical 1965–8 period of U.S. troop buildup and high inflation, we estimate that 38 percent of potential budgetary support aid was lost for that purpose. Where did it go? Some was drained off to windfall gains from importing because of the exchange rate policy of the period. Given our previous calculation of windfall gains, 30–40 percent of the lost aid could have been captured by importers. Another large percentage of the loss in budget revenues was due to the subsidy on rice. In 1965–8, Vietnam imported about $360 million in U.S. rice under PL 480. This rice was sold in the market at a price considerably below its market value. We do not know what the free market price would have been during the period, but the subsidy was somewhere between 75 and 200 piasters per dollar of imported rice. At 100 piasters per dollar, we can account for another 40 percent of loss in budget support. Subsidization of other commodities could round out the difference. Subsidization was not necessarily a bad policy. Some argued at the time that subsidizing imported rice was a factor in the decline in domestic production, or at least had a powerful disincentive effect regarding raising output. However, the politicians accepted the economic losses as the price for political stability, to which they thought the subsidy contributed. Besides, they frequently acted as though there were no limit on aid.

The data show that U.S. aid to Vietnam would have been sufficient to eliminate the deficit completely from 1965 on if different economic policies had been pursued. Thus, the rate of inflation might have been much lower than it was. Once again, it could be argued that although different policies regarding the exchange rate and subsidization might have reduced inflation, they might have undermined political stability. The subsidies were to the benefit of the urban population and to the disadvantage of farmers, and it is not clear whether or not they had a positive effect overall. In any event, the government reversed its income redistribution policy later on, as we documented in Chapter 5. With regard to exchange rate policy, one doubts that any major group besides the privileged importers benefited.

Finally, it is apparent that U.S. aid was sufficient to finance the entire military budget had it been used effectively. There is no particular economic meaning attached to this observation. The point is that the war was adequately financed by the United States, which supplied billions of dollars in ordnance and ample economic aid to pay the troops and otherwise run the military establishment.

We conclude that much of Vietnam's potential budgetary aid did not actually support the budget. In this sense, aid was not used efficiently. Nor do the data indicate any improvement in aid efficiency over time. The last period in Table 11.6 was one of frequently announced economic reforms. Yet, the ratio of budget aid lost to potential did not improve. Improving the "efficiency of aid" was not the goal of these "reforms," but one unintended consequence of effective reforms (particularly those dealing with exchange rate policy and tariffs) would have been to improve the efficiency of aid in budget support. Some readers might be puzzled over why Vietnamese and U.S. officials continued to tolerate the situation we have described, because it can reasonably be assumed that they understood the costs of their policies. An understanding of the short-run/long-run dilemma is an essential starting point in solving this puzzle, and the following chapter deals with one aspect of this dilemma.

Table A11.1. *Counterpart funds for Vietnamese use, 1955–74ᵃ (billion piasters)*

Year	Series A	Series B	Series C	Average A and C
1956	8.1			8.1
1957	8.4			8.4
1958	6.7			6.7
1959	5.5			5.5
1960	5.8			5.8
1961	4.2			4.2
1962	7.6			7.6
1963	8.8			8.8
1964	8.3	7.8	7.7	8.2
1965	11.7	11.9	11.0	11.4
1966	20.1	23.9	21.5	21.1
1967	15.0	38.8	34.7	24.9
1968	20.1	29.2	24.6	22.3
1969	24.7	31.6	26.8	25.8
1970	28.0	33.0	28.3	28.2
1971	30.8	41.0	36.1	33.5
1972	101.2	109.0	104.3	102.0
1973		133.0	128.0ᵇ	128.0
1974		258.0	253.0ᵇ	253.0

ᵃData sources:
Series A: 1956–61, AID-VN (annual, 1966, Table H–7, "Deposits to counterpart funds");
   1962–5, AID-VN (annual, 1965, pt. B, Table 1, row C, "Counterpart"); 1966–72, AID-
   VN (annual, 1973, pt. B, Table 1, row C, "Counterpart").
Series B: AID (1976, pt. A, Table 7, row D). The data in this source overestimate counterpart funds for Vietnamese use, because the calculations were not made net of "trust fund"
   deposits. Trust fund deposits were reserved for U.S. use.
Series C: These figures were derived by subtracting trust fund deposits for each year from the
   data in series B.
ᵇAssumes trust fund deposits of 5 billion piasters.

Table A11.2. *Sources of deficit financing, 1962–74ª (billion piasters)*

Year	(1) Deficit after aid	(2) Advanced by National Bank	(3) Net sale of treasury bonds	(4) Residual
1962	2.5	1.4		1.1
1963	4.2	2.6		1.6
1964	7.4	6.3	1.0	0.1
1965	15.0	15.8	2.1	-2.9
1966	-2.4	11.5ᵇ	0.7	-14.6
1967	18.0	0.6	1.2	16.2
1968	43.3	31.1	6.2	6.0
1969	33.1	31.6	4.8	-3.3
1970	57.1	38.0	2.7	16.4
1971	59.9	45.0	18.2	-3.3
1972	97.5	60.0ᶜ	36.4	1.1
1973	134.9	85.0	18.0	31.9
1974	127.4	29.0	90.0	8.4

ªData sources:
(1) Table 11.4, column (6).
(2) 1962–4, VN-NIS (annual, 1970, Table 243, "Temporary advance to government," annual differences); 1965–72, VN-NBVN (annual, various issues); 1973–4, AID (1976, pt. A, sect. xii).
(3) 1964, VN-NIS (annual, 1970, Table 197); 1965–72, VN-NBVN (annual, various issues); 1973–4, AID (1976, pt. A, sect. xii).
(4) Column (1) − column (2) − column (3).
ᵇThis does not include a "special" advance of 22 billion piasters made by the National Bank to the Ministry of Finance to import (subsidize) PL 480 rice. Excludes 6.8 billion piasters "repaid" by the central government to the National Bank that it gained because of devaluation of the piaster. The figure according to the primary source is 4.7 billion piasters.
ᶜExcludes 62.0 billion piasters "repaid" by central government, made possible by devaluation. The figure according to the primary source is −2.1 billion piasters.

Table A11.3. *Potential value of foreign aid for budget support, 1962–72*[a]

Year	(1) Total ($ million)	(2) Net resources transferred not generating counterpart ($ million)	(3) Net resources transferred generating counterpart ($ million)	(4) Value of piaster (d/$)	(5) Potential aid for budgetary use (d billion)	(6) Potential aid lost (d billion)
1962	217.4	33.8	183.6	78	14.3	3.0
1963	220.2	68.6	151.6	78	11.8	-0.2
1964	270.5	53.6	216.9	81	17.6	6.1
1965	316.1	51.2	264.9	94	24.9	9.6
1966	479.5	53.0	426.5	146	62.3	24.6
1967	550.7	72.9	477.8	189	90.3	43.1
1968	405.5	109.6	295.9	201	59.5	11.5
1969	610.1	152.1	458.0	229	104.9	41.8
1970	614.6	75.2	539.4	325	175.3	95.7
1971	568.9	79.8	489.1	388	189.8	83.2
1972	516.8	59.8	457.0	439	200.6	66.5

[a]Data sources:

(1) Table 10.3.

(2) This includes U.S. Food for Peace grants (Title II), Project Aid (commodities), and third-country aid; 1962–71, VN-NIS (annual, 1972, p. 136); 1972, AID-VN (annual, 1973, p. 25) and AID (1974a, p. 49) for Third World country aid.

(3) Column (1) – column (2).

(4) Table 9.5.

(5) Column (3) × column (4).

(6) Column (5) – column (5) in Table 11.4.

CHAPTER 12

The fiscal dilemma

As relations between the two Vietnams grew increasingly hostile, a major fiscal problem in the South became its chief dilemma. Fiscal and other unpopular measures in self-reliance, it was thought, would alienate the population in the short run and reduce the probability of survival of the government. Yet, postponement of those measures would cause more serious problems eventually, because self-reliance is essential to economic development and viability of democratic governments in the long run. The options open to the Vietnamese government were to make the first move toward self-reliance, and then proceed step by step, or to become more and more dependent on aid. Both appeared to be risky and unpromising.

In the late 1950s and early 1960s, South Vietnam was a relatively poor country. Though almost self-sufficient in food, it had a large trade deficit that it was able to manage thanks to U.S. aid. The country had a poor central administration, with little skill or motivation to cope with internal financial problems. The internal war in the early sixties, and later the external war, brought insecurity to the countryside, along with a siphoning of manpower and other resources to military operations. How to meet the military payroll and to provide for some of the local military personnel needs, how to pay for more education and pacification of the civilian population, how to pay for additional public projects, and how to pay for these expenditures out of domestic resources in a relatively poor country *without alienating the masses and various influential groups* posed a difficult problem. To finance the large and expanding budget solely out of domestic taxation clearly was not a possibility. Foreign aid appears to have been the only solution. Internal efforts were minimal. Yet, one can question that the rather minimal efforts undertaken by the government to increase domestic taxation would have served the government very well in the long run. The fiscal crisis in the period of cease-fire was due partly to tax policy neglect during the "pre-Vietnamization" period, when it must have appeared to the Vietnamese that American aid was a never-ending flow. When real U.S. aid began to decline, the Vietnamese economy stagnated. The effort to assure a gradual increase in consumption in all earlier years probably only raised expectations that could not be met in the long run. If this is true, the government undoubtedly would have been in for hard times even if the war had not come to an abrupt end.

231

The previous chapter recorded facts about expenditures and revenues. This chapter deals with wartime fiscal policy. The task is to define the dimensions of the fiscal problem and then to point out the likely long-run effects of policies that were undertaken with very short term objectives in mind.

12.1 Dimensions of fiscal policy

The fiscal policy pursued by the Vietnamese government during the war can be described as shortsighted and defensive. Although the needs of the government increased enormously, we have seen that there was little apparent effort to raise the domestic tax burden. Our present concern is with the question why the government did not take more aggressive action in attacking its internal fiscal problem. We offer the following hypotheses:

1. The GVN had no incentive to raise taxes or reduce expenditures, because they conjectured that the U.S. government would fill the expenditure gap with aid.
2. The government lacked administrative skills to collect taxes.
3. The effective tax base, excluding agriculture, was so poor that even a large effort would not have provided a large amount of additional revenues, and the central government did not want to tax agriculture for reasons related to pacification.
4. The U.S. government did not make a big issue over taxes, because even raising taxes to some maximum feasible level would have reduced the aid requirement only fractionally (and the total cost of the war imperceptibly). At the same time, such action would have increased the probability of civil and military discontentment significantly. In other words, given overall U.S. objectives, the cost–benefit ratio of a major tax effort, as calculated by the State Department, appeared high.

Although we know of no numerical way to verify any of these hypotheses, we think that each contributed to keeping taxes low. The many formal attempts made by the GVN to raise the domestic tax burden were undertaken more for show than for effect. Neither the GVN or the responsible U.S. officials wanted to see a significant decline in the consumption standards of the people, for they believed that a reduction in the standard of living would undermine the huge military effort under way.

12.1.1 The tax base

The actual tax base in Vietnam was severely circumscribed during the war because agriculture was exempted and industrial activity was relatively minor.

The exemption of agriculture followed from historical conditions and the realities of insurgency operations. Historically, land taxes were reserved for local governments, whose revenue needs were small. The central government could have preempted this source of revenue during the war but was reluctant to do so, probably for the following reasons: (1) It had no way to collect them. (2) Land taxes would have been contrary to its major goal of pacification of the countryside. (3) The central government did not want to continue the Viet Cong institution of agricultural taxation. (4) The central government was probably influenced by large landowners who supported the GVN and were opposed to land taxes. Excluding agriculture, which accounted for one-third to one-half of private national income, from the tax base left few good alternative tax options.

Essentially, the tax base was confined to industrial activity and services. Manufacturing in Vietnam contributed only minimally to the GNP, between 5 and 7 percent in most years. The government levied an ad valorem production tax on some manufactured products and relatively high excise taxes on some goods. The production and excise taxes, including the tax on gasoline, accounted for two-thirds of all domestic taxes. In addition, the workers in the major industrial firms paid a disproportionate share of the personal income taxes simply because it was easy to collect from them by withholding income taxes.

To demonstrate how restrictive the tax base actually was, it has been observed that taxes on tobacco, beer, carbonated beverages, petroleum, and the share of income and production taxes contributed by nine companies accounted for about 60 percent of total taxes collected in all of Vietnam. Combined, these nine companies employed approximately 6,000 workers, maybe one-half of 1 percent of the total work force of Vietnam (Dacy 1969a, p. 66).[1] All of these companies operated principally in Saigon. Thus, whereas it was easy to tax the products of manufacturing and the people engaged in it, the tax base was very small.

Taxes on service outputs were also limited. On the tax books, one notes taxes on entertainment, restaurants, dancing, and so forth, but these were relatively minor activities. Furthermore, taxes on such activities were meager because of poor bookkeeping (or double bookkeeping) and no practical way to collect them.

12.1.2 Tax advice and tax administration

The GVN had many official and unofficial tax advisors. Much "technical assistance" was available. A legitimate question arises: Why did the government not move faster and more purposefully toward the tax reform advocated by some advisors? There are three basic answers to the question: (1)

Tax advisors frequently did not understand the political constraints imposed by the wartime conditions or chose to work in a theoretical context. In those cases, the reform recommendations were politely "studied" by the government, but ignored. (2) Some tax advisors acted as if they did not fully appreciate the low level of tax administration and the inherently difficult problems of tax collection in an underdeveloped country, particularly one at war. With respect to advice from these advisors, the Vietnamese made some effort to please the advisors. (3) The government was politically oversensitive about any kind of economic policy that appeared to impose a burden on the people. In those cases, it simply rationalized inaction.

12.1.2.1 Tax administration: American tax advisors generally recognized that Vietnam was poorly equipped to handle a comprehensive tax reform effectively. Nevertheless, some tax recommendations did not adequately consider the Vietnam context. For example, much effort was expended in designing and enforcing a complicated graduated income tax. It was not a very fruitful effort, because the success of a progressive income tax depends critically on reliable accounting and a favorable tax attitude, two preconditions that were absent. Perhaps they would have developed in due course in South Vietnam, but an expectation of such development did not solve the wartime finance problem. The income tax was hardly worth the collection cost until a withholding provision was instituted in 1967. Because withholding could be enforced only against the employees of large employers, particularly American employers, this tax was discriminatory at first.

With the withholding provision, income tax collections were more than doubled in the first year. However, in the next five years the total take rose barely faster than the rate of inflation. During this period, revenues from the income tax increased 3.5-fold, whereas prices almost tripled. One would have expected more from a progressive income tax with built-in "bracket creep" in an inflationary environment. Evidently, the government was not able to broaden the base beyond those relatively few workers who were employed by a few withholding employers.

A major problem of tax policy was institutional. In 1966, a U.S. Internal Revenue Service study (IRS 1966, p. 59) found that

the problem lies in non-compliance by the Vietnamese taxpayers with a rather complex and sophisticated system of laws and inadequate tax administration. The non-compliance . . . is the result of tax personnel inadequate as to numbers, ability and authority.

This situation did not change much over the next five years. Thus, Stockfisch (1971, p. 29) wrote that

The Finance Ministry has around 2,200 employees, with about 900 of them functioning in the field. No more than 50 or 60 of them have training in auditing techniques.

There is a lack of rigor in collection and enforcement in both the excise and "direct" fields. By standards prevailing in other countries, including those in Asia, this tax collection enforcement capacity is inadequate by a factor of from three to five ...

Poor tax administration cannot be transformed in a short time. In addition, the transformation requires more than formal training and proper remuneration. Even if these had been the only prerequisites, Vietnam could not have solved them during the war, and so the problem of having to collect a large amount of revenues from a relatively small tax base would have remained. In any event, formal training of tax collectors is not the major prerequisite for an efficient collection system. According to Stockfisch (1971, p. 30), "The Executive Branch and the courts must vigorously back up the tax collecting arm, to prosecute cases of tax evasion fairly and without regard to a violator's political affiliations." This latter condition, clearly, requires resolve and will.

12.1.2.2. Tax attitude: Up until the summer of 1973, when the Vietnamese put into effect a value-added tax, the government showed little in the way of resolve and will regarding tax policy.[2] It appears not to have been willing to tackle any economic issue with strong political overtones. Within the area of tax policy, this means that it was willing only to make marginal changes in tax rates without any genuine reform of the tax system. However, even within this limited context it seems that the government used double standards in raising the rates on various products.

The government's attitude on two specific taxes illustrates the point. In the case of beer, one of Vietnam's best excise tax earners, the government never hesitated to raise the rate per liter. Over the period of this study, the implied rate on a liter of beer rose over twelvefold. By contrast, in the case of gasoline, the implied rate per liter rose only threefold, including import duties. Was there an economic justification for this apparent contradiction in tax attitude? Obviously, the distinction could not have been made on the basis of economic criteria such as demand elasticities and maximum tax revenues or from consideration of tax incidence and income distribution. We believe that the distinction was made on the basis of moral preconceptions and out of concern for political sensitivity. The government believed it could tax beer heavily because it was a "luxury," whereas, at one time, gasoline had been listed as a "necessity" in the Vietnamese taxonomy of taxes. When U.S. officials on occasion complained about the relatively low gasoline tax, their Vietnamese counterparts claimed that a high price on gasoline would cause much urban unrest and hence would be politically destabilizing. This seems to have been an all too frequent rationale for inaction.

One student of the Vietnamese tax system put the blame for lack of tax reform squarely on tax administrators, who, he claimed, almost invariably gave a negative response to any new tax proposal. He thought that "if tax reform depended on the ready acquiescence of tax administrators, there probably would be little reform. Nevertheless, it is also likely that the combination of administrative limitations, political procrastination, and the level of tax morality on the part of the public constitutes a greater barrier to tax reform than the technical problem of devising a better tax system" (Taylor 1968, p. 62). This statement suggests that intermediate-level bureaucrats were psychologically incapable of thinking about substantive reform measures. Certainly there was little pressure put on them by high-level officials of the government, who undoubtedly thought that American aid was the answer to short-run fiscal problems.

Vietnamese officials undoubtedly had a negative tax attitude. They were not willing to try much in the way of new taxes and were unwilling to raise rates significantly on some potentially good tax earners. It is understandable that tax officials, on behalf of the government, would not want to alienate the urban population. Besides, they were able to follow a very cautious policy in the short run because they were effective in lobbying for foreign economic aid. Thinking about the possible adverse long-run consequences of short-run tax policies was not their job. This disagreeable task was the responsibility of strategic economic planners, who, if they existed at all, kept their thoughts to themselves.

12.2   Some consequences of wartime tax strategy

Given the overwhelming financial burden imposed by the war, it seems unlikely that any tax scheme could have solved both the long-run and short-run political and economic problems. Faced with this fiscal dilemma, the Vietnamese government (and their American advisors) opted for short-run solutions, probably under the very realistic assumption that if the short-run financial difficulties could not be resolved without lowering the standard of living of the people, then there would be no chance to tackle the long-run problem – that of raising taxes in a peaceful environment. The main policy thrust had two prongs: to contain inflation within the bounds of political stability and to keep the standard of living from falling. This strategy seemed sensible to the American advisors, ever concerned with political stability, and it was easy for the Vietnamese government to accept and pursue because it reduced their political problems.

Perhaps the stabilization-consumption strategy that implied low tax effort and high foreign aid was the only way to face the dilemma. We do not believe it would have worked in the long run, even had the war been brought to a successful conclusion. History, of course, will not provide the necessary test.

Speculation on what might have been is interesting, but not very useful. Here we briefly discuss some of the consequences of pursuing the tax strategy that minimized tax effort.

12.2.1 Political credibility

One sign of political credibility is the power to tax. The power to tax indicates that a government has a strong hold on the people. In a democratic society it means that the people generally approve the programs for which they are taxed and therefore approve of the government to some extent. In a nondemocratic society it usually means that the government has sufficient military support to assure tax collections, and sometimes the people support the goals of the government.

It is not reasonable to apply this criterion of credibility strictly in the case of wartime Vietnam. In that situation, no government could have imposed on the people the heavy burden required to finance the war. The war, which was hardly a popular people's war, was simply too big for any underdeveloped country to finance. With respect to political allegiance, there were small groups on the left and right, with a huge mass of population caught in the middle.[3] Over the years, the central government gained the support of a larger share of the population, but gaining it may have come at a very high cost for the future. In effect, the government used foreign aid to buy the support of the population. Although this method may have had a salutary pacification effect in the short run, it hardly established political credibility, because it displayed a lack of international independence.

The credibility problem had no easy solution. On the one hand, the government needed a pacified populace to conduct the war. If it pacified without demonstrating a capacity to rule, it would lose a certain amount of credibility. The easiest way to pacify was to rely on U.S. aid. Taxation and its effect of reducing consumption would indicate a capacity to rule, but at a high risk of losing popularity. Somewhere within this spectrum the central government had to make a choice. Theoretically, there was an optimal mix of taxation and aid. It is most difficult, even in retrospect, to specify that mix. We simply speculate that the availability of massive aid presented the Vietnamese government with little incentive to face up to their internal economic problems. By taking all the aid they could get, we believe the GVN lost the chance to enhance its political credibility. As it developed, they lost their major advantage in justifying continued support of the U.S. Congress. With declining aid in the last few years, consumption dropped anyway, and the government appears to have relied on more repressive measures to maintain itself.[4]

12.2.2   Income distribution

Some evidence on income distribution was presented in Section 5.3. The conclusion reached there was that farmers gained in relation to the urban population over the 1956–74 period as a whole. Improvement in the economic status of farmers was not an uninterrupted process. We have seen that the rice price policy in the critical 1965–8 period worked against the farmers. Major gains were registered in the period following the Tet attack, when price policy was reversed and land reform became a reality. The previous analysis was undertaken without consideration of the impact of taxation. The present task is to make a reasoned guess as to how the tax system affected income distribution.

It is probable that the formal tax system discriminated against the urban population. Provincial taxes levied against the rural population were negligible and even declined by about 50 percent in real terms from 1965 to 1972.[5] By contrast, almost all of the slight real increase in the tax revenues of the central government was collected in the cities. It has been established that about 90 percent of all internal revenues were collected in the Saigon/Cholon/Gia Dinh area (IRS 1966, p. 66). It is probable that some of these taxes were shifted to the rural population, but there can be little doubt that most of the burden fell on urban dwellers.

It is probably true, also, that almost all of the inflationary tax was borne by the urban population. There are two strong reasons for making this assumption: (1) Farmers consumed a very large part of their produce; that is, they "paid" themselves in kind. Therefore, the inflationary tax would affect their real income less than the income of urban people. (2) Holders of money balances lose part of their wealth in an inflationary environment. In Vietnam, it is very likely that most of the money stock was held by the urban population, because theirs was almost completely an exchange society. Thus, the billions of piasters raised by printing money reduced the real income (and wealth) of the urban population much more than for the rural population.

Finally, the import tariffs placed on agricultural inputs were considerably lower than those on consumer goods that found major outlets in the urban areas. Fertilizer, as an example, was subsidized over most of the period of this study, and there was no tariff on agricultural machinery. Thus, the import tariff structure also discriminated against the urban population in comparison with farmers. This aspect of tax policy was, of course, no accident. President Thieu made a major effort to appeal to the rural population.

12.2.3   Economic development

Most developed countries have overall tax rates in excess of 20 percent. Tax rates of this order appear to be necessary for development of infrastructure and the advancement of human capital. Because these promote productivity and sustained growth, the institution of taxation has to be well established before growth can be taken for granted.

Taxation is hardly ever a positive feature of the public attitude. It takes years for its acceptance, even as a necessary evil. In extraordinary circumstances a government is able to impose and collect more taxes than would be the case in uneventful periods. Surely, all-out war is an extraordinary event. In an extraordinary situation, the degree of public acceptance is improved, and the act of paying taxes, if it becomes habitual, helps to promote longer-run public acceptance. The tax institution can be strengthened during war.

Wartime tax policy in South Vietnam did little to strengthen an essential institution of economic development. Given the extraordinary situation and the demonstrated capability of the government to act when it felt under pressure (e.g., when it devalued the piaster in 1966 and instituted the value-added tax in 1973), we believe that the GVN lost a good opportunity to raise the probability for successful future development by its lack of interest in raising the performance of its tax system before it became too late.

12.3   The dilemma restated

A small underdeveloped country was engulfed in a costly war that it could not possibly finance out of local resources. The question, therefore, was not what kind of fiscal policy it might pursue to completely finance the war but how large a share of the total the government thought it could impose on the people. A major constraint, other than the availability of resources, was political – the pacification of the people. It could achieve an immediate political advantage with a higher probability of success by shifting the incidence of taxation away from the people (and accepting aid from a foreign nation) rather than by increasing the domestic burden of taxation. But by pursuing a policy of short-run advantage, it would have to give up something in the way of longer-term political credibility and, very likely, longer-term economic development. That was the fiscal dilemma of wartime Vietnam. Evidently, the government opted for the short-run gain. Undoubtedly, the rationale was that if it could not solve the short-run problem, it would have no chance to solve the long-run problem.

CHAPTER 13

Foreign aid and economic development in an environment of high military threat

One of the long-standing arguments during the Vietnam war concerned the prospects for economic development while the war was in progress. In essence, the pessimists thought that the combined military-political problem had to be resolved in advance of economic development, because the latter depended on a stable military-political environment. Optimists thought that substantial development could occur while the war was being fought. On this view, foreign aid could stabilize the economy and promote development simultaneously. To the optimists, the relevant question pertained to the *amount* of aid required to put Vietnam on the path of self-sustaining growth, and studies were commissioned to determine the amount of aid needed.

We have argued that not much economic development occurred during the war. If this is correct, should one then conclude that the pessimists were right?[1] We do not think so. A demonstration that significant development did not occur during the war is no proof that it could not have occurred.

This chapter deals with a wider question than the one that concerned Vietnam optimists and pessimists. Here we face the general question whether or not it is reasonable to expect significant economic development to take place over a relatively short period of time, say two decades, in an environment of high military threat if other conditions are favorable. In the period since World War II, U.S. foreign policy regarding the underdeveloped nations in the world has been focused on the high-threat environments in four small countries: Israel, South Korea, Taiwan, and South Vietnam. These nations have been referred to as U.S. "client" states, and aside from being sponsored by the United States, they had much in common. Our purpose is to compare Vietnam and these other countries with respect to an important economic variable and a critical political variable. The economic variable is the ratio of domestic saving to income. The political variable is the leadership commitment to development. One does not need to look much beyond these variables to explain the economic failure of Vietnam, in contrast to the successes of South Korea and Taiwan and to a lesser extent Israel. The comparison reveals that substantial development can take place in an environment of high military threat if certain economic and political conditions are met.

240

13.1   Aspects of high military threats

13.1.1   What is a high military threat?

In the 1950–75 period, there were several underdeveloped nations that operated under the cloud of a real or imagined military threat. The two Vietnams,
several Middle Eastern countries, Taiwan, the two Koreas, and Cuba would
be included on the lists of many observers, even without a formal definition
of "high military threat." To our definitional purpose it is useful to distinguish
between a "threatened nation" and an "aggressor nation," because no nation
can be threatened unless there is an aggressor to threaten it. Depending on
differing points of view, any nation can fit into both categories. For example,
whether Israel has been a threatened nation or an aggressor depends on one's
point of view. Most "threatened" nations probably have been considered
aggressors by the peoples across their borders. Our definition of a threatened
nation follows from these characteristics of a threatening situation:

1. The threat is external. One sovereign nation is threatened by another.
   Civil or guerrilla wars will meet this criterion if the sides in the
   struggle are seen to be proxies for aggressor nations. Both Vietnams
   qualify under this criterion. The GVN considered the Viet Cong to
   be a proxy for the North Vietnamese and the Russians, and the North
   Vietnamese considered the government of South Vietnam to be
   "lackeys" of the United States.
2. There is geographic proximity between the threatened and aggressor
   countries.
3. The aggressor nation must actually have the power to significantly
   harm the threatened nation. A situation in which an aggressor nation
   can only conduct occasional raids against a border does not qualify
   as a high-threat situation.

A high military threat does not imply actual combat between nations. The
major point is that a threatened nation has a genuine fear of an aggressor who
is capable of inflicting physical damage and, most likely, would severely alter
existing institutions if victorious. A threatening situation usually involves a
superpower, at least indirectly, but there is no necessity of such involvement.

It is difficult to distinguish between a high military threat and an ordinary
one. Most nations sense some potential military threat, and they maintain
armed forces for protection. Although a feeling of threat is a state of mind
that cannot be observed directly, there are some objective manifestations of
it. Underdeveloped countries that feel threatened maintain armed forces that
are large relative to the sizes of their populations and spend relatively large

Table 13.1. *Defense spending and relative size of armed forces in high-threat underdeveloped nations, 1963 and 1968*

	1963		1968	
Country	Percentage of GNP spent on defense	Percentage of population in armed forces	Percentage of GNP spent on defense	Percentage of population in armed forces
Cuba	5.6	1.1	5.8	1.3
Egypt	8.6	0.5	8.9	0.6
Iraq	10.2	1.1	12.3	1.0
Israel	8.6	2.7	17.7	3.4
Jordan	15.3	2.5	19.5	2.6
Korea, North	12.2	3.1	17.4	3.1
Korea, South	4.2	2.3	4.1	2.0
Syria	8.7	1.5	11.2	1.1
Taiwan	10.2	4.6	10.6	3.9
Vietnam, North	17.9	1.5	25.0	2.4
Vietnam, South	13.5	2.8	18.7	4.2
Median, 87 LDCs	2.1	0.3	2.4	0.3

Source: U.S. Arms Control and Disarmament Agency (undated).

shares of their GNPs on defense. There is considerable sacrifice of resources to guard against the perceived threat. This fact permits a crude determination of high-military-threat nations by statistical means.

The statistical measures are based on percentage of population in the armed forces and percentage of GNP spent on defense. Some high-threat nations in the 1950–75 period are listed in Table 13.1. All the nations shown in the table were threatened according to the criteria given earlier, in addition to qualifying statistically. In comparison with the median values for eighty-seven underdeveloped nations, each nation listed spent a large percentage of its GNP on defense and maintained relatively large armed forces. The figures shown probably understate relative military preparedness, because most of the nations listed had considerable outside military assistance in comparison with the median for underdeveloped countries.

13.1.2 Potential impacts on development

The economic effect of a threat, military or other, is assumed to be negative. To defend one's self from a threat requires the use of time and resources that must be diverted from other uses. It is possible, however, that threats will produce some unexpected positive outcomes or positive indirect effects. If it had been possible to have improved the pre-threat developmental environment by more knowledge, better incentive structures, and better organization, then positive outcomes would be possible if a threatening situation should induce improvements in those development-augmenting factors. But if an economy were operating efficiently (in a Paretian manner) before the threat, it could only be worse off after reallocating resources to counter the threat.

The fact that any nation is not developing satisfactorily is prima facie evidence that its economy is not operating in a Pareto-optimal manner. There is room for improvement. Even so, there is no reason to presume that a military threat will jolt a nation in the direction of economic efficiency. The presumption still must be that a military threat is an additional obstacle to economic development.

The reasons for this probable outcome are numerous. A threat can turn into actual conflict, with physical destruction of a country's population and productive capacity, as exemplified by the Korean War. Even without physical damage, a military threat spreads uncertainty, which has a depressing effect on local investment and also is likely to alter the composition of the reduced investment toward inventory accumulation and away from plant and equipment. The impact on foreign investment can be even more devastating. A military threat usually induces the government to shift its priorities to short-run, counterdevelopmental programs and to increase its regulations throughout the economy under the guise of security, interfering with migration and stifling private initiatives and economically efficient practices. Wherever a threat is met by a military buildup, the drain of skilled manpower into the armed forces creates an additional problem for industrial development. Further, the military buildup requires an expansion of the military budget, creating a larger government deficit. The deficit is financed usually by printing money. This causes inflation, which, if not checked, tends to undermine the authority of the government. Finally, a military threat can increase social tensions, depending on how well the aggressor nation plays to the various divisions that exist in all societies.

On the other hand, it is conceivable that a military threat can have some favorable effects on behavior. It can serve as a catalyst to improve social cohesion of the population by promoting patriotism and presenting a set of common objectives. A military threat can strengthen government without making it more repressive, under favorable circumstances. Under a cloud of war, efficiency can become a major interest of government. Obsolete capital is likely to be replaced more quickly by more modern capital. Military training usually improves the skills of people called to serve and improves work discipline. Growth-retarding institutions are more likely to disintegrate in a threatening environment than under the status quo. Finally, a military threat can create conditions for the rise of a charismatic leader. If such a leader is interested in economic development, a stagnant economy can be turned around in a relatively short period.

13.2   U.S. foreign aid to high-threat nations and economic development

The role of military aid is to permit a buildup of security forces with minimal budgetary impact and without sacrificing foreign exchange earnings. However, military aid causes economic problems in recipient nations, which creates the need for economic assistance. Specifically, U.S. military aid to other nations, called *security assistance*, is not "free" to the recipient country. Ordnance supplied under the Military Assistance Program (MAP) requires maintenance and, not infrequently, a buildup of forces. Where a buildup of forces is a complement to MAP aid, the adverse budgetary impact can be significant. On the other hand, it is possible that MAP grants can be used to substitute virtually free military capital for labor. If better equipment allows a country to reduce the size of its forces, it is conceivable that the budgetary impact could be positive. Although there is a theoretical possibility to the contrary, we accept the popular view that military assistance, particularly to underdeveloped countries, induces a rise in the local defense budget. This, of course, aggravates the development problem.

Evidently, the adverse budgetary implications of security assistance are recognized by the U.S. State Department. For those countries in which the United States has a keen security interest, *supporting assistance* is made available. The purpose of this economic aid is to promote and maintain economic and political stability. An assumption used to justify supporting assistance to preferred nations is that a rapidly expanding budget, for whatever reason, will cause inflation, other economic problems, and political instability. These conditions are deemed to be inimical to national security and undermine the purpose for which supporting assistance is given to counterbalance the presumed adverse economic effects of military aid.

In the underdeveloped world, four countries dominated U.S. security interests in the 1950–75 period. These countries, South Vietnam, South Korea, Taiwan, and Israel, faced formidable economic as well as national security problems. They received 20 percent of all U.S. economic aid and 45 percent of all U.S. military aid in 1953–74, and that excludes billions of dollars spent to maintain U.S. forces in two of those countries. The dollar values are shown in Table 13.2. Vietnam received half of the four-country total.

Of all the underdeveloped countries in the early 1950s, Taiwan and South Korea present possibly the best examples of economic development, and Israel's progress would be considered high on the list by many economic

Table 13.2. *U.S. economic and military assistance, 1953–74 (billion dollars)*

	1953–61		1962–74	
Country	Economic assistance	Military assistance	Economic assistance	Military assistance
All countries	24.053	24.240	52.469	43.302
Four-country total	5.610	4.279	9.242	26.106
Israel	0.507	nil	0.714	3.912
Korea	2.579	1.561	2.447	4.830
Taiwan	0.979	2.145	0.311	1.798
Vietnam	1.545	0.572	5.770	15.566

Source: AID (undated).

development analysts. Vietnam, as we argued in Chapter 4, presents a mixed picture. Many of its indicators of development were positive, but, overall, it failed to achieve the momentum or self-reliance to assure self-sustaining growth before its defeat.

Considering the successes of Taiwan, South Korea, and Israel, it is evident that a highly threatening situation is not necessarily a bar to economic development. The presumed adverse economic effects of threats can be overcome. It also seems evident that high-threat nations require large amounts of foreign aid if they are to develop despite the threat. In the special case of the four U.S. client states, it is also clear that massive foreign aid was not a sufficient condition for development. Vietnam received the most aid and developed the least satisfactorily.

13.3   High-threat group and comparison group

13.3.1   Method of analysis

It would be desirable to compare economic development in a group of threatened countries with development in another group similar in significant ways, with the exception of the threat. Such a comparison of groups would be instructive in assessing the developmental contribution of the threat. The problem is that no ideal comparison group exists, because the threatened nations differ from most other countries in that they are also highly aided, and it is difficult to disentangle the effects of foreign aid and high military threat. As an aid in thinking about the problem of comparison, consider the following matrix:

	High threat	No threat
High-aid countries	A_{11}	A_{12}
Moderate-aid countries	A_{21}	A_{22}
Low-aid countries	A_{31}	A_{32}

Included in group A_{11} are Israel, South Korea, South Vietnam, and Taiwan. Assuming that two groups are alike in other ways, we would like to compare group A_{11} with group A_{12}. As stated earlier, this comparison should indicate whether a threat is a positive or negative factor in development. Unfortunately, we are not able to identify a group such as A_{12}. A different approach is required.

Let us assume for the moment that a high military threat to a poor nation inhibits economic development and that a generous application of foreign aid promotes it. For a threatened/highly aided underdeveloped country, we further assume that the effect of aid cancels out the effect of the threat, so that, on balance, a group of such countries should perform as "normal" underdeveloped countries (A_{22} in the matrix). On this assumption it would be legitimate to compare a group of threatened/aided countries (A_{11}) with a "normal" group (A_{22}) under the further assumption that the "normal" group is similar in other essential characteristics to the threatened/aided group. In such a comparison, differences in development performance between the two groups would contradict the assumption that high threat and high aid offset each other. For example, if it were found that the threatened/aided group performed worse than normal, one would infer, almost certainly, that the high military threat was the cause. On the other hand, if it were found that the threatened/aided group performed better than the normal group, one of two conclusions could be drawn: (1) A threatening environment does not bar development, or (2) an abundance of aid can more than offset the negative impact of a threatening environment. This result would be inconclusive. An additional step of conducting a within-group analysis of the threatened/aided group would be required. The purpose of the within-group study would be to uncover factors other than threat that could account for the varied performances within the group.

Our strategy is to compare South Vietnam, South Korea, Taiwan, and Israel as a group of threatened/highly aided countries with another group of non-threatened/moderately aided countries. For simplicity of expression we shall refer to the two groups as threatened and nonthreatened, although aid is a critical feature. The first order of business is to select the nonthreatened group of countries. This is followed by a brief comparison of various performance indicators or group averages.

13.3.2   Selecting the comparison group

There are several criteria that could serve as a basis for picking countries in the nonthreatened group. One would want the comparison group to be similar to the threatened group in essential characteristics other than aid and military threat environment. The first two criteria for selection into the comparison group were percentage of GNP spent on defense and percentage of population in the armed forces. A specific requirement for a nonthreatened group is that these percentages be significantly lower than in the threatened group. As a double check, we decided to select countries from relatively nonthreatening regions of the world. The two qualifying regions in the 1950–75 period were black Africa and South America. Of course, each underdeveloped country has special problems; but, as a continental group, the South American countries appeared to be more similar to the four threatened countries than the black African countries were. To further narrow the list, it was necessary to choose from numerous country characteristics those that are most important for understanding economic development. We assumed that sociopolitical characteristics were more important than geographic characteristics.

The information contained in Adelman and Morris's book *Society, Politics, and Economic Development* (1972) is very useful for distinguishing country characteristics. As input data for their factor analysis, Adelman and Morris ranked seventy-four developing countries with scores (generally) of A, B, C, and D in twenty-four sociopolitical characteristics. Among the twenty-four designations are characteristics such as economic dualism, social mobility, cultural and ethnic homogeneity, modernization of outlook, strength of traditional elite, administrative efficiency, and so forth. We compared the rankings of each of our threatened countries in each sociopolitical characteristic with every South American country to determine which South American country paired best with each threatened country. "Best" was measured as lowest total score. The score in a particular characteristic was computed by assigning zero points if the two countries being compared had the same rank in that characteristic, one point if they were one rank apart, and two points if they were more than one rank apart. The total score is the sum over twenty-four characteristics. By this method of matching, Israel paired very well with Venezuela (they had the same rank in sixteen of the twenty-four characteristics), Taiwan matched best with Chile and Paraguay (tie), South Korea with Ecuador and Paraguay (tie), and South Vietnam with Ecuador. Israel's second best match was with Colombia, and Korea's was with Brazil and Peru. In general, Argentina and Brazil were poor matches with the group of threatened countries and were excluded from the comparison group, which included the six Andean countries and Paraguay.

To determine if we could do much better in selecting a comparison group, we paired some non–South American countries with the four defense-oriented countries. For example, Lebanon and the Philippines seemed good candidates. Surprisingly, Israel paired better with Venezuela (in the characteristics compared) than with Lebanon, and Korea and Taiwan paired much better with Paraguay and Chile than with the Philippines. The major objection to our comparison is lack of consideration given to the geographic and demographic factors. South Vietnam, Israel, South Korea, and Taiwan are relatively small countries in physical size, with relatively high population densities. We could not deal with those undefined "personal faculties and attitudes" stressed always by Professor P. T. Bauer. Per capita incomes in 1961 were not so different as to raise an additional objection.

13.3.3   Threatened and nonthreatened groups compared

Table 13.3 presents data for comparing the threatened and nonthreatened groups. The differences with respect to defense expenditure and population in the armed forces (1960–73) should be noted as a definitional matter. These differences were the bases for the original distinction. In regard to development performance, the threatened nations clearly outperformed the nonthreatened group. This claim is verified in a general way by comments from numerous investigators of economic development. Most analysts would place Taiwan, South Korea, and Israel in the group of development success stories in the post–World War II era. The seven Latin American countries we picked as a comparison group, with perhaps one or two exceptions, fell within the large set of poor performers in development.

The GDP growth figures in Table 13.3 support the general impression of superior performance by the threatened group in comparison with the Latin American countries. The per capita growth rate of real GDP in the threatened group in the 1960–73 period was 2.5 times the average rate achieved in the comparison group. The country growth rates achieved by Israel, South Korea, and Taiwan as a trio were still better. It is of special interest to note the acceleration in growth rates in the cases of South Korea and Taiwan between the 1955–63 and 1960–73 periods. The Israeli economy grew very fast in both periods, although the growth rate was reduced in the latter period. Measured by growth rate alone, Vietnam fell more in the class of the comparison group than in the threatened group. With the passage of time, Vietnam's growth rate not only fell further behind that of its own group but also fell relative to that of the comparison group.

Investment usually is associated with growth of GNP. Gross investment as a percentage of GNP does not seem to be a distinctive feature in comparing the two groups. The average rates of gross investment for the 1955–63 period are practically the same for the two groups; yet the growth rate in the threatened countries was 50 percent higher than for the comparison group during that period. In the 1960–73 period, gross investment was slightly higher in the threatened nations than in the Latin American group, but the growth rate, as before, was much higher. We are not concerned with why or how the threatened group managed to achieve a higher rate of growth out of comparable gross investment rates. It is of interest, though, to point out that the data for Vietnam more closely resemble those for the comparison group than for its own group. Why this should be so is our major concern.

To conclude this section on group comparison, it is evident that a high military threat is not necessarily a bar to development. Yet, it is possible that the threatened group performed better than the unthreatened group because the former was also a highly aided group. In other words, the presumed advantage of foreign aid might outweigh the presumed disadvantage of a high-threat situation. To test this proposition, it is necessary to take a closer look at the countries listed in the highly threatened/highly aided group.

13.4 Vietnam, South Korea, Taiwan, and Israel compared

13.4.1 Early conditions

Among the four selected threatened nations, South Vietnam, South Korea, and Taiwan in the early 1950s were strikingly alike in many cultural characteristics and past economic history. First and foremost, they shared a common Chinese heritage. Mason and associates (1980)[2] emphasized the role of Confucian values in Korean economic development. Little (1979, p. 461) thought that these values were important in the economic development of Taiwan. These values include high regard for education and self-improvement, respect for leaders, and acceptance of social discipline. Vietnam, perhaps, was somewhat removed from Confucianism, but not distant. As was true of Taiwan and Korea, it had a homogeneous and industrious population. The fact that about 10 percent of its population was Catholic did not lead to an unmanageable division there.[3] These three countries clearly were candidates for successful development, given the motivation and attitudes of their populations in the early 1950s.

A second major similarity is that each of these countries had just recently been freed from colonial domination. The Japanese ruled Taiwan from 1894 to 1945 and Korea from 1910 to 1945. The French decided to subdue Vietnam in 1857 under the pretext of protecting French missionaries, and they attached Tourane in 1858 and gained a tenuous foothold in Saigon in 1859. Three provinces of Cochin China came under French rule in 1862, and three more were added in 1867.[4] The French governed all of Indochina until 1954. The

Table 13.3. *Comparative data on gross investment, foreign investment, and defense-related variables for South Vietnam, Israel, South Korea, Taiwan, and average of seven Latin American countries, 1955–73*

Variable	South Vietnam	Israel	South Korea	Taiwan	Average of threatened nations	Average of seven Latin American countries
1955–63						
Defense expenditures/GNP[a]						
Armed forces/Population[a]						
Real GDP (average annual growth rate)[b]	0.038	0.099	0.054	0.067	0.064	0.043
Real GDP (average per capita growth rate)	0.012	0.049	0.028	0.031	0.030	0.019
Gross investment/GNP[c]	0.088	0.288	0.132	0.186	0.174	0.175
Foreign investment/GNP[d]	0.102	0.174	0.099	0.080	0.114	0.030
Foreign investment ($ annual average per capita)[e]	13.50	178.60	12.10	9.90		
1960–73						
Defense expenditures/GNP[a]	0.159	0.191	0.041	0.099	0.122	0.022
Armed forces/Population[a]	0.044	0.033	0.020	0.040	0.034	0.005
Real GDP (average annual growth rate)[b]	0.041	0.084	0.091	0.097	0.078	0.050
Real GDP (average per capita growth rate)	0.015	0.050	0.065	0.070	0.050	0.019
Gross investment/GNP[c]	0.109	0.275	0.203	0.233	0.205	0.181
Foreign investment/GNP[d]	0.129	0.168	0.090	−0.013	0.094	0.029
Foreign investment ($ annual average per capita)[e]	23.50	261.50	16.40	−3.10		

[a] Data from U.S. Arms Control and Disarmament Agency (undated, Table II). Comparable data compiled by the agency begin in 1962.

[b] For the 1955–63 period: These figures are averages of annual rates as computed from data in the United Nations *Yearbook* (1965), except for South Vietnam. Data for South Vietnam refer to net domestic product as computed by the author. Average rate of growth of GNP for Bolivia covers the period 1958–63, and this shorter-period average received equal weight in the average for the seven Latin American countries. For the 1960–73 period: Except for South Vietnam, Taiwan, and Ecuador, these data were taken from the United Nations *Yearbook* (1972, vol. III, International Tables, Table 4A), and they cover the period 1960–71. The figure for South Vietnam was computed from the source cited for the 1955–63 period and covers the period 1960–72. The figure for Ecuador used as a component in the entry for the seven Latin American countries is an unweighted average for the period 1965–70 taken from the United Nations *Statistical Yearbook* (1974, Table 186), and 1960–5 data were computed from real GDP data in the United Nations *Yearbook* (1965–6). The figure for Colombia covers 1960–70, and for Paraguay 1962–71.

[c] Gross investment as a percentage of GNP is the ratio of the two items of the two items undeflated. Original data from the United Nations *Yearbook* (1965) and International Monetary Fund (monthly, various issues). Data for Bolivia used to compute the average for seven Latin American countries began in 1958.

[d] Foreign investment is defined as import surplus on current account in dollars multiplied by the local currency/dollar foreign exchange rate for each country. Data are from International Monetary Fund (monthly, various issues).

[e] These figures were computed as annual average dollar value of foreign investment as defined in footnote d divided by average population over the period.

colonizers were exploiters. The Japanese used Taiwan and Korea as sources of cheap food (primarily rice), and the French used Indochina as a marketplace for French manufactures that were paid for by Indochinese rice exports to other Asian countries (Robequain 1944, p. 322).

The Japanese appear to have been more efficient colonizers than the French. This might be due to the fact that the Japanese depended on Taiwan and Korea to help feed the Japanese. In any event, they paid much attention to agricultural development and did not suppress industrial development. As a result, Taiwan national income grew at approximately 4 percent per year from 1903 to 1940 (Ho 1978, p. 26), and Korea experienced about the same annual rate of growth over the shorter period 1910–40 (Mason et al. 1980, p. 75). Vietnam's economy was not stagnant. One measure shows that rice exported from Saigon increased from 284,000 tons in 1880 to 1,548,000 in 1937 (Robequain 1944, p. 220), an annual growth rate of 3 percent. However, it is most unlikely that the rest of the economy grew anywhere near as fast as rice exports, so that the overall rate of growth probably did not exceed population growth. Another positive aspect of Japanese rule was educational achievement. The Japanese favored primary education, whereas the French in Indochina were ambivalent toward it, at best.[5] Thus, just prior to independence, Taiwan and Korea were closer to "takeoff" than Vietnam.

World War II wiped out much of Taiwan's advantage. It was heavily bombed. During the Korean War, about 75 percent of Korea's capital was destroyed. These destructive wars undoubtedly reduced the advantage that Taiwan and Korea had gained over Vietnam, so that their starting points in the early 1950s probably were not as uneven as the previous growth patterns indicate.

Although the problems facing Israel at the beginning of its nationhood were basically different,[6] there were some similarities. Palestine had also been under colonial rule and had developed agriculturally. Unlike the Asian countries, it had a culturally divided population. Many of the Arabs, who had been heavily engaged in agriculture, left Israel when it was formed as a nation in 1948. The exodus of agricultural workers and the ensuing massive immigration of Jews from Europe, Asia, and Africa, doubling the population by 1952, were severe disruptions to the economy. Also, many of the non-European immigrants were illiterate and did not fit neatly into the existing structure. Much effort was expended by the government to integrate the immigrants in new settlements and to find external financial support, principally through donations. Coping with a huge import surplus became and remained one of Israel's major economic problems. On the positive side, Israel was well endowed with trained administrators, managers, and technicians, and its population possessed what Bauer (1972, p. 133) referred to as the "faculties and motivations appropriate to successful development."

South Vietnam, South Korea, Taiwan, and Israel shared the following characteristics: (1) Each was a newly independent, small, underdeveloped country in the early 1950s. (2) Each faced external threats that required disproportionately large expenditures on defense. (3) Each received large amounts of security assistance to help finance defense expenditures, as well as economic supporting assistance and other foreign aid to help finance their trade deficits. (4) None developed a single resource, such as oil, that would greatly mitigate its budgetary and trade burdens. Aside from their peculiar military situations, they resembled many other underdeveloped countries and were not so unusual in nondefense characteristics.

A major distinction is that Korea and Taiwan were not engaged in armed struggles with their adversaries, even though the threat of armed conflict was real and had to be accepted as a major factor in formulating domestic policies. There is, of course, the question to what extent physical violence inhibits development more than does the threat of violence, which only affects incentives. In placing South Korea and Taiwan in the same group with Israel and South Vietnam, we have made the judgment that the motivational and economic impacts due to violence, in contrast to probable violence, are quantitative rather than qualitative. The drain of human resources (labor) away from economically productive activities and into military pursuits was of the same order in all four countries. The warring countries, Israel and Vietnam, made rapid progress in the development of human resources (education), and these two countries had relatively easy access to real (capital) resources. Israel was not physically destroyed, and South Vietnam's major productive areas were not physically destroyed. The effect of physical violence on the motivation of the people is harder to measure. In the case of Israel, it may have been positive, but it probably was negative in South Vietnam. However, Vietnam furnished a curious historical example of how the proximity of armed struggle does not necessarily create an insurmountable barrier to economic development. The war was fought primarily in rural areas, and only to a limited extent in urban centers; yet agricultural development clearly outpaced industrial development during the last decade of the war.

These countries were sufficiently alike in the early 1950s to justify the expectation that they should perform approximately alike in subsequent years. Three did perform much better than average, and one did not. The following discussion focuses on two important characteristics that separate Vietnam from Israel, South Korea, and Taiwan. It is these characteristics that explain essentially why Vietnam developed slower than the other three and why its development more resembled that of the Latin American countries than that of the threatened/aided group. Consequently, the conclusion that foreign aid was the major determinant of development cannot be drawn.

13.4.2   Commitment to development

At the times the four countries embarked on their national development courses, Taiwan, South Korea, and Israel probably were closer to "takeoff" than South Vietnam. From the early 1950s to 1970, Vietnam fell more and more behind the other three countries in that very important indicator of development called "leadership commitment to economic development," to use Adelman and Morris's characterization. These writers graded Israel A+ and Taiwan B for the 1957–62 period, while assigning a grade of C to South Korea and South Vietnam (Adelman and Morris 1972, p. 80). Most analysts probably would agree that Taiwan's and South Korea's leaders attained the highest grade in commitment to development later on, whereas Vietnam under Thieu probably would not receive a much higher mark than it did under Diem. This lack of interest in development by Vietnam's leaders goes far in explaining why it fell so far behind the others.

Commitment to development is not necessarily forthcoming from strong governments. Israel, Taiwan, and South Korea have had strong governments for most of their independence. Yet, in the 1950s, South Korea was not a model of economic development. In fact, in the fifties, the development path of South Korea resembled that of Vietnam in a later period. Each country was concerned with maximizing U.S. aid and importing consumer goods. President Syngman Rhee of South Korea was a strong political leader, but his administration was unenthusiastic about matters of development. President Chiang Kai-shek was another strong leader, but he was concerned primarily with military matters during the first decade of Nationalist rule on Taiwan. It was not until the late fifties in Taiwan and the early sixties in Korea that economic development became the focus of attention. Competent and energetic people were appointed to key economic positions. Reasonable plans were formulated and vigorously pursued.

In South Korea, the overthrow of Syngman Rhee in 1960 by a student-led revolt brought an inept government into power. This government was overthrown in a military coup in 1961. The new Park military government established as its principal goals rapid economic development and reduced dependence on the United States. The first five-year plan (1962–6) called for an annual growth rate of 7 percent. In the light of previous economic performance, this target seemed "absurdly high," but, in fact, it was exceeded. "South Korea, in whose future American advisers had nearly abandoned hope, was on the verge of one of the most rapid sustained growth experiences known to economic history" (Mason et al. 1980, p. 464).

Economic development in South Korea was a crucial element in the maintenance of power for its president, Park Chung Hee. He considered development as the "principal legitimizer" of his holding power (Mason et al.

1980, pp. 48, 136). Little, writing about Taiwan and Singapore as well as South Korea, claimed that the governments of these countries "perceived economic development as a primary means of establishing their legitimacy and consolidating their support" (1979, p. 466).

On Taiwan, Chiang Kai-shek had ample reason to support economic development. He was convinced that economic mismanagement on the mainland, particularly that leading to rampant inflation and an unfavorable land tenure system, had contributed to his defeat there. However, this concern for economic development was subordinate to his military goal of recapturing the mainland. For some reason – probably lack of interest in his most ambitious vision – the idea of "developing Taiwan into a 'showcase' of Chinese development under free economic institutions became increasingly appealing to Nationalist Chinese leaders" around 1956 (Jacoby 1966, p. 36).[7] According to Jacoby, it was thought that this strategy would "vindicate" the Nationalist regime in world opinion and, in addition, would be true to the teaching of their first leader, Sun Yat-sen, of improving the livelihood of his people (1966, pp. 36, 136).

The situation in Vietnam was different. There is was taken for granted that the people would be provided for adequately by U.S. aid. The "legitimizer" of President Thieu's power was his demonstrated relationship with the United States. If he could be seen by his people as an "equal partner," with access to the center of power in the United States, he would be accepted by the majority of Vietnamese as a legitimate ruler.[8] Given this perception of the road to power, there was little incentive for Vietnamese officials to consider seriously all the necessary and painful economic reforms required for economic development. Nor did they have the personal disposition to make the attempt. As a footnote, it is interesting that when Thieu lost access to the center of power in the United States toward the end of the war, the government had to become more repressive to maintain itself in power.

Of course, there was an understandable reason for the leaders of Vietnam to take this view of legitimacy. With a major war in progress, the government was fully occupied with military affairs. With respect to the assignment of priorities, Vietnamese officials took their cues from their American counterparts. The American government was occupied with two immediate (related) problems. The first, obviously, was conducting the war. The second was convincing the American people that U.S. participation in the war was worthwhile. The economic development of South Vietnam was remote from both of these immediate problems. Consequently, there was no sense of urgency about development to motivate Vietnamese leaders.

There was no lack of urgency with respect to political development in South Vietnam. American leaders had to be concerned with political development in Vietnam in order to sell their war policies to the American public. Therefore, political development toward democracy was forced on the Vietnamese government, rather than policies for economic development. There was a kind of tacit agreement: Thieu would hold elections, and the Americans would continue to "legitimize" his power by supplying consumer goods through aid. While the governments of South Korea and Taiwan were designing policies for attracting foreign private capital and promoting exports to reduce dependence on the U.S. government, Vietnamese officials had to be concerned with how to appease the American public. The legitimizing processes were different. One promoted economic development; the other did not.[9]

The government of Israel stood in sharp contrast to the totalitarian regimes in South Korea and Taiwan. But, like them, it had a definite commitment to development, even if for different reasons. This indicates that development prospects are independent of the form of government. It can take place in democracies or dictatorships so long as aggressive development attitudes prevail.

Pack made a strong case that "government motivation" was a "sufficient" condition for development in Israel (1971, ch. 8).[10] The leaders of Israel in the 1950s and 1960s were members of the Second Alliyah.[11] They came into Palestine possessed with strong views about social democracy.

Being strongly imbued with the concept of strengthening both the economic and social structure of Palestine, they eventually formed the administrative nucleus of the key institutions, both economic and political. They thus entered positions of power not as representatives of particular group interests, but with a perception of themselves as the embodiment of national interests. [Pack 1971, p. 227]

Development was the vehicle by which the leadership group could achieve the goals they defined. After the formation of Israel in 1948, their first task was to settle the new immigrants. With this achieved by 1954, they set out to provide their new countrymen with sufficient incomes to assure social integration. This required rapid economic growth. Thus, economic growth was a necessary condition for achievement of the broader vision held by the leaders of Israel. Their commitment to the broader vision, in turn, virtually assured its success.

We presume that this committed leadership was acutely aware of the hostile regional environment in which they operated. Achievement of their vision depended on the cooperation of the recent immigrants, the masses who were needed to protect their country from hostile neighbors. Thus, the leadership depended on social integration to protect their country, and major social divisions in this context might have proved disastrous for Israel. Therefore, economic development was imperative not only for social integration but also, perhaps, for survival.

"Commitment to development" is much more than issuing five-year plans or announcing economic reforms. It usually involves some plan, but the plan is not its essential feature. Its essential feature is vigorous pursuit of stated economic goals, usually by a committed leader or, as in the case of Israel, by a group. Many countries have developed without plans and explicit goals on the Western model. Development in those cases has been an extended process. In the face of a high military threat, time is of the essence, and the development process must be rushed. In this situation, "commitment to development" might be the single most important variable in economic development. Certainly in our study of four underdeveloped countries facing high military threats, it is evident that the one that did not develop satisfactorily in a short twenty-year period, despite enough foreign aid to close all of the "gaps" discussed in the literature, was also the one in which there was an absence of leadership commitment to development.

13.4.3 Domestic saving and economic development

A major indicator of economic development is the behavior of the *domestic saving ratio*. With reference to the role of saving in economic development there is a vast literature, but most of this does not touch on the critical distinction between *total* saving and *domestic* saving.[12] In this literature, a positive correlation between economic growth and total saving is postulated. Although there are some questions about the exact quantitative character of this relationship,[13] there is nevertheless a rough correspondence. The problem is that growth does not necessarily imply development over any time period except the long run.

Total saving is composed of domestic saving and foreign saving. A superpower like the United States could raise total saving in an underdeveloped country like Vietnam almost at will. This clearly will promote growth of national income, while at the same time it may hinder development. Development must imply a move in the direction of economic independence. A rise in total saving will not necessarily signal such a move. Therefore, it may be misleading to focus attention on this variable. The proper variable to observe for the purpose of monitoring development is the domestic saving ratio. Economic development implies that this ratio is growing both absolutely and relative to total saving.

Emphasis on domestic saving also directs attention to practical issues of domestic economic policy. Suppose that a country has a committed leadership, so that investment is truly the engine of growth. Investment can be increased by raising any of the components of total saving, which can be divided into private domestic saving, government saving, and foreign saving. Increased taxation instantly raises government saving, but it lowers private domestic saving. However, increased taxation raises the sum of private domestic saving and government saving, which is designated as total domestic saving. This is true because most of the increased tax revenues come from private consumption rather than private domestic saving. Thus, tax reform, insofar as it is directed toward raising total domestic saving and total investment, is a major way accessible to underdeveloped countries to promote economic development.

Foreign saving (including foreign aid) is closely associated with the country's deficit on current account, that is, the import surplus. Policies designed to increase exports or reduce imports (import substitution), while maintaining investment at some existing level, are development-oriented, even though they are not directed at raising total saving and investment, because they serve the purpose of shifting the distribution of total saving away from foreign saving and toward domestic saving. Thus, foreign trade policy can promote *development* if it encourages domestic saving at the expense of foreign saving, even if it does not promote *growth* of income.

In contrasting the development records of Israel, South Korea, Taiwan, and South Vietnam, it is most useful to compare behaviors in their domestic saving ratios. For this purpose, domestic saving has been derived by subtracting the import surplus in local currency – a measure of foreign saving – from gross investment, which is a measure of total saving. The period of analysis is 1955–73. The cutoff date was not dictated by the fall of South Vietnam shortly afterward, but by the world oil crisis. The rapid rise in the price of oil greatly increased import surpluses in almost all underdeveloped countries. Thus, extending the analysis a few years beyond 1973 would introduce an element that would dominate the statistics but would not be relevant to the point to be made.

Figure 13.1 displays time series in domestic saving ratios over the 1955–73 period. For Vietnam, the domestic saving ratio was negative for most of the period, whereas it was strongly positive for the other entries. A negative domestic saving ratio does not mean that individuals within a country do not save anything. It does mean that the citizens are consuming well beyond their own means to support it out of domestic resources, and if the foreign source of saving is eliminated, consumption, gross investment, and national income will fall. The domestic saving ratio was low in Korea and Taiwan in the mid–1950s. Starting in 1958, it grew steadily in Taiwan, reaching about 32 percent after 1972, when the country achieved a very significant export balance. As the chart indicates, South Korea floundered from 1956 to 1962, but from 1962 its domestic saving grew rapidly, indicative of a strong movement in the direction of economic independence and self-sustained growth.

The domestic saving ratio in Israel exhibited no upward trend over the period. It rose rapidly to a plateau of 12–14 percent, declined drastically after the 1967 war, subsequently attained a new high level, and plunged to around 5 percent at the time of the Yom Kippur war in 1973. It seems evident that

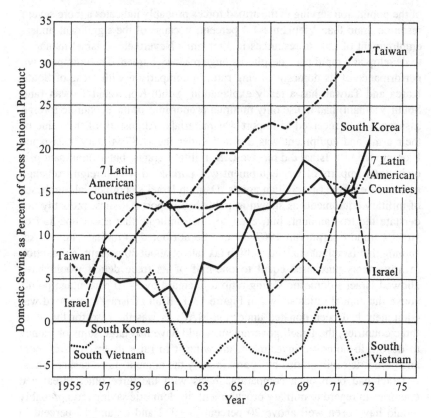

Figure 13.1. Domestic saving as percentage of gross national product for South Vietnam, Israel, South Korea, Taiwan, and seven Latin American countries, 1955–73. *Source*: Based on data in International Monetary Fund, *International Financial Statistics* (various issues). Domestic saving is defined as gross investment less import surplus on current account.

Israel's high growth rate could not have been maintained without massive (private) foreign assistance. However, despite the intermittent, relatively short wars and pervasive military threat from neighboring Arab countries, the Israeli government took measures to build up its defense and develop its economy simultaneously. The government realized that its very high defense burden ultimately would have to be financed out of domestic economic growth; therefore, rapid sustainable growth was a high-priority item on the Israeli agenda. The data in Table 13.1 show that the Israeli defense burden, measured by percentage of GNP spent on defense or armed forces as a percentage of population, was approximately the same as that of South Vietnam. (For a very small country with virtually no underemployment Israel's 3.3 percent of the population serving in the armed forces probably indicates a more severe resource drain than Vietnam's 4.4 percent, because of the significant underemployment of human resources in Vietnam.) Nevertheless, Israel managed to develop at a rapid pace despite its huge military burden. The unimpressive performance of its domestic saving ratio in comparison with those of South Korea and Taiwan has a ready explanation. South Korea and Taiwan (and South Vietnam) had to use only minimal proportions of the economic foreign assistance they received to import war materials. Almost all of the value of their arms and equipment was donated under the U.S. Military Assistance Program (MAP). Israel did receive U.S. military grants, but a significant part of its total imports of war equipment was purchased with foreign exchange in the same manner as civilian goods. Data on Israel's commercial purchases of military equipment, as shown in published import statistics, probably understate the true amount, but, even so, they indicate that about one-half of Israel's import surplus in 1967–73 can be attributed to military items. Assuming that Israel maintained its high tax rate of about 30 percent, a reduction in armaments purchases equal to one-half of its trade deficit would have allowed Israel's domestic saving ratio to increase by 8–10 percentage points above the annual ratios shown in Figure 13.1. If all of Israel's imported war equipment had been donated under the MAP, as was the case for the other three countries, the Israeli government would have had large sums of money to devote to domestic investment, allowing it to raise its gross investment and domestic saving ratios by approximately the amount stated earlier. Thus, if Israel had been on a comparable basis with the three other threatened countries in regard to military procurement, its domestic saving ratio probably would have been well above 20 percent in 1972 and around 15 percent in 1973, the year when its ratio fell drastically because of a huge increase in military imports and government spending on the war.

Using the roughly adjusted figures for Israel, and those actually computed for South Korea and Taiwan, it is evident that a rising domestic saving ratio is an indicator of development. The data for Vietnam show no progress in that important indicator. Once again, the Vietnam record of no growth is more similar to that of the Latin American group than to that of the other three threatened nations. Although we cannot state that the domestic saving ratio is a major *cause* of development, we do assert that countries are not likely to be developing unless their domestic saving ratios are rising absolutely and as percentages of their total saving ratios.

13.4.4 Note on leadership, saving, and development

What is the relationship between leadership commitment to development and growth in the domestic saving ratio? Because a major function of leadership is to establish the rules of the game or to influence the environment in which development takes place, leadership has a causal influence on domestic saving. In some instances the causal nexus is direct, as, for example, when taxes are changed. In most cases the connection is indirect. A typical example is the attempt by government to finance infrastructure through inflation. Whether successful or not, this method has an adverse effect on private saving and, most likely, on domestic saving.

Theoretically, "neutral" leadership, meaning leadership that does not establish rules to discourage saving, is all that is required for development if time is not a critical element. On the whole, the leadership in the United States during the time of its development might be considered to have been neutral. In such a society, domestic saving as a percentage of national income will tend to grow without prodding whenever the marginal propensity to save is larger than the average propensity to save.

When time is a critical factor in development, as it is with underdeveloped nations under threat, neutral leadership will be incompatible with development. Specifically, it is not likely that the domestic saving ratio will rise or, at least, rise fast enough under this condition to generate the momentum required for these countries to survive. The leaderships in South Korea, Taiwan, and South Vietnam in the 1950s and early 1960s, and that of Vietnam later on (periods of only moderate development), were not worse than those typical of traditional societies, and they did not govern explicitly with the intent of maintaining the status quo. However, the rules of the game (institutions) that get established in the histories of traditional societies are negative with respect to development. Overcoming these rules requires a long evolutionary period, which is consistent with neutral leadership, or else revolutionary change in the rules, which requires committed leadership. Obviously, when time is a critical factor, the normal evolutionary process will not work. The role of committed leadership is to change the traditional rules so that domestic saving will rise rapidly.

Examples from the histories of South Korea, Taiwan, and Vietnam are readily available. By traditional practices, governments frequently attempt to control interest rates, other prices, investment, intracountry trade, and foreign trade. Consider the interest rate problem. In these three countries, the necessity to maintain a large military force suggested the use of inflationary finance. With nominal interest rates fixed at historical levels, the real rates fell to negative values. This discouraged private saving and encouraged capital flight. Vietnam never quite solved this problem of low or negative real interest and therefore was not able to raise domestic saving, but it was solved in South Korea and Taiwan in the early sixties, when genuine reforms were put into effect.

Domestic saving is the engine for economic development in the normal evolutionary process. Compound interest applied to the growth in the domestic saving ratio may be sufficient to overcome the unfavorable rules established in the period of traditional society. Indeed, those rules gradually change in successfully developing societies, and, in time, neutral leadership ceases to act as a drag on development. But when development must occur rapidly to free a high-threat country from unreliable foreign grant aid, committed leadership is required. In this situation, the causal connection flows from leadership through domestic saving to development, with another channel directly from leadership to development.

13.5   The role of foreign aid

What, then, is the role of foreign aid in the context of a high military threat? To answer this question, it is useful to divide foreign aid into three classes: (1) military aid, (2) government-to-government grants of economic aid, (3) regular commercial aid. Under a narrow definition of foreign aid, the third class, comprising loans and direct investments, would be excluded. It is included here only because we have used a country's import surplus, including commercial aid, as our operational definition of foreign saving.

The role of loans and direct foreign investment in economic development is not a controversial subject. Obtaining commercial aid is the normal way that developing countries fill their saving–investment gap and foreign trade gap. Loans are taken advisedly, and the projects they finance must meet the ability-to-pay criterion. This gives some assurance, although no guarantee, that the loans will not be misused. This kind of "aid" has an unquestioned role in development. However, the availability of commercial loans to a nation under threat is likely to be restricted.

Military aid is an essential requirement for development for a high-threat underdeveloped country. Military aid includes hardware, war supplies, and, most frequently, "technical assistance" with planning, training, and operations. It is inconceivable that a country could develop satisfactorily under a defense burden that included foreign purchases of the equipment and materials of war. Furthermore, there would be no practical way a poor country could finance such purchases. It might be able to raise the financing for a very short period by drastically restricting normal commercial imports and raising taxes, but most countries would find this method difficult even without excessive requirements. Whereas it seems evident that military grants to developing countries facing a high threat may not promote economic development, it is equally clear that no such country will develop satisfactorily in the absence of military aid. Jacoby, in analyzing the contribution of aid to the development of Taiwan, came to a similar conclusion (1966, p. 126).

The role of free government-to-government grants is clear in theory but ambiguous in practice. As stated earlier, U.S. military assistance frequently is accompanied by economic *supporting assistance*. It can be argued that the budgetary consequence of a situation requiring military assistance is so unfavorable that a country receiving free military equipment and supplies is in need of budgetary support as well. South Korea, South Vietnam, and Taiwan received budgetary support in the form of commodity imports and PL 480 (Food for Peace) aid. Counterpart funds accumulated from the sale of these products within the aided country were set aside to support their budgets. Regarding Vietnam, there was a formal agreement that PL 480 counterpart was to be used to support the military budget. Presumably, this arrangement freed the government to spend its domestically generated revenues on pacification and development. The theory behind *supporting assistance* is persuasive.

There are two practical problems with this approach that are particularly relevant here: (1) PL 480 commodities usually are sold below market clearing prices, and (2) this kind of aid is so attractive to the host country that government officials spend too much time thinking of ways to increase aid. By selling surplus commodities below market prices, the government stifles local production, when its main interest should be to promote production. One reason that free aid is attractive is that it relieves the government of the immediate need to implement reforms conducive to development. If free aid, or foreign saving, added to total saving on a one-for-one basis and did not present government officials with the motive to delay needed reforms, it would not be objectionable on macro grounds. (The micro or price effects would still hold.) However, as Griffin and Enos (1970) and others have shown, foreign aid tends to decrease domestic saving. Also, if it promotes "government consumption," it can result in a fall in the growth rate in future years (Dacy 1975). But these concerns are minor compared with the effect free aid has on the government's incentive to take the difficult and unpopular measures that promote development. A leadership "partly committed" to development may be tempted away from that commitment by the receipt of free foreign aid.

For example, in their analysis of Korean development, Mason and associates (1980, p. 458) stressed the fact that President Rhee's "primary objective was to maximize receipts of foreign aid and to rehabilitate the economy with the smallest possible burden placed on Korean taxpayers." The same was true of all the governments of South Vietnam. In both countries, as well as Taiwan, the pace of development was relatively slow so long as the attitude of maximizing foreign aid prevailed. Korea and Taiwan were successful in shedding this attitude, and thereafter developed rapidly.

P. T. Bauer, a critic of foreign aid, thinks that grant aid is almost always antidevelopmental. His theme is that the prime requirements for development are the economic attitudes of the people and their social institutions and political arrangements. He stresses the importance of "personal faculties and attitudes." Because foreign aid cannot affect these determinants to any significant degree (except, perhaps, adversely), it cannot be very helpful in development. Thus, if a country "cannot develop readily without external gifts, it is unlikely to develop with them" (Bauer 1972, p. 100). There is one exception to this dictum. Countries that face a "crisis in confidence" due to a major threat (Taiwan is Bauer's example) may have confidence restored if the receipt of foreign aid is taken as a signal that a superpower (the United States) will not allow the recipient country to be taken over by the aggressor nation (Bauer 1972, p. 132). However, the effect of aid in this case is due to what it signals rather than what it can achieve directly.

Jacoby's assessment of aid to Taiwan suggests that it had a direct linkage with development. He stated that "aid more than doubled the annual rate of growth of Taiwan's GNP, quadrupled the annual growth of per capita GNP, and cut thirty years from the time needed to attain 1964 living standards" (1966, p. 152). This very favorable assessment was derived from simulations with a Harrod-Domar growth model, but this kind of exercise misses the essential point of the critics of aid. The Taiwan environment, including the "personal faculties" of the people and the ambitions of those who ruled, was extremely favorable for utilizing aid. A proper lesson to be drawn from the Taiwan "miracle" is that "economic policies are far more important than the amount of external aid for any country that aspires to make rapid progress" (Jacoby 1966, p. 129).

Another lesson is that aid can be used to a certain extent to gain leverage over economic policy. This is usually referred to as the issue of "strings." One of the major complaints of critics of American aid to South Vietnam was that the U.S. Embassy there did not use its full power to influence economic events in the country. Embassy officials often protested that they did not have the leverage attributed to them. They had much leverage, undoubtedly, but were handicapped by their substantial agreement with Vietnamese officials that nothing should interfere with the conduct of the war, including economic reforms that they thought were necessary for development. U.S. leverage on economic matters was definitely exercised in Taiwan, where the U.S. mission used its influence to elevate development to the level of national purpose (Jacoby 1966, ch. 10).

Free foreign aid can have beneficial effects even though it may promote some disincentives. Much of the physical overhead capital and improvements in education and health in the three Asian countries can be attributed to foreign aid. When free foreign aid to Korea and Taiwan was finally cut off or reduced, these countries had in place expensive infrastructures for which there were no foreign debts. Not only were these infrastructures vital for future development, but the relative lack of foreign indebtedness conserved foreign exchange in subsequent years and was a factor in securing private loans and direct investments in both countries.[14]

In Israel, South Korea, South Vietnam, and Taiwan, military assistance was essential for success. Some grant aid was useful, and maybe essential. But no amount of military and grant aid can substitute for effective leadership. For promoting development, the form of government is not as important as the attitude of public officials toward development. Economic development can take place in an environment of high military threat whenever the leadership is committed to it. Unfortunately, billions of dollars cannot buy this commitment, as we observed in South Vietnam, and its poor performance in comparison with Israel, South Korea, and Taiwan can be explained in large degree by that fact.

Notes

Chapter 1

1. For background reading, one can choose from a wide selection touching on virtually all aspects of South Vietnam's political history. Some books recommended are Buttinger (1967), Fall (1963), Halberstam (1969), Kahin and Lewis (1967), Karnow (1984), and Shaplen (1965).
2. A more complete view of the economy for this period is given in Buttinger (1967, vol. 2, ch. 12), Fall (1963, ch. 14)), Lindholm (1959), Scigliano (1963, ch. 5), and Taylor (1961). Most independent analysts of this early period are highly critical of the policies of the Diem regime and, by implication at least, of the American "complicity" in his economic (and political) management. For a contrary report, see U.S. Department of State (1961).
3. Operations by the U.S. Navy are given in detail in Commander in Chief, U.S. Pacific Fleet (1959).
4. The best discussion on refugee resettlement is in Lindholm (1959).
5. Deciding what constituted U.S. aid to Vietnam is a complicated matter. There is a discussion of this matter in Chapter 10. The figures given here are those reported by the U.S. Agency for International Development and shown in Table 10.2.
6. See Taylor (1961). The best overall discussion of U.S. aid programs to Vietnam for this early period is that of Montgomery (1962).
7. Data on rice production for the 1955–60 period should be accepted with caution, because information presented in various sources is inconsistent. Compare, for example, the data in Table A4.2 with those given in Fall (1963, p. 294).
8. Crop production figures are given in Table A4.2.
9. Muslof (1963) argued that whereas the Diem government stressed development through public enterprises, it did not pursue the goal aggressively.
10. For a discussion of the IDC, see Trued (1960).
11. See American Friends of Vietnam (1958) for an overly optimistic interpretation of such public declarations.
12. Scigliano and Fox (1965) have written on the role of the Michigan State Advisory Group with respect to these matters.
13. GNP figures are given in Table 3.1.
14. See Table 6.1.

266

15. For a much more pessimistic appraisal stressing development rather than growth, see Hendry (1962).
16. Buttinger has described and speculated on the causes of this failure (1967, vol. 2, pp. 930–46).
17. Killings of village officials were reported to be 700 in 1957, 2,500 in 1959–60, 4,000 between May 1960 and May 1961, and 13,000 in 1961–3 (Fall 1963, p. 360). Kahin and Lewis (1967, p. 138), using U.S. State Department sources, indicated that the number of assassinations increased by 50% from 1960 to 1963, while the number of kidnappings rose tenfold.
18. The concept of "regular equivalent" forces is defined in Chapter 3, and data are given in Table 3.7.
19. Any statement such as this that requires a dollar–piaster comparison should always be read with suspicion. Usually one observes that the translation was made using the official exchange rate, which for most of the period of our account grossly overstated the value of the piaster. This issue is treated in Chapter 9.
20. For these data and a view of the war from the perspective of the American commander, see Westmoreland (undated).
21. See Table 4.1.
22. Cooper (1970) described this conference and its achievements in detail.
23. A good account is given in Sansom (1970).
24. Corson (1968, chs. 8–10) wrote a blistering attack on the U.S. pacification efforts in South Vietnam.
25. Black market and other corrupt activities were the focus of attention in many economic reports from Vietnam during the war. This was particularly true of U.S. congressional investigations, weekly news magazines, and newspaper articles. For a scratch at the surface of this reporting, see U.S. Senate (1966, 1971a), *Newsweek* (1967), Aarons in the *Washington Post* (1969), and Randall in the *Washington Post* (1972).
26. An ambivalent appraisal of this austerity measure was provided by AID (1967, pt. A, pp. 55–6).
27. There was much dissatisfaction in the U.S. Congress that American troops were being forced to give "aid" to South Vietnam when they purchased piasters at the prevailing "inequitable" exchange rate. See U.S. House of Representatives (1971). In fact, many U.S. soldiers and civilians were purchasing piasters on the black market at a rate of about 400 per dollar at the time.
28. Hazilla (1973, pp. 55–7) gave an optimistic assessment of the financial reforms and the GVN's attempt to attract foreign investment.
29. Other studies accepted this explanation, and repetition tended to "confirm" this mistaken view. See, for example, Boarman (1973, p. 33) and Hazilla (1973, p. 54). In fact, the latter suggested that the recession came a whole year after the fact.
30. These data are taken from Table 3.2.
31. Koehler and Williams (1974, pp. 5–6) characterized the recession of 1974 as one of "uncertain depth" and supported their observation with comments on falling wages and "numerous stories" of significant excess capacity in textiles, shrimp, fishing, fish meal, plywood, logging, and construction.

32. The major causes of the recession, accompanied by inflation, and what to do about it were contested by analysts. The three points of view are adequately represented in AID (1976, pt. A, pp. 136–7).
33. It was not uncommon for writers at that time to claim that poverty was Vietnam's major problem, ahead of development. See Dalby (1973).
34. Income to farmers is compared with income to urban workers in Chapter 5. Domestic rice prices rose rapidly during this period, although not as fast as the world price for rice. The government controlled the domestic price of rice by direct purchases, and for several months in 1973 it became practically the sole purchaser of rice at the wholesale level and controlled interprovincial deliveries. This kind of market intervention and other prohibitions on commerce were criticized to the end by economic analysts on the grounds that they were major sources of inefficiency in the economy.
35. This calculation was made from data in Tables 11.1 and 11.2.
36. Treaster (1973, sec. 3, p. 41) reported in the *New York Times* that investors were "waiting to see" how the cease-fire would work.
37. We estimated from data in Wu (1982, Tables 3 and 4) that Taiwanese manufacturing in 1968 required $6,375 in capital stock per worker. Given the relative wage rates in Taiwan and Vietnam, this figure probably would be too high for Vietnam. Even if we took a conservative figure of $4,000 per worker in Vietnam, it would have required $400 million in investment each year to employ 100,000 workers.

Chapter 2

1. See especially Chenery and Strout (1966) and Fei and Paauw (1965). A good critical discussion of the basic approaches to foreign aid and requirements is given in Mikesell (1968).
2. However, if the desired rate of per capita growth exceeds the long-run rate of growth of capital, aid will not be self-terminating. See Fei and Paauw (1965, p. 256).
3. It is possible to construct a model in which the saving–investment gap and the foreign exchange gap are complementary and lead to the same result. See Balassa (1964).
4. The concept is discussed in Adler (1965). Chenery and Strout (1966), using "skill limit" as the measure of absorptive capacity, incorporated it in their model. Mikesell (1968, pp. 99–104) vigorously criticized the usual treatment of the concept.
5. The "state of the art" in modeling today has advanced considerably beyond the models referred to here. But advanced models such as those of Taylor and associates (1980) add no new insights regarding the theory of foreign aid.
6. An obvious example is Hollis Chenery, a long-time leader and innovator in the theory of foreign aid. In his book *Structural Change and Development Policy* (1979) one observes continual advancement in modeling techniques and some concern for poverty, but no change in the treatment of foreign assistance.
7. With specific reference to the United States, see Chenery (1964), Little and

Clifford (1965), Mason (1955, 1964), Mikesell (1968), Millikan and Rostow (1957), Montgomery (1962), Morgenthau (1962), Wolf (1960), Jordan (1962), and U.S. Senate (1957).

8. In his inaugural address, President John F. Kennedy said: "To those people in the huts and villages of half the globe struggling to break the bonds of mass misery, we pledge our best efforts . . . not because the communists may be doing it, not because we seek their votes, but because it is right" (Kennedy 1962, p. 1). Then, to strengthen the aid prospects in Congress, Kennedy appointed a committee with the title "Committee to Strengthen the Security of the Free World." Reported by Mason (1964, p. 28).

9. Data from U.S. Senate (1971b, p. 392).

10. I have not been able to find a printed statement that explicitly expresses this insurance view of the role of Vietnam economic aid. However, this view was implied once in a conversation I had with a relatively high official about excessive rice imports in 1967. To my estimate that the United States might save $70 million, he replied (paraphrase): "Why are you worried about such a small amount? That's only a fraction of one percent of the thirty billion dollars we spend a year on this war."

11. The same was true with the early aid program in Taiwan. See Jacoby (1966, p. 30).

12. This conference is reported in Cooper (1970, pp. 296ff.) and U.S. Department of Defense (1971, book 6, ch. 8, sect. II).

13. This well-known offspring of Keynesian demand analysis is described and analyzed in Friedman (1942).

14. In more refined analyses, these assumptions could be relaxed or replaced by specific information or other assumptions, and USAID did try to handle these requirements in more sophisticated ways in their annual forecasts.

15. There was much speculation about what a "tolerable" rate of inflation might be. Most U.S. advisors thought 30% per year would be safe, and this estimate is reported by Ayres (1969b, p. 1).

16. AID officials frequently tried to persuade the GVN to raise taxes and devalue the piaster in an effort to reduce the monetary gap. On one occasion when the United States withheld aid to force the GVN to institute certain antiinflationary reforms, the *New York Times* reported: "In the discussions, the Saigon officials were said to have argued frankly that the new tax measures and reduction of luxury imports would be dangerous to the carefully balanced government" (Ayres 1969a, p. 1).

17. MACV is an acronym for the U.S. Military Assistance Command Vietnam.

18. See Table 10.2.

19. This topic is discussed in Chapter 8.

20. For an early criticism of this same practice, see Taylor (1961).

21. This problem is analyzed in Beazer et al. (1972, ch. 2).

22. This point was made explicitly by Charles A. Cooper, then minister-counselor for economic affairs at the U.S. Embassy in Saigon. See his testimony in U.S. House of Representatives (1971, pp. 7–8).

Chapter 3

1. Pearsall and Petersen "corrected" the GNP estimates up to 1967 and also produced their own for 1967, 1968, and 1969. For these three years, the NBVN estimates of GNP in current prices fall within a standard deviation of the Pearsall-Petersen estimates, but the NBVN measures in constant prices are considerably below those of Pearsall and Petersen (1971, pp. 64–5). This comparison cannot be considered as a test of the validity of the NBVN's estimates. In fact, there are good (nonstatistical) reasons for believing that the NBVN's estimates for the three years are better than those of Pearsall and Petersen.

2. See Hill (1971). Double deflation is a procedure for deriving a deflated value of income originating in a sector by subtracting the deflated value of intermediate inputs from the deflated value of output of the sector.

3. See equation (3.1).

4. In years for which Saigon and total South Vietnam data are available, the percentage of building activity reported in Saigon is fairly consistent at about 45% of the total for Vietnam. Partly because the Saigon percentage is so large, the standard deviation of the proportion is small.

5. Except for the years prior to 1962. The index for 1956–61 was constructed by the author from partial data.

6. The classification system and the range of compensation are described in Elliott, Uyen, and Wilhelm (1968).

7. These weights are based on median gross compensation for each group as of January 1, 1965. Gross compensation for career civil servants with a GVN index rating of 560 was 14,481 piasters per month. We took the index or "step" 560 to be the median. Similar GVN index medians and monthly gross compensations for other categories were 770 and 16,805 piasters for contractual workers, C(2/6) and 5,013 piasters for daily workers, and D2 and 3,217 piasters for temporary workers or "floaters." See Elliott, Uyen, and Wilhelm (1968, Appendix Tables A–26, A–27, and A–28). In all cases, these data apply to a married person with three children.

8. In the period before 1964, regional and popular forces did not exist. Instead of these designations, there were units called Civil Guards and Self-Defense Corps. We have excluded a number of paramilitary groups such as the Civil Irregular Defense Group (CIDG), Armed Combat Youth, and the People's Self-Defense Forces because either their numbers or pay were relatively insignificant. The Police Field Forces are included in the national police under civilian employment.

9. For the regular forces, we considered the median rank to be corporal-I/6/REG (index 160), with compensation of approximately 9,000 piasters per month. For the regional forces, we took a private-I with compensation of 5,500 piasters per month as the average, and we assumed that the compensation of the average PF was equivalent to a private in the RF whose compensation was about 3,500 piasters per month as of January 1, 1965. See Elliott, Uyen, and Wilhelm (1968, Tables C-7 and C-8). I am grateful to Mr. V. L. Elliott for his suggestions regarding the median ranks for compensation comparison.

10. In 1960, there were approximately 200,000 fishermen, compared with 5,400,000 in general agriculture.
11. See the extended discussion on the valuation of the piaster in Chapter 9.
12. Okubo (1974, II and III) described these indexes.
13. Although we consider it highly unlikely that agriculture declined as much as the deflated NDP series indicates.
14. Imported raw materials data taken from Dacy, Piekarz, and Watkins (1971, Table 2.2).
15. This was the percentage of total government expenditures commonly thought by accountants in Saigon during the war to be spent on personnel. Of course, any constant percentage of total government expenditures would yield the same index value results.
16. For 1971, the implicit government consumption deflator was 347. Using NBVN data on wages and salaries, the wage index in 1971 for all employees was 409, and for permanent civil equivalent employees 410. Using our constructed data on total compensation, the "compensation" index in 1971 for all employees was 420, and for permanent civil equivalent employees 421. The ratio of the implicit government consumption deflator to our constructed indexes based on average consumption is 0.8. If our constructed compensation index is realistic, then real estimated NDP in public administration overstates its true value by 20%, and that is approximately the amount that the deflated series on NDP exceeds the physical index on government employment.
17. Computed from a regression on the natural logarithms of NDP, the rate of growth is 4.7% per year, but using simple compounding with the beginning and ending values, the rate is 4.2%.
18. For short periods, we computed the average rate of growth as the mean of the growth rate for the individual years included in the period.
19. According to the official statistics, the area under cultivation was less in 1959 than in 1957. Thus, the increase in rice production was due to improved yields per hectare from an average of 1.2 tons in 1957 to 2.1 tons in 1959. See VN-NIS (annual, 1964–5, Table 98).
20. See note 17 in Chapter 1.
21. The effect on crop production is clear from Table 3.5, but the data in Table 3.2 on NDP in agriculture indicate a slight increase in 1967 over 1961. Our data simply are not good enough to support a definitive statement on the changes in agricultural production for this subperiod, although we would guess that the data in Table 3.5 paint a truer picture of the period than those in Table 3.2.
22. Another contradiction between Tables 3.2 and 3.5 is noted in the case of construction. In the former, construction activity in 1968 increased slightly over 1967, whereas it just about halved in the latter. This and other contradictions are very likely due to faulty deflators.
23. These exact figures should not be taken too seriously. It is very likely that growth was not as high as 11.6% in 1970 and somewhat higher than 0.9% in 1971. The physical composite index and GNP data reinforce this precautionary remark.
24. Note that Kuznets computed sectoral shares of GDP rather than NDP. For Vietnam, the sectoral shares based on GDP were very close to those based on NDP.

Therefore, a comparison of the two sets of data is valid. Vietnam was one of the countries excluded from Kuznets's sample because of its special circumstances.

Chapter 4

1. This change in emphasis occurred over a relatively short period of time. To realize how rapid the change was, one needs only to consult the second and third editions of Meier's *Leading Issues in Economic Development*. In the second edition, economic development is defined as "the *process* whereby *real per capita income* of a country increases over a *long period* of time" (Meier 1970, p. 7). In the third edition, the leading issues "coalesce in a central theme: policies which are designed to eradicate poverty, reduce inequality, and deal with problems of unemployment" (1976, p. vii). In his recent writings, Amartya Sen (1983) has characterized development in terms of expansion of "entitlements." This approach deemphasizes both growth of income and income distribution.
2. One well-known textbook on economic development states that "Growth and development are often used synonymously in economic discussion and this usage is entirely acceptable" (Kindleberger 1965, p. 1). When this text was revised, the clause "and this usage is entirely acceptable" was dropped (Kindleberger and Herrick 1977, p. 3). These authors cited the book by Clower et al. (1966) on Liberia with the intriguing title *Growth Without Development* as supplying an example of the distinction between growth and development. Today, writers make a point of distinguishing between the two terms. See, for example, Streeten (1981).
3. Economic events contributed to the reported illicit practices. Between January 1973 and May 1974, prices in Vietnam doubled, but military pay increased by only 25%. The drastic reduction in real income invited military personnel to appropriate whatever they safely could from local farmers and individuals engaged in commerce (U.S. Senate 1974, p. 8). Inflationary pressure could have been responsible for many of the estimated 100,000 "flower soldiers" reported in the same Senate study who paid their superiors to ignore their military absence while they were working at civilian jobs. The most pernicious corrupt act alleged to have taken place within the military was the "selling" of artillery support by some commanders. See Snepp (1977, p. 118) and Donnell (1976, p. 1).
4. This analysis is based on numerous statements in Snepp (1977, last chapter in Part I and early chapters in Part II).
5. The reader should be cautioned about statements made by public officials at the time. It is not possible to determine to what extent they served as propaganda. The author's own opinion, based on many off-the-record conversations with public officials, is that most really thought that significant development was taking place.
6. By contrast, see the simulated results given in Section 4.9.
7. See, for example, Silver (1971).
8. Our statement of Rostow's view of economic development in South Vietnam is based on Rostow (1972, pp. 470–6).
9. The major crops omitted from the list are three fruits (citrus), vegetables, and bananas (AID-VN 1973, Table 1).
10. Estimate based on foregoing report (AID-VN 1973).

11. Previously we had estimated pig production to be 45% of the value of rice production (Dacy 1969b, 40–1).
12. Controlled slaughterings are not the proper statistics for measuring pig production, because most pigs were slaughtered outside of the tax-collecting government-controlled slaughterhouses. In using those data, we assume that the ratio of controlled slaughtering to total slaughtering was constant over the period. Thus, an index of controlled slaughtering will also be a proper index of total slaughtering. We doubt that the ratio was invariant to local conditions, but for the purpose of making general statements covering a number of years, we think the assumption is less objectionable. On the whole, this series probably understates the growth in pig production, because commercial (feedlot) production was growing rapidly toward the end of the war.
13. The figures in Table A4.4 understate the rise in the ratio of rice prices to other commodity prices because the price of rice was a major item in the implicit GNP deflator.
14. The value of the piaster is treated in Chapter 9.
15. In Chapter 10, we calculate the value of exported Vietnamese services. These exports were due to the American military presence and could not be relied on for long-run growth. Thus, the figures in Table A4.5 are the relevant ones for the discussion here.
16. See, for example, International Rice Research Institute (1978).
17. See David and Barker (1978, p. 183). Specifically, we have taken an average of three production functions (modern varieties of rice in irrigated fields, modern varieties in rain-fed fields, and traditional varieties in irrigated fields). The composite production foundation is as follows: yield $= 1,900 + 18(\text{nitrogen}) - 0.11(\text{nitrogen})^2$. The measure is kilograms per hectare. Our calculations substitute total fertilizer for nitrogen, although only two-thirds (by weight) of all fertilizer used in Vietnam was nitrogenous in 1972.

    Sansom estimated a yield response function for data collected in two villages. In Long Binh Dien, the quadratic curve $Y = 759 + 12.2N - 0.026N^2$ was a reasonable fit to the data. In another village, Than Cuu Nghia, a linear response curve, $Y = 1,572 + 2.68N$, was a reasonable fit (Sansom 1970, p. 184). Neither of these equations is as good a predictor for all of Vietnam as the function we adopted from David and Barker.
18. Usually, installed capacity is measured in kilowatts (KW) rather than the flow, kilowatt-hours (KWH). We assume that there is some conversion factor such as 2,000 hours per year to translate KW into KWH. Thus, we assume that the Adelman-Morris figure of 25–80 KWH is a measure of electricity production rather than installed capacity, and in comparing these countries with Vietnam, we shall use Vietnam production rather than installed capacity.
19. For a review of the growth of electrical power in Vietnam, see AID (1976, pt. D).
20. But note that the increase in electricity consumption was much more rapid than the increase in industrial production as measured by the index of industrial production.
21. Eighty percent of the members of the Viet-Nam Confederation of Industry and Handicrafts were located in the Saigon area in 1970 (Moody 1975, p. 86). Moody

suggested that the firms located outside of Saigon were mostly handicraft enterprises. Thus, the figures based on electricity use probably are quite valid indicators of regional industrial location.

22. This paragraph is a summary of Dacy (1971, pp. 32–6).

23. The data in Tables 4.3 and A4.7 were compiled primarily by the Vietnamese customs office and pertain to arrivals and departures. Balance-of-payments data for merchandise trade do not exactly correspond with customs office data for each year, although the figures are not so different as to necessitate greatly qualifying any general statement made about trade activities. Exports, according to balance-of-payments statements, were greater than those shown in Table A4.7 for the years 1967–9; but even in those three years exports were only 5% of imports, using balance-of-payments reports, rather than the 2% shown in Table 4.3. For data on trade in the balance-of-payments accounts, see Table 9.2.

24. See AID (1976, pt. A, p. 113) for this and other data.

25. The Development and Resources Corporation thought that rubber production could be restored. Vietnam's rubber plantation managers and small holders were knowledgeable about their business. Although Vietnam had an excellent natural environment for rubber, it was rightly assumed that revival of production would be dependent on much capital investment (in new plantings and facilities), and that would be forthcoming only in a secure political setting. See McIndoe (1969).

26. See also Delaplaine (1967, p. 10).

27. The exchange rates are given in AID (1974b, Apr.–June).

28. d was the Vietnamese symbol for their unit of account, the "dong," almost universally called the "piaster."

29. Using 1970 as the base year, our estimated export price index numbers for South Vietnam were 145 and 171 for 1973 and 1974, respectively. This index was based on four commodities, tea, rubber, wood pulp, and shrimp, with weights 0.1, 0.3, 0.3, and 0.3, respectively. Deflated by this index, exports in 1972, 1973, and 1974 were $14.6, $40.0, and $49.6 million, respectively.

30. This is Silver's estimate (1971, p. 339); however, the definition of urban population is arbitrary. Writing on the subject, Louie (1970) stated that 25% of the population were urban in 1964, and 32 percent in 1968, if all those living in the provincial capitals and the autonomous cities, such as Saigon and Danang, were defined as urban. Goodman (1971, p. 350) defined "urban population" as that of cities with 20,000 or more and estimated that only 10% to 15% were urban in 1964. On the basis of their separate definitions, the Louie and Goodman estimates should not be as far apart as they are. If we accept the figures cited by Silver, the urban population grew from 2.3 million in 1958 to 6.0 million in 1970, a change that is not implausible.

31. This is from Scigliano (1963, p. 70). Adelman and Morris (1972, p. 39) classified South Vietnam's literacy rate in the range of 16% to 22% of the adult population for 1958.

32. See VN-NIS (annual, 1972, p. 372).

33. Data from VN-NIS (annual, various issues).

34. VN-NIS (annual, 1972, p. 85).

35. VN-NIS (annual, 1972, pp. 74–5).

36. Data on total U.S. military expenditures on infrastructure-type projects are not known with accuracy because of the nature of wartime accounting in combat zones. The figures cited in this paragraph were taken from Beazer et al. (1972, p. 24).
37. Some of this information is in Dacy (1985).
38. These figures and those cited in the next two paragraphs were taken from AID's *Terminal Report* (AID 1976, pt. D).
39. It has been reported that the crash program for highway construction in some instances resulted in "substandard" highways (AID 1976, pt. D, pp. 5–6). Whether "substandard" was defined in relation to military or normal civilian usage is not clear. Frank Snepp thought that the poor condition of Route 7B from Pleiku to the coast contributed to the debacle of the Vietnamese withdrawal from the central highlands in March 1975. Snepp's reference clearly is military.
40. This has been reported in AID (1976, pt. D, p. 39).
41. In Vietnam, much of the doubling of the urban ratio from 1958 to 1970 was due to refugees from war zones.
42. This is discussed in more detail in Chapter 7.
43. See AID (1976, pt. A, pp. 66–1).
44. Data in this paragraph were taken from AID (1976, pt. A, pp. 121–2).
45. For a discussion of "personalism," see Donnell (1959).
46. The Catholic influence was stressed by Scigliano (1963, p. 76).
47. See AID (1976, pt. A, p. 115).
48. The aid reduction scheme still would have left about $3.5 billion in aid over ten years. In 1969, a more optimistic study reported that with $2 billion in aid spread over ten years, Vietnam should be able to achieve "independence" and sustain a rate of growth of 6%. See Lilienthal (1969, p. 330).

Chapter 5

1. This view of Adelman was influenced by her findings in an earlier work with Morris to the effect that those policies useful in promoting more equal income distribution would not necessarily be the same as those to promote growth (Adelman and Morris 1973, ch. 5).
2. According to Little (1982, p. 210), the shift in emphasis from growth to equity was greatly influenced by "Western intellectuals and a few international civil servants from LDCs." It would appear, too, that this movement received a push from Indian economists, dating to the mid–1950s and the five-year plans. See India (1956, p. 33).
3. Dorner (1972) argued in favor of land reform in this general context.
4. P. T. Bauer questioned that land reform is the best way for achieving many of the benefits it is frequently argued to have (1972, pp. 208ff.).
5. Discussion in the following few pages is based primarily on Bredo et al. (1968, ch. 1) and Sansom (1970, ch. 3). See also AID (1976, pt. C). Discussions of pre–1960 land reform programs are in Lindholm (1964, pt. III) and Gittinger (1959).
6. These goals were contained in Articles 19–21 of the constitution.

7. Calculated as area between the 1955 and 1966 Lorenz curves divided by area under the 1955 curve.
8. According to AID (1976, pt. C, p. 40), the total cost was estimated to be $420 million. Evidently the writer of this report used the official exchange rate to translate the piaster cost into dollars, with the result that the estimate grossly overstates the dollar cost. Unfortunately, there is no clear statement about those costs actually covered. Landlords were to receive 20% in cash, with the rest to be paid in government "land reform bonds" to be retired in eight years. (In 1971, this period was reduced.) The bonds carried a 10% rate of interest. If the 52 billion piasters was the total landlord compensation to the 48,255 landlords for 753,000 hectares (AID-VN 1972a, p. 12), the implicit price per hectare was 69,000 piasters, on average. Depending on assumptions regarding the expected inflation rate, prevailing rents, etc., this comes to 2.7–3.4 times the year's rental payments.
9. These figures are from AID (1976, pt. C, pp. 45–7). Between July and October 1970, as required by law, there were 48,225 landowners who declared land subject to expropriation and compensation. The average expropriation per landlord was 15.6 hectares, and that accommodated about thirteen tenants.
10. This is Sansom's estimate (1970, p. 222). GVN land taxes were negligible.

Chapter 6

1. Meier (1976, p. 250) explained the relative loss of interest in capital as a reaction to the "excessive" attention it received early in comparison with other components of development.
2. The importance of saving and investment in development has been downplayed by the new breed of equity-minded economists such as Mahbub ul Haq, who listed the "investment illusion" as one of the "seven sins of development planners" (1976, pp. 17–20). Also, they have been degraded repeatedly by Professor Bauer, a conservative (1972, 1981, 1984).
3. "Rent seeking" is not Bauer's expression. The expression was made popular by Anne O. Krueger (1974) and has become a descriptive device for explaining economic activities that avoid the discipline of competitive markets. There is much literature on this subject by economists and other social scientists. See, for example, Bates (1981, ch. 6).
4. Although the author is sympathetic to some of these arguments, he does not endorse the hypothesis that aid is *necessarily* counterproductive. In some obvious cases it has been productive, but perhaps not for the reasons usually given in the theory of foreign aid.
5. Papanek (1973) found a negative relationship between aid and domestic saving, but did not necessarily think the relation is causal.
6. These methods are not independent. Tariffs intended to promote import substitution make exports less competitive, and subsidies intended to promote exports act to reduce effective tariffs on imports and place additional burdens on import-competing industries.
7. There is discussion of interest rates in Chapter 7.

Chapter 7

1. For this purpose, see Table A7.1.
2. The implicit deflators appear dubious for the three-year period 1968–70. In the author's opinion, the rate of change in the implicit deflator is much too low in 1968, too high in 1969, and too low in 1970.
3. See Table 11.6.
4. Much of this section has been reported in Dacy (1984).
5. Besides Fisher (1963), see Angell (1937), Ellis (1938), and Warburton (1946, 1949).
6. As, for example, that developed in Branson (1979).
7. Another aspect of U.S. troop in-country expenditures may be called the "market basket" problem. Americans did not buy the same market basket as the Vietnamese, and their purchases may not have been reflected adequately in the consumer price index. This is an index number problem that we cannot resolve here.
8. See Selden (1956, p. 229) on this point.
9. For a fascinating discussion of the effects of American Civil War battles on the value of U.S. greenbacks, see Mitchell (1903).
10. It seems that the decline in American troop strength, and their disengagement from land combat after 1970–1, had a serious effect on the morale of the Vietnamese people. In particular, the cease-fire that went into effect in early 1973 seems to have been taken as a signal of withdrawal of American support and seriously affected the confidence of the Vietnamese military and important segments of the civilian population. See Hosmer et al. (1980) and Snepp (1977).
11. If there were a time trend, the use of this kind of adaptive expectations would not be rational. In wartime South Vietnam, the rate of inflation before 1965 was relatively low, but constant. After 1965, the policy of "programmed inflation" assumed that it would be relatively high, but constant. Therefore, the use of an adaptive model in the case of Vietnam does not preclude rational expectations.
12. See, for example, Hanson and Vogel (1973) and Vogel (1974).
13. The National Bank of Vietnam started compiling figures on GNP in 1960. We have estimated GNP for previous years (see Table 3.1), but have less confidence in those figures than the official GNP estimates. Nevertheless, the longer series was also used for regressions, but the results were poorer than for the series beginning in 1960.
14. Regressing percentage change in the deflator index on percentage change in the working-class index (average for the year) yields an R^2 of 0.85. This high correlation is expected, because much of the deflator was determined by using the working-class index.
15. Chow tests indicate that the estimated velocity functions are stable even though the data for the first five years were generated in a guerrilla war environment rather than in one of conventional war with large deficits. See Dacy (1984).
16. In regression form, the quantity theory can be expressed as $d \ln P = a_0 + a_1 d \ln M + a_2 d \ln V + a_3 d \ln Q + u$. According to a strict interpretation of the quantity theory, the parameter values a_0, a_1, a_2, and a_3 are expected to be 0, 1, 1, and -1, respectively.

Chapter 8

1. "Rent seeking" is a term used to describe activities giving rise to economic rents or incomes that do not derive from productive effort. The term is associated with Krueger (1974).
2. The program was resumed in 1971.
3. This problem is not peculiar to Vietnam. See discussion on overvaluation in Allen and Ely (1953, p. 97).
4. In fact, licensing was accelerated at the time of the October 1969 reforms.
5. Following the 1966 devaluation, importers would not be likely to raise their orders in anticipation of a devaluation, because after the 1966 event the government collected a retroactive "equalization" tax on goods in pipeline (Dacy 1969a). Before the 1966 devaluation, there probably was considerable ordering in anticipation of the devaluation. The unanticipated equalization tax and the high demurrage charges on goods held on ships in the overcrowded Saigon harbor reduced importers' profits well below what they had expected.
6. Comparable data for licenses requested for GVN financing are not available. Assuming a two-month lag between request and issuance at the time, requests fell from $164 million to $92 million between the first and second half of 1966. Assuming a one-month lag, they fell from $134 million to $115 million (AID-VN annual, no. 11, Table D–10).
7. See Table 10.5.
8. Cancellations on requests for licenses made before devaluation were generally not allowed. Thus, import speculators were stuck with their prior requests. For this information I am thankful to Mr. John Wilhelm.
9. See Appendix 8.1.
10. See column 1, Table A8.2.
11. The National Bank of Vietnam did discount commercial loans at official interest rates, but it certainly is not clear that commercial banks charged only the official interest rate. Unfortunately, the annual reports of the National Bank give practically no information on this subject. See, for example, VN-NBVN (annual, fiscal year 1966), particularly pp. 30ff., which pertain to the bank's credit situation and policies.
12. We have tested the sensitivity of the results to changes in this b_2 index and have found, not unexpectedly, that wide differences from the assumed conditions would affect the calculation of windfall profits by only a couple of piasters per dollar at most.

Chapter 9

1. This symbol appeared prominently on South Vietnamese stamps.
2. For a discussion of the monetary gap, see Section 2.4 in Chapter 2.
3. See Section 2.3 in Chapter 2.
4. U.S. Senate (1966a, p. 49). Whether or not import duties were "a tax on the people of Vietnam" is discussed in Chapter 11.
5. Earl Rolph has argued that the burden of import duties falls on the domestic

owners of resources, principally those engaged in export trade, not on the consumers (people) in the exporting country, as Mill, Edgeworth, Marshall, and Pigou thought (Rolph 1946, 1947). However, in an aid economy – one in which almost all imports are financed out of aid rather than exports – there is no domestic incidence of the tax (or very little), because the net revenue generated by import taxes is zero (or very small). Rolph has developed this theme in an unpublished paper (1971). In this case, the people of the aid-giving nation bear the burden of their gift, and the people in the receiving country have no burden to bear, because they give up no resources, no matter what the nominal tariff rate. This matter is developed further in Chapter 11.

6. It was widely assumed that U.S. contractor employees and the firms themselves were the major sources of supply.

7. To the extent that risk is an important cost in procuring foreign exchange on the black market, this perceived cost must be taken into account. In that case, underinvoicing would be profitable whenever the official exchange rate plus tariff exceeded the black market rate for exchange plus the perceived risk factor. For a discussion of underinvoicing and an attempt to measure the extent of it in Turkey (1961), see Bhagwati (1964).

8. Imports of some commodities would increase and others would decline with a single exchange rate, but there is no presumption that the probable total volume of trade would change. It could, of course, rise or fall depending on the demand elasticities of the separate commodities.

9. This holds true only under fully competitive conditions. The theory presented in Chapter 8 was based on the assumptions of imperfect competition and the expectation of continually rising prices. Under these assumptions, the government could not remove all excess profits by taxation, or by raising the exchange rate.

10. Actual tariff collections are contrasted with those specified in the customs regulations in Appendix 8.1, and a series of the implicit effective exchange rate for various time periods is given in Table A8.2.

11. Although the piaster was officially devalued on June 18, 1966, the rate of d35/$ was continued in use through July 1966.

12. For practical purposes, the 118 rate broke down in October 1970 when the rate on some imports was raised to d275/$.

13. For convenience, the adjective "approximate" will be dropped from this designation.

14. Though limited, the data in Table 9.2 can be used in regression analysis. Regressing the market clearing rate/black market rate ratio (RATIO) on the percentage GVN financing (PGVNF) and the political situation entered as a dummy variable (DUMMY) yields the following results:

$$\text{RATIO} = 0.42 + 0.99\text{PGVNF} + 0.10\text{DUMMY}$$
$$\qquad\quad (4.13) \quad (3.20) \qquad\quad (1.11)$$

The t statistics are in parentheses. The adjusted R^2 is 0.76. The signs on the independent variables are those expected (because $S = 1$, $U = 0$), but the coefficient on the DUMMY is not statistically significant.

15. In index form, the "consistency" condition is

$$y'(t)/y'(0) = y*(t)/y*(0) \tag{a}$$

By definition,

$$y'(0) = Y'(0) \tag{b}$$

and

$$y'(t) = Y'(t)/P'(t) \tag{c}$$

$$y*(t) = Y'(t)/\text{VOP}(t)/P*(t) \tag{d}$$

$$y*(0) = Y'(0)/\text{VOP}(0)/1.0 \tag{e}$$

Substitute (b) through (e) into (a) to obtain

$$\text{VOP}(t)/\text{VOP}(0) = P'(t)/P*(t)$$

$$\text{VOP}(t) = [P'(t)/P*(t)]\text{VOP}(0)$$

Chapter 10

1. These percentages may not be strictly comparable to ours.
2. See also Hosmer et al. (1980).
3. These data have been arranged in much greater detail in Dacy (1985).
4. Undetermined amounts of the aid expenditures attributed to highways and roads (and other projects to a lesser extent) were reimbursed by the U.S. Department of Defense. One expert on AID projects, Mr. Ray Wateski, estimated that at least $50 million was reimbursed for services that AID performed for the military in highway construction. Thus, there is some double accounting in the data on aid to South Vietnam presented in Table 10.2.

Chapter 11

1. Percentages computed from data in VN-NIS (annual, 1972, Table 185).
2. There are numerous pamphlets and studies dealing with the tax system. Some of use to a reader interested in more detail than we shall present are Chinh (1967), Dacy (1969a), VN Directorate General of Taxation (1968), Geddes (1969), Taylor (1959a, 1959b, 1959c, 1960a, 1960b, 1968).
3. See Section 8.1.
4. On this point, see Rolph (1946).
5. There is discussion of tax effort in Bird (1964, pp. 303–8).
6. The interested reader is referred to Chelliah (1971) for an update of the rank ordering for the period 1969–71.
7. Testimony of Charles Hylander in U.S. House of Representatives (1971, p.7).
8. This is a questionable assumption. If inflation is a consequence of a continued deficit, then the deficit will constitute a burden, because inflationary finance is known to have adverse welfare implications. A seminal work on this subject is that of Bailey (1956).

Chapter 12

1. This rather startling finding surprised a principal Vietnamese tax advisor and the director general of the National Bank of Vietnam when it was presented to them.
2. Milton Taylor (1968, p. 59) stated that "war finance has consisted of muddling through, increasing rates as revenue-raising devices, but not altering the basic structure of the tax system."
3. John Kenneth Galbraith quipped at a Senate hearing, "I am perfectly persuaded that if the peasants of Vietnam were given the choice to vote as between the Viet Cong and the Saigon Government they would enthusiastically vote to have neither of them. The greatest desire as it has been for the last thousand years is to be left alone." (U.S. Senate 1966b, p. 245) Of course, this is a belief that was held by many writers, particularly during the early stages of the war.
4. Shaplen (1975, p. 542) claimed that the United States "acquiesced" if not "encouraged" the movement toward repression as a practical solution.
5. Nonmunicipal revenues, excluding subsidies from the central government, rose from 0.2 billion piasters in 1962 to 0.8 billion in 1971, or a drop of 50% when deflated by the working-class price index (VN-NIS annual, 1964–65, 1972).

Chapter 13

1. The answer to this question has foreign policy implications for the United States or any donor nation that takes sides in regional conflicts. If significant economic development does not occur while a poor nation is being propped up by, say, a superpower, the requirement for external assistance will not decline. In effect, the donor will have taken on an open-ended commitment that it is likely to regret in time. This was a major problem for the United States in its relations with South Vietnam.
2. There are eighteen references to Confucian values in this book.
3. Although President Ngo Dinh Diem (1956–63) was Catholic, he was called by one writer "The Last Confucian." See Warner (1963).
4. For the history of this period, see Buttinger (1958, ch. 6) and Karnow (1984, pp. 72–8).
5. Section 4.5.
6. This discussion is based primarily on Pack (1971).
7. As their goal of reclaiming control over the mainland faded, it would seem natural that the Nationalist leaders would consider other ways to unite the people in Taiwan.
8. A U.S. congressional staff reporting on the status of Vietnam in 1974 made this same point. "Unofficial observers" thought that "if the day ever comes when [it is believed] that Thieu can no longer deliver American aid, he will be finished" (U.S. Senate 1974, p. 13).
9. Regarding Taiwan, Jacoby commended the United States for not using aid as a lever for bringing about political reforms (1966, p. 148).
10. For caveats, see Pack (1971, p. 232).
11. The Second Immigration refers to those who immigrated to Israel between 1905 and 1914.

12. See Chapter 6.
13. Indeed, Pack raised a question about the relationship between investment and growth in regard to Israel (1971, pp. 221–3).
14. This point is stressed by Mason et al. (1980, p. 458) for South Korea.

References

Aarons, Leroy F. 1969a. "Blackmarket Perils Vietnam, Senators Told," *Washington Post* (November 20), A2.

1969b. "Currency Rackets Undermine Saigon Economy, Panel Told," *Washington Post* (November 19), A2.

Adelman, Irma. 1975. "Development Economics – A Reassessment of Goals," *American Economic Review*, Papers and Proceedings (May).

Adelman, Irma, and Cynthia Taft Morris. 1972. *Society, Politics, and Economic Development*. Baltimore: Johns Hopkins University Press.

1973. *Economic Growth and Social Equity in Developing Countries*. Stanford University Press.

Adler, John H. 1965. *Absorptive Capacity: The Concept and Its Determinants*. Washington, D.C.: The Brookings Institution.

AID. 1974a. United States Agency for International Development, Fiscal Year 1975 Submission to Congress: "Indochina Postwar Reconstruction Program." Washington, D.C.: AID.

1974b. United States Agency for International Development, Bureau of Supporting Assistance. *Vietnam Economic Data* (quarterly). Washington, D.C.: AID.

1976. United States Agency for International Development, *Terminal Report, United States Economic Assistance to South Vietnam, 1954–1975*, separate sections classified here as (A) "Economic Overview," (B) "Industry," (C) "Land Reform," (D) "Public Works," (E) "Rural Development and Field Operations." Washington, D.C.: AID.

Undated. United States Agency for International Development, *U.S. Overseas Loans and Grants from International Organizations: Obligations and Loan Authorizations, July 1, 1945–September 30, 1977*, Washington, D.C.: AID.

AID-VN. 1972a. United States Agency for International Development, Vietnam, Agricultural Economics Division, "Agriculture in the Republic of Vietnam" (staff paper). Saigon: AID.

1972b. United States Agency for International Development, Vietnam, *Report to the Ambassador from the Director of the United States Agency for International Development, Vietnam*. Saigon: AID.

283

1973. United States Agency for International Development, Vietnam, Office of Domestic Production, *Agricultural Production Memo No. 26* (January 9). Saigon: AID.

AID-VN. Annual. United States Agency for International Development, Vietnam, Office of Joint Economic Affairs, *Annual Statistical Bulletin*. Saigon: AID.

Monthly. United States Agency for International Development, Vietnam, Office of Joint Economic Affairs, *Monthly Bulletin of Statistics*. Saigon: AID.

Allen, R. G. D., and J. Edward Ely. 1953. *International Trade Statistics*. New York: Wiley.

American Friends of Vietnam. 1958. *Conference on Investment Conditions in Vietnam*, New York: AFV.

Angell, J. W. 1937. "The Components of Circular Velocity of Money," *Quarterly Journal of Economics*, 51:2 (February).

Ayres, B. Drummond, Jr. 1969a. "Aid to Vietnam Delayed to Force Inflation Control," *New York Times* (June 9), 1.

1969b. "Inflation in Vietnam is Raising Fears of a Crisis," *New York Times* (September 22), 1.

Bailey, Martin J. 1956. "The Welfare Cost of Inflationary Finance," *Journal of Political Economy*, 64:2 (April).

Balassa, Bela. 1964. "The Capital Needs of Developing Countries," *Kyklos*, 18:2.

Bates, Robert H. 1981. *Markets and States in Tropical Africa: Political Basis of Agricultural Policies*. Berkeley: University of California Press.

Bauer, P. T. 1968. "International Development Policy: Two Recent Studies," *Quarterly Journal of Economics*, 82:3 (August).

1972. *Dissent on Development*. Cambridge: Harvard University Press.

1981. *Equality, the Third World and Economic Delusion*. Cambridge: Harvard University Press.

1984. *Reality and Rhetoric: Studies in the Economics of Development*. Cambridge: Harvard University Press.

Baumol, William J. 1952. "The Transactions Demand for Cash: An Inventory Theoretic Approach," *Quarterly Journal of Economics* 66:2 (May).

Beazer, W. F. 1970. "Piasters and Dollars: A Theory of the Black Market in Vietnam" (unpublished). Arlington, Va.: Institute for Defense Analyses.

Beazer, William F., D. C. Dacy, R. Piekarz, and H. Williams. 1972. "The Economic Development of South Vietnam: Policy Issues" (unpublished study). Arlington, Va.: Institute for Defense Analyses.

Bhagwati, Jagdish. 1964. "On the Underinvoicing of Imports," *Bulletin of the Oxford University Institute of Economics and Statistics*, 26 (November).

Bird, Richard. 1964. "A Note of 'Tax Sacrifice' Comparisons," *National Tax Journal*, 17:3 (September).

Boarman, Patrick M., (ed.) 1973. *The Economy of South Vietnam: A Beginning*. Los Angeles: Center for International Business.

Branson, William H. 1979. *Macroeconomic Theory and Policy*. New York: Harper & Row.

Bredo, William, et al. 1968. *Land Reform in Vietnam*. Menlo Park: Stanford Research Institute.

Bronfenbrenner, Martin, and Franklyn D. Holzman. 1973. "A Survey of Inflationary Theory," *American Economic Review*, 63:4 (September).

Brunner, Karl, and Alan Meltzer. 1971. "The Uses of Money: Money in the Theory of an Exchange Economy," *American Economic Review*, 61:5 (December).

Buttinger, Joseph. 1958. *The Smaller Dragon: A Political History of Vietnam*. New York: Praeger.

_____. 1967. *Vietnam: A Dragon Embattled*, vols. 1 and 2. London: Pall Mall Press.

Callison, C. Stuart. 1974. "The Land-to-the-Tiller Program and Rural Resource Mobilization in the Mekong Delta of South Vietnam," paper prepared for the Mekong Development Panel of the Southeast Asia Development Group of the Asia Society meeting at Ithaca, N.Y., March 22–4.

Chandavarkar, Anand G. 1977. "Monetization of Developing Economies," *IMF Staff Papers*, 24:3 (November).

Chelliah, Raja J. 1971. "Trends in Taxation in Developing Countries," *IMF Staff Papers*, 18:2 (July).

Chenery, H. B. 1964. "Objectives and Criteria of Foreign Assistance," in G. Ranis, ed., *The United States and the Developing Countries*. New York: W. W. Norton.

Chenery, Hollis. 1979. *Structural Change and Development Policy*. Oxford University Press.

Chenery, Hollis B., and Peter Eckstein. 1970. "Development Alternatives for Latin America," *Journal of Political Economy*, 78:4, part II (July–August).

Chenery, Hollis B., and Alan Strout. 1966. "Foreign Assistance and Economic Development," *American Economic Review*, 56:4 (September).

Chinh, Nguyen Cao. 1967. *The Current Tax Regime in Vietnam*. Vietnam: American Chamber of Commerce.

Clower, Robert W., George Dalton, Mitchell Harwitz, and A. A. Walters. 1966. *Growth Without Development: An Economic Survey of Liberia*. Evanston: Northwestern University Press.

Cole, David C. 1959. "Economic Setting," in Richard W. Lindholm, ed., *Viet-Nam: The First Five Years*. East Lansing: Michigan State University Press.

Commander in Chief, U.S. Pacific Fleet. 1959. "The Role of the United States Navy," in Richard W. Lindholm, ed., *Viet-Nam: The First Five Years*. East Lansing: Michigan State University Press.

Cooper, Chester. 1970. *The Lost Crusade*. New York: Dodd, Mead.

Corson, William R. 1968. *The Betrayal*. New York: W. W. Norton.

Dacy, Douglas C. 1967. "The United States Wage Sector Problem," memorandum to the deputy ambassador, June 13.

_____. 1969a. *The Fiscal System of Wartime Vietnam*, S–337. Arlington, Va.: Institute for Defense Analyses.

_____. 1969b. *Total Availability of Goods in South Vietnam from 1964 through 1967*, S–366. Arlington, Va.: Institute for Defense Analyses.

_____. 1971. "The Economic Development of South Vietnam: Problems and Prospects" (unpublished). Arlington, Va.: Institute for Defense Analyses.

1973. "An Experimental Index of Current Economic Activity in Vietnam with Comments on the Recession of 1972-1973" (unpublished). Arlington, Va.: Institute for Defense Analyses.

1975. "Foreign Aid, Government Consumption, Saving and Growth in Less-Developed Countries," *Economic Journal*, 85 (September).

1984. "The Effect of Confidence on Income Velocity in an Unstable Environment: Wartime South Vietnam," *Kyklos*, 37:3 (December).

1985. "Memorandum on Uses of Project Aid in Vietnam, 1955-1975" (unpublished).

Dacy, Douglas C., Rolf Piekarz, and Nancy Watkins. 1971. "Protection of Industry and Tariff Reform in South Vietnam: Measurement and Policy Recommendations" (unpublished). Arlington, Va.: Institute for Defense Analyses.

Dalby, Stewart. 1973. "Send the Bill to Washington," *Far Eastern Economic Review*, 74 (January 29).

David, C. C., and R. Barker. 1978. "Modern Rice Varieties and Fertilizer Consumption," in *Economic Consequences of the New Rice Technology*. Los Banos: International Rice Research Institute.

Delaplaine, John W. 1967. "The Vietnamese Industrial Sector," working paper no. 2. New York: Development and Resources Corporation.

Development and Resources Corporation. 1969. *Export Prospects for Vietnam: Market Demand for Selected Products*, vol. II. New York: Development and Resources Corporation.

Donnell, John C. 1959. "National Renovation Campaigns in Vietnam," *Pacific Affairs*, 32 (March).

1976. "South Vietnam in 1975: The Year of Communist Victory," *Asian Survey*, 16:1 (March).

Dorner, Peter. 1972. *Land Reform and Economic Development*. Baltimore: Penguin.

Easterlin, Richard A. 1968. "Economic Growth," in *International Encyclopedia of the Social Sciences*, vol. 4. New York: Macmillan.

Elliott, Vance L. 1971. "The Agricultural Marketing/Finance System of Vietnam" (manuscript). Arlington, Va.: Institute for Defense Analyses.

Elliott, V. L., Nguyen Uyen, and J. K. Wilhelm. 1968. "Vietnamese Compensation Structures: Inter and Intra-Sectoral Analysis of Compensation Structures in Basic Employment Sectors of the Republic of Viet-Nam, January 1, 1965 through January 1 1968" (manuscript). Saigon: U.S. Agency for International Development.

Ellis, Howard. 1938. "Some Fundamentals in the Theory of Velocity," *Quarterly Journal of Economics*, 52:3 (May).

Emery, Robert F. 1970. *The Financial Institutions of Southeast Asia*. New York: Praeger.

Fall, Bernard. 1963. *The Two Vietnams*. New York: Praeger.

Fei, John C., and Douglas S. Paauw. 1965. "Foreign Assistance and Self-Help: A Reappraisal of Development Finance." *Review of Economics and Statistics*, 47:3 (August).

Fields, Gary S. 1980. *Poverty, Inequality, and Development*. Cambridge University Press.

Fisher, Irving. 1963. *The Purchasing Power of Money*. New York: Augustus M. Kelley (reprint).

Friedman, Milton. 1942. "Discussion of the Inflationary Gap," *American Economic Review*, 32:2 (June).

——— 1956. "The Quantity Theory of Money: A Restatement," in Milton Friedman, ed., *Studies in the Quantity Theory of Money*. University of Chicago Press.

Frisch, Helmut. 1977. "Inflation Theory 1963–1975: A 'Second Generation'," *Journal of Economic Literature*, 15:4 (December).

Galenson, Walter, ed. 1979. *Economic Growth and Structural Change in Taiwan*. Ithaca: Cornell University Press.

Geddes, Ronald. 1969. "A Practical Guide to Taxes in Viet-Nam" (mimeographed). Saigon.

Gittinger, Price. 1959. "Agrarian Reform," in Richard W. Lindholm, ed., *Viet-Nam: The First Five Years*. East Lansing: Michigan State University Press.

Goodman, Alan E. 1971. "The End of the War as a Setting for the Future Development of South Vietnam," *Asian Survey*, 11:4 (April).

Goodman, Alan E., and Lawrence M. Franks. 1975. "The Dynamics of Migration to Saigon, 1964–1972," *Pacific Affairs*, 48:2 (summer).

Griffin, K. G., and J. L. Enos. 1970. "Foreign Assistance: Objectives and Consequences," *Economic Development and Cultural Change*, 18:3 (April).

Grimm, Bruce, and Rolf Piekarz. 1971. "A Macroeconomic Planning Model for Vietnam" (manuscript). Arlington, Va.: Institute for Defense Analyses.

Gurley, John G., and E. S. Shaw. 1967. "Financial Structures and Economic Development," *Economic Development and Cultural Change*, 15:3 (April).

Halberstam, David. 1969. *The Best and the Brightest*. New York: Random House.

Hanson, James S., and R. C. Vogel. 1973. "Inflation and Monetary Velocity in Latin America," *Review of Economics and Statistics*, 55:3 (August).

Harnett, Joseph J. 1959. "The Work of the Roman Catholic Groups," in Richard W. Lindholm, ed., *Viet-Nam: The First Five Years*. East Lansing: Michigan State University Press.

Hazilla, Michael. 1973. "Vietnam and Postwar Development: An Economic Analysis" (manuscript). Paper dated November 21.

Haq, Mahbub ul. 1976. *The Poverty Curtain: Choices for the Third World*. New York: Columbia University Press.

Hendry, James B. 1962. "Economic Development Under Conditions of Guerrilla Warfare: The Case of Viet Nam," *Pacific Affairs*, 2:4 (June).

Hill, T. P. 1971. *The Measurement of Real Product: A Theoretical and Empirical Analysis of the Growth Rates of Different Industries and Countries*. Paris: Organization for Economic Cooperation and Development.

Ho, Samuel P. 1978. *Economic Development of Taiwan, 1860–1970*. New Haven: Yale University Press.

Hoan, Buu. 1958a. "Vietnam: Economic Consequences of the Geneva Peace," *Far Eastern Economic Review* (December 11).

——— 1958b. "Vietnam: Structure of a Dependent Economy," *Far Eastern Economics Review* (December 18).

288   References

1958c. "Impact of Military Expenditure on the South Vietnamese Economy," *Far Eastern Economic Review* (December 25).

Hosmer, Stephen T., Konrad Kellen, and Brian M. Jenkins. 1980. *The Fall of South Vietnam: Statements by Military and Civilian Leaders*. New York: Crane, Russak.

Houthakker, H. S. 1965. "On Some Determinants of Savings in Developed and Underdeveloped Countries," in E. A. G. Robinson, ed., *Problems in Economic Development*. London: Macmillan.

Huntington, Samuel P. 1972. "Foreign Aid: For What and For Whom," in Robert E. Hunter and John E. Rielly, eds., *Development Today*. New York: Praeger.

India, Government of. 1956. Planning Commission, *Second Five Year Plan*.

Institute for Strategic Studies. Annual. *The Military Balance*. London: ISS.

International Monetary Fund. Monthly. *International Financial Statistics*. Washington, D.C.: IMF.

International Rice Research Institute. 1978. *Changes in Rice Farming in Selected Areas of Asia: Interpretative Analyses of Selected Papers*. Los Banos: IRRI.

IRS. 1966. United States Internal Revenue Service, Foreign Tax Assistance Staff, "Vietnamese Tax Administration."

Jacoby, Neil M. 1966. *U.S. Aid to Taiwan*. New York: Praeger.

Jones, Leroy. 1971. "Impediments to Industrial Development" (working paper). Arlington, Va.: Institute for Defense Analyses.

Jordan, Amos A. 1962. *Foreign Aid and the Defense of Southeast Asia*. New York: Praeger.

Kahin, George M., and John W. Lewis. 1967. *The United States in Vietnam*. New York: Dial Press.

Karnow, Stanley. 1984. *Vietnam: A History*. New York: Penguin.

Kennedy, John F. 1962. *Papers of the Presidents of the United States – John F. Kennedy, January 20 to December 31, 1961*. Washington, D.C.: U.S. Government Printing Office.

Kindleberger, Charles P. 1965. *Economic Development*, 2nd ed. New York: McGraw-Hill.

Kindleberger, Charles P., and Bruce Herrick. 1977. *Economic Development*, 3rd ed. New York: McGraw-Hill.

Kissinger, Henry. 1972. "Memorandum for the Secretary of Defense," July 25.

Koehler, John E., and Albert P. Williams, Jr. 1974. "The Vietnam Economy in 1974: An Assessment with Policy Recommendations" (manuscript). Santa Monica: The Rand Corporation (November).

Krueger, Anne O. 1974. "The Political Economy of Rent Seeking Society," *American Economic Review*, 64:3 (June).

Kuznets, Simon. 1955. "Economic Growth and Income Inequality," *American Economic Review*, 35:1 (March).

1971. *Economic Growth of Nations*. Cambridge: Harvard University Press.

Laidler, D. E. W., and J. M. Parkin. 1975. "Inflation – A Survey," *Economic Journal*, 85:4 (December).

Lerner, Daniel. 1958. *The Passing of Traditional Society*. Glencoe, Ill.: The Free Press.

Lewis, W. Arthur. 1954. "Economic Development with Unlimited Supplies of Labor," *Manchester School of Economics and Social Studies*, 22 (May).

Lilienthal, David. 1969. "Postwar Development in Viet Nam," *Foreign Affairs*, 47:2 (January).

Lindholm, Richard W., ed. 1959. *Viet-Nam: The First Five Years*. East Lansing: Michigan State University Press.

Lindholm, R. W. 1964. *Economic Development Policy: With Emphasis on Viet-Nam*. Eugene: University of Oregon Press.

Little, Ian M. D. 1979. "An Economic Reconnaissance," in Walter Galenson, ed., *Economic Growth and Structural Change in Taiwan*. Ithaca: Cornell University Press.

1982. *Development Economics: Theory, Policy, and International Relations*. New York: Basic Books.

Little, I. M. D., and J. M. Clifford. 1965. *International Aid*. Chicago: Aldine.

Logan, William J. C. 1971. "How Deep is the Green Revolution in South Vietnam?" *Asian Survey*, 11:4 (April).

Lotz, Jorgan R., and Elliott R. Morss. 1967. "Measuring Tax Effort in Developing Countries," *IMF Staff Papers*, 14:3 (November).

Louie, Richard, 1970. "Population Definitions" (manuscript). Arlington, Va.: Institute for Defense Analyses.

McIndoe, K. G. 1969. "A Preliminary Survey of Rubber Plantations in South Vietnam," Vietnam working paper no. 3. New York: Development and Resources Corporation (September).

Mason, Edward S. 1955. *Promoting Economic Development: The United States and Southern Asia*. Claremont, Calif.: Claremont College.

1964. *Foreign Aid and Foreign Policy*. New York: Harper & Row.

Mason, Edward S., et al. 1980. *The Economic and Social Modernization of the Republic of Korea*. Cambridge: Harvard University Press.

Meier, Gerald M., ed. 1970. *Leading Issues in Economic Development*, 2nd ed. Oxford University Press.

1976. *Leading Issues in Economic Development*, 3rd ed. Oxford University Press.

Melitz, Jacques, and Hector Correa. 1970. "International Differences in Income Velocity," *Review of Economics and Statistics*, 52:1 (February).

Mikesell, Raymond F. 1968. *The Economics of Foreign Aid*. Chicago: Aldine.

Millikan, Max E., and W. W. Rostow. 1957. *A Proposal: Key to Effective Foreign Policy*. New York: Harper & Brothers.

Mitchell, Wesley C. 1903. *A History of Greenbacks*. University of Chicago Press.

Montgomery, John D. 1962. *The Politics of Foreign Aid: American Experience in Southeast Asia*. New York: Praeger.

Moody, Dale Linder. 1975. "The Manufacturing Sector in the Republic of Viet-Nam: Its Structure, Productivity and Development," Ph.D. dissertation, University of Florida.

Morgenthau, Hans. 1962. "A Political Theory of Foreign Aid," *American Political Science Review*, 56:2 (June).

Morrison, Lawrence. 1959. "Industrial Development Efforts," in Richard W. Lindholm, ed., *Viet-Nam: The First Five Years*. East Lansing: Michigan State University Press.

holm, ed., *Viet-Nam: The First Five Years*. East Lansing: Michigan State University Press.

Muslof, Lloyd D. 1963. "Public Enterprise and Development Perspectives in South Vietnam," *Asian Survey*, 3:8 (August).

Newsweek. 1967. "The Fat Cats of Lam Phat" (May 1).

New York Times. 1973. "Saigon Baits Hook for Big Investors" (January 21, Sec. 3), 49.

Niehans, Jurg. 1971. "Money and Barter in General Equilibrium with Transactions Costs," *American Economic Review*, 61:5 (December).

Oberdorfer, Don. 1971. *Tet!* New York: Doubleday.

Okubo, Sumiye. 1974. *National Income Accounts of Vietnam*, IDA P–1028. Arlington, Va: Institute for Defense Analyses.

Pack, Howard. 1971. *Structural Change and Economic Policy in Israel*. New Haven: Yale University Press.

Papanek, Gustav F. 1973. "Aid, Foreign Private Investment, Savings and Growth in Less Developed Countries," *Journal of Political Economy*, 81:1 (January–February).

Papanek, G. F., S. C. Jakubiak, and E. Levine, 1969. "Aid, Foreign Private Investments, Savings and Growth in Less Developed Countries," statistical appendix to *Economic Development Report* (no. 195), Development Research Group, Harvard University.

Parker, Maynard. 1975. "Vietnam: The War That Won't End," *Foreign Affairs*, 53:2 (January).

Pearsall, Edward S., and Dietrich Petersen. 1971. "Estimates of the National Income and Product of South Vietnam" (manuscript). Arlington, Va: Institute for Defense Analyses.

Pearson, Lester B., chairman. 1969. *Partners in Development*, report of the Commission on International Development. New York: Praeger.

Popkin, Samuel L. 1979. *The Rational Peasant: The Political Economy of Rural Society in Vietnam*. Berkeley: University of California Press.

Rahman, Mohammed Anisure. 1968. "Foreign Capital and Domestic Savings: A Test of Haavelmo's Hypothesis with Cross Country Data," *Review of Economics and Statistics*, 50:1 (February).

Randall, Jonathan C. 1972. "Saigon Downshift in the Honda Economy," *Washington Post* (September 3).

Robequain, Charles. 1944. *The Economic Development of French Indo-China*. Oxford University Press.

Rolph, Earl. 1946. "The Burden of Import Duties," *American Economic Review*, 36:5 (December).

1947. "The Burden of Import Duties with Fixed Exchange Rates," *American Economic Review*, 37:4 (September).

1971. "Effects of Import Duties and U.S. Aid on the Vietnam Economy" (manuscript). Arlington, Va.: Institute for Defense Analyses.

Rosebery, Frank D. 1959. "Experiment in Planning Economic and Social Development," in Richard W. Lindholm, ed., *Viet-Nam: The First Five Years*. East Lansing: Michigan State University Press.

Rosenstein-Rodan, Paul N. 1961. "International Aid for Underdeveloped Countries," *Review of Economics and Statistics*, 43:2 (May).

Rostow, Walt W. 1972. *The Diffusion of Power: An Essay in Recent History*. New York: Macmillan.

Sansom, Robert L. 1970. *The Economics of Insurgency in the Mekong Delta of Vietnam*. Cambridge: M.I.T. Press.

Scigliano, Robert. 1963. *South Vietnam: Nation Under Stress*. Boston: Houghton Mifflin.

Scigliano, Robert, and Guy H. Fox. 1965. *Technical Assistance to Vietnam: The Michigan State University Experience*. New York: Praeger.

Seers, Dudley. 1969. "The Meaning of Development," *International Development Review*, 2 (December).

Selden, Richard. 1956. "Monetary Velocity in the United States," in Milton Friedman, ed., *Studies in the Quantity Theory of Money*. University of Chicago Press.

Sen, A. K. 1983. "Development: Which Way Now?" *Economic Journal*, 93 (December).

Shaplen, Robert. 1965. *The Lost Revolution*. New York: Harper & Row.

1975. "Southeast Asia – Before and After," *Foreign Affairs*, 53:3 (April).

Shaw, Edward S. 1973. *Financial Deepening in Economic Development*. Oxford University Press.

Silver, Solomon. 1971. "Changes in the Midst of the War," *Asian Survey*, 11:4 (April).

Smithies, Arthur. 1970. "Economic Problems of Vietnamization" (manuscript). Arlington, Va.: Institute for Defense Analyses.

1972. "Yet Another Model of Aid and Development" (manuscript). Arlington, Va: Institute for Defense Analyses.

1974. "Inflation and Depression in Vietnam" (manuscript). Arlington, Va: Institute for Defense Analyses.

Snepp, Frank. 1977. *A Decent Interval*. New York: Random House.

Stockfisch, J. A. 1971. "The Domestic Tax System" (manuscript). Arlington, Va.: Institute for Defense Analyses.

Streeten, Paul. 1972. *The Frontiers of Development Studies*. London: Macmillan.

1981. *Development Perspectives*. London: Macmillan.

Sulzberger, C. L. 1955. "Teaching the Sultan's Horse to Speak," *New York Times* (January 17), 22.

Taylor, Lance, Edmar L. Bacha, Eliana A. Cardosco, and Frank J. Lysy. 1980. *Models of Growth and Distribution in Brazil*. Oxford University Press.

Taylor, Milton C. 1959a. *The Patente (Business License Tax) in Viet-Nam*. Saigon: Michigan State Advisory Group.

1959b. *The Taxation of Income in Viet-Nam*. Saigon: Michigan State Advisory Group.

1959c. *The Taxation of Real Property in Viet-Nam*. Saigon: Michigan State Advisory Group.

1960a. *The System of Excise Taxes in Viet-Nam*. Saigon: Michigan State Advisory Group.

1960b. *The System of Indirect Taxes in Viet-Nam*. Saigon: Michigan State Advisory Group.

1961. "South Vietnam: Lavish Aid, Limited Progress," *Pacific Affairs*, 34:3 (Fall).

1968. *Tax Policies for the Postwar Development of Vietnam*, working paper 28. Saigon: Joint Development Group.

Tobin, James. 1956. "The Interest Elasticity of Transactions Demand for Cash," *Review of Economics and Statistics*, 38:3 (August).

Treaster, Joseph B. 1973. "South Vietnam's Optimism Goes Sour," *New York Times* (January 21, Sec. 3), 49.

Trong, Le Hoang. 1975. "Survival and Self-reliance: A Vietnamese Viewpoint," *Asian Survey*, 15:4 (April).

Trued, M. N. 1960. "South Vietnam's Industrial Development Center," *Pacific Affairs*, 33 (September).

United Nations. 1973. *United Nations Yearbook of National Account Statistics*, vol. 2.

1975. *Monthly Bulletin of Statistics*, 29:4 (April).

U.S. Arms Control and Disarmament Agency. Undated. *World Military Expenditures and Arms Trade, 1963–1973*. Washington, D.C.: ACDA.

U.S. Department of Defense. 1971. *United States Vietnam Relations*. Washington, D.C.: U.S. Government Printing Office.

U.S. Department of State. 1961. *A Threat to the Peace: North Vietnam's Effort to Conquer South Vietnam*. Washington, D.C.: DOS.

U.S. Department of State and Department of Defense. 1957. *The Mutual Security Program, Fiscal Year 1958*. Washington, D.C.: International Cooperation Administration.

U.S. House of Representatives. 1966. Foreign Assistance Act of 1966, *Hearings Before the Committee on Foreign Affairs*, 89th Congress, 2nd Session, Part 1 (March 16, 17, 22–4).

1967. Foreign Assistance Act of 1967, *Hearings Before the Committee on Foreign Affairs*, 90th Congress, 1st Session, Part 1 (April 1).

1970. Committee on Government Operations, "A Review of the Inequitable Monetary Rate of Exchange in Vietnam," 91st Congress, 2nd Session, House Report No. 91–1228 (June 25).

1971. "Vietnam and the Hidden Subsidy (Inequitable Currency Exchange Rate)," *Eighth Report on the Committee on Government Operations*, House Report No. 92–760 (July 8).

1974. Committee on Foreign Affairs, *United States Aid to Indochina: Report of a Staff Survey Team to South Vietnam, Cambodia and Laos, July 1974*. Washington, D.C.: U.S. Government Printing Office.

U.S. Senate. 1957. *Mutual Security Act of 1957*, Senate hearings, 85th Congress, 1st Session.

1963. Testimony by David Bell, *Hearings Before the Committee on Foreign Relations*, 88th Congress, 1st Session (June 12).

1966a. Foreign Assistance Act of 1966, *Hearings Before the Committee on Foreign Relations*, 89th Congress, 2nd Session (April 6).

1966b. Foreign Assistance Act of 1966, *Hearings Before the Committee on Foreign Relations*, 89th congress, 2nd Session (April 25).

1966c. Committee on Government Operations, *An Investigation of the U.S. Economic and Military Assistance Program in Vietnam*. Washington, D.C.: U.S. Government Printing Office.

1969. Foreign Assistance Act of 1969, *Hearings Before the Committee on Foreign Relations*, 91st Congress, 1st Session (July 14).

1971a. Committee on Government Operations, *Fraud and Corruption in Management of Military Club Systems (Illegal Currency Manipulations Affecting South Vietnam)*. Washington, D.C.: U.S. Government Printing Office.

1971b. Foreign Assistance Legislation, Fiscal Year 1972, *Hearings Before the Committee on Foreign Relations*, 91st Congress, 1st Session (June 10, 11, 14).

1974. Committee on Foreign Relations, *Vietnam May 1974*, a staff report for the use of the Committee on Foreign Relations, 93rd Congress, 2nd Session (August 5).

VN Department of Agriculture. Annual. *Agricultural Statistics Yearbook*.

VN Directorate General of Taxation. 1968. *Taxation in Vietnam: A Handy Guide for Professionals, Business and Salaried Taxpayers*. Saigon: DGT.

VN-NBVN. Annual. National Bank of Vietnam, *Vietnam Annual Report*.

VN-NIS. Monthly. Vietnam National Institute of Statistics, *Monthly Bulletin of Statistics*.

Annual. Vietnam National Institute of Statistics, *Vietnam Statistical Yearbook*.

Vogel, Robert C. 1974. "The Dynamics of Inflation in Latin America," *American Economic Review*, 64: 1 (March).

Warburton, Clark. 1946. "The Quantity and Frequency of the Use of Money in the United States," *Journal of Political Economy*, 54:5 (October).

1949. "The Secular Trend in Monetary Velocity," *Quarterly Journal of Economics*, 63:1 (February).

Warner, Dennis. 1963. *The Last Confucian*. New York: Macmillan.

Weisskopf, Thomas. 1972. "The Impact of Foreign Capital Inflow on Domestic Savings in Underdeveloped Countries," *Journal of International Economics*, 2:1 (February).

Westmoreland, W. C. Undated. "Report on Operations in South Vietnam, January 1964–June 1968," in *Report on the War in Vietnam*. Washington, D.C.: U.S. Government Printing Office.

Wolf, Charles, Jr. 1960. *Foreign Aid: Theory and Practice in Southeast Asia*. Princeton University Press.

Wu, C. S. 1982. "Analysis and Estimation of Productivity of the Industrial Sector" (translation), *Quarterly Journal of Bank of Taiwan*, 34:4 (December).

Wurfel, David. 1957. "Agrarian Reform in the Republic of Vietnam," *Far Eastern Survey*, 26:6 (June).

Zasloff, Joseph. 1962–3. "Rural Resettlement in South Vietnam: The Agroville Program," *Pacific Affairs*, 35:4 (winter).

Index

295